Lynda Weinman's

Adobe®
Premiere® Pro 2

Includes Exercise Files and Demo Movies

lynda.com

By Jeff Schell

Adobe® Premiere® Pro 2: Hands-On Training

By Jeff Schell

lynda.com/books | Peachpit Press
1249 Eighth Street • Berkeley, CA • 94710
800.283.9444 • 510.524.2178 • 510.524.2221(fax)
www.lynda.com/books
www.peachpit.com

lynda.com/books is published
in association with Peachpit Press,
a division of Pearson Education
Copyright ©2006 by lynda.com, Inc.

ISBN: 0-321-39774-6

0 9 8 7 6 5 4 3 2 1

Printed and bound in the
United States of America

H•O•T Credits

lynda.com Director of Publications: Tanya Staples

Editor: Karyn Johnson

Production Coordinator: Tracey Croom

Compositors: Myrna Vladic, David Van Ness

Copyeditor: Kimberly Wimpsett

Proofreaders: Haig MacGregor, Jennifer Danner

Interior Design: Hot Studio, San Francisco

Cover Design: Don Barnett

Cover Illustration: Bruce Heavin (bruce@stink.com)

Indexer: Julie Bess, JBIndexing Inc.

Video Editors and Testers: Steven Gotz, Scott Cullen, Eric Geoffroy

H•O•T Colophon

The text in *Adobe Premiere Pro 2 H·O·T* was set in Avenir from Adobe Systems Incorporated. The cover illustration was painted in Adobe Photoshop and Adobe Illustrator.

This book was created using QuarkXPress and Microsoft Office on an Apple Macintosh using Mac OS X. It was printed on 60 lb. Influence Matte at Courier.

Table of Contents

Bonus chapters on the Premiere Pro 2 HOT DVD-ROM:

Introduction

A Note from Lynda Weinman

Most people buy computer books to learn, yet it's amazing how few books are written by teachers. Jeff Schell and I take pride this book was written by experienced teachers who are familiar with training students in this subject matter. In this book, you'll find carefully developed lessons and exercises to help you learn Adobe® Premiere® Pro 2—one of the most robust and feature-rich video-editing applications available for the PC.

This book is targeted to beginning- to intermediate-level video editors who are looking to capture and edit video and to produce movies in a variety of formats with titles, transitions, and effects. The premise of the hands-on approach is to get you up to speed quickly with Premiere Pro 2 while actively working through the lessons in this book. It's one thing to read about a program, and it's another experience entirely to try the product and achieve measurable results. Our motto is "Read the book, follow the exercises, and you'll learn the program." I have received countless testimonials, and it is our goal to make sure this motto remains true for all our Hands-On Training books.

This book doesn't set out to cover every single aspect of Premiere Pro 2. What we saw missing from the bookshelves was a process-oriented tutorial teaching readers core principles, techniques, and tips with hands-on exercises.

We welcome your comments at **pp2hot@lynda.com**. If you run into any trouble while you're working through this book, check out the technical support link at **www.lynda.com/books/HOT/pp2**.

Jeff Schell and I hope this book will improve your skills in video editing with Premiere Pro 2. If it does, we have accomplished the job we set out to do!

—Lynda Weinman

About lynda.com

lynda.com was founded in 1995 by Lynda Weinman and Bruce Heavin in conjunction with the first publication of Lynda's revolutionary book, *Designing Web Graphics*. Since then, **lynda.com** has become a leader in software training for graphics and Web professionals and is recognized worldwide as a trusted educational resource.

lynda.com offers a wide range of Hands-On Training books, which guide users through a progressive learning process using real-world exercises. **lynda.com** also offers a wide range of video-based tutorials, which are available on CD and DVD and through the **lynda.com Online Training Library**™. **lynda.com** also owns the Flashfoward Conference and Film Festival.

For more information about **lynda.com**, check out **www.lynda.com**. For more information about the Flashforward Conference and Film Festival, check out **www.flashforwardconference.com**.

Product Registration

Register your copy of the *Adobe Premiere Pro 2 Hands-On Training* book today, and receive the following benefits: a *free* 24-hour pass to the **lynda.com Online Training Library**™ with more than 10,000 professionally produced video tutorials covering more than 150 topics by leading industry experts and teachers; news, events, and special offers from **lynda.com**; and the **lynda.com** monthly newsletter.

To register, visit **www.lynda.com/register/HOT/pp2**.

Additional Training Resources from lynda.com

To help you further develop your skills with Premiere Pro 2 and digital video, use the *free* 24-hour pass to the **lynda.com Online Training Library**™ and check out the following video-based training resources:

Digital Video Principles
with Larry Jordan

Premiere Pro 2 Essential Training
with Jeff Schell

Premiere Pro 2 New Features
with Jeff Schell

After Effects 7 Essential Training
with Lee Brimelow

After Effects 7 New Features
with Lee Brimelow

Photoshop CS2 Essential Training
with Michael Ninness

Illustrator CS2 Essential Training
with Jeff Van West

About Jeff Schell

Jeff Schell is a video editor, comedy writer, author, Web designer, technical trainer, actor, and amateur physics geek. Jeff has produced and edited video for local news programs, network television programs, Emmy award–winning programs, and nationally syndicated shows. As an ACE (**A**dobe **C**ertified **E**xpert) and an ACI (**A**dobe **C**ertified **I**nstructor) since 1999, Jeff travels across the United States teaching video production classes in Premiere Pro, Adobe After Effects, Adobe Encore DVD, Adobe Audition, Adobe Photoshop, and Adobe Illustrator. Jeff strives to infuse his real-world experience and humor into every lesson.

Jeff is the author of the *Premiere Pro 1.5 Hands-On Training* book and the *Premiere Pro 2 New Features* and *Premiere Pro 2 Essential Training* video-based resources in the **lynda.com Online Training Library**. He has also written questions for the Adobe certification exams for Premiere Pro and After Effects.

When not teaching others how to create videos, Jeff can be found tinkering with his own video projects to support his comedy jones. Jeff has written for and performed at comedy clubs and festivals throughout the United States and Canada. When not writing, teaching, performing, or designing Web sites, Jeff spends his free time in a quixotic quest to find the best Mexican food north of the border.

As an added bonus, Jeff has dotted this book with hidden references to sixteenth-century Renaissance English literature.

Acknowledgments from Jeff

This book would not have been possible without a strong team of dedicated, enthusiastic, and talented individuals. Most notably:

Our families and friends. Mom and Dad, I owe everything to you. Maria, you are the best Oma. Jack, thanks for watching over us.

Profound thanks to Brian, Gehrig, Luke, Johnny, Mark, Ryan, and Dave—thanks for lending me your sparkling faces.

Everyone at lynda.com: Garo, Lynda, Jonathan, Paavo, Brian, and the rest of the Ojai Muni Brigade. Most of all, a heartfelt thank you to Tanya Staples, the benevolent mastermind behind this book. Thanks for putting up with me.

Karyn Johnson, Kim Wimpsett, Jennifer Eberhardt, and the fine folks at Peachpit Press.

Outstanding work by the beta testers, Steven Gotz and Scott Cullen. Thank you for your thoroughness, dedication, and amazing insight.

My best friend and the love of my life, Jennifer. You keep me grounded and laughing. And thanks for doing my share of the chores while I wrote the book.

Special thanks to Digital Juice (**www.DigitalJuice.com**) for the excellent audio and video content graciously provided for the exercise files in this book.

How to Use This Book

The following sections outline important information to help you make the most of this book.

Understanding the Formatting in This Book

This book has several components, including step-by-step exercises, commentary, notes, tips, warnings, and video tutorials. Step-by-step exercises are numbered. File names, folder names, commands, keyboard shortcuts, and URLs are boldface so they pop out easily: **filename.htm**, the **images** folder, **File > New**, **Ctrl+S**, and **www.lynda.com**.

Commentary is in gray text.

This is commentary text.

Viewing the Interface Screen Captures

All the illustrations in the book were captured on a Windows computer using Windows XP because Premiere Pro 2 runs only on the Windows operating system.

What's on the HOT DVD-ROM?

You'll find a number of useful resources on the **Premiere Pro 2 HOT DVD-ROM**, including exercise files, video tutorials, and information about product registration. Before you begin the hands-on exercises, read the following section so you know how to set up the exercise files and video tutorials.

And if that's not enough, the DVD-ROM also contains two bonus chapters—Chapter 18, *"Editing Video from Multiple Cameras,"* and Chapter 19, *"Collaborating with Clip Notes."*

Copying Exercise Files to Your Hard Drive

The files required to complete the exercises are on the **Premiere Pro 2 HOT DVD-ROM** in a folder called **exercise_files**. It is *highly* recommended you copy the entire **exercise_files** directory from the **DVD-ROM** to the root directory of your C drive before beginning any of the hands-on exercises.

Premiere Pro 2 expects to find all necessary exercise, video, audio, and graphic files in one of the subdirectories of **c:\exercise_files**. (For example, Premiere Pro 2 will look for Exercise 1 of Chapter 3 in **c:\exercise_files\chap_03**.)

1 Double-click the **My Computer** icon on your **Desktop**, or choose the **My Computer** item from your **Start** menu.

My Computer

2 Double-click the DVD drive that has the **Premiere Pro 2 HOT DVD-ROM**.

3 Click the **exercise_files** directory to select it. Choose **Edit > Copy to Folder** to open the **Copy Items** dialog box.

---

4 In the **Copy Items** dialog box, select **Local Disk (C:)**, and click the **Copy** button. This opens a dialog box displaying the progress of the copy.

If you choose to copy the files to any other hard drive location (this is *not* recommended), each time you open a new exercise file, Premiere Pro 2 will prompt you to locate the video, audio, and graphic files before you can proceed with each exercise.

On Windows, when files originate from a DVD, they automatically become write protected, which means you cannot alter them. Fortunately, you can easily change this attribute. For complete instructions, refer to the "Making Exercise Files Editable on Windows Computers" section on the next page.

NOTE:

Copying to the C Drive

This book asks you to copy the hands-on exercise and supporting files to the **C:** directory only for the purposes of instruction; in other words, this ensures compatibility with all readers. However, when you are using Premiere Pro 2 in a real-world situation, you should *definitely avoid* capturing to or editing from the **C:** directory. If you have only one hard drive in your system, then you should use a subfolder of your **My Documents** directory, such as **My Documents\Project Name**. This will help keep your files organized.

If you have a separate storage drive, then you should use that drive for all your future Premiere Pro 2 projects for increased system performance.

Viewing the Video Tutorials

Throughout the book, you'll find references to video tutorials. In some cases, these video tutorials reinforce concepts explained in the book. In other cases, they show interesting bonus material you'll find useful. To view the video tutorials, you must have Apple QuickTime Player installed on your computer. If you do not have QuickTime Player, you can download it for free from the Apple Web site: **www.apple.com/quicktime**.

To view the video tutorials, copy the videos from the **Premiere Pro 2 HOT DVD-ROM** to your hard drive. Double-click the video you want to watch, which opens it in QuickTime Player. Make sure the volume on your computer is turned up so you can hear the audio content.

If you like the video tutorials, refer to the previous "Product Registration" section, and register to receive a free pass to the **lynda.com Online Training Library**, which is filled with more than 10,000 video tutorials covering more than 150 topics.

Making Exercise Files Editable on Windows Computers

By default when you copy files from a DVD to a Windows computer, the files are set to read-only (write protected). To follow the exercises in this book, you should remove the read-only property by following these steps:

1 Double-click the **My Computer** icon on your **Desktop**, or choose the **My Computer** item from your **Start** menu.

2 Double-click **Local Disk (C:)** to view its contents.

3 Right-click the **c:\exercise_files** directory, and choose **Properties**.

Note: If the directory has not been copied, see "Copying Exercise Files to Your Hard Drive" on page xiii.

4 In the **Properties** dialog box, turn off the **Read-only** check box.

5 Click **OK**. In the **Confirm Attribute Changes** dialog box, select **Apply changes to this folder, subfolders and files**. Click **OK**.

Making File Extensions Visible on Windows Computers

By default, you cannot see file extensions, such as **.avi**, **.jpg**, **.mp3**, or **.psd** on Windows computers. Fortunately, you can change this setting easily. Here's how:

1 Double-click the **My Computer** icon on your **Desktop**, or choose the **My Computer** item from your **Start** menu.

2 Select **Tools > Folder Options** to open the **Folder Options** dialog box. Select the **View** tab.

3 Turn off the **Hide extensions for known file types** check box. This makes all file extensions visible.

Understanding the Premiere Pro 2 System Requirements

The following are the minimum requirements you need to run Premiere Pro 2:

Processor: Video is actually a series of 24–30 images played in 1 second. To our human eye, this creates the illusion of motion. Adobe's minimum requirement is an Intel Pentium 4 1.4 GHz (**G**iga**H**ertz) processor—although that seems a bit low. We recommend at least a 2.8 GHz processor.

Operating system: Premiere Pro 2 runs only on Microsoft Windows XP Professional or Home Edition with Service Pack 2. The biggest pitfall is having too many background applications running on your **Desktop**. Playing all that video is hard work, and your system will be begging for processing power. Background applications (such as all those little icons in your system tray) take away resources from Premiere Pro 2. The moral is this: Be cautious about what you allow to run in your system tray, be vigilant about ending unnecessary background applications, and try not to run too many other tasks while editing video. (Like oil and water, Web surfing and video editing do not mix!)

Memory: At a minimum, Adobe recommends 512 MB (**M**ega**B**ytes) of RAM (**R**andom **A**ccess **M**emory). And this will suffice, but 1 GB (**G**iga**B**yte) of memory gives your computer some "breathing room." If you're editing HDV (**H**igh-**D**efinition **V**ideo), then 2 GB is a must.

Hard drive: For the application install, Adobe requires 4 GB of available hard drive space for installation. However, for capturing and editing video, a separate 7,200 rpm (**r**evolutions **p**er **m**inute) hard drive is recommended. Note that internal drives tend to be faster than external drives. For high-definition video, you will definitely need multiple hard drives, professionally configured.

CD/DVD drive: Premiere Pro 2 ships on DVD, so a DVD drive is a must. If you plan to create DVD movies, then you need either a DVD+R burner or a DVD-R burner.

Computer monitor: Adobe recommends a 1,280 x 1,024 pixel video display with a 32-bit color adapter. (This is fancy talk for "a monitor that was built in the last 5 years.") Many professionals have workstations that can display the software across two monitors. This is a function of your graphics card.

Graphics card: Adobe lists recommended/certified graphic cards at **www.adobe.com/products/premiere/dvhdwrdb.html**. Some cards that work with Premiere Pro 2 are not on this list—but it's always a gamble if you venture from the list.

Capture card: To communicate with a DV or HDV camera, your system needs an OHCI-compatible IEEE 1394 video interface card. This is confusing jargon for "a FireWire or i.Link port." Most FireWire/i.Link ports are OHCI-compatible.

Getting Demo Versions of the Software

If you'd like to try the demo versions of the software used in this book, you can download them at the following location:

www.adobe.com/products/tryadobe/main.jsp

See, you've already made it to the end of the introduction. Way to go! Just two more chapters until you know how to edit your video. (Seriously!) Now that you have installed and prepared the exercise files, it's about time you get around to using them. The first step in any Premiere Pro 2 venture is to create a new project. And that is exactly where your training begins in Chapter 1, *"Getting Started"* (just as soon as you turn the page).

1

Getting Started

Adobe Premiere Pro 2 is one of the most powerful video-editing programs on the market. In this chapter, you will learn how Premiere Pro 2 helps you capture, edit, and export video. You will dive in by creating your first project while sorting through the potentially confusing project options. (Of course, with this book, nothing will be confusing!) This chapter also introduces the completely redesigned user interface in Premiere Pro 2.

Introducing Premiere Pro 2

Video editing is the process of taking a long video recording—such as that four-minute panorama from your tropical vacation that puts friends to sleep—and whittling it down so it tells a more concise, clear story. The term video editing is also used as a catchall to include the process of combining many separate video recordings to create one new recording—complete with titles, pictures, and special effects. In other words, video editing means both editing a single recording and undertaking the entire process of creating new video. From start to finish, Premiere Pro 2 provides tools to help you every step of the way.

Premiere Pro 2 is video-editing software that aids you in creating video for playback on television,

DVDs, the Web, and many other formats. From television producers to wedding videographers to home hobbyists, many people use Premiere Pro 2 for an even wider array of projects.

Premiere Pro 2 allows you to accomplish three main tasks: You can capture and collect video, audio, and graphics in one location; you can assemble your video and add titles, graphics, transitions, and effects; and you can export your video to formats appropriate for television, DVDs, or the Web.

For each of these tasks, you will use a project file, which you will learn about in the next section.

NOTE:

The "Pro" in Premiere Pro 2

One popular question users ask about Premiere Pro 2 is, is it professional? The short answer is yes. The long answer goes like this...

Premiere Pro 2 will not make your video professional or unprofessional. It's professionally ambiguous. Premiere Pro 2 is no different from any other video-editing software on the market in this respect. If you give it professional video, it will give you professional video. If you give it lousy video, it will give you lousy video. In other words, Premiere Pro 2 has little to do with the question of professionalism. It is as professional as you need it to be.

Creating a Premiere Pro 2 Project

A Premiere Pro 2 **project** is a single file containing all your work. A project holds all the audio, video, and graphics you plan to use. It remembers which files were captured from your camera. Most important, it contains the blank canvas you will use to create your program.

Before you can begin using Premiere Pro 2, you must first create a **project file**. Every task you perform in Premiere Pro 2 takes place within a

project file. In fact, Premiere Pro 2 will not allow you to do *any* work unless you make a new project or open an existing one. Every time you want to capture video from your camera or export video to DVD, you must have a project open. That's why the first task you will learn in this chapter is how to make a new project. Without a project, you can't do much else.

Video Geek Vocabulary

If you're new to video editing, you may discover yourself surrounded by strange video-editing vocabulary. Specifically, you'll find two words sprinkled throughout this chapter:

Program: A **program** refers to your creation. Similar to a television program, a program is the final piece of video you are producing. A program can be a slide show, a wedding video, a commercial, a movie...anything!

Clip: A **clip** is any video file, audio file, or still image imported into your project. A clip can be a snippet of a larger video file, or it can refer to the entire file. It just depends on how you use the video file in your project.

Choosing Project Presets

As mentioned, you must create a project file before you begin working. Premiere Pro 2 asks you (OK, it *forces* you) to choose the type of project you want to create. Every project file has at least a dozen settings you need to specify before Premiere Pro 2 will create the project. These settings include frame size, pixel aspect ratio, editing mode, color depth, audio sample rate, field priority, and more! Whew. Don't worry. Using project presets makes this daunting task much easier.

A **project preset** is a preconfigured template that automatically chooses the optimal settings for your project. When you choose a preset, Premiere Pro 2 specifies and locks each setting so you don't accidentally choose incompatible options. Of course, you can customize the project settings if you want; however, this is usually unnecessary—and can be downright risky! With so many settings that must perfectly match your video, choosing a preset is not only the easiest thing to do but also the safest.

When you choose a preset, you must do so with care because after you choose the project settings, you cannot change them. (Insert ominous clap of thunder to underscore this point.) Although this may cause little concern when you're five minutes into a project, you'll find it much harder to start over when you're five days into a project. For this reason, choose wisely! (Of course, if you do choose incorrectly, a workaround can salvage your project; Chapter 16, *"Working with 16:9, HDV, and 24p Video,"* discusses this workaround.)

In the first exercise, you will create a new project and learn how to properly choose a project preset.

1 | Creating a New Project

Creating a project is similar to writing an e-mail. To write an e-mail, you first create a blank e-mail letter and then fill it with words. In Premiere Pro 2, you create a blank project and fill it with audio and video. In this exercise, you will learn how to create a new project.

---

1 Start Premiere Pro 2 if you do not already have it open.

When you open Premiere Pro 2, you'll see a Welcome Screen, which lets you start a new project or open an existing project.

---

2 Click **New Project** to open the **New Project** dialog box, which contains a list of available presets.

Tip: If you have existing projects, the most recent ones will appear below the Recent Projects heading. This is a quick way to open an existing project without having to navigate through the Open Project folder.

3 Under **Available Presets**, click the plus sign to expand the **DV – NTSC** preset folder, and click the **Standard 48kHz** preset to select it.

When selecting a preset, it is important to select a preset matching the video you'll be editing—this is not the format of the final video you want to produce but is the format of the source video you will be using. Throughout this book, you'll be using video Premiere Pro 2 thinks came from a standard DV (**D**igital **V**ideo) camera. For a more in-depth explanation, please see the tip at the end of this exercise.

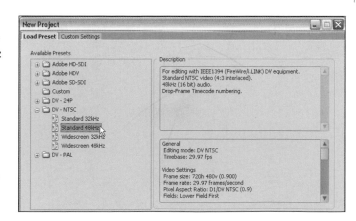

Premiere Pro 2 ships with six groups of presets, each represented by a folder. You can expand (or minimize) a folder by clicking the plus (or minus) sign next to the folder icon.

To the right of the Available Presets area, you will see a description of each preset. In the pane below that, you will see a list of the preset settings. If you scroll through the settings, you will see exactly how many settings any given project has. The preset saves you from having to specify each of these settings.

Note: If your video-capture card came bundled with Premiere Pro 2, you may see additional presets in the Available Presets list.

4 Click the **Browse** button. In the **Browse For Folder** dialog box, navigate to the **c:\exercise_files\chap_01** folder, click to select it, and click **OK**. This returns you to the **New Project** dialog box.

When creating your own projects, make sure you know exactly where you are creating your file, because you will need to refer frequently to the file location. Pick a location you can remember and easily find.

Some editors like to save their project files in the same folder with all the video they capture from their camera—so everything is in one convenient location. Other editors like to have projects in one folder and captured video from their camera in another folder. Each method has its merits, and you'll discover the method most comfortable for you. You'll learn more about organizing video content in Chapter 14, "Capturing Digital Video."

5 In the **Location** field, you will see the folder you chose. At the bottom of the **New Project** dialog box, type **exercise01** in the **Name** field, and click **OK**.

This creates a new project file with the chosen settings on your hard drive and automatically opens your new project. Now your project is ready for use.

6 Choose **File > Save**.

This saves your project and leaves it open. Although at this point it's really unnecessary to save your file, this step shows you how to save a project because at the end of each exercise in this book, you will be prompted to save your project. It's also a good idea to save frequently because you never can predict when a dreaded crash will occur.

7 Choose **File > Save a Copy**. In the **Save Project** dialog box, the file name is appended with *Copy*. Click **Save**. Leave the project open before moving on to the next exercise.

The Save a Copy command creates a duplicate copy of your project but leaves the original open. This allows you to create a backup of your project while continuing to work on the original. Many editors use this as a restore point and name their copies "backup 7/18 3:11pm" or "backup 7/18 4:05pm" and so forth.

At the end of each exercise, you will be prompted to close your project or leave it open. Of course, you can always close it and open it later when you are ready to continue.

You have just created and saved your first project using a preset. The preset contains detailed information for more than 20 possible settings. At this point, you do not need to worry about any of those settings, just as long as you choose the proper preset. However, the list of presets and their settings can be overwhelming. So which is the right one to choose?

The project settings should match the format of the source video as closely as possible. For example, if you shot footage on a 16:9 DV NTSC camera with 48 kHz sound quality, then you would use the DV – NTSC Widescreen 48kHz preset.

Some cameras can shoot multiple sizes and multiple formats. For example, if your DV camera shoots both widescreen and standard size, you should pick your screen size before shooting and stick with it. Unless you are looking for a specific effect, avoid mixing and matching formats in the same Premiere Pro 2 project.

For a brief primer on widescreen and standard size videos, as well as HDV (**H**igh-**D**efinition **V**ideo), see Chapter 16, *"Working with 16:9, HDV, and 24p Video."*

If you'd like to understand what is going on "under the hood" when choosing a project preset, the following table provides a simple overview of the most important settings defined by each preset. This table is extra credit—refer to it if you need to, but this table is not required in order to successfully complete the exercises in this book.

Note: Do not operate heavy machinery after reading this table.

What About Those Other Settings?	
Setting	**Description**
Editing Mode	Tells Premiere Pro 2 what type of source files you will be using and how to play them. Available options include DV NTSC, DV PAL, DV 24p, HDV 720p, and a few more. These are all different "flavors" of video that Premiere Pro 2 will accept. It's important to choose an editing mode matching your source video so Premiere Pro 2 doesn't have to work as hard to convert from your camera's format to the project format.
Timebase	Specifies the time divisions of your video. NTSC is divided into 30 frames per second of video. (Actually it's 29.97 frames per second, but 30 is easier to remember.) PAL is divided into 25.0 frames per second. Some editing modes, such as 24p, have a unique Timebase mode of 23.976 frames per second. Other editing modes, such as HDV 1080i, use a Timebase setting of 25.00 frames per second.

continues on next page

What About Those Other Settings? *continued*

Setting	Description
Frame Size	Specifies the width and height of your video. The frame is the container holding the video. Frames at a movie theater are measured in feet. Frames on a big-screen television are measured in inches. Frames of video displayed on a computer monitor are measured in pixels. A frame of NTSC DV video is 720 pixels wide by 480 pixels tall (even if it's widescreen video).
Pixel Aspect Ratio	Describes the shape of the video frame. You will deal with three common aspect ratios in video editing: **1.0 aspect ratio pixel (computer monitor)** A pixel in a computer monitor is perfectly square, so the ratio of its width to height, or **aspect ratio**, is 1:1, the same as 1÷1, which equals 1.0. **0.9 aspect ratio pixel (NTSC DV standard 4:3)** A pixel of DV video is not square but slightly skinny. Here's why: NTSC DV video is always 720 pixels × 480 pixels, which is a ratio of 720 ÷ 480 = 1.5. But standard televisions have a ratio of 4:3 = 1.333. This means that 1.5-ratio DV video is too wide to fit on a 1.333-ratio television screen. To fix this problem, each pixel of DV video is a bit thinner, by 0.9 to be exact, which helps it squeeze into a standard 4:3 television screen. Hence, you have a "0.9 pixel aspect ratio." **1.2 aspect ratio pixel (NTSC DV widescreen 16:9)** A pixel of widescreen DV video, on the other hand, is *wider* than a square pixel. Since NTSC DV video is always 720 × 480 pixels—yes, even widescreen NTSC DV video—this poses a unique problem. How do you get the same number of pixels to fill a 16:9 ratio screen? Answer: Make the pixel *wider*! This is how 720 × 480 pixels expand to fit a 16:9-ratio television screen. For you mathaholics: (16:9) ÷ (720:480) = 1.2.
Color Depth	Specifies how many possible colors can be used in your video. DV video is always "millions of colors," and it cannot be changed.

continues on next page

What About Those Other Settings? *continued*	
Setting	**Description**
Quality	Sets the quality to a value between 0–100 where 100 is the maximum. DV can be set only to 100%.
Compressor	Compresses and decompresses the video stream so it plays smoothly on your computer. Uncompressed video is very large (25 MB/sec), and the average computer would choke trying to play such a massive file size. Compression is a method of efficiently condensing the video into a smaller size so that your computer can handle playing it smoothly. DV video always uses DV compression. DVDs and HDV use MPEG-2 compression. Other compressors do exist, and you will learn which ones are best for exporting your program to the Web, CD, DVD, and more.
Fields	Upper field + Lower field = Full frame A full DV frame is divided into two fields. Every odd-numbered line is stored in the upper field, and even-numbered lines are stored in the lower field. This is called **interlacing fields** (picture the teeth of a zipper). DV video is interlaced with its lower field first. If you could slow down an interlaced television screen when playing DV video, you would see the lower field drawn and then the upper field. DV video is sometimes called **60i**, short for "60 frames interlaced" (30 frames per second × 2 fields per frame). Computer monitors are not separated into fields, so each horizontal line of the frame is drawn progressively in numeric order (1, 2, 3, 4, 5…). This is called **progressive scan**. Why does this matter? When you watch interlaced video on an interlaced television screen, you don't see the interlacing; the video plays smoothly. But, when you watch interlaced video on a progressive scan computer screen, the interlacing effect becomes apparent. In Chapter 13, *"Exporting to Files and Tape,"* you will learn how to convert interlaced video to progressive video for playback on the Internet or CDs.

Exploring the Premiere Pro 2 Workspace

Based on the task you are accomplishing, Premiere Pro 2 provides different workspaces. A **workspace** is a collection of panels tailored to the task at hand. The **Editing** workspace, for example, prominently displays panels for trimming your video footage. The **Effects** workspace gives you easy access to panels for adding and modifying special effects. The specific arrangement of panels is what makes each workspace unique.

Think of the workspace like your neighborhood. Your neighborhood comprises many houses, and the exact location and size of each house is what makes your neighborhood unique. Each house contains neighbors. Some houses have one neighbor, and some have many neighbors.

Returning to reality, you can apply this analogy to workspaces. Your workspace comprises many panels, and the exact location and size of each panel is what makes your workspace unique. Each panel contains tabs. Some panels have one tab, and some have many tabs.

Note: By default, Premiere Pro 2 uses the **Editing** workspace. However, because Premiere Pro 2 remembers the most recently opened workspace, if you have been playing with Premiere Pro 2 already, you may have made changes to your workspace. To ensure your workspace matches the workspace shown in this book, choose **Window > Workspace > Editing**. Also note the illustrations in this book were created on a monitor with resolution of 1024 × 768. If you have a different resolution, your screen may look slightly different.

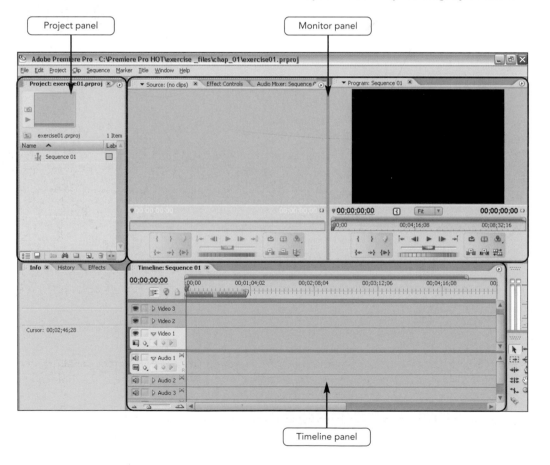

Project panel

Monitor panel

Timeline panel

The **Editing** workspace, as shown in the illustration here, is the primary layout in Premiere Pro 2 and is where you will do most of your work. The three primary panels of the **Editing** workspace are the **Project**, **Monitor**, and **Timeline** panels. The next few chapters discuss each of these panels in detail. In this chapter, you will get an overview of these panels and understand how they fit into the big picture.

The **Project** panel is the holding area for all your video clips. You must first import every audio, video, and graphic clip you plan to use in your project into the **Project** panel before you can use the clip. When you capture video from your camera, the video file is stored on your hard drive and imported into the Project panel automatically. (You'll learn more about importing in Chapter 2, *"Importing and Editing."*)

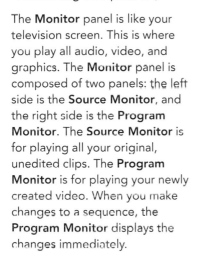

All Premiere Pro 2 projects come with one item, named **Sequence 01**. You can see the sequence patiently sitting in your **Project** panel. A **sequence** is the blank canvas where you will do your editing. (You'll find more about sequences in Chapter 3, *"Assembling a Sequence."*)

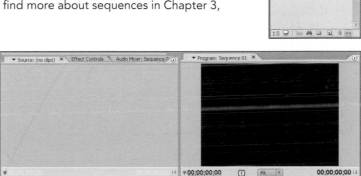

The **Monitor** panel is like your television screen. This is where you play all audio, video, and graphics. The **Monitor** panel is composed of two panels: the left side is the **Source Monitor**, and the right side is the **Program Monitor**. The **Source Monitor** is for playing all your original, unedited clips. The **Program Monitor** is for playing your newly created video. When you make changes to a sequence, the **Program Monitor** displays the changes immediately.

The **Timeline** panel is where you assemble your sequence. Whereas the **Monitor** panel shows the visual representation of a sequence, the **Timeline** shows what is happening *in time*. The **Timeline** starts at zero seconds on the far left and increases to infinity. (Actually, the **Timeline** stops at 24 hours in length, but a movie that is 24 hours long will *feel* like infinity.)

Before going any further, I'll summarize these panels: You import clips into the **Project** panel. You preview the original clips in the **Source Monitor**. You assemble the clips in a sequence in the **Timeline** panel. You preview the sequence in the **Program Monitor**.

Since you're now familiar with the default workspace, you can begin customizing it.

Arranging Panels

In Premiere Pro 2 you can dock and group multiple panels in a single pane, as well as turn any panel into a floating panel. Most editors start with a basic workspace as a template and then customize the layout of the panels to fit their needs. (Like snowflakes, no two editors are alike!) Because this is a radical change to the previous Premiere Pro interface, it's important to learn how to dock and group your panels in a pane.

Grouped panels show up as tabs along the top of a pane. You can see the contents of only one panel at a time when they are grouped in a pane. In the illustration shown above, the **Info**, **History**, and **Effects** panels are grouped into one pane. To access each panel, simply select the tab you want to bring to the foreground. In the illustration shown above, the **Info** panel is in the foreground.

Docked top to bottom   *Docked side by side*

Unlike grouped panels, **docked panels** allow you to see the contents of multiple panels all at once in a single pane. You can dock panels side by side or top to bottom. In the illustration shown here on the left, the **History** panel is docked to the bottom of the pane. In the illustration shown here on the right, the **History** panel is docked to the right of the pane. The overall pane size remains the same, no matter how you dock the panels.

A series of dots appears on the tab at the top of each panel. To move a panel, you must click and drag its tab (these dots) to a new location.

So how exactly do you group or dock a panel in a pane? The trick is to grab the panel's tab, represented by the dots at the top of the panel, and drag it to one of the five target panels. The target panel on which you drop the panel determines its position in the pane.

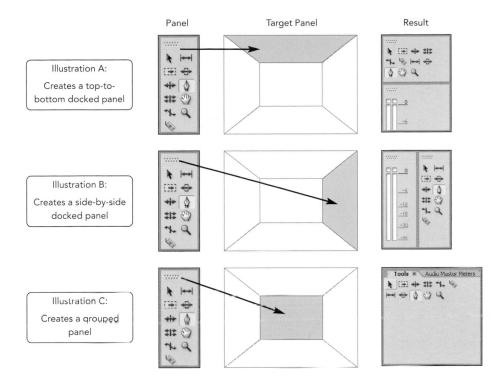

Panel	Target Panel	Result

Illustration A:

Creates a top-to-bottom docked panel

Illustration B:

Creates a side-by-side docked panel

Illustration C:

Creates a grouped panel

The illustration shown here demonstrates the three scenarios for docking a panel inside a pane.

Illustration A: If you drag the panel tab to the top or bottom target panel, you create a **top-to-bottom docked panel**.

Illustration B: If you drag the tab to the left or right target panel, you create a **side-by-side docked panel**.

Illustration C: If you drag the tab to the center target panel, you create a **panel group**.

You can also create **floating panels**, which appear on top of other panel. In the illustration shown here, the **History** panel floats over the **Info** panel. Floating panels are especially useful if you have multiple computer monitors because you can float the panel on the second monitor and then dock additional panels to the floating panel.

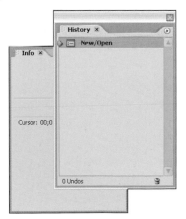

In the next exercise, you will practice the art of docking, grouping, and floating panels.

2 | Docking, Grouping, and Floating Panels

So many verbs all at once! In this exercise, you will learn how to dock and group panels, how to create a floating panel, and how to save a custom workspace for quick access in future projects.

---

1 If you followed the previous exercise, **exercise01.prproj** should still be open in Premiere Pro 2. If it's not, click **Open Project** on the **Welcome Screen**. Navigate to the **c:\exercise_files\chap_01** folder, click **exercise02.prproj** to select it, and click **Open**.

---

2 Choose **Window > Workspace > Editing** to ensure you are using the default workspace: **Editing**.

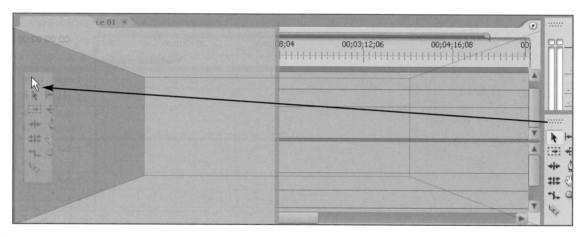

3 Click and drag the tabs of the **Toolbar** panel from the lower-right corner of the workspace to the left of the **Timeline** panel to dock the panel. Hold down the mouse until you see the new location in the left target panel, and then release.

Tip: If you accidentally let go of the mouse in the wrong location, simply repeat Step 2 to reset your workspace, and then try Step 3 again.

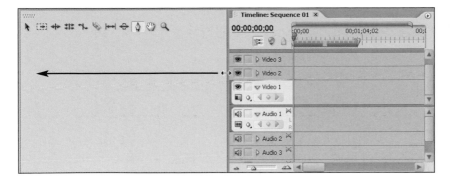

4 Click and drag the yellow bar between the **Toolbar** and **Timeline** panels all the way to the left.

The pane size doesn't change, but the division of real estate between the panels changes. This gives the Timeline panel a little more breathing room.

---

5 Click the tab (dots) once at the top of the **Audio Master Meters** panel. You can find the **Audio Master Meters** panel at the far right of the **Timeline** panel.

Tip: Clicking the tab of a panel once brings the panel into focus, indicated by the yellow high-light around the panel. **Focus** means a panel is the active panel. Throughout this book, you'll be instructed to bring a panel into focus before performing certain actions. In Premiere Pro 2, the same command can cause different results depending on which panel is in focus, so it's a good habit to explicitly click the panel you want to work in before you try working in it.

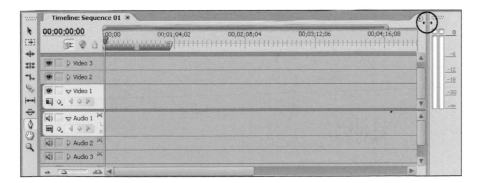

6 Click and drag the yellow bar between the **Audio Master Meters** and **Timeline** panels to the left, just enough to see the **Audio Master Meters** panel more fully.

You have just docked and resized panels within a pane. Now it's time to make a panel group in a pane.

---

7 In the lower-left pane, select the **Effects** panel to bring it into focus.

8 Click and drag the **Effects** panel straight up to the center of the **Project** panel. Release the mouse when you see the new location in the center target panel.

Releasing the mouse in the center target panel creates a panel group, with tabs along the top of the pane for each panel in that group.

9 Select the **Info** panel to bring it into focus. Hold down the **Ctrl** key, and then click and drag the **Info** panel to the center of your screen to create a floating panel. Release the mouse when you see the panel floating by itself.

Tip: You can close a floating panel by clicking the familiar red-and-white Close button in the upper-right corner of the panel. Conversely, you can open any panel from the Window menu.

After you customize your panels, you may want to save the custom configuration. Premiere Pro 2 allows you to save your custom workspace for use in future projects. You'll learn how in the next steps.

10 Choose **Window > Workspace > Save Workspace**.

---

11 In the **Save Workspace** dialog box, type **My Workspace** in the **Name** field, and click **Save**.

Tip: You can delete a custom workspace from the same menu. Simply choose Window > Workspace > Delete Workspace.

Once a workspace is saved, it's easy to switch between workspaces. Next you will open one of the additional workspaces that comes with Premiere Pro 2, and then you will learn how to return to the saved My Workspace.

---

12 Choose **Window > Workspace > Color Correction**.

Notice the panels are in a completely different configuration—this is a strange layout indeed. What if you want to return to the workspace you created in this exercise? Since you saved the workspace, you can return to it easily. You'll learn how in the next step.

---

13 Choose **Window > Workspace > My Workspace**.

The panels return to the custom workspace you created and saved.

---

14 Choose **File > Save**. Next, choose **File > Close** to close this project before moving on to the next chapter.

VIDEO: | **interface.mov**

To learn more about the Premiere Pro 2 interface, including how to customize the workspace, check out **interface.mov** in the **videos** folder on the **Premiere Pro 2 HOT DVD-ROM**.

Congratulations! You just finished the first step in any Premiere Pro 2 project: creating a new project file. Since you are now familiar with starting a new project, choosing a project preset, and working with the primary panels of a project file, you're ready to move on to the next step: importing and editing your clips.

2

Importing and Editing

Once you create a new project in Adobe Premiere Pro 2, the next step is to import and edit your video. To accomplish these tasks, you need to go in-depth with the **Project** and **Source Monitor** panels. In this chapter, you'll learn how to import videos, audio files, and still images in the **Project** panel, and you'll learn how to organize your clips with bins. Finally, you will preview and edit the clips in the **Source Monitor** panel.

What Is Importing?

Importing is the process of bringing a file from your hard drive into your Premiere Pro 2 project. It is important to note that the original file stays on your hard drive, and you are only linking to the original file. For example, when you download a 3 MB file from the Web to your computer, you are **copying** the entire 3 MB file to a specific location on your hard drive. Now at least two instances of that file exist: the original 3 MB file on the Web site and the 3 MB copy on your hard drive.

However, when you import a file into Premiere Pro 2, you make a link to the original file, not a copy. Every time you preview the file in the **Source Monitor** panel, Premiere Pro 2 follows the link, finds the file on your hard drive, and plays it from its original location. Because the project file links to other files on the hard drive, the project file stays very small. In addition, Premiere Pro 2 auto-matically reflects updates to the original file in the Premiere Pro 2 project.

Linking has one main disadvantage: If you move the original file to a different folder on your hard drive, Premiere Pro 2 needs help locating the file because moving the original file breaks the link—the link no longer exists.

Importing Versus Capturing

Importing is often confused with capturing. As discussed, **importing** is the process of bringing the file on your hard drive into your Premiere Pro 2 project. **Capturing** is the act of transferring video from videotape and saving it to a file on your hard drive. In Chapter 14, *"Capturing Digital Video,"* you will learn how Premiere Pro 2 helps you capture video from your camcorder. In this chapter, you will import files already on your hard drive.

NOTE:

What File Types Can You Import?

Beyond video, Premiere Pro 2 can import graphics and audio files. This capability allows you to add company logos, text, music, and much more to your project. Here are some of the most common graphic and audio types Premiere Pro 2 can import:

Common Graphic Types	Common Graphic Formats
Photos from digital cameras	JPEG, BMP, TIF, PNG
Images from the Web	JPEG, GIF, BMP, TIF, PNG
Mac graphics	PICT
Layered Adobe Photoshop images	PSD
Computer-drawn artwork	AI (Adobe Illustrator)
Logos, titles, and text	Formats with an alpha channel (more on this later in the book)

Common Audio Types	Common Audio Formats
CD audio	**Note:** Premiere Pro 2 cannot copy directly from CDs. Instead, use a CD-copying program, such as Windows Media Player, to capture the audio to one of these compatible formats: MP3, WAV, AIF, WMV, or WMA.
Audio from a microphone	Can be recorded directly into a Premiere Pro 2 project
Audio from the Internet	MP3, WAV, AIF, WMV, WMA
Mac audio file	AIF

Exploring the Project Panel

If you remember nothing else from this section, remember this: *You cannot use a file unless you first import it into the Project panel.* The **Project** panel has two primary functions: to collect and organize all the clips you plan to use and to preview and display the properties of a clip.

Once you import a file, you can then use it to make your program.

Displaying a Clip's Properties

Each video clip you work with has unique characteristics, or **properties**. The properties define the size of the clip on the screen, the duration of the clip, and the quality of its audio, among a few other attributes. One of the functions of the **Project** panel is to display vital information about each clip.

The top portion of the **Project** panel is called the **preview area**. This is where important properties of the currently selected clip display. Here's a brief rundown of what the **Project** panel displays:

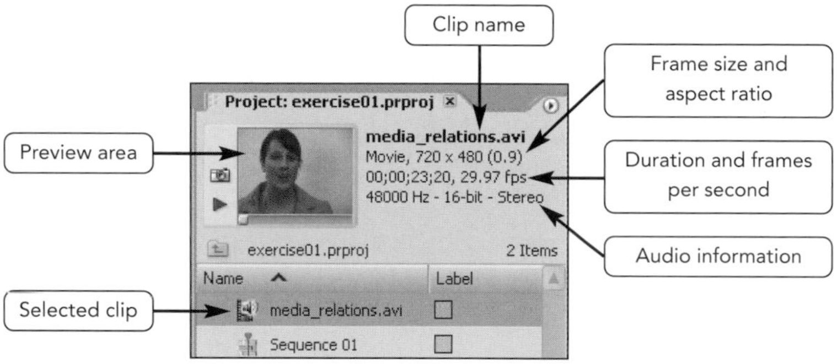

Preview area: This is where the selected clip plays.

Frame size and aspect ratio:
Premiere Pro 2 expresses the frame size in terms of pixels wide by pixels high and displays the aspect ratio in parentheses. In this case, the frame size is 720 x 480 pixels with an aspect ratio of 0.9.

Duration and frames per second: Duration is expressed in terms of *hours;minutes;seconds;frames*, whereas the frames per second value is expressed in...well...frames per second. (This video stuff is easy!)

Audio information: Video clips with sound and audio files display important audio information such as quality, bit depth, and channel (Stereo or Mono).

Displaying Clips

You can display clips in the **Project** panel using one of two methods.

Clicking the **List** button, in the illustration shown here on the left, puts the **Project** panel in **List view**. Clicking the **Icon** button, in the illustration shown here on the right, puts the **Project** panel in **Icon view**.

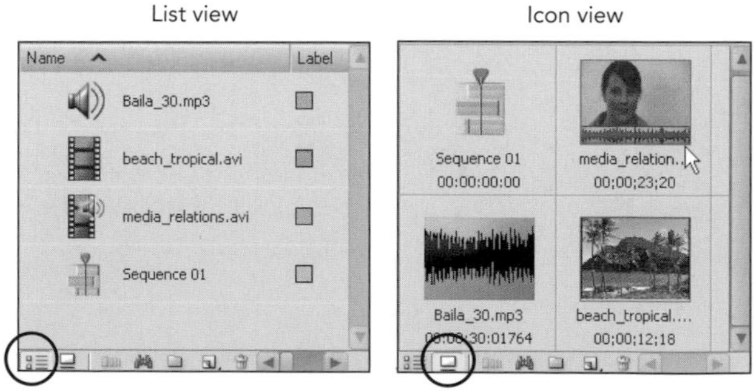

List view: Displays a list of imported clips. When you use List view, the emphasis is on the file name because you see a generic icon indicating the type of clip and the name or file name of the clip. You can sort List view by clicking the column heading. If you click the **Name** column, you sort from A to Z. Clicking it again reverses the sort, from Z to A. **List view** has many other hidden columns, but you can display them by scrolling the **Project** panel to the right.

Icon view: Displays all the clip icons in a grid view. When you use **Icon view**, you see a thumbnail preview of the clip so you can quickly identify the content of the clip. You can sort **Icon view** by dragging clips to squares on the grid (like a checkerboard).

VIDEO: **columns.mov**

When the **Project** panel is in **List view**, you can view about 30 columns, each one chock-full of different information. To learn more about how to expand and sort through the column options in the **Project** panel, check out **columns.mov** in the **videos** folder on the **Premiere Pro 2 HOT DVD-ROM**.

Organizing Clips

A bin in Icon view

An expanded bin
in List view

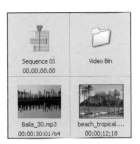

A bin in List view

When you're importing and editing clips, you'll often have numerous clips and may find it overwhelming to see them all in the **Project** panel. To help organize the clips, you can use **bins**, which behave similarly to the folders you are accustomed to using in Windows XP. (Premiere Pro 2 calls them bins because movie film used to be stored in real bins.) To organize clips into bins, you simply drag and drop clips in a bin. You can display—or **expand**—the contents of a bin by clicking the arrow to the left of the bin. Conversely, you can close—or **collapse**—a bin by clicking the arrow again.

In the following exercise, you will import files, change views, and expand and collapse bins.

NOTE: **Dutch Harbor Resort and Casino**

Throughout the remainder of this book, you'll create a promotional DVD for the Dutch Harbor Resort and Casino, a fictional resort. The exercises in this book help you assemble a program you will eventually export to a DVD movie with menus.

1 | Importing and Organizing Clips

When you start any project, your first step is to import all the media files you plan to use to create your program. In this exercise, you will import and organize your clips in a variety of ways.

1 On the **Welcome Screen**, click **Open Project**. In the **Open Project** dialog box, navigate to the **c:\exercise_files\chap_02** folder, click **exercise01.prproj** to select it, and click **Open**.

Tip: Notice the project opens with a custom workspace. This is a workspace I've created for you to use in this exercise. It is based on the default Editing workspace, but the Project panel has been enlarged, which helps you see more clips at once.

A useful feature of Premiere Pro 2 is that it saves the workspace with the project file. If you were to open this project a year from now, the same workspace would display.

Since you may want to refer to this workspace again, it's a good idea to save it permanently so you can quickly choose it in the future.

2 Choose **Window > Workspace > Save Workspace**. In the **Save Workspace** dialog box, type **HOT** in the **Name** field, and click **Save**.

Note: You'll use the HOT workspace throughout this book. If you move the panels, you can always return to the HOT workspace so your screen matches the exercises in this book by choosing Window > Workspace > HOT.

3 Choose **File > Save As**. Navigate to the **c:\exercise_files\dutch_harbor** folder. Name the file **dutch harbor promo**, and click **Save**.

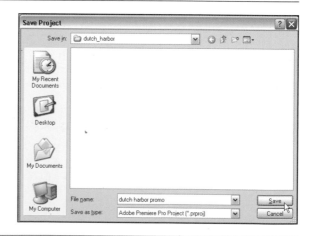

Tip: The Save As command creates and opens a new file. The Save a Copy command creates a new file but leaves the original file open. Saving a copy is useful for making backups or creating restore points.

Now that you have the workspace set up and you've saved the project file, it's time to start importing clips into the project. You'll learn how in the next steps.

4 Choose **File > Import**. In the **Import** dialog box, navigate to the **c:\exercise_files\media_files\video** folder, click **beach_tropical.avi** to select it, and click **Open**.

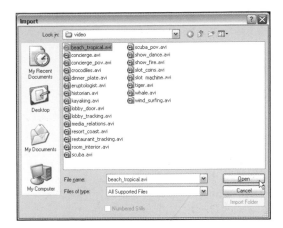

You can now see the beach_tropical.avi clip in the Project panel. In the preview area, you can see the first frame of the video clip and its properties.

5 Choose **File > Import**. In the **Import** dialog box, navigate to the **c:\exercise_files\media_files\video** folder, click **historian.avi** to select it, and click **Open**.

Both the beach_tropical.avi and historian.avi clips display in the Project panel.

Tip: Premiere Pro 2 remembers the last folder you imported from, so you shouldn't need to navigate all that far to find the file!

Clicking Open is just one way to import a clip. In the next step, you'll import a clip by double-clicking a file name.

6 In the **Project** panel, double-click anywhere in the large gray area, as shown in the illustration here, to open the **Import** dialog box. In the **Import** dialog box, double-click **concierge.avi** to import it.

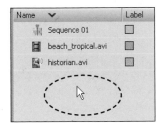

Double-clicking in the empty region of the Project panel is an alternative method of importing a file and works exactly like the Import command but is much faster. Throughout this book, you'll notice Premiere Pro 2 offers many ways to perform the same task.

7 In the **Project** panel, click the **Name** column head to sort the list alphabetically by name, from A to Z.

If you look at the illustration shown here, you'll see that Premiere Pro 2 displays the clips in the order they were imported. Although the clips are currently sorted alphabetically, new clips will display at the bottom until you sort them again.

So far, you've imported single clips into the Project panel. What if you want to import multiple clips from the same folder? Premiere Pro 2 lets you import multiple clips. You'll learn how next.

---

8 In the **Project** panel, double-click anywhere in the large gray area. In the **Import** dialog box, click **concierge_pov.avi** to select it. Hold down the **Shift** key, and click **eruptologist.avi** to select all the files in between. Click **Open**.

The Import dialog box lets you import multiple clips simultaneously. If you are familiar with the Windows operating system, this should make you feel right at home.

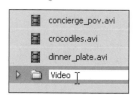

You may have noticed the Project panel is getting a bit crowded. Creating a bin helps you effectively organize your clips.

---

9 Choose **File > New > Bin**. When the bin icon appears, type **Video**, and press **Enter**.

Note: If you click somewhere else before naming the bin, Premiere Pro 2 automatically names the bin Bin 01 (or Bin 02, Bin 03, and so on, depending on how many bins you created). You can rename a bin by right-clicking the folder icon next to the bin, choosing Rename, and pressing Enter.

With the new Video bin in place, you can begin moving your clips into the bin.

---

10 Click the filmstrip icon to the left of **dinner_plate.avi** to select it, and drag it onto the **Video** bin icon.

As you position your mouse over the bin icon, the cursor changes as shown in the illustration shown here to indicate you are about to place a clip in a bin.

11 To see the clip you placed in the Video bin, click the **arrow** to expand the contents of the **Video** bin.

The contents of the bin display with an indentation below the bin. If you want to put more than one video clip into a bin, you can use the Ctrl key to select multiple clips. You'll learn how in the next step.

---

12 Click **eruptologist.avi** to select it. Hold down **Ctrl**, and click **concierge_pov.avi** and **crocodiles.avi** to select all three clips. When all three files are selected, release **Ctrl**. Drag the selected files onto the folder icon next to the **Video** bin.

You just placed multiple clips into a bin all at once. Because all three clips are selected, dragging any one of the clips moves all three clips. This is a huge time-saver, especially with large projects. If you have trouble selecting multiple clips, choose Edit > Undo, and try again.

To access, or **step inside**, clips in a bin, you can double-click the folder icon of a bin.

---

13 Double click the folder icon next to the **Video** bin.

This method is similar to double-clicking a folder in Windows to view the contents of that folder.

---

14 Choose **File > Import**. In the **Import** dialog box, click **kayaking.avi** to select it. Hold down the **Shift** key, click **wind_surfing.avi** to select all the files in between, and click **Open**.

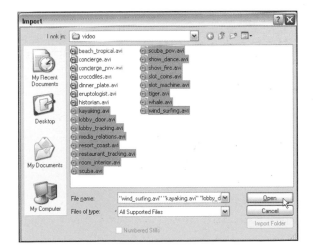

Notice the clips were imported into your Video bin automatically because you were "inside" the bin at the time of import.

15 To return to the top level, click the **Parent Bin** button.

While you are "inside" the Video bin, you can see only the clips that have been placed or imported into the bin. However, you cannot see a few clips because they were left "outside" the bin. When you return to the top level, you are **stepping out** of the Video bin, which allows you to see the other clips.

Tip: In the illustration shown here, notice the Video bin contains 20 Items. This is a quick way to figure out how many items are currently displayed in the Project panel.

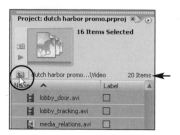

---

16 Next to the **Video** bin, click the **arrow** to collapse the contents of the **Video** bin.

The Project panel now displays five items. Although the project contains many more items, you are viewing only five.

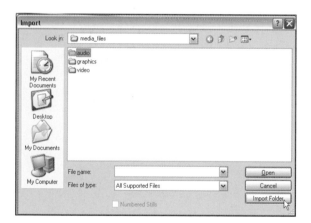

17 Choose **File > Import**. In the **Import** dialog box, navigate to the **c:\exercise_files\media_files** folder, click the **audio** folder to select it, and click the **Import Folder** button.

Importing a folder allows you to import all the files in that folder at one time. In this step, Premiere Pro 2 converts the audio folder on your hard drive to an audio bin in your project. Plus, all of the files in the audio folder are imported as clips in the audio bin.

So far, you've done all this importing and organizing in List view. Next, you'll learn how to import and organize in Icon view.

---

18 At the bottom of the **Project** panel, click the **Icon** button.

When you switch to Icon view, Premiere Pro 2 places each item in a square. In the illustration shown here, you can see many empty squares. In addition, more squares appear to the right, beyond the width of the Project panel.

Tip: You can position your mouse over (almost) any button, and after a brief pause, a tool tip pops up. If a button has a keyboard shortcut, the shortcut displays in parentheses.

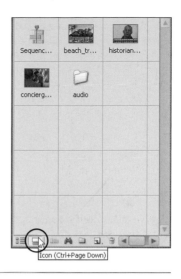

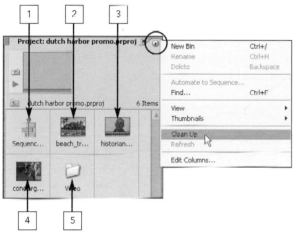

Before using the Clean Up command,
only five of the six items are visible.

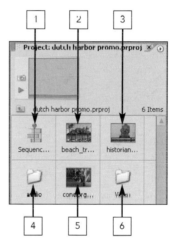

Now all six items can be seen
in the panel.

19 Depending on the size and resolution of your computer monitor, you may not be able to see all the items because of the width of the **Project** panel. To resolve this, click the **wing menu** in the upper-right corner of the **Project** panel, and choose **Clean Up**.

The Clean Up command removes any empty squares in Icon view and arranges items so they display within the width of the Project panel. Keep in mind, the number of items visible on your own system may differ from that shown here because this is based on the resolution and size of your computer monitor. No matter how your screen currently looks, the Clean Up command should rearrange everything to be visible on your own monitor.

Note: Wing menu is a fancy name for a menu containing additional commands for a particular panel. In Premiere Pro 2 (and other Adobe applications), you can usually find wing menus represented by an arrow within a tiny circle in the upper-right corner of a panel.

20 Drag and drop each of the remaining three video clips—**beach_tropical.avi**, **historian.avi**, and **concierge_pov.avi**—into the **Video** bin.

In List view you sort by clicking the column heads. In Icon view, you sort by dragging and dropping a file or bin to a different grid square.

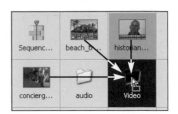

---

21 From the **Project** panel **wing menu**, choose **Clean Up**.

When finished, the Icon view should show Sequence 01, the audio bin, and the Video bin.

---

22 At the bottom of the **Project** panel, click the **New Bin** button to create a new bin, name it **Graphics**, and press **Enter**.

This is yet another way to create bins.

---

23 Double-click the **Graphics** bin to step inside the bin and view its contents.

A downside of using Icon view is you can only view the contents of bins by going into the bins.

You can probably guess what you're going to import into the Graphics bin (hint hint). In the next step, you'll import two JPEGs.

Tip: When you want to select multiple files that are not next to each other, press Ctrl instead of Shift.

---

24 You are currently viewing the "inside" of the Graphics bin. In the **Project** panel, double-click any empty grid square to import more clips. Navigate to the **c:\exercise_files\media_files\ graphics** folder. Hold down the **Ctrl** key, click **coral_reef.jpg**, and then click **resort_map.ai** to select both files. Click **Open**.

You just imported two types of image files: two JPEGs (.jpg) and an Adobe Illustrator file (.ai). Just like in List view, clips are imported into the bin you are viewing at the time of import.

If you have trouble seeing the icons because of their small sizes, you can increase their thumbnail sizes, as described in the following step.

25 From the **Project** panel **wing menu,** choose **Thumbnails > Medium.**

26 Click the **Parent Bin** button to return to the top level of the project. Now that the Icon view squares are much larger, this is an ideal time to use the **Clean Up** command again. From the **Project** panel **wing menu,** choose **Clean Up.**

With that, it's time to return to List view.

27 In the lower-left corner of the **Project** panel, click the **List** button.

28 In the **Project** panel, click the **wing menu,** and choose **Thumbnails > Medium.**

This increases the size of the List view icons, making them easier to see.

29 Click the arrow next to the **Video** bin to expand its contents. In the Project panel, click the **wing menu,** and make sure **Thumbnails > Off** is unchecked. If it is already unchecked, press **Esc** twice to close the wing menu.

Turning on thumbnails in List view displays pictures of each clip, rather than generic icons. This setup gives you the best of both worlds. You have the alphabetized order of List view and the thumbnail graphics of Icon view—which are now large enough to see clearly, thanks to the previous step.

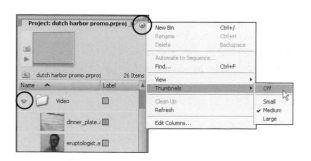

30 Choose **File > Save**, or press **Ctrl+S**. Leave **dutch harbor promo.prproj** open for the next exercise.

Although this exercise had many steps, it was quick and painless. The purpose of this exercise was to get you familiar with the layout and features of the Project panel. To recap, you imported by choosing File > Import or by double-clicking the gray area of the Project panel; you imported video, audio, and graphic files and entire folders; you used the Ctrl and Shift keys to select multiple clips; you created and named bins; you switched between List and Icon views; and you sorted clips alphabetically in List view and graphically in Icon view.

This concludes your journey of the Project panel. Now that you have your clips imported and organized, it's time to preview and edit them in the Source Monitor.

VIDEO:

adobe_bridge.mov

As if you didn't have enough ways to import files into Premiere Pro 2, you may want to try one more method new to Premiere Pro 2: Adobe Bridge.

Bridge is a completely separate application from Premiere Pro 2 that installs on your computer at the same time you install Premiere Pro 2. The function of Bridge is to act as a media library: it helps to organize and catalog all of the media files on your hard drive. You can quickly navigate and preview media files on your hard drive and also add metadata and keywords to any clip.

Metadata is information about the file, such as the author's name, resolution, copyright—*anything!* Many of the powerful Bridge features that allows you to organize, search, and keep track of your files rely on the metadata information for each file. For example, if you've added the keyword *Holland* to your video clips and still images from your vacation to Amsterdam, you can quickly search and display any files associated with the keyword *Holland*.

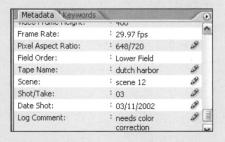

Bridge also helps you share files with Premiere Pro 2. You can import clips into Premiere Pro 2 by dragging them from Bridge to the Premiere Pro 2 Project panel. To launch bridge directly from within Premiere Pro 2, choose **File > Browse**.

To learn more about navigating, previewing, adding metadata, and sharing media files with Bridge, check out **adobe_bridge.mov** in the **videos** folder on the **Premiere Pro 2 HOT DVD-ROM**.

Working with the Monitor Panel

The **Monitor panel** is a built-in video player within Premiere Pro 2. The primary functions of the **Monitor panel** are to preview and edit your original video (called the **source video**) and preview the sequences you assemble.

To aid you in these two tasks, the **Monitor** panel is divided into two split views. The left side, or **Source Monitor**, helps you preview and edit your source video. The right side, or **Program Monitor**, is for previewing sequences in the **Timeline**. In this chapter, you will focus on the **Source Monitor** and its functions. In the next chapter, you will get to know the **Program Monitor**.

Source Monitor   Program Monitor

Understanding the Source Monitor

The left side of the **Monitor** panel is the **Source Monitor**.

Here is how the **Source Monitor** fits into the overall Premiere Pro 2 workflow:

1. Import clips into the **Project** panel. This is what you did in Exercise 1.

2. Drag clips from the **Project** panel to the **Source Monitor**, and *trim off the fat* (that is, get rid of unwanted video). You accomplish this by adding **In** and **Out** points.

3. Drag clips from the **Source Monitor** to the **Timeline** panel, and assemble your program.

4. The **Source Monitor** has various buttons for previewing and trimming your video. In the next exercise, you will explore the primary features of the **Source Monitor**.

Adding In and Out Points

In and **Out** points are the bookends of your source clip. When you import a clip into the **Project** panel, it's not necessary to use the entire clip. You can trim some material from the beginning and end of the source clip, or you can use just a small segment from the middle. The process of whittling down your video to only the part you want to use is the heart and soul of video editing.

The most common workflow in Premiere Pro 2 is to set **In** and **Out** points in the **Source Monitor**. The idea is to watch your original clip and then choose which portions you want to use. Keep in mind, specifying **In** and **Out** points does not permanently delete any video from a clip. The **In** and **Out** points affect only the temporary copy of the clip that lives in your project, never the original file on the hard drive. You can change **In** and **Out** points as often as you'd like or remove them. In other words, you are doing no damage to any of your clips, so don't worry about practicing with your own video.

One more fact you should know about **In** and **Out** points: They don't like to share. A video clip can have only one **In** point and only one **Out** point. If you set a new **In** point, it destroys the old **In** point.

2 | Setting In and Out Points

In this exercise, you will learn to use the basic features of the **Source Monitor** and learn how to set **In** and **Out** points in a video file.

1 If you followed the previous exercise, **dutch harbor promo.prproj** should still be open in Premiere Pro 2. If it's not, click **Open Project** on the **Welcome Screen**. Navigate to the **c:\exercise_files\chap_02** folder, click **exercise02.prproj** to select it, and click **Open**.

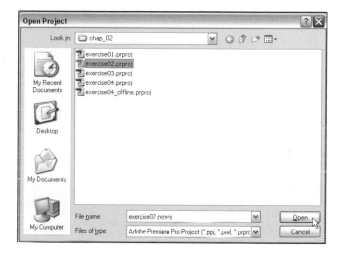

2 Choose **File > Save As**. Navigate to the **c:\exercise files\dutch_harbor** folder. Name the file **dutch harbor promo**, and click **Save**.

Note: If a previous version of dutch harbor promo.prproj already exists, you may be asked to replace it. Click Yes.

3 In the **Project** panel, click the **arrow** next to the **Video** bin to expand its contents, if it is not already expanded.

4 Scroll down to **historian.avi**, and drag its thumbnail from the **Project** panel to the **Source Monitor**.

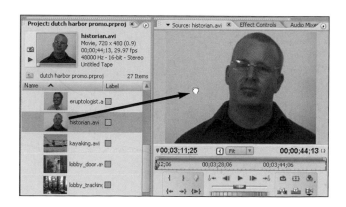

Note: If you have the title safe/action safe margins activated, you will see two thin boxes around the perimeter of the Source view. These serve as guides, primarily used as boundaries when creating text. You can temporarily hide these guides by clicking the Safe Margins button until the guides disappear. You will use these guides for creating titles in Chapter 5, *"Adding Titles."*

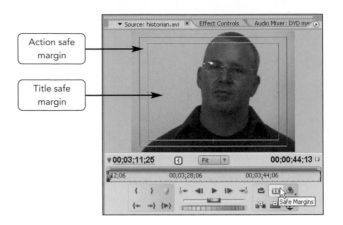

5 In the **Source Monitor**, click the **Play** button. Play the clip for a few seconds, and click the same button to stop the playback.

Your video plays in the Source Monitor. Notice the Play button switches to a Stop button during playback.

Tip: You can press the spacebar on your keyboard to begin playback. Pressing the spacebar a second time stops the playback.

The Play button begins playback.

During playback, the button changes to a Stop button.

6 Click the **Play** button. Play the clip until you locate the CTI (**C**urrent **T**ime **I**ndicator), and click the **Stop** button to stop.

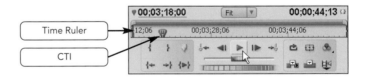

Notice the CTI moves across the Time Ruler as the video plays. The Time Ruler represents the entire duration of your clip. The far left is the beginning, and the far right is the end of the clip. The CTI, represented as a blue tab, shows you the exact frame being displayed in the Source Monitor.

Another way to change the current time is to drag the CTI left or right in the Time Ruler.

7 Click and drag the **CTI** to the far left of the **Time Ruler**, which is the beginning of the clip.

Notice the Monitor panel displays the frame at which the CTI is positioned in the Time Ruler.

Now it's time to set **In** and **Out** points to trim off some of the excess video at the beginning and end of this clip.

---

8 Click the **Play** button. Play the clip until right before the speaker begins his "good" take, and then click the **Stop** button.

Tip: If you go too far, use the Step Back and Step Forward buttons to move the CTI one frame at a time. To match this exercise, move the CTI to 00;03;19;23.

Tip: The Current Time Display setting shows the frame number being viewed. The format is *Hours;Minutes;Seconds;Frames*. Keep in mind there are 30 frames per second, just like there are 60 seconds per minute.

Tip: You can also use the left and right arrow keys on your keyboard to move one frame at a time.

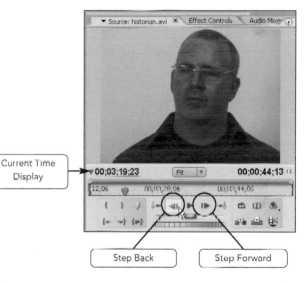

Current Time Display

Step Back

Step Forward

---

9 Click the **Set In Point** button, or press the **I** key on the keyboard.

This sets an In point at the position of the CTI, which is 00;03;19;23. Notice a dark-gray bar appears in the Time Ruler, indicating the segment of the clip you plan to use. Everything to the left of the dark-gray bar is the excess that will not be included in your final program.

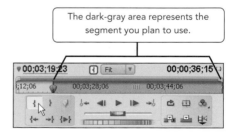

The dark-gray area represents the segment you plan to use.

10 Click the **Play** button. Play the clip until the actor gets to the end of his speech, and then stop the CTI.

This example uses 00;03;54;20. Don't forget the Step Forward and Step Back buttons if you want to move one frame at a time.

---

11 Click the **Set Out Point** button, or press the **O** key on your keyboard.

You just made your first edit! You now have some video at the beginning and the end of the clip you are trimming off. Notice the dark-gray bar extends only to the Out point.

---

12 In the **Project** panel, locate the **Video** bin, and double-click the thumbnail next to **media_relations.avi** to open it in the **Source Monitor**.

With this clip, you want to do the same task—trim off the excess at the head and tail of the video clip.

---

13 In the **Source Monitor**, click the **Play** button. Play the clip until the actor says her first word, and then click the **Stop** button at approximately **00;17;14;04**.

Tip: Head and **tail** are video-geek lingo for the beginning and end of a clip.

Next, you should set an In point before the speaker begins speaking, which is slightly before the current position of the CTI.

Another method for slowly moving backward and forward in time is the Jog Wheel. The Jog Wheel is great for quickly shuttling forward and backward over small amounts of time. Just in case you are wondering, it's supposed to look like a thin wheel or disk, like the volume dial on a Walkman. (Remember *those* ancient things?)

---

14 Position your mouse anywhere over the Jog Wheel, and slowly drag your mouse to the left, until immediately before the actor takes her breath, at approximately **00;17;13;10**.

15 In the **Source Monitor**, click the **Set In Point** button.

Notice the dark-gray bar in the Time Ruler extends from the In point to the end of the clip. Why the end? All clips *require* a beginning and an end. By default, the first frame is the In point, and the last frame is the Out point. You modified the In point, but the default Out point is still the end of the clip.

---

16 In the Source Monitor, click **Play** until the actor finishes speaking and puts down her hands. Click the **Stop** button. Use the **Step Back** and **Step Forward** buttons (frame by frame) or the **Jog Wheel** to move the **CTI** to **00;17;32;12**. Click the **Set Out Point** button.

Now that you are getting the hang of this, the next step includes a complete set of instructions.

---

17 In the **Project** panel, locate the **Video** bin. Drag the thumbnail next to **eruptologist.avi** to the **Source Monitor**. Using your preferred method of playback, set an **In** point and an **Out** point around the actor's speech.

In this example, I chose 00;07;47;03 as the In point and 00;07;57;13 as the Out point.

Time to learn a new button! In the next step, you'll practice using the Play In to Out button. As the name implies, this button plays your video from the In point and stops it on the Out point.

---

18 In the **Source Monitor**, click the **Play In to Out** button.

Tip: The regular Play button begins playing at the CTI and stops playing at the end of the clip. The Play In to Out button, however, starts playing at the In Point and stops at the Out Point, regardless of the CTI location.

Bonus question: What does the Play In to Out button do if your clip has no set In and Out points? **Answer:** It plays the entire clip because the default In and Out points are the first and last frames of the clip.

---

19 Choose **File > Save**, or press **Ctrl+S**. Leave **dutch harbor promo.prproj** open for the next exercise.

Here is a review of the exercise you just completed: You used the Source Monitor to trim clips before assembling them in the Timeline panel. The Play button becomes a Stop button during playback. Your keyboard's spacebar doubles as a Play/Stop button. You can move the CTI by dragging the CTI to a new point in time, by using the Jog Wheel, by clicking the Step Back and Step Forward buttons to move frame by frame, and by using the left and right arrow keys to move frame by frame.

The good news is you can edit all source clips—music, video, graphics, everything—this way. You have much more in-depth editing to learn, but you now understand the basics and are well on your way to efficient editing.

Using Subclips

Subclips are new to Premiere Pro 2. A **subclip** is a copy of a clip—not just an exact copy but a copy of only a small segment of a clip.

For example, if you have a two-minute clip and want to use only ten seconds of that clip, the two-minute clip is the **master clip**. You can set **In** and **Out** points around the ten-second segment of the master clip you plan to use. You can then turn that ten-second segment into a subclip in the **Project** panel. In the **Project** panel, you'll see two clips: the master clip and the subclip.

Subclips reside in the **Project** panel and behave exactly like master clips. Everything you can do to a master clip, you can do to a subclip.

Why are subclips so great? In the real world, it is not uncommon to capture a DV (**D**igital **V**ideo) tape as one *loooooong* master clip. Searching for a particular scene in a very long clip is like searching

for a needle in a video haystack. Subclips to the rescue! You can divide the master clip into multiple smaller and more manageable subclips. There's no searching. You know exactly where the segment of video is that you want because it's represented as a separate clip in the **Project** panel.

The steps for making a subclip are simple:

1. In a master clip, set an **In** point and an **Out** point.

2. Drag the master clip from the **Source Monitor** to the **Project** panel.

In the next quick exercise, you will see for yourself how easy it is to make multiple subclips from a single file.

NOTE:

Dutch Harbor Promotional DVD

By the end of this book, you will create a mock promotional DVD for the fictional Dutch Harbor Resort and Casino. This DVD will have three components: a short introductory video, a narrated map of the resort, and a brief history of the island.

Unfortunately, the DVD narration for all three components is currently one very long audio file. In the next exercise, you'll turn the lengthy narration into four smaller subclips.

3 | Creating Subclips

In this exercise, you will learn how to turn a long audio clip into multiple subclips. You will find that navigating through the smaller clips is easier, and additionally, having the clips separated in the **Project** panel makes locating a subclip much quicker.

---

1 If you followed the previous exercise, **dutch harbor promo.prproj** should still be open in Premiere Pro 2. If it's not, click **Open Project** on the **Welcome Screen**. Navigate to the **c:\exercise_files\chap_02** folder, click **exercise03.prproj** to select it, and click **Open**.

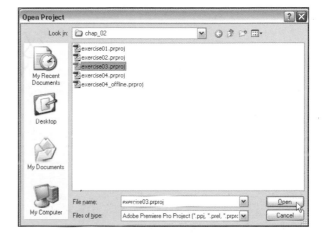

---

2 Choose File > Save As. Navigate to the **c:\exercise_files\dutch_harbor** folder. Name the file **dutch harbor promo**, and click **Save**.

Note: If a previous version of dutch harbor promo.prproj already exists, you may be asked to replace it. Click Yes.

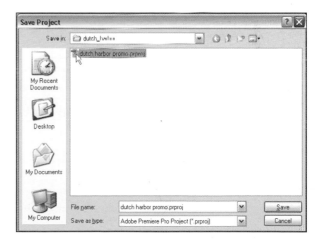

3 In the **Project** panel, click the **arrow** next to the **audio** bin to expand its contents. Click the icon next to **voiceover.wav**, and drag it to the **Source Monitor**.

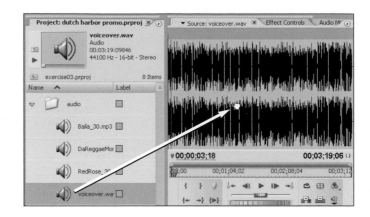

Audio clips are trimmed in the Source Monitor, just like video clips. However, instead of seeing a preview of the video clip, you see the audio waveform. A **waveform** is a graph of the audio's loudness—the louder the sound, the taller the sine wave (like a seismograph of an earthquake).

---

4 In the **Source Monitor**, click the **Current Time Display** shown in blue, type **3620**, and press **Enter**.

The first segment of audio ends at 00;00;36;20. This moves the CTI to 00;00;36;20.

Just when you thought you were done learning new ways to move around in the Source Monitor, along comes a completely new method, out of the blue. (Get it? Blue?) Typing the Current Time Display is useful when you know the exact time to which you want to go.

Tip: Even though the time displays with a semicolon, it is not required when typing the current time display. Typing 3620 is the same as typing 36;20 but is much quicker!

---

5 In the **Source Monitor**, click the **Set Out Point** button.

Tip: Because you didn't manually set your own In point, Premiere Pro 2 automatically uses the first frame of the audio clip as the default In point. You have now officially set both your In and Out points.

It is hard to discern where the speaker starts and stops speaking because you are viewing the entire audio file at once. To remedy this, you will zoom in closer to the CTI.

6 Drag the tapered handle of the **Viewing Area Bar** (either the right or the left) very slowly toward the **CTI** to zoom in. Continue dragging until the **Viewing Area Bar** is about half its original size.

As you drag the Viewing Area Bar to zoom in, the waveforms become clearer. You can easily see where the narrator pauses between syllables, words, and sentences, indicated by a flat line. You can now verify your Out point is positioned in a silent area, between words.

Note: Keep in mind, when you zoom in, you do not affect the clip. You change only how much of the file displays in the panel. Think of it like viewing the earth from outer space versus viewing it from the roof of your house. You can see much more detail from your roof, but you can't see the entire planet at once (unless you have a very tall house!).

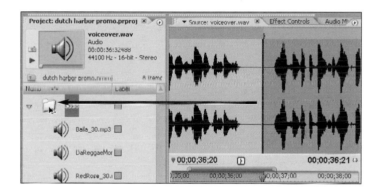

The flat line indicates silence, such as a pause.

Viewing Area Bar

---

7 Drag and drop the **Source Monitor** preview onto the **audio bin icon** in the **Project panel**.

This is the first step in creating a subclip of the In to Out section. When your mouse is positioned on the audio bin icon, the cursor changes, and the bin name is highlighted. This indicates you are about to create a subclip in the bin.

---

8 In the **Make Subclip** dialog box, name the subclip **DVD intro**, and click **OK**.

You should now see a DVD intro subclip, with a special subclip icon, at the end of the audio bin.

Tip: If you "missed the mark" and accidentally created the subclip *outside* the bin, don't fret. You can always drag and drop the subclip from its accidental location in the Project panel onto the audio bin icon, just like you practiced in Exercise 1.

With the first subclip finished, it's time to create your next subclip.

9 Click the **Go to Out Point** button.

This snaps the CTI to the Out point you set in Step 5.

Note: If your CTI was already placed at the Out point, then you probably didn't see much happen when you clicked the Go to Out Point button.

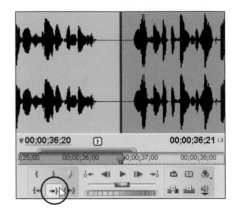

---

10 In the **Time Ruler**, right-click, and choose **Clear Clip Marker > Out**.

You use the Clear Clip Marker command to clear In and Out points you have manually set.

---

11 With the **CTI** still at 00;00;36;20, click the **Set In Point** button to set a new **In** point.

---

12 Click and drag the **Shuttle Slider** to the right until the CTI is at **00;01;37;23**.

The Shuttle Slider is another method of moving in time. Playback is accelerated the farther you drag from the center position. Left of center is reverse; right of center is forward. (No, that's not a political joke.)

Tip: If you overshoot your destination, you can drag the slider slowly to the left to reverse.

---

13 Click the **Set Out Point** button.

The In to Out Duration now reads 00;01;01;04 (1 minute, 1 second, 4 frames).

14 In the **Project** panel, click the **audio** bin icon to select it. In the **Source Monitor** preview, right-click, and choose **Make Subclip**. In the **Make Subclip** dialog box, name the subclip **DVD map**, and click **OK**.

This is an alternative method of creating the subclip. The new subclip should display in the audio bin list.

Tip: Clicking the bin icon before making the subclip this way ensures the subclip is placed in the desired bin (just in case somebody else came along and clicked another bin while you weren't looking).

15 In the **Project** panel, click the icon next to **voiceover.wav** to select it. Click the **Clear** button to delete the clip from the project.

This step highlights two important facts about clips: Although you deleted the master clip from the project, the two subclips remain. Deleting a clip from your project doesn't delete it from your hard drive. (In fact, almost nothing you do to a clip in Premiere Pro 2 can harm the original file on your hard drive.)

It's important to mentally distinguish between the "clip" in the project and the original file on the hard drive. Remember, the clip *points* to the file on the hard drive. Each time you play the clip, you are really playing the file from the hard drive. This holds true for subclips. Hence, deleting a clip from your hard drive removes the audio/video content of the clip from the project, and all that remains is an empty clip placeholder, called an **offline file**. For a complete description, check out the next section and exercise.

16 Save and close **dutch harbor promo.prproj**. If prompted to save changes, click Yes.

As you've experienced, subclips allow you to chop bigger clips into smaller clips, as well as turn In and Out points into separate clips in the Project panel, which allows for easy access later.

Here is a review of Exercise 2: Subclips are copies of a master clip segment. In and Out points are exclusive. A clip can have only one of each. If you set an In point, Premiere Pro 2 uses the last frame as the Out point, unless you specify a custom Out point. Vice versa, if you set an Out point, Premiere Pro 2 assumes the first frame as the In point.

Using Online Versus Offline Clips

If Premiere Pro 2 cannot find a file that has already been imported into a project, then the clip is considered to be **offline**. It is important to know how to find clips that are offline so you can to turn them into online clips and safely export your finished program.

At its most basic, an **offline clip** is a placeholder. It indicates a clip in a project Premiere Pro 2 cannot find. Perhaps you deleted the file from your hard drive. Perhaps you moved the file to a new location. Or, perhaps you are using an external hard drive that is temporarily disconnected.

Each time Premiere Pro 2 comes across a clip it cannot find, it asks you for help. You can choose to manually locate the file for Premiere Pro 2, or you can choose to convert the online clip into an offline clip. To understand the difference between online and offline clips and to understand what you should do in these situations, take a moment to review how clips are stored in a project.

Each clip in a project (as shown in the illustration here on the left) links to a file on the hard drive (as shown in the illustration here on the right). When you play the clip in the project, Premiere Pro 2 follows the link and plays the file on the hard drive.

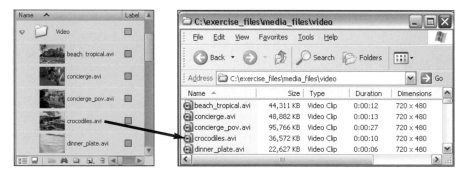

As you learned at the beginning of this chapter, when you import a file from your hard drive into a Premiere Pro 2 project, you are not really importing the entire file. Rather, you are importing a link to the file. The link tells Premiere Pro 2 where to find the file. In the illustration shown here, the clip **crocodiles.avi** *links to* the file **crocodiles.avi** in **c:\exercise_files\media_files\video**.

Each time you play the clip in the project, Premiere Pro 2 follows the link, locates the file on the hard drive, and plays the file that exists on the hard drive. If Premiere Pro 2 successfully finds the file, it is considered **online**. Furthermore, every time you *open* a project, Premiere Pro 2 checks every clip in the project and verifies each one of the links to ensure each file can be found and is therefore online.

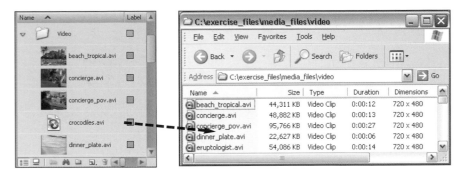

If Premiere Pro 2 *cannot* find a file on the hard drive, the clip cannot be played in the project. Clips with missing or broken links are considered to be **offline**. Premiere Pro 2 displays offline clips with a special icon. In the illustration shown here on the left, Premiere Pro 2 is displaying **crocodiles.avi** as an offline clip in the Project panel because it is missing in the Windows Explorer window (in the illustration shown above on the right).

If you try to play the offline clip, Premiere Pro 2 displays a generic **Media Offline** image in the **Monitor** panel. Until you restore the link to the file on the hard drive, the clip in the **Project** panel will display as offline, and any attempts to play the clip will result in the **Media Offline** screen.

Linking Offline Clips

When a clip's link is broken, the clip displays as offline. What causes a link to break? Usually, it's because the file has been deleted from the hard drive or moved to a new location. Unfortunately, Premiere Pro 2 has no way of knowing what happened. You need to tell Premiere Pro 2 how to find the clip, or you will not be able to export your final product.

Upon opening a project, Premiere Pro 2 checks the link of every clip to make sure it can play all the files. If Premiere Pro 2 comes across a broken link, the process of opening the project halts. Premiere Pro 2 then asks you what to do in the **Where is the File 'X'?** dialog box (as shown in the illustration on the next page). At this point, you have several choices: If the file has been moved to a different directory on your

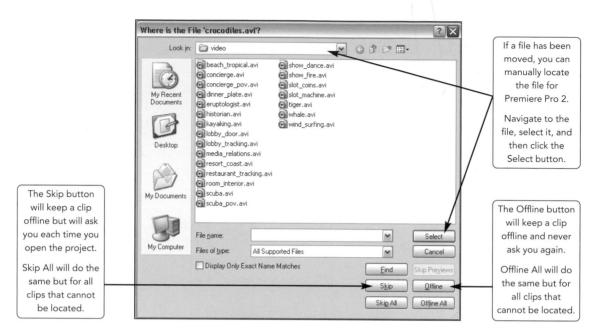

If a file has been moved, you can manually locate the file for Premiere Pro 2.

Navigate to the file, select it, and then click the Select button.

The Skip button will keep a clip offline but will ask you each time you open the project.

Skip All will do the same but for all clips that cannot be located.

The Offline button will keep a clip offline and never ask you again.

Offline All will do the same but for all clips that cannot be located.

hard drive, you can point the link to the new location right away, so Premiere Pro 2 will stop asking you to find it. If the file is not on the hard drive yet—perhaps it's on an external device that is not connected, or perhaps you deleted it—you can tell Premiere Pro 2, "I'd like to keep this clip offline for now." You can further choose whether Premiere Pro 2 asks you next time you open the project, or if it should leave you alone until you are ready to restore the link yourself.

The following are the available choices in the **Where is the File 'X'?** dialog box, as well as a brief description of when to choose them.

Select: If you want to find the file right away, you can navigate to the new location of the file in the dialog box, select it, and then click the **Select** button. Premiere Pro 2 will restore the link, and the clip will show as online in the project. You should use this option when you have moved a clip to a new location.

In addition, if you have multiple clips that have moved, you need to select only the first clip, and Premiere Pro 2 will automatically find any other missing files that happen to be in the same directory.

Skip/Skip All: The Skip button will leave the clip as offline. When the project finishes opening, you will see the offline icon in the **Project** panel. When you open the project next time, Premiere Pro 2 will once again ask you to find the file. **Skip All** performs the same task but will do it for all missing files, instead of asking you about them one at a time. You should use this option when you have a clip temporarily unavailable but you know it will be available the next time you are working on the project—such as having an external hard drive that is temporarily disconnected from the computer.

Offline/Offline All: The **Offline** button will leave the clip as offline, just like **Skip**. However, Premiere Pro 2 will *never* prompt you again to find the file. If you click **Offline**, the clip stays offline until you manually decide to fix the link. **Offline All** does the same but for all broken links. This option is the most dangerous, since you will never be prompted again. Use this option when you don't plan to make a clip online in the near future, or if you are comfortable enough to manually link the clips yourself.

In the next exercise, you will walk through each of these options so you better understand how each button works and when to use them.

4 | Restoring Offline Clips

Sometimes when you open a project, a clip you previously imported is no longer on your hard drive. Perhaps you deleted the file or moved the file to a new location. When you open the project, Premiere Pro 2 can no longer find the file and alerts you to this problem. At this point, you have two choices—you can help Premiere Pro 2 locate the file, or you can ask Premiere Pro 2 to keep the clip as offline in the project. In this exercise, you will learn how to restore a link to an offline clip and also how to keep a clip offline until you are ready to restore its link.

---

1 On the **Welcome Screen**, click **Open Project**. In the **Open Project** dialog box, navigate to the **c:\exercise_files\chap_02** folder, click **exercise04.prproj** to select it, and click **Open**.

Two video clips in this project file were moved to a different location. When opening the project, Premiere Pro 2 discovers the two broken links and asks you what to do next. In this first series of steps, you will skip the file to keep the clip as offline in the project.

---

2 After you open the project file, Premiere Pro 2 displays the **Where is the File 'X'?** dialog box, as shown in the illustration here. As you can see, Premiere Pro 2 is looking for the **chef_kitchen.avi** file. Click **Skip**.

Instead of trying to locate the file, the Skip button will open the project with the clip chef_kitchen.avi as offline.

> Premiere Pro 2 displays the name of the file it cannot find in the bar along the top of the dialog box.

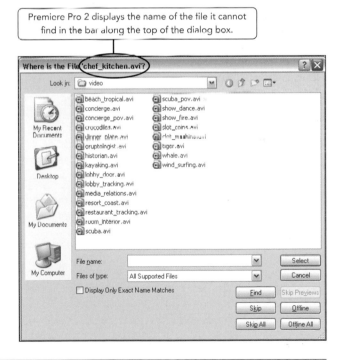

3 Because there is another file missing, Premiere Pro 2 displays the next file in the **Where is the File 'X'?** dialog box, as shown in the illustration here. It is looking for the **blackjack.avi** file. Click **Skip**.

Tip: If you want to work offline with all the video clips you're trying to open, click Skip All.

Note: Clicking Cancel performs the same task as Skip All.

Once you have told Premiere Pro 2 what to do with all the missing files (two in this case), the project finishes opening. In the Project panel, the two skipped clips each display with an offline icon, as shown in the illustration here.

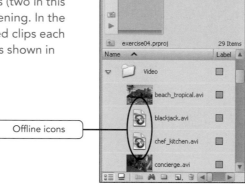

Offline icons

---

4 Choose **File > Close**. In the **Save** dialog box, click **Yes** to save the changes to **exercise04.prproj** before closing.

When you open the project next time, you will again be prompted to find, skip, or make the clips permanently offline. In the following steps, you will tell Premiere Pro 2 where to find the missing files.

---

5 On the **Welcome Screen**, click **Open Project**. In the **Open Project** dialog box, navigate to the **c:\exercise_files\chap_02** folder, click **exercise04.prproj** to select it, and click **Open**.

---

6 Just like last time, Premiere Pro 2 opens the **Where is the File 'X'?** dialog box and asks you to locate the **chef_kitchen.avi** file. Navigate to the **c:\exercise_files\chap_03** folder. Click **chef_kitchen.avi** to select it. Verify the selected clip matches the clip name in the top bar, and click the **Select** button to link the clip.

> When locating a file that has been moved, the clip displayed along the top bar should match the clip you are selecting.
>
> Always double-check before clicking Select, or you may link to the wrong clip!

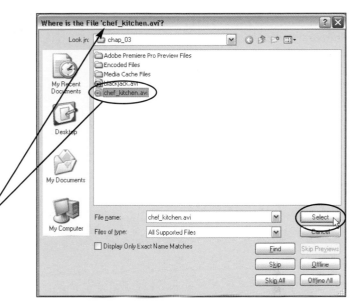

The project opens, and *both* clips are now online, as shown in the illustration here. (You can tell they are online because you can see their thumbnail images.) Even though you selected only *one* of the clips, Premiere Pro 2 was smart enough to find the other clip in the same directory.

> A thumbnail icon indicates the clips are online.

7 Choose **File > Close**. In the **Save** dialog box, click **Yes** to save the changes to **exercise04.prproj** before closing.

You have learned how to point Premiere Pro 2 to the new file location. Each time you open this project, these files will be online (unless you move the files *again*).

In both of these scenarios, Premiere Pro 2 *prompted* you to find the file upon opening the project. On the other hand, if the two clips are permanently offline, you will not be prompted. The next series of steps shows you how to manually link to a file if a project is already open.

8 On the **Welcome Screen**, click **Open Project**. In the **Open Project** dialog box, navigate to the **c:\exercise_files\chap_02** folder, click **exercise04_offline.prproj** to select it, and click **Open**.

This time, you were not prompted to find the two broken links because both clips are permanently offline, as indicated by the offline icons in the Project panel. This means someone chose Offline/Offline All when this project was previously opened.

In the Project panel, the offline clips will stay offline until you manually link them yourself (which you will do in the next step).

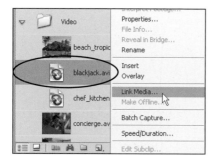
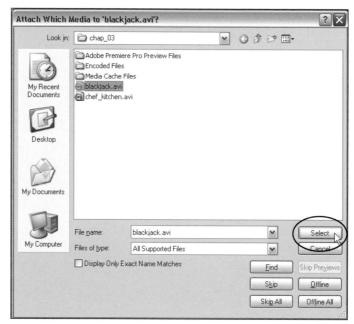

9 Right-click the offline icon for **blackjack.avi**, and choose **Link Media**. Premiere Pro 2 asks you **Attach Which Media to 'blackjack.avi'?** As you did in Step 6, navigate to the **c:\exercise_files\chap_03** directory. Select **blackjack.avi**, and click **Select**.

After selecting the file, you can see it is again online, indicated by its thumbnail image in the Project panel.

Tip: The Attach Which Media to 'X'? dialog box is identical to the Where is the File 'X'? dialog box.

10 Right-click the other offline clip, **chef_kitchen.avi**, and choose **Link Media**. Premiere Pro 2 asks you **Attach Which Media to 'chef_kitchen.avi'?** Navigate to the **c:\exercise_files\chap_03** directory. Select **chef_kitchen.avi**, and click **Select**.

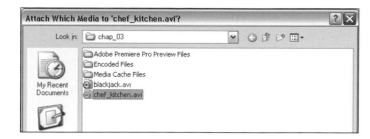

After selecting the file, you can see it is again online, indicated by its thumbnail image in the Project panel.

---

11 **Choose File > Close** to close the current project. If prompted to save changes, click **Yes**.

In this exercise, you learned how to restore broken links to files that have moved. You also learned how to manually link files. Overall, if you're not sure where a file is, clicking Skip/Skip All is the safest because you will continue to be prompted each time you open the project.

During the course of this chapter, you learned how to start with a blank project; import video, audio, and graphics; and edit your clips by specifying In and Out points. You also learned how to resolve the issue of clips showing as offline. Now that you have all this material ready and waiting, what do you do with it? It all comes together in the next chapter, as you learn the ins and outs of assembling a sequence.

3

Assembling a Sequence

In a sequence, you can arrange, rearrange, edit, copy, transition, and add special effects to clips. You assemble sequences in the **Timeline** panel, which is where you do most of your work on a project. In this chapter, you will create and assemble multiple sequences and learn the primary functions of the **Timeline** panel.

Introducing Sequences

Sequences are the blank canvas where you assemble your program. When you add clips to the **Timeline** panel, you are actually adding clips to a sequence. Without a sequence, you can't assemble your program. Adobe Premiere Pro 2 lets you create as many sequences in a project as you'd like.

In the **Project** panel, sequences appear and behave like any other clip—you can rename, sort, and place sequences in bins.

In the **Program Monitor** (the right side of the **Monitor** panel), you preview sequences such as video and audio clips so you can watch them as you assemble them.

Sequences help divide a program into logical "chunks." For example, if you are working on a movie with 20 scenes (Scene 1: The cat burglar prepares for the heist, Scene 2: The museum security guard falls asleep, and so on), each scene can be a sequence, so you'd end up with 20 sequences in your project. This helps keep your **Timeline** in shorter, manageable chunks as you edit and allows you to work on Scene 20 before working on Scene 4.

Later in this chapter, you will encounter another example of how to use multiple sequences. In your Dutch Harbor Resort and Casino DVD, you will create three sequences, one for each DVD menu item.

Viewing Sequences in the Timeline Panel

Remember timelines from your grade-school history book? The far left of a timeline represents many years ago, and the right side of the timeline represents the present day. Sequences in Premiere Pro 2

behave the same way. When you open a sequence in the **Timeline** panel, the far left of the Timeline is the beginning of the sequence (0 seconds), and time increases as you scroll to the right.

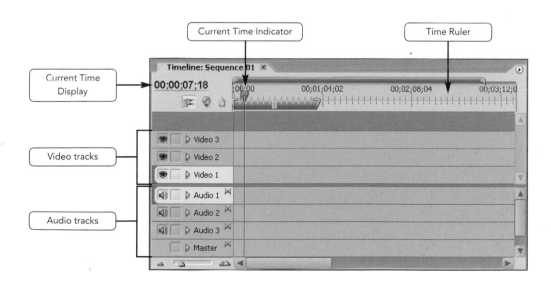

Sequences, when displayed in the **Timeline** panel, are divided into audio and video tracks, like a highway with divided lanes. When you place a clip in a sequence, you place it into one of the predefined audio or video tracks. When you drive your car on the interstate, you can drive only in one of the predefined lanes (or I hope you do!).

You can place only video and graphic clips into video tracks, and you can place only audio clips into audio tracks. A sequence can have up to 99 video/audio tracks.

Just like the **Monitor** panel, which you came to know and love in Chapter 2, *"Importing and Editing,"* the **Timeline** panel has a **Time Ruler**, **CTI** (**C**urrent **T**ime **I**ndicator), and **Current Time Display**. So already you are familiar with how the **Timeline** panel works because it's really just one big **Time Ruler**. Even the blue tab of the **CTI** looks the same.

Viewing Sequences in the Program Monitor

The **Program Monitor** is the same as the **Source Monitor**—with one notable exception. Instead of showing source clips from the **Project** panel, the **Program Monitor** shows sequences from the **Timeline** panel. Other than this, the two sides of the **Monitor** panel are nearly identical, right down to their **Shuttle Sliders**, **Jog Wheels**, **Time Rulers**, and everything else you learned about in Chapter 2, *"Importing and Editing."*

Enough talk. Time to get cracking on that promotional DVD because the client wants it soon!

1 | Creating and Organizing Sequences

Creating multiple sequences in Premiere Pro 2 allows you to divide the tasks of editing long projects into smaller, more manageable chunks. You can also use multiple sequences if you are creating a DVD with multiple menu choices. These are just a couple of the many, many uses of sequences. In this exercise, you will create multiple sequences and organize them in the **Project** panel. In Chapter 12, *"Authoring DVDs,"* you will turn each sequence into a DVD menu choice.

1 On the **Welcome Screen**, click **Open Project**. In the **Open Project** dialog box, navigate to the **c:\exercise_files\chap_03** folder, click **exercise01.prproj** to select it, and click **Open**.

This project file begins where you left off at the end of Chapter 2, *"Importing and Editing."* So far, you have imported a handful of clips and organized them into different bins in the Project panel. If you're unsure of this process, review the exercises in Chapter 2, *"Importing and Editing."*

2 Choose **File > Save As**. Navigate to the **c:\exercise_files\dutch_harbor** folder. Name the file **dutch harbor promo.prproj**, and click **Save**. Or, if this file already exists, click the project file once to select it, and then click **Save**.

Note: In the last chapter, you saved your project with the same name, dutch harbor promo.prproj. When saving the file in this step, you may be asked to replace the file already on your hard drive from the previous chapter. Click Yes.

All projects, by default, start with a single sequence, Sequence 01. However, you can rename this to make it more appropriate to the project on which you are working.

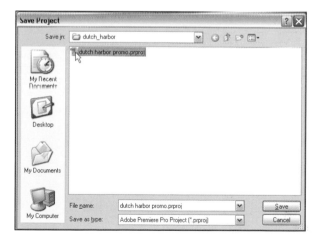

3 In the **Project** panel, right-click **Sequence 01**, and choose **Rename**. Name the sequence **DVD history**, and press **Enter**.

Of course, you are not confined to the single sequence included with each project file. You can create as many as you'd like. In the next two steps, you will create two additional sequences.

4 At the bottom of the **Project** panel, click the **New Item** button to expand the **New Item** pop-up menu. Choose **Sequence**, as shown in the illustration here.

When creating a new sequence, Premiere Pro 2 lets you specify how many video and audio tracks you'd like to include in the sequence. You can always add and subtract tracks in the sequence later, so it's safe to leave the default option of three video tracks and three stereo audio tracks.

5 In the **New Sequence** dialog box, name the sequence **DVD intro,** and click **OK** to add a new sequence to the **Project** panel.

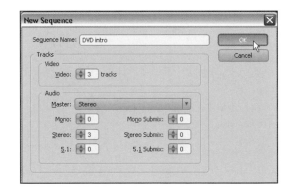

The newly created sequence appears in the Project panel, as shown in the illustration here.

Tip: Each sequence can have from 1 to 99 audio/video tracks, and each sequence can have a different number of tracks. In some sequences, you may require only one video track. In others, if you are loading it with lots of titles and graphics, you may find yourself needing four or five video tracks.

Premiere Pro 2 lets you create sequences using a number of methods. In the next step, you'll learn an alternative method of adding a new sequence. In addition, you will specify you want only one video track and one audio track.

6 Choose **File > New > Sequence**. In the **New Sequence** dialog box, name the sequence **DVD map**. In the **Tracks** section, type **1** in the **Video** field, and type **1** in the **Stereo** field. Click **OK**.

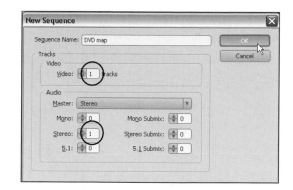

The third sequence appears in the Project panel, as shown in the illustration here.

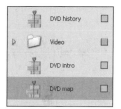

In the previous chapter, you learned how to organize clips into bins. Just like with clips, you can also organize sequences by dragging them into bins. When you have multiple sequences, it is often helpful to move them into a single bin so you can quickly find the sequences. The first step is to make a new bin to hold your sequences.

7 Choose **File > New > Bin**. When the new bin appears in the **Project** panel, the default bin name is highlighted, and the cursor blinks, indicating the bin is ready to be named. Type **Sequences** to name the bin, and press **Enter**.

Tip: Before creating a new bin, the Project panel must be "active" (indicated by a yellow border around the panel). Click anywhere on the panel tab to make it the active panel.

Now you have a bin for sequences. The next step is to drag the existing sequences into the bin.

8 In the **Project** panel, drag and drop each of the three sequence icons on the **Sequences** bin icon to place them in the bin. You can drag and drop the sequences one at a time, or you can hold down **Ctrl** to select all three sequences and drag them to the bin all at once.

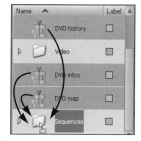

This places the DVD history, DVD intro, and DVD map sequences into the Sequences bin. When you're finished, you should see only four bins in the Project panel: audio, Graphics, Video, and Sequences.

9 Click the **Name** column heading to sort your bins alphabetically. The audio bin should be the top bin, as shown in the illustration here.

Note: You may need to click twice, since the first click may sort the list in reverse alphabetical order (from Z to A).

---

10 Choose **File > Save**, or press **Ctrl+S**. Leave **dutch harbor promo.prproj** open for the next exercise.

In this exercise, you learned how to create and organize sequences. You can create sequences at any time while you're working on a project. If you are prepared enough to create them ahead of time, even better. But no law says you have to decide on all of your sequences before starting. Also remember, each project can have multiple sequences, and each sequence can have multiple tracks. And, like with audio and video clips, you can sort sequences into bins.

Assembling Clips in the Timeline

Once you've created an empty sequence, you can begin to fill it with audio, video, and graphic clips as you construct a final product (or **program**). This process is called **assembling**; assembling a sequence is one of the primary functions of Premiere Pro 2.

To assemble clips in a sequence, you must open the sequence in the **Timeline** panel. Once you have a sequence open in the **Timeline** panel, Premiere Pro 2 provides many ways to assemble clips. One of the easiest methods is to drag a clip directly from the **Source Monitor** and place it in a sequence's video or audio track, directly in the **Timeline** panel.

The sequence currently open in the **Timeline** panel appears as a tab at the top of the **Timeline**. Notice, as shown in the illustration here, that the **DVD history** tab appears in the foreground of the other tabs, indicating it is currently open.

As shown in the illustration here, an audio clip is being dragged from the **Source Monitor** to track **Audio 2** of the **DVD history** sequence, which is open in the Timeline panel. In addition, it's being dragged to the *beginning* of the sequence (the far left is the beginning). Keep in mind, you can place only audio clips in audio tracks; you can place only video and graphic clips in video tracks.

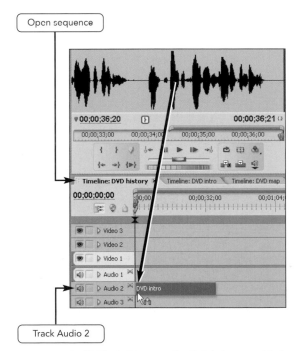

In this illustration, an audio clip is being assembled into the DVD history sequence.

The clip is being dragged from the Source Monitor, into the sequence's Track Audio 2 in the Timeline panel.

Dragging a clip to the **Timeline** panel takes skill and precision. You should be aware of three pitfalls:

Pitfall #1—Putting a clip in the wrong sequence:
The top of the Timeline panel has a tab for each sequence you create. If you start clicking all willy-nilly, you may accidentally open the wrong sequence. Whichever tab displays as bold and in the foreground is the sequence you currently have open.

Pitfall #2—Dragging the clip to the wrong time or the wrong track: When you drag a clip into the Timeline, you drop it on one of the predefined tracks. The instant you release your mouse, the clip is placed. For this reason, you should hold down the mouse until you are positive the clip is where you would like it to go.

As you drag and position the clip (before releasing the mouse), you will see a ghost clip attached to your cursor, as shown in the illustration here on the left. The **ghost clip** indicates the position of the clip when you release the mouse. The clip isn't actually "placed" into the sequence *until* you release the mouse. As shown in the illustration here on the right, you can see how the same clip appears once you release the mouse and drop the clip on the sequence's track.

Pitfall #3—Not dragging to the start of the sequence: When you drag your *first* clip into a sequence, you normally drag it to the far left of the Timeline, which is the beginning of the sequence. As you drag the clip to the left, you eventually run into an imaginary wall, where the clip refuses to move farther left to indicate you are at the beginning of the sequence. When you "feel" the imaginary wall, double-check you are in the proper video or audio track and then release the mouse.

In this next exercise, you will experience for yourself how to drag clips into the **Timeline** panel. And of course, be careful to *avoid the pitfalls!* (Insert ominous clap of thunder.)

NOTE:

Misbehaving Timelines

Along with avoiding the pitfalls of dragging clips into the **Timeline**, you might accidentally click a few other places in the **Timeline** panel, causing the panel to behave in strange ways:

Snap toggle: Premiere Pro 2 designers like to place the **Snap** toggle (like a light switch) in the one place where you are sure to accidentally click it. You normally want it turned on.

Track Lock toggle: Premiere Pro 2 allows you to lock a track by clicking the **Track Lock** toggle to the left of the track name. Sometimes this is a good thing. A locked track displays a series of diagonal lines in the track, indicating it is locked. However, if a track is locked, you cannot place any clips in the track. So usually you want this unlocked.

In and Out points: Although it's hard to accidentally set **In** and **Out** points in a sequence, I've seen students do it in every class. To clear them in the **Timeline** panel, right-click in the **Time Ruler**, and choose **Clear Sequence Marker > In and Out**.

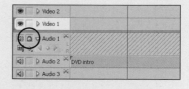

2 | Dragging Clips to the Timeline

In the previous exercise, you learned how to create and organize sequences. Once you have an empty sequence, the next step is to begin filling the sequence with audio, video, and graphic clips. In this exercise, you will learn how to drag clips into the **Timeline** from the **Source Monitor** to place them in one of the sequence's audio or video tracks.

---

1 If you followed the previous exercise, **dutch harbor promo.prproj** should still be open in Premiere Pro 2. If it's not, click **Open Project** on the **Welcome Screen**. Navigate to the **c:\exercise_files\chap_03** folder, click **exercise02.prproj** to select it, and click **Open**.

---

2 Choose **File > Save As**. Navigate to the **c:\exercise_files\dutch_harbor** folder. Name the file **dutch harbor promo**, and click **Save**. Or, if this file already exists, click the project file once to select it, and then click **Save**.

Note: If a previous version of dutch harbor promo.prproj already exists, you may be asked to replace it. If so, click Yes.

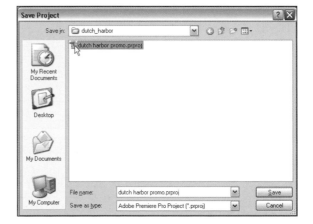

---

3 In the **Project** panel, click the **arrow** icon next to the **Sequences** bin to expand its contents. Double-click the **DVD map** sequence to open it in the **Timeline** panel.

This highlights a major difference between regular clips and sequences. When you double-click a clip in the Project panel, the clip opens in the Source Monitor. When you double-click a sequence, *it opens in the Timeline panel.*

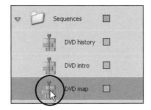

Now you have a sequence open in the Timeline panel, ready to be assembled. You can place clips in a sequence in a couple of ways. The first method is to open a clip in the Source Monitor and then drag it to a sequence track.

---

4 In the **Project** panel, click the **arrow** icon next to the **audio** bin to expand its contents. Double-click the **DVD map** subclip to open it in the **Source Monitor**.

Once a clip is open in the Source Monitor, you can click its preview in the Source Monitor and drag it to a sequence track in the Timeline.

5 Drag the **Source Monitor preview** all the way to the left of Track **Audio 1** in the **Timeline** panel. When you are confident the clip is *all the way* to the left and you see its ghost clip on Track **Audio 1**, release the mouse.

Remember, Premiere Pro 2 shows you a ghost clip of where the clip will appear. It is not truly placed in the sequence until you release the mouse.

Tip: If you are unhappy with the placement of the clip, you can undo it by choosing Edit > Undo.

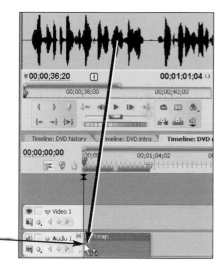

> One method to assemble a clip in a sequence is to drag it from the Source Monitor to the Timeline.
>
> In the illustration shown here, the DVD map audio subclip is being placed in the sequence's Track Audio 1.

6 In the **Program Monitor** (the monitor on the right side), click the **Play** button.

This allows you to preview your sequence. You don't have to listen to the entire sequence; you can click the Stop button once you are satisfied.

The Program Monitor should look familiar because it behaves just like the Source Monitor.

Now that you have begun to assemble a sequence in the Timeline, it's important you understand the connection between the Timeline CTI (Current Time Indicator) and the Program Monitor.

7 In the **Timeline** panel, drag the **CTI** tab left and right.

Notice as you move the CTI in the Timeline panel, you also move the CTI in the Program Monitor—they are one and the same. Also notice the CTI in the Timeline panel has a vertical red line. The Program Monitor always previews the sequence at the red line. In other words, wherever the red line is positioned, that's the exact frame of video you will see in the Program Monitor.

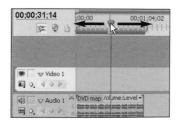

8 With the Timeline panel active (displayed with the yellow border around it), press the **spacebar** to play the sequence.

Tip: The spacebar is a keyboard shortcut for the Play button. In Premiere Pro 2 terminology, a **keyboard shortcut** is any key that does the same task as a button or menu option. If you tap the spacebar again, it stops the playback.

---

9 In the **Project** panel, scroll down to the **Sequences** bin. Double-click the **DVD intro** sequence to open it in the **Timeline** panel.

---

10 In the **Project** panel, scroll to the **audio** bin. Double-click the **DVD intro** subclip to open it in the **Source Monitor**.

---

11 In the **Source Monitor**, drag the display handle all the way to the left.

This zooms out as far as possible so you can view the entire subclip in the preview area.

---

12 In the **Source Monitor**, move the **CTI** to **00;00;14;26**. Click the **Set In Point** button.

There's no right or wrong way to move the CTI. Feel free to use your favorite method from Chapter 2, *"Importing and Editing."*

---

13 The **DVD Intro** sequence should still be open in the Timeline. Drag the **DVD intro** subclip from the **Source Monitor** to the beginning of the Track **Audio 2** in the **Timeline** panel.

When a clip has In and Out points specified, only the In to Out segment is placed in the Timeline.

Right now the clip looks tiny in the Timeline panel because you are zoomed out. You'll fix this in the next step.

14 To zoom in closer, click the **Zoom In** button several times until the clip takes up about three quarters of the Timeline panel.

Tip: If you zoom too far, you can always zoom out by clicking the Zoom Out button.

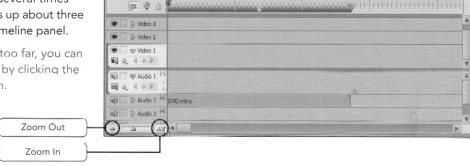

Zoom Out

Zoom In

15 Press the **spacebar** to play the sequence.

16 Choose **File > Save**, or press **Ctrl+S**. Leave **dutch harbor promo.prproj** open for the next exercise.

In this exercise, you began the baby steps of assembling a sequence by dragging two clips to a sequence in the Timeline panel. If you remember nothing else from this exercise (I hope not!), just remember this: As you drag a clip into the Timeline, do not release your mouse until you are in the proper track and at the proper time.

This exercise represents the tip of the iceberg. Although there is much more to learn about placing clips in the Timeline, the good news is you've pretty much got the gist of it. You set In and Out points in the Source Monitor and then drag them to the Timeline. At the most basic, this is all you ever need to do (but you're going to do it about a zillion more times!).

You've now laid down your audio. The next step is to start filling in the sequence with some video that matches what you hear in the audio.

3 | Trimming in the Timeline

Once you assemble a clip in a sequence, frequently you will want to edit it further, to make sure the video matches the existing audio, and vice versa. Editing clips directly in the **Timeline** is called **trimming**; this allows you to remove a snippet of unwanted audio or video from the start or end of a clip.

A common method of editing, used heavily at your local television station, is first to assemble some audio (as you have done) and then to add video to match, sentence by sentence, what the narrator is saying. In this exercise, you will assemble video clips in your sequences; at the same time, you will trim the clips to match the existing audio.

---

1 If you followed the previous exercise, **dutch harbor promo.prproj** should still be open in Premiere Pro 2. If it's not, click **Open Project** on the **Welcome Screen**. Navigate to the **c:\exercise_files\chap_03** folder, click **exercise03.prproj** to select it, and click **Open**.

---

2 Choose **File > Save As**. Navigate to the **c:\exercise_files\dutch_harbor** folder. Name the file **dutch harbor promo**, and click **Save**. Or, if this file already exists, click the project file once to select it, and then click **Save**.

Note: If a previous version of dutch harbor promo.prproj already exists, you may be asked to replace it. Click Yes.

---

3 In the **Project** panel, scroll to the **Sequences** bin, and double-click the **DVD intro** sequence to open it in the **Timeline** panel, which may already be open. In the **Timeline** panel, make sure the **Snap** toggle is activated.

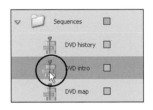

When you turn on snapping, the clip edges become "sticky." As you drag clips in the Timeline, they **snap** to the edges of other clips, like two magnets.

One of the easiest ways to trim clips in the Timeline is to move the Timeline CTI to where you want a clip to finish playing. Then, you drag a clip to the Timeline and trim it by snapping its Out point to the CTI. This is what you'll do in the next series of steps.

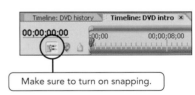

Make sure to turn on snapping.

---

4 In the **Timeline** panel, drag the **CTI** to the beginning of the sequence. Press the **spacebar** to play the sequence. Play the sequence until the narrator says, "...with over 800 rooms," and then press the **space-bar** again to stop at **00;00;02;10**.

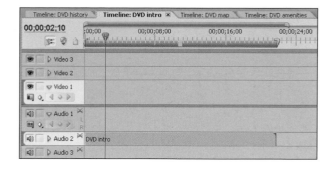

This is the point in the Timeline where the narrator's description of the rooms finishes. This means it should *also* be the point where the video about the rooms finishes. Moving the CTI to this point acts as a guideline so you know where to end the video.

Next you will add some video of the hotel rooms to match the audio you just heard.

---

5 In the **Project** panel, scroll to and expand the **Video** bin. Double-click **room_interior.avi** to open it in the **Source Monitor**. Drag the clip from the **Source Monitor** to the beginning of Track **Video 1** in the **Timeline** panel.

The video of the hotel room is longer than it needs to be. Remember, you want it to finish playing at the same time the narrator finishes talking about the rooms. In the previous step, you designated this point in time by moving the Timeline CTI. In the next step, you will trim the long video clip so it finishes playing at the CTI.

---

6 Before you trim the video clip, make sure you have the **Selection** tool chosen in the **Tools** panel.

The Selection tool is the default tool. This tool should be chosen at all times—unless you are purposefully using one of the other tools. This is because Premiere Pro 2 behaves differently based on the tool you have chosen. You may *think* you are trimming, but if a different tool is chosen, who knows what result you might get!

7 In the **Timeline** panel, position your cursor—but don't click it yet—over the **Out** point of **room_ interior.avi** on Track **Video 1**, as shown in the illustration here.

Notice your cursor changes to the Trim Out cursor. Be careful to keep your cursor positioned over the clip; otherwise, you may lose the Trim Out cursor.

The Trim Out cursor allows you to get rid of excess video/audio in the Timeline. The Trim Out cursor appears only while you position your cursor over the end of a clip with the Selection tool chosen.

---

8 Click and drag the end of the clip slowly to the left. Hold down the mouse until you feel the clip snap to the red line of the **CTI**. Release the mouse when you see the black snapping line.

The black snapping line indicates you have snapped to the CTI. Snapping "sticks" your cursor to the Timeline CTI as the cursor draws near.

In this case, you trimmed the video by snapping it to the CTI. This doesn't mean you are *near* the CTI, rather, this means you are 100 percent, without a doubt, at the *exact point* of the CTI. This is the power of snapping. It allows you to make precise trims in the Timeline.

Time to take stock of what you just did. You first determined where the video should finish playing, and you used the CTI to remember the spot. You then assembled video in the sequence. And finally, you trimmed the video to the desired length by snapping it to the CTI.

Now you understand the basics. It's time to hammer it home by assembling video to match the entire audio clip, one video piece at a time.

---

9 Press the **spacebar** to play the **Timeline** panel. Play the sequence until the narrator says, "...15,000 slot machines," and then press the **spacebar** to stop the playback at **00;00;04;09**.

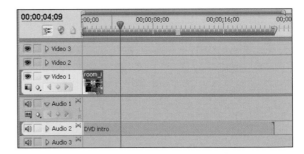

Note: Pressing the spacebar plays the active panel. (The active panel is the one with a yellow border.) If you press the spacebar and the Source Monitor plays instead of the Timeline panel, all you have to do is click in the Timeline to make it the active panel and press the spacebar again.

Using the Timeline CTI, you have marked where the slot machine video should end, by listening to the narrator. Once again, it's time to trim video by snapping it to the CTI.

10 In the **Project** panel, scroll to the **Video** bin. Double-click **slot_machine.avi** to open it in the **Source Monitor**. Drag the clip from the **Source Monitor**, and snap it to the **Out** point of the clip in the Track **Video 1**.

More fun with snapping! Not only can you snap to the CTI when you are trimming, but you can snap clips *to other clips* when assembling them in the Timeline.

Why is this so important? This ensures the new clip you have just placed in the Timeline is butted up against the first clip *as close as it can be*. This prevents any gaps between your clips. (Gaps in the Timeline are bad because they result in quick flashes of **black video**, which are very distracting and nonprofessional.)

11 Position your cursor over the **Out** point of the second clip on Track **Video 1** until you see the **Trim Out** cursor. Drag the **Out** point of the second clip, and snap it to the **CTI**.

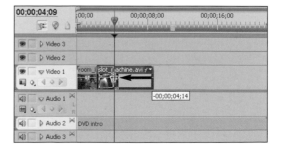

12 Press the **spacebar** to play the **Timeline** panel. Play the sequence until you hear the narrator say, "...and three miles of sandy beaches," and then press the **spacebar** again to stop the playback at **00;00;06;25**.

Another way of assembling clips into a sequence is to drag them directly from the Project panel.

---

13 In the **Project** panel, click the **arrow** icon next to the **Graphics** bin to expand its contents. Drag the **coral_reef.jpg** image to the **Timeline**, and snap it to the **Out** point of the second clip on Track **Video 1**. Look for the black, vertical line to indicate you are snapping the new clip to the endpoint of the last clip.

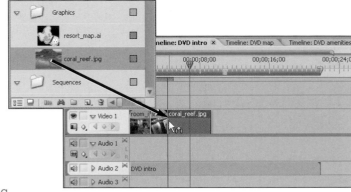

In this step, you are using an image file instead of a video clip, but that doesn't change anything—you can do everything you've done to video clips so far also to images.

---

14 With the **Trim Out** cursor, snap the **Out** point of the **coral_reef.jpg** clip to the **CTI**.

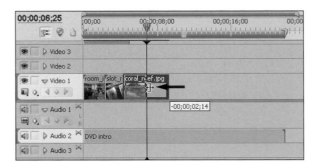

Just as you trimmed video clips, you can also trim still images. This image clip is now the proper duration to match the narrator's audio.

You have now assembled three video clips, matching the narrator's audio each time. It's time to check out the sequence you've built so far to see how you're doing.

---

15 Drag the **CTI** to the beginning of the sequence. Click **Play**, or press the **spacebar**, to play the sequence. Stop the playback after the last video clip plays.

No time to stop, there's more video to assemble!

---

16 In the **Timeline** panel, drag the **CTI** to any point above the **coral_reef** clip in the Timeline. Play the **CTI** until the narrator says, "...biggest destination resort in the world," and then click the **Stop** button at **00;00;11;24**.

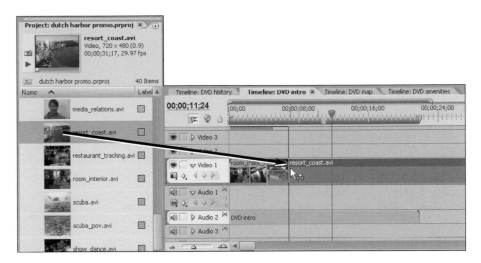

17 From the **Project** panel **Video** bin, drag and snap **resort_coast.avi** to the **Out** point of coral_reef.jpg on Track **Video 1**.

Based on your monitor resolution, the Out point of resort_coast.avi may be outside the viewing area of the Timeline panel. Not to worry—you'll fix that in the next step.

---

18 Slowly drag the **horizontal scroll bar** at the bottom of the **Timeline** panel to the right, until you can see the end of the clip.

The scroll bar doesn't need to go very far, so drag with care.

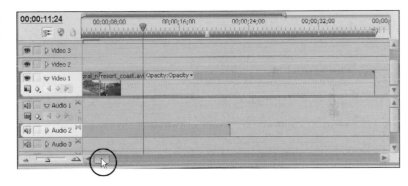

---

19 Position your cursor over the **Out** point of resort_coast.avi on Track **Video 1**. With the **Trim Out** cursor, snap the **Out** point to the **CTI** at **00;00;11;24**.

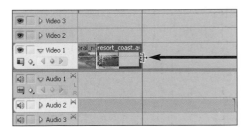

20 Play the **Timeline** panel until the narrator says, "...wherever your sense of adventure leads you," and then click the **Stop** button at **00;00;14;08**.

---

21 Drag **scuba.avi** from the **Project** panel **Video** bin, and snap it to the **Out** point of **resort_coast.avi** on Track **Video 1**.

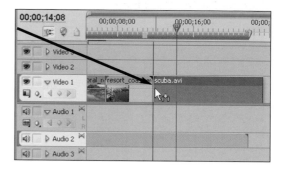

---

22 Position your cursor over the **Out** point of **scuba.avi** on Track **Video 1**. With the **Trim Out** cursor, snap the **Out** point to the **CTI** at **00;00;14;08**.

---

23 Play the **Timeline** panel until the narrator says, "...a variety of recreational," and then click the **Stop** button at **00;00;17;04**.

---

24 In the **Project** panel **Video** bin, double-click **whale.avi** to open it in the **Source Monitor**. Play the **Source Monitor** to preview the clip.

More often than not, instead of dragging a video clip from the Project panel to the Timeline, you will first review the video in the Source Monitor. It's useful to decide what part of the video you want to bring into the sequence, before trimming.

In this step, you will play the clip of the whale and trainer and try to use only the portion where the trainer has his hands down (so his motions don't distract from the intent of the video, which is to show the whale).

---

25 Click the **Play** button in the **Source Monitor**. Play the sequence until the trainer puts his hands down, and click the **Stop** button at **00;00;03;21**.

26 Click the **Set In Point** button, and click the **Play** button again. Play the sequence until right before the trainer raises his hands again, and click the **Stop** button at **00;00;05;13**. Click the **Set Out Point** button.

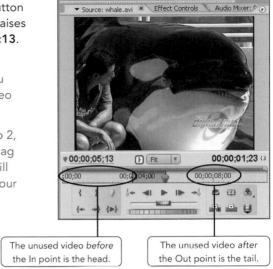

Tip: The section of video *before* the In point (which you chose not to use) is called the **head**. The section of video *after* the Out point is called the **tail**.

Remember, setting In and Out points tells Premiere Pro 2, "I want to use only this portion of video." When you drag the clip to assemble it in a sequence, Premiere Pro 2 will use only the portion of video you have specified with your In and Out points.

> The unused video *before* the In point is the head.

> The unused video *after* the Out point is the tail.

27 Drag the clip from the **Source Monitor**, and snap it to the **Out** point of the last clip on Track **Video 1**.

In this instance, the In to Out you chose is too short because your clip does not extend all the way to the CTI. Instead of using the Trim Out cursor to shorten the clip, you can use it to *lengthen* the clip as well.

28 Position your cursor over the **Out** point of scuba.avi on Track **Video 1**. With the **Trim Out** cursor, snap the **Out** point to the **CTI** at 00;00;17;04.

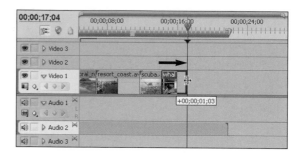

Note: It is important to understand *how* you lengthened the clip. In reality, you chose not to use only about 5 seconds of tail material in the whale source clip. When you lengthened the clip in the Timeline, you were telling Premiere to use some of the excess tail material to help fill in the empty space before the CTI.

---

29 In the **Project** panel **Video** bin, double-click **show_dance.avi** to preview it in the **Source Monitor**.

---

30 Move the **CTI** in the **Source Monitor** to **00;00;00;26**. Click the **Set In Point** button.

---

31 Drag the **show_dance.avi** clip from the **Source Monitor** to the **Out** point of the last clip on Track **Video 1**.

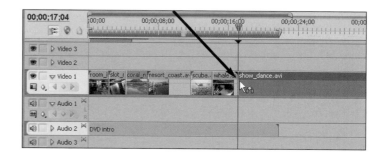

---

32 Because the show_dance.avi clip is so long, the **Out** point may not be visible in the **Timeline** panel. This time, instead of scrolling, try clicking the **Zoom Out** button in the lower-left corner of the **Timeline** panel. Zoom out until the entire clip appears in the **Timeline** panel.

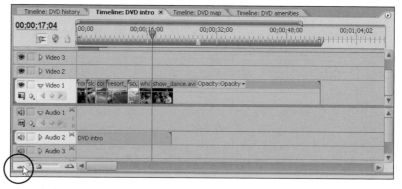

With the last clip of a sequence, instead of snapping it to the CTI, you can also snap it to the end of the audio clip so the video and audio finish at the same time.

---

33 Position your cursor over the **Out** point of **show_dance.avi** on Track **Video 1**. With the **Trim Out** cursor, snap its **Out** point to the **Out** point of the **DVD intro** clip on Track **Audio 2**.

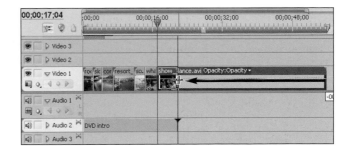

That's right! Video can snap to audio, audio can snap to video, images can snap to audio, video can snap to images, and so on, and so on. Premiere Pro 2 is an equal-opportunity snapper.

Now, run to the kitchen, and get some popcorn because it's time to preview your sequence. The next step shows you the quickest way to watch your sequence from the beginning.

---

34 In the **Program Monitor**, click the **Play In to Out** button.

Tip: Unless you have specified In or Out points in the *sequence* (which you have not learned to do yet), the Play In to Out button plays the entire sequence from the beginning.

Yikes! Did you notice the flash frames at the end of the slot machine video? If you didn't see them, repeat this step, and look for a quick flash of video.

Flash frames are brief flashes of unwanted video, and they are the sworn enemies of every editor. It is your job to hunt them down and destroy them. You will learn how to do that in the next exercise.

---

35 Choose **File > Save**, or press **Ctrl+S**. Leave **dutch harbor promo prproj** open for the next exercise.

Whew. This exercise contained a lot of steps for only a handful of video clips. (You can see why editing video can be a time-consuming process.) Remember, the method taught in this exercise is but one way to assemble a sequence. As you get more comfortable with the program, you will definitely find work-flows that work better for you.

Moving and Inserting Clips in the Timeline

The real power of editing on a computer is the ability to assemble your clips in any order you'd like. In a perfect world, you neatly assemble your sequence from left to right in the **Timeline**. However, it's common to need to insert, replace, and rearrange clips even after they are assembled in a sequence. In this exercise, you will learn how to move individual and multiple clips, as well as insert clips at the beginning (or any point) of a sequence.

1 If you followed the previous exercise, **dutch harbor promo.prproj** should still be open in Premiere Pro 2. If it's not, click **Open Project** on the **Welcome Screen**. Navigate to the **c:\exercise_files\chap_03** folder, click **exercise04.prproj** to select it, and click **Open**.

2 Choose **File > Save As**. Navigate to the **c:\exercise_files\dutch_harbor** folder. Name the file **dutch harbor promo**, and click **Save**. Or, if this file already exists, click the project file once to select it, and then click **Save**.

Note: If a previous version of dutch harbor promo.prproj already exists, you may be asked to replace it. Click Yes.

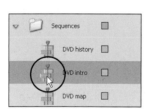
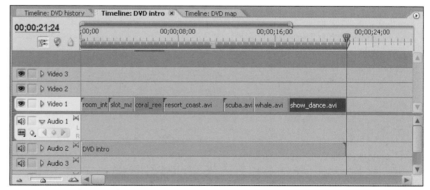

3 In the **Project** panel **Sequences** bin, double-click the **DVD intro** sequence to open it in the **Timeline** panel. Press the **backslash (\)** key to zoom the sequence to fit inside the **Timeline** panel.

The **backslash (\)** key automatically zooms in a sequence as far as it can while keeping every clip visible in the Timeline panel. Premiere Pro 2 automatically determines the maximum zoom level to allow you to see all of the clips inside a sequence.

4 In the **Timeline** panel, click the arrow next to Track **Video 1** to collapse it.

When you collapse a track, the track options are hidden, and the track appears "thinner." In this exercise, because you are clicking and moving many clips, hiding the track options prevents any accidental *clickitis*.

In Exercise 3, you discovered some accidental flash frames (quick frames of another clip that can be jarring to a viewer). In this exercise, you will eliminate the flash frames and then move all the clips to the left to cover the "hole" where the frames used to be.

---

5 Select the **Zoom** tool from the **Tools** panel. In the **Timeline** panel, click and drag the **Zoom** tool from the upper-left corner of **slot_machine.avi** to the lower-right corner of **coral_reef.jpg**.

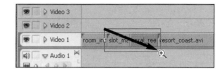

A thin, gray box indicates the zoom area. This zooms in the Timeline panel to the width of the zoom area.

---

6 Select the **Selection** tool from the **Tools** panel, or press the **V** key.

Tip: It's good to get in the habit of immediately choosing the Selection tool after performing a task with a different tool. When clicking in the Timeline, different tools yield wildly different results. And as every editor who has ever used Premiere Pro 2 can testify, it's incredibly easy to forget you have a different tool selected!

Unfortunately, although the zoom "distance" changed, the CTI is still where you left it.

---

7 Click anywhere in the **Time Ruler** to see the **CTI** in the **Timeline** panel.

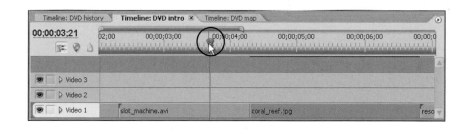

When you click in the Time Ruler, the CTI instantly moves to your cursor.

Now you are zoomed in around the area of the flash frames. The next step is to find the first flash frame so you can remove all of them.

8 Slowly drag the **CTI** over the last three frames of **slot_machine.avi** to identify the flash frames. Move your CTI to the first flash frame. Your CTI should be at **00;00;04;06**.

Moving the CTI to the first frame of the flash frames acts as a guideline so you can trim the few flash frames at the end of the clip by snapping them to the CTI.

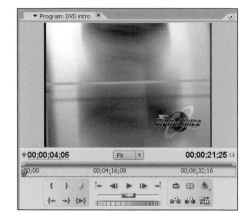

9 Position your cursor over the **Out** point of **slot_machine.avi** until you see the **Trim Out** cursor. Drag and snap the **Out** point of **slot_machine.avi** to the **CTI**.

A yellow box appears to indicate you are moving -00;00;00;03 frames to the left.

Note: Make sure the arrow is pointing to the *left*. If it's pointing to the *right*, you are positioned over the In point of the next clip with the Trim *In* cursor. Move your cursor subtly to the left of the edit point until you see the Trim *Out* cursor.

An **edit point** is the point where two clips meet on the Timeline.

You have successfully removed the flash frame, but now you are left with a three-frame gap—equally problematic. You'll resolve this in the next steps.

10 Click in the center of **coral_reef.jpg**, and move it to the left, snapping it to the **Out** point of **slot_machine.avi**.

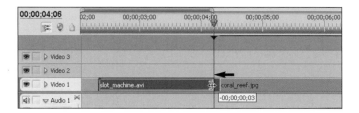

You can directly click and drag any clip in the Timeline panel to move it. Notice the selected clips display darker than the surrounding clips.

Tip: It's important to click in the center of a clip when moving it. If you click too close to the edge of the clip, Premiere Pro 2 may think you want to use the Trim In/Trim Out cursor instead.

Now that you have moved coral_reef.jpg to the left, you have created a new gap.

11 Scroll the **Timeline** panel to the right until you can see the gap between **coral_reef.jpg** and **resort_coast.avi**.

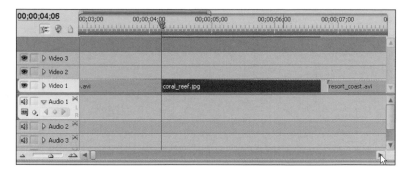

You may see a frustrating pattern develop. Each time you move a clip to close the gap to its left, you will create a gap to its right. You could always continually move clips one at a time, but if your Timeline is complex, this could take more time than you'd like. If only Premiere Pro 2 offered some way to move multiple clips simultaneously! (Hint hint! Keep reading.)

---

12 Press the **backslash** (\) key to zoom the **Timeline** out far enough to see all the clips.

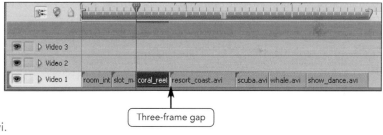

Three-frame gap

It's hard to see when you're zoomed this far out, but if you squint just right, you can see the sliver of a gap between coral_reef.jpg and resort_coast.avi.

---

13 Select the **Track Select** tool from the **Tools** panel.

The Track Select tool selects all clips on a track to the right of wherever you click it.

---

14 Click anywhere inside **resort_coast.avi** on Track **Video 1**.

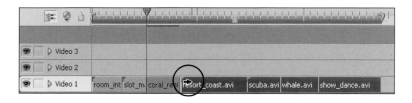

Since you have the Track Select tool chosen, every clip to the right of and including the resort_coast.avi clip is selected.

Tip: When the Track Select tool is active, the cursor displays as a black, horizontal arrow.

15 Click and snap **resort_coast.avi** three frames to the left, until it snaps to the **Out** point of **coral_reef.jpg**.

When the Track Select tool is active, all selected clips move at one time.

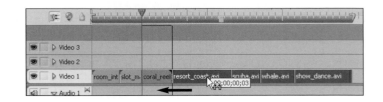

16 Select the **Selection** tool from the **Tools** panel, or press the **V** key.

Notice all five clips are still selected in the Timeline panel, even though the Track Select tool is no longer active. This can be very dangerous. The quickest way to unselect your clips is to click in any *empty* area of the Timeline panel.

17 In the **Timeline** panel, click any empty (gray) area.

This deselects the clips. Remember— whenever you're done selecting multiple clips, it's a good idea to click an empty area of the Timeline to deselect them.

Tip: You can also choose Edit > Deselect All.

You've successfully moved all the remaining clips three frames to the left. However, this means the last frame of the sequence is three frames *too short*. You can quickly rectify this by using the Trim Out cursor to extend the clip.

18 Position your cursor over the **Out** point of **show_dance.avi** on Track **Video 1**, and snap it to the **Out** point of the **DVD intro** clip on Track **Audio 2**.

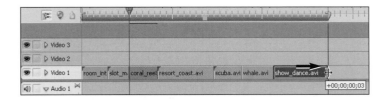

19 In the **Program Monitor**, click the **Play In to Out** button to preview your sequence.

In the next series of steps, you will learn how to insert a clip at the beginning of the Timeline.

20 In the **Project** panel **audio** bin, double-click the **DVD intro** subclip to open it in the **Source Monitor**.

---

21 Click the **Go to In Point** button in the **Source Monitor** to snap the **CTI** to the **In** point.

This subclip already has In and Out points specified; in Exercise 2, you chose to use only the second half of this clip. Now, you will modify the In and Out points and insert this audio clip at the beginning of the sequence.

The first step is to clear the existing In and Out points.

---

22 In the **Source Monitor**, right-click the **Time Ruler**, and choose **Clear Clip Marker > In**.

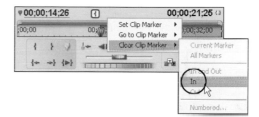

---

23 Click the **Set Out Point** button.

Without moving the CTI, you removed the In point and created an Out point in its place. So, instead of using everything to the *right* of the CTI—as you were previously doing—you are now using the media to the *left* of the CTI.

---

24 Drag the audio clip from the **Source Monitor**, and snap it to the beginning of Track **Audio 2**.

Did you notice the existing clip was overwritten? When dragging clips to the Timeline panel, the default behavior is to **overwrite** (replace) anything already existing on the track. In this case, that's not exactly what you wanted to do.

---

25 Choose **Edit > Undo**.

This undoes the last action, so the audio clip on Track Audio 2 should be restored to normal.

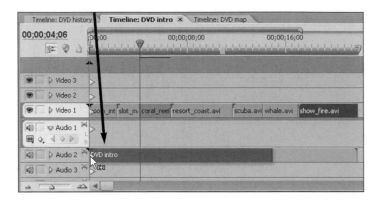

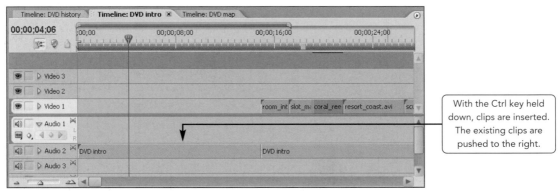

With the Ctrl key held down, clips are inserted. The existing clips are pushed to the right.

26 Hold down the **Ctrl** key, and drag the audio clip from the **Source Monitor** to the beginning of Track **Audio 2**.

When you let go, the new clips are inserted, and the existing clips slide to the right.

When you hold down the Ctrl key, Premiere Pro 2 inserts the clip instead of overwriting. With Ctrl held down, you should see small, white triangles at the snap indicator, which signify you are inserting instead of overwriting.

---

27 Choose **File > Save**, or press **Ctrl+S**. Leave **dutch harbor promo.prproj** open for the next exercise.

In this exercise, you used the Zoom tool to zoom in closely on the Timeline and make minor edits, such as removing three frames from a clip. Remember, when you see a flash frame, the initial step is to position the CTI on the first "bad" frame and then trim the Out (or In) point of the clip by snapping it to the CTI. Then select all the remaining clips, and close the gap.

Also keep in mind the difference between overwriting and inserting clips in a sequence. If you hold down the Ctrl key, the clip will be inserted, and everything will scoot over to the right. If you do not hold down the Ctrl key, the new clip will overwrite the existing clips.

---

5 | Using Only the Video or Audio of a Clip

So far you've worked with clips containing audio and others containing video. However, most of the clips you will work with in the real world (outside this book) will contain both audio and video. Sometimes you will want to use only the video portion of a clip and sometimes only the audio portion of a clip. This exercise shows you how to assemble a clip with both audio and video into a sequence, as well as how to separate the audio from the video, and vice versa.

---

1 If you followed the previous exercise, **dutch harbor promo.prproj** should still be open in Premiere Pro 2. If it's not, click **Open Project** on the **Welcome Screen**. Navigate to the **c:\exercise_files\chap_03** folder, click **exercise05.prproj** to select it, and click **Open**.

---

2 Choose **File > Save As**. Navigate to the **c:\exercise_files\dutch_harbor** folder. Name the file **dutch harbor promo**, and click **Save**. Or, if this file already exists, click the project file once to select it, and then click **Save**.

Note: If a previous version of dutch harbor promo.prproj already exists, you may be asked to replace it. Click Yes.

---

3 In the **Project** panel **Sequences** bin, double-click **DVD history** to open it in the **Timeline**.

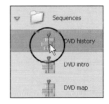

---

4 In the **Project** panel **Video** bin, double-click **historian.avi** to open it in the **Source Monitor**.

If you look at the Time Ruler of the Source Monitor, you will see Premiere Pro 2 *still* remembers the In and Out points you specified for this clip, way back in Chapter 2, *"Importing and Editing."*

5 Drag **historian.avi** from the **Source Monitor** to the beginning of Track **Video 1** in the **Timeline**.

When you drag this clip to the Timeline, notice it appears as two clips—one for the video and one for the audio. These two clips are linked, and they move as one clip.

You have just assembled a clip that has both audio and video. Sometimes, you want to take only the video portion of a clip that has both audio and video. To do this, you must tell Premiere Pro 2 which portion of the clip to "take."

6 In the **Project** panel **Video** bin, double-click **eruptologist.avi** to open it in the **Source Monitor**. Click the **Toggle Take Audio and Video** toggle.

When you click the Toggle Take Audio and Video toggle, it displays the filmstrip icon.

The toggle button lets you toggle among three modes: Take Video Only (filmstrip icon), Take Audio Only (speaker icon), and Take Audio and Video (filmstrip and speaker icon). This controls which part of the clip you assemble into the Timeline.

7 Drag and snap the clip from the **Source Monitor** to the end of the clip on Track **Video 1**.

Notice only the video portion of the clip was inserted in the Timeline. This is because you specified Take Video Only in the previous step.

Suppose you come across a clip that has audio you want to assemble, but you do not want to use the video. Similarly, you can use the same Toggle Take Audio and Video toggle to assemble only the audio portion. Just make sure the toggle button is showing the speaker icon only.

8 In the **Source Monitor**, click the **Toggle Take Audio and Video** toggle until you see just the **speaker** icon.

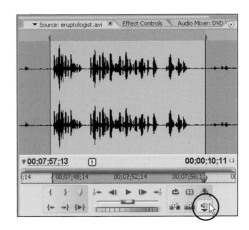

9 Snap the clip from the **Source Monitor** to the end of the audio clip on Track **Audio 1**.

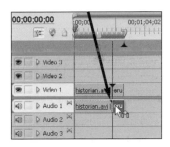

The eruptologist.avi clip now appears as two clips. Because they were brought to the Timeline separately, they are *not* linked to each other and can be moved independently.

On the Timeline you have two clips independent of each other. As far as Premiere Pro 2 knows, they are two separate clips entirely. However, you may want to link them so Premiere Pro 2 views them as one clip.

10 Click the **eruptologist.avi** clip once on Track **Video 1**. Hold down **Shift**, and click the **eruptologist.avi** clip once on Track **Audio 1**. Choose **Clip > Link**.

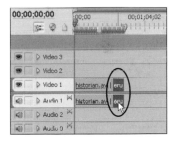

The Shift key allows you to select multiple clips in the Timeline. The Link command links the two clips as if they were one.

11 From the **Project** panel **Video** bin, drag **media_relations.avi**, and snap it to the end of **eruptologist.avi** on Track **Video 1**.

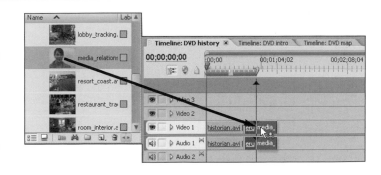

Although you did not bring this clip to the Source Monitor for the traditional "pit stop," Premiere Pro 2 *still* remembers the In and Out points you set in Chapter 2, *"Importing and Editing"*—even when dragging a clip directly from the Project panel.

12 Choose **File > Save**, or press **Ctrl+S**. Leave **dutch harbor promo.prproj** open for the next exercise.

In this exercise, you worked with three clips containing both audio and video. In each case, you placed the clip in the sequence using a different method. Premiere Pro 2 doesn't really care *how* you get the clip(s) in the Timeline—that should be based on what you feel most comfortable doing. If a clip has both audio and video, Premiere Pro 2 will move these elements as if they are one clip. If you separate the audio and video, Premiere Pro 2 will recognize them as separate clips and treat them as such.

---

6 | Trimming with the Ripple Edit Tool

As you have learned so far, the **Trim In/Trim Out** cursor helps you to shorten or lengthen a clip in the **Timeline**. When you trim the **In** or **Out** point of a clip, you leave a gap behind. Sometimes you want the gap there—perhaps you plan to fill the gap with other video. Other times, you may not want to leave a gap. Premiere Pro 2 provides a convenient way of trimming to automatically close the gaps for you; the tool is called the **Ripple Edit** tool. It behaves just like the **Trim In/Trim Out** cursor, with the added bonus that it moves all of the remaining clips to close any gaps. In this exercise, you'll learn the ease of using the **Ripple Edit** tool to trim and close your gaps in one easy step.

---

1 If you followed the previous exercise, **dutch harbor promo.prproj** should still be open in Premiere Pro 2. If it's not, click **Open Project** on the **Welcome Screen**. Navigate to the **c:\exercise_files\chap_03** folder, click **exercise06.prproj** to select it, and click **Open**.

---

2 Choose **File > Save As**. Navigate to the **c:\exercise_files\dutch_harbor** folder. Name the file **dutch harbor promo**, and click **Save**. Or, if this file already exists, click the project file once to select it, and then click **Save**.

Note: If a previous version of dutch harbor promo.prproj already exists, you may be asked to replace it. Click Yes.

---

3 In the **Project** panel **Sequences** bin, double-click **DVD history** to open it in the **Timeline**.

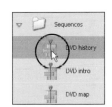

---

4 In the **Program Monitor**, click the **Play In to Out** button.

This allows you to preview the sequence from the beginning. After the first historian clip, you may notice a bit of a pause before the next clip begins, which slows the pace of the sequence. In the next series of steps, you will use the Ripple Edit tool to remove the pauses and unwanted dead space before or after the clips.

---

5 In the **Program Monitor**, drag the **CTI** to the beginning of the sequence, and click the **Play** button. Play the sequence until right after the historian finishes talking, and click the **Stop** button at **00;00;33;15**.

As you can see in the Timeline, not much is left of this clip before the next clip starts. To clearly see the edit you are about to make, you need to zoom in.

6 In the lower-left corner of the **Timeline**, click the **Zoom In** button repeatedly until the three clips take up most of the viewable area of the **Timeline**.

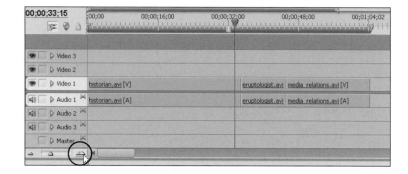

7 Select the **Ripple Edit** tool from the **Tools** panel.

The Ripple Edit tool is like two commands in one. It is similar to the Trim In/Trim Out cursor you used in Exercise 3. In addition, it automatically "closes" the gap for you by shifting all clips to the left.

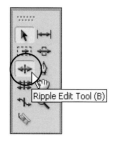

8 Position your cursor at the **Out** point of **historian.avi**.

Notice the Ripple Edit tool's cursor is much larger than the regular Trim Out cursor you've used previously. Make sure the arrow is pointing to the left.

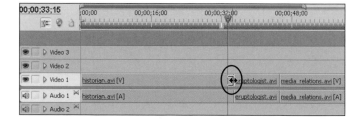

Note: It is important that the pointer points to the *left*, as shown in the illustration here. If the pointer is pointing to the *right* instead, you will end up trimming the clip to the right. Think of it like this: Pointing to the left = clip to the left; pointing to the right = clip to the right. Simple!

9 Click and drag the **Out** point of **historian.avi**, and snap it to the **CTI**.

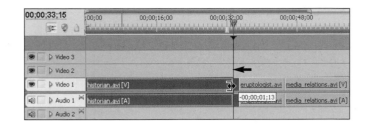

When you release the mouse, the remaining clips automatically shift to the left to close the gap. Notice the audio and video portions of the clips are trimmed as a single clip. This is because they are linked.

You can also use the Ripple Edit tool on the beginning of a clip.

---

10 In the **Program Monitor**, click the **Play** button. Play the sequence until right before the media relations woman begins to speak, and click the **Stop** button at **00;00;44;01.**

Now it's time to get *really* picky. As you can see in the Timeline, you are trimming off only about five frames, or about 1/6 of a second.

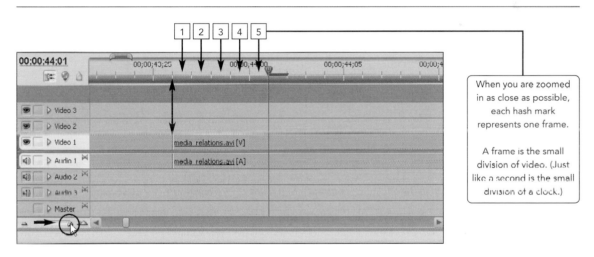

When you are zoomed in as close as possible, each hash mark represents one frame.

A frame is the small division of video. (Just like a second is the small division of a clock.)

---

11 In the **Timeline** panel, drag the **Zoom** slider as far to the right as it will go.

You may notice the Zoom controls in the Timeline zoom in "around" the CTI. In other words, the CTI is always at the center of the Timeline as you zoom.

Tip: This may be the first time you've zoomed in as far as you can. Each **hash mark** in the Time Ruler represents one frame. As shown in the illustration here, you can count off five frames from the CTI to the clip's In point (to the left of the CTI).

12 Position your cursor over the **In** point of the **media_relations.avi** clip until you see the **Ripple Edit** tool pointing to the *right*. Click and drag the **In** point, and snap it to the **CTI**.

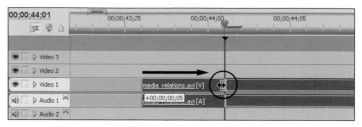

If it looks like nothing happened, don't panic. This one can be deceiving. Here's what happened behind the scenes: When you released the mouse, Premiere Pro 2 automatically closed the gap by sliding the entire clip to the left. So to you, it may appear as if the clip remained the same, but in reality, you trimmed five frames.

---

13 Press the **backslash** (\) key.

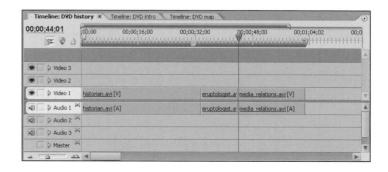

---

14 Select the **Selection** tool from the **Tools** panel.

To prevent unexpected behaviors when clicking the mouse, immediately select the Selection tool when you finish using the Ripple Edit tool.

---

15 Choose **File > Save**, or press **Ctrl+S**. Leave **dutch harbor promo.prproj** open for the next exercise.

The Ripple Edit tool is really two tools in one: It trims and moves clips at the same time. You should use this tool when you are trimming a clip and you *do not* plan to fill the gap with any other clips. On the other hand, if you want to ensure no gap is left behind, the Ripple Edit tool can be your best friend.

Using Three-Point Editing

You may not realize this, but what you've been doing throughout this chapter is formally called **three-point editing**, which is a fundamental technique of video editing—widely used from news stations to movie studios. So far in this book, you have been making many of your edits directly in the **Timeline**— by trimming clips. However, three-point editing teaches you to trim all your clips in the **Source Monitor** and then to place the trimmed clip in the **Timeline** with the click of a button (or the stroke of a key, if you prefer the keyboard).

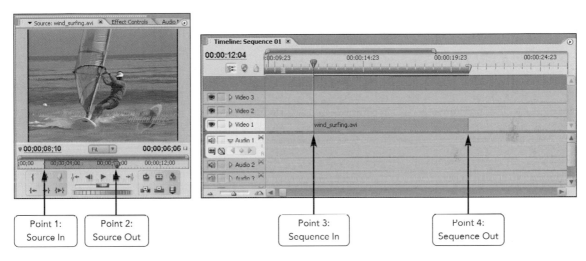

Point 1: Source In

Point 2: Source Out

Point 3: Sequence In

Point 4: Sequence Out

The idea behind three-point editing is that it takes three points to edit video. So what are the points, and how do they help you edit? When you assemble video into a sequence, you can specify a total of four possible points. *Only* four points are involved in any edit:

Point 1—Source In: The first frame of the source video you plan to use

Point 2—Source Out: The last frame of the source video you plan to use

Point 3—Sequence In: The point in time in the sequence where you plan to start playing the source video

Point 4—Sequence Out: The point in time in the sequence where you plan to stop playing the source video

Specifying any three of the four points allows you to successfully edit ({1,2,3} or {1,2,4} or {1,3,4}, and so on). All it takes is three points, any three.

So far in this book, you've assembled clips in a sequence by dragging them from the **Project** panel or from the **Source Monitor**. When you set **In** and **Out** points in the **Source Monitor**, you specified points 1 and 2. Instead of dragging a clip to the **Timeline** panel, you can click the **Insert** or **Overlay** buttons in the **Source Monitor** to automatically place clips in the **Timeline**.

But, you may ask, "If I'm not dragging the clip to the **Timeline**, how does it know where to go? Where does it start playing?" This is the job of the third point when using three-point editing. You can tell Premiere Pro 2 where to *start* playing a clip in the **Timeline**, or you can tell it where to *stop* playing a clip in the **Timeline**. Either way, you've specified a total of three points.

Remember, you can set any combination of points, just as long as you set at least *three* of the points. All along you've primarily been setting points 1 and 2 in the **Source Monitor**. In the next exercise, you will learn how to also set points 3 and 4 in the **Timeline** panel.

7 | Making a Three-Point Edit

As mentioned previously, you have many, many ways to assemble a sequence. So far, you have learned how to use your mouse to drag clips from the **Source Monitor** to the **Timeline**. Another popular way of editing is three-point editing, which emphasizes the technique of always specifying three points before assembling a sequence. In this exercise, you will learn how to make traditional three-point edits in Premiere Pro 2.

Note: In this exercise, you will be switching back and forth between working in the **Program Monitor/Timeline** and then working in the **Source Monitor**. Please pay special attention to the instructions for each step when setting **In** and **Out** points and when moving the CTI. It's important that you are working in the correct monitor/panel.

---

1 If you followed the previous exercise, **dutch harbor promo.prproj** should still be open in Premiere Pro 2. If it's not, click **Open Project** on the **Welcome Screen**. Navigate to the **c:\exercise_files\chap_03** folder, click **exercise07.prproj** to select it, and click **Open**.

---

2 Choose **File > Save As**. Navigate to the **c:\exercise_files\dutch_harbor** folder. Name the file **dutch harbor promo**, and click **Save**. Or, if this file already exists, click the project file once to select it, and then click **Save**.

Note: If a previous version of dutch harbor promo.prproj already exists, you may be asked to replace it. Click Yes.

---

3 In the **Project** panel **Sequences** bin, double-click the **DVD intro** sequence to open it in the **Timeline** panel, if necessary.

---

4 In the **Timeline** panel, click directly on Track **Video 1** until it has a lighter background than the other video tracks. Click Track **Audio 1** until it has a lighter background than the other audio tracks. (They may already appear this way.)

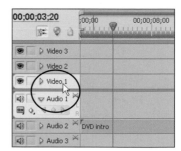

Your track "coloring" should match the illustration shown here. You just specified Tracks Video 1 and Audio 1 as your target tracks. The **target tracks** are the tracks in a sequence where any inserted clips are placed when making a three-point edit.

---

5 In the **Program Monitor**, drag the **CTI** to the beginning of the sequence.

Do you remember what the 00;00;36;22 number on the right side of the Program Monitor indicates? It's the total duration of the sequence. (Good job. I'm just making sure you're paying attention.)

---

6 In the **Program Monitor**, click the **Set In Point** button.

It's hard to see, but behind the CTI is an In point marker.

Tip: In and Out points in the Program Monitor behave the same as in the Source Monitor. Because you didn't specify an Out point, Premiere Pro 2 assumes the last frame of the sequence is your Out point.

---

7 In the **Program Monitor**, click the **Play** button. Play the sequence until the narrator says, "...a vacation to your own tropical paradise," and then click the **Stop** button at **00;00;03;20**. Click the **Set Out Point** button.

You just specified two points toward your three-point editing. In the Timeline panel, shown in the illustration here, you can see the gray In to Out bar in the Time Ruler, as well as the blue shading in the target tracks.

The illustration shown here helps to underscore the use of target tracks. The light-blue shading shows you where new clips will be inserted. This shading appears only in your target tracks. In this case, video clips will go in Video 1, and audio clips will go in Audio 1.

The In to Out bar shows you where in time clips will be inserted.

The blue region shows you into which tracks the clips will be inserted.

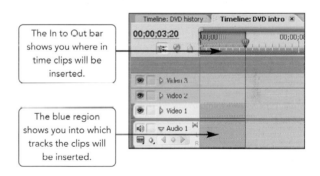

---

8 In the **Project** panel **Video** bin, double-click **beach_tropical.avi** to open it in the **Source Monitor**. Move the **Source Monitor CTI** to **00;00;04;20**, and click the **Set In Point** button.

You just specified the third point needed for a successful three-point edit.

9 In the **Source Monitor**, click the **Overlay** button.

The clip from the Source Monitor is inserted into Track Video 1 because it is the target track. Premiere Pro 2 uses only as much video as is needed to fill the space between the sequence In and Out points (the blue region).

As shown in the illustration here, you can see the Source Monitor has 7 seconds and 28 frames of available video. But, because you specified In to Out points in the sequence, Premiere Pro 2 did not use all of the source video.

Notice the Timeline CTI was automatically positioned at the end of the inserted clip. Every time you insert a clip in the Timeline panel with three-point editing, Premiere Pro 2 moves the CTI to the end of the clip.

---

10 In the **Program Monitor**, with the **CTI** still at **00;00;03;21**, click the **Set In Point** button to start your next three-point edit. In the **Program Monitor**, play the sequence until the narrator says, "...white sand and turquoise water," and then stop the playback at **00;00;06;25**. Click the **Set Out Point** button.

The sequence In to Out duration is 3 seconds and five frames. This means Premiere Pro 2 will insert only 3 seconds and five frames of video.

---

11 In the **Project** panel **Video** bin, double-click **kayaking.avi**. In the **Source Monitor**, move the **CTI** to **00;00;05;17**, and click the **Set Out Point** button.

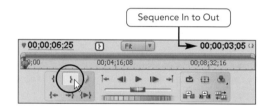

This time, you specified the source Out point instead of its In point. When you insert it into the sequence, you will use the 3 seconds and five frames *ending* at the source Out point.

---

12 In the **Source Monitor**, click the **Overlay** button.

This inserts 3 seconds and five frames of video into the target track.

---

13 In the **Program Monitor**, click the **Set In Point** button. Play the **Program Monitor** until **00;00;09;15**, and click the **Set Out Point** button.

Your In to Out duration is 2 seconds and 20 frames.

---

14 In the **Project** panel **Video** bin, double-click **wind_surfing.avi**. In the **Source Monitor,** move the **CTI** to **00;00;6;23**, and click the **Set In Point** button. Move the **CTI** to **00;00;10;12**, and click the **Set Out Point** button.

Your In to Out duration is 3 seconds and 20 frames. This presents an interesting scenario. Instead of specifying three points, you manually specified all four points. In the Timeline panel, you're expecting to fill only 2 seconds and 20 frames. However, in the Source Monitor, you chose 3 seconds and 20 frames—that's 1 second more. What will Premiere Pro 2 do with that extra second of video? You'll learn more in the next steps.

---

15 In the **Source Monitor**, click the **Overlay** button. In the **Fit Clip** dialog box, select the **Trim Clip's Tail (Right Side)** option, and click **OK**.

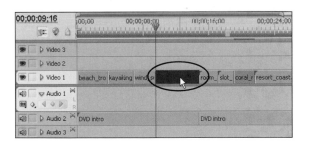

You just told Premiere Pro 2 to ignore the source Out point. (Or, as Premiere Pro 2 phrases it, you chose to "trim the extra video off the tail of the source clip.") For a description of all five choices, see the Note at the end of this exercise.

Premiere Pro 2 provides another way to specify In and Out points in the Timeline panel. You can right-click inside any gap and ask Premiere Pro 2 to use the gap as the sequence In to Out points. This is extremely useful when you want to fill an entire gap with a new piece of video.

---

16 In the **Timeline** panel, locate track **Video 1**, and click the gap between **wind_surfing.avi** and **room_interior.avi**.

17 Choose **Marker > Set Sequence Marker > In and Out Around Selection.**

In the Timeline panel, you can see sequence In and Out points set for the duration of the gap. When you insert your next clip, the entire gap will be filled.

Tip: You can also press the **slash** key (/) to perform this command.

---

18 In the **Project** panel **Video** bin, double-click **resort_coast.avi**. In the **Source Monitor**, click the **Overlay** button.

This fills the gap in the Timeline panel.

Tip: Because no source In or Out point was specified, Premiere Pro 2 assumed the source In point as your third point.

---

19 In the **Program Monitor**, click the **Play In to Out** button to preview the entire sequence.

Nice work. The only nagging issue is the resort coast video being used twice. Before calling it a day, why not quickly replace one of the two instances of the video?

When the sequence finishes, you may notice Premiere Pro 2 scrolling the Timeline panel to the end of the sequence. It appears as if your clips have been deleted, but they are really just out of view of the Timeline panel. The next step shows you how to view the rest of the clips you cannot currently see.

---

20 If you can't see the beginning of the sequence in the Timeline panel, click the **horizontal scroll bar**, and drag it all the way to the left, to the beginning of the sequence.

---

21 In the **Timeline** panel, click the second instance of **resort_coast.avi** to select it.

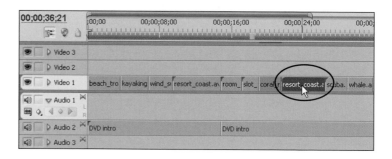

22 Right-click the **Timeline** panel **Time Ruler**, and choose **Set Sequence Marker > In and Out Around Selection**.

In Step 17, this command placed sequence In and Out points around the selected *gap*. In this step, it places sequence In and Out points around the selected *clip*. This command works the same, no matter what you have selected.

---

23 In the **Project** panel **Video** bin, double-click **lobby_door.avi**. In the **Source Monitor**, move the **CTI** to **00;00;05;19**. Click the **Set Out Point** button.

Perhaps you decided it was more important to show what happens at the *end* of the source clip rather than at the beginning. This is a real-world example of why you might use the source Out point in three-point editing. In this scenario, for example, you wanted the couple to walk all the way through the screen before the edit point.

---

24 In the **Source Monitor**, click the **Overlay** button.

This replaces the clip in the Timeline panel with the clip from the Source Monitor.

---

25 In the **Program Monitor**, click the **Play In to Out** button to preview the entire sequence.

---

26 Choose **File > Save**, or press **Ctrl+S**. Choose **File > Close** to close this project.

People who spend hours and hours each day editing in a darkened room—besides having enlarged, mole-like eyes—will tell you three-point editing is the fastest method possible. Now, at this point in your education, this may not be the case. But when you become comfortable using keyboard shortcuts exclusively when editing, you may someday agree with the Mole People. Just remember the principles behind three-point editing: Always set your target tracks, and always specify at least three points. As long as you remember to do both of these tasks, you can successfully make three-point edits.

Congratulations. You have reached a milestone! You now know the basics of editing video in Premiere Pro 2. You can assemble clips in a sequence, move them around in the Timeline panel, and trim In and Out points. Even more exciting is that every exercise in this chapter applies to audio clips and still images. This means you not only know how to assemble video, but you know how to assemble every type of clip—and you're only at Chapter 3.

Of course, you still have plenty left to learn, such as importing special graphic clips with alpha channels and modifying fixed effects, which you will learn in the next chapter.

Fit Clip

For three-point editing, you need only three points. However, if you select four points, Premiere Pro 2 easily gets confused—especially if the source and destination durations don't match. When this happens, Premiere Pro 2 asks you how it should handle the different durations.

To help illustrate your choices and how they affect your edit, imagine you have an 8-second source clip and a 4-second gap in your sequence. (Each second of the source clip has been colored for emphasis.) When you attempt to fit an 8-second source clip into a 4-second gap in a sequence, Premiere Pro 2 prompts you to ignore one of the 4 points. After all, it only wants 3 points when 3-point editing. Here are the choices Premiere Pro 2 presents to you, with a description of how they affect the edit:

- **Trim Clip's Head (Left Side):** Premiere Pro 2 ignores the **source In** point, as if you never set it. In other words, it *trims away the beginning of the clip (its "head")*. As shown in the illustration here, Premiere Pro 2 uses the *last* 4 seconds of the source clip.

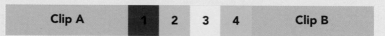

- **Trim Clip's Tail (Right Side):** Premiere Pro 2 ignores the **source Out** point and trims away the end of the clip (its "tail"). Only the *first* 4 seconds of the source clip are used.

- **Ignore Sequence In Point:** Premiere Pro 2 ignores the **sequence In** point. All 8 seconds of the source clip are used, and it finishes playing at the end of the gap.

- **Ignore Sequence Out Point:** Premiere Pro 2 ignores the **sequence Out** point. All 8 seconds of the source clip are used, and it begins playing at the start of the gap.

- **Change Clip Speed (Fit to Fill):** Premiere Pro 2 doesn't ignore *any* points. Instead, it changes the speed of the source clip until it fits in the gap. In the illustration here, the 8-second clip plays twice as fast because it is squeezed into 4 seconds.

4

Adding Graphics

A **graphic** is a broad category of items including pictures, logos, photographs, and video with transparency. There's really no mystery to using graphics in Adobe Premiere Pro 2 because Premiere Pro 2 treats them like video and audio clips. Nearly everything you've learned about importing and trimming clips in the **Timeline** up to this point applies to graphics. In fact, if you return to previous chapters, scratch out the phrase **video clip**, and replace it with **graphic clip**, most of the exercises will still hold true.

Although most of the clips you work with in Premiere Pro 2 are video clips, graphics can spice up a project with logos, text, photographs, and still images layered on top of video. In this chapter, you will work with a few types of graphics, including video clips containing alpha channels. You will learn some of the properties unique to graphics and how to best handle them in your projects.

Displaying Still Images

The primary difference between video and still images is size. Size in the video world is measured in pixels. For example, video from a standard DV (**D**igital **V**ideo) camera in North America is exactly 720 pixels wide by 480 pixels tall—*always*. So it was no coincidence 720 x 480 pixels was the size of the project preset you chose way back in Chapter 1, *"Getting Started."* (If you live in Europe or Australia, the video size is 720 x 576 pixels.)

Still images, on the other hand, have no size restrictions because they come from many different sources. Some images could be twice the size of your project; others could be half. Some could be the same rectangular shape as your project; others could be square. This lack of size restriction presents a unique set of problems (and also opportunities) when working with still images.

Large image

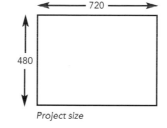

Project size

Full screen
(The image is cropped.)

You can play images equal to or larger than your Premiere Pro 2 project at **full screen**, meaning the images take up the entire display, just like the video clips you've worked with so far. If an image is larger than your project screen size, the part of the image falling outside the Program Monitor is **cropped**, which means only a portion of the original image displays during playback, since the excess falls outside the Program Monitor **canvas**. Cropping is similar to baking cookies with a cookie cutter; when you press the cookie cutter into the dough, any part of the dough falling outside the cookie cutter is cropped (and then quickly eaten when nobody is looking!).

Premiere Pro 2 doesn't discard the excess video—it just hides it because it's too big to fit within the screen. In the example shown in the illustration here, the cropping results in an awkward composition because the image is so large.

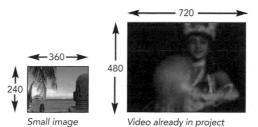

Small image

Video already in project

Image overlayed on top
of video

Images smaller than your project can be **overlayed**, meaning they take up just a small section of the screen and play on top of existing video. This allows the video "under" the image to still be seen. In addition, you get to decide where on the screen you want to overlay the image. Premiere Pro 2 provides you with precise controls to move the image around, so it can overlay in the upper-left, the lower-right, or anywhere on top of the video you desire.

Understanding Fixed Effects

The good news is Premiere Pro 2 gives you the ability to resize your images so you can scale them to match any project size. In addition, you can rotate images, move them all around the screen, and even play them back slightly transparently, like a ghost.

The secret to modifying images lies within fixed effects. **Fixed effects** are attributes of a clip that cannot be removed—they are *fixed*. In other words, fixed effects are properties inherent to every clip. You can modify these properties, but you can never get rid of them. All clips have some basic properties you cannot remove.

Image and video clips have six fixed effects: **Position**, **Scale**, **Rotation**, **Anchor Point**, **Anti-flicker Filter**, and **Opacity**. These six properties define the look of the clip during playback in the **Program Monitor**.

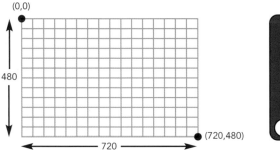

Here is a quick explanation of these properties:

Position: The **Position** property defines the location of the clip in the Program Monitor. Premiere Pro 2 expresses a clip's position as a coordinate, such as (360,240), where the first number is the horizontal position and the second is the vertical position. The horizontal and vertical values of the **Position** property behave just like an Etch A Sketch: The first knob moves the image left and right, and the second knob moves it up and down. (Please do not turn your monitor upside down and shake it to undo your work!)

Scale 100% (Original size)   *Scale 75%*   *Scale 125%*

Scale: The **Scale** property defines the relative size of the clip, as shown in the illustration here. By default, Premiere Pro 2 imports a clip at its original size, which is 100 percent. Any scale value less than 100 percent reduces the size of the clip, and values greater than 100 percent increase the size of the clip. If the image is too big to fit inside the **Program Monitor**, you can scale it down until the entire picture is visible.

An important caveat about scaling: If you scale to more than 100 percent, the image quality will start to degrade. If you want to experience this, press your nose up against your television while you're watching a show: You will notice the image really consists of a series of dots, or **pixels**, and the illusion of a smooth image is lost. The same is true for still images in Premiere Pro 2. Granted, this may not be noticeable when you are at 105 percent, but the more you enlarge an image, the more noticeable this will become. It is always best to stay at 100 percent or less than 100 percent for optimal still image quality.

Rotation 0°

Rotation 90°

Rotation 180°

360° or 1 x 0°

Rotation: The **Rotation** property changes the angle of the clip, in degrees—90 degrees is sideways, 180 degrees is upside-down, and 360 degrees is one full revolution, back to where you started. Premiere Pro 2 expresses the rotation value as *Revolution x Rotation*, where 1 x 0 degrees means one revolution and zero degrees.

Anchor Point: This is often the most difficult property to understand. An **anchor point** is the pivot point of the image when you position, scale, or rotate. For example, lift your arm up like you are flapping a wing. In this example, your arm is rotating, and your shoulder is the anchor point. Now try this: In your chair, kick your leg out like you're kicking a ball. Your leg is rotating, and the anchor point is your knee. (One more for you astronomy fans: The anchor point of the Earth is the sun, and the anchor point of the moon is the Earth.)

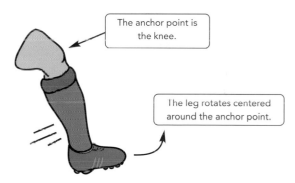
The anchor point is the knee.

The leg rotates centered around the anchor point.

In terms of Premiere Pro 2, this is helpful when you are trying to rotate or scale an image. By default, the anchor point is the center of an image. However, you might want an image to rotate around one of its corners, instead of the center. Or, you might want an image to appear to "grow" from one of its corners, rather than expand from the center. In both of these cases, moving the anchor point to the desired corner helps achieve these effects.

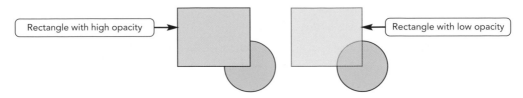

Rectangle with high opacity

Rectangle with low opacity

Opacity: The **Opacity** property changes the overall transparency of the clip. In other words, it defines how much the object allows other objects to "show through" from behind. For example, if you stand behind a brick wall, which has a high opacity, an observer on the other side of the wall cannot see you. However, if you stand behind a clear shower curtain, which has a lower opacity, anyone on the other side can see you (and will think you're a little creepy). In your Premiere Pro 2 project, opacity allows you to create interesting visuals by combining images with the underlying video. You can create a ghost-like appearance, in which the image appears to be semitransparent. You can also use opacity to help blend an image into the underlying video so it doesn't seem to stand out so much in stark contrast.

Anti-flicker Filter: This property adds a slight blur to your images to help reduce any flickering/twittering/jumping/bouncing/sparkling pixels in your image. The higher the filter amount, the more blur applied. Keep in mind, this (almost) exclusively applies to video playing on a regular television monitor. For a complete description, see the "Understanding Image Flicker" sidebar.

You can view and modify all fixed effects properties in the **Effect Controls** panel.

NOTE:

Understanding Image Flicker

To understand what causes image flicker, it's important to understand how video monitors and computer monitors display images differently.

Computer monitors display video relatively simply compared to television monitors. Like an ink-jet printer sweeping back and forth across a piece of paper, a computer monitor "prints" the image from top to bottom, one line at a time. (This happens so fast, your eye usually cannot detect it.) This is called **progressive scan** because each horizontal line is displayed progressively, in order, such as 1, 2, 3, 4, 5, 6, and so on.

Lower Field + Upper Field = Full Frame

Lower Field + Upper Field = Full Frame

Television monitors are not so neat. Most televisions print every other line in the first pass and then fill in the missing lines in the second pass.

The lines are stored in two separate fields. All of the odd-numbered lines are stored in one field (1, 3, 5, 7, 9...), and all of the even-numbered lines are stored in the second field (2, 4, 6, 8, 10...). The two fields interlock, like a zipper, to form a full frame of video. Hence, half of the frame's information is stored in the lower field, and half is stored in the upper field. This is called **interlaced**, and it is the standard for television all over the globe. (Computer monitors have no fields because every line is "printed" progressively in the first pass.)

continues on next page

Understanding Image Flicker *continued*

This process is akin to someone giving you every other word in a paragraph and then supplying you with the missing words a little bit later.

Keep in mind, a slight delay exists between the printing of the two fields. Premiere Pro 2 prints the first field, and when done, it prints the second field. Luckily, this happens so fast your eye normally cannot detect it.

So what exactly causes flicker? Sometimes very thin lines, mostly those near horizontal, are *so* incredibly thin they don't fit neatly in a field. Sometimes Premiere Pro 2 displays them on the upper field, and sometimes they display on the lower field. Because a slight delay exists between printing the two fields, the thin line of the image appears on and then off. On, then off. And so on. When you do this fast enough, the screen appears to flicker.

How do you prevent flicker? If you are working with a title, thick fonts are best, and don't make fonts too small because the thin lines may flicker. Avoid **serif fonts** (fonts with "feet" like Times New Roman) because the serifs tend to be thin as well.

If you are working with a still image, the **Anti-flicker Filter** adds a slight blur. This softens the edge of the thin lines and makes them blend with the surrounding pixels. This means the thin line no longer exists in only one field—but it is thicker because of the blur, so it spans multiple fields, which reduces the flicker.

You will get a chance to experience, firsthand, the **Anti-flicker Filter** in Exercise 5.

Viewing Fixed Effects in the Effect Controls Panel

You can view and modify each of the fixed effect properties in the **Effect Controls** panel. In the same way you use the **Source Monitor** to display source video and the **Program Monitor** to display sequences, you use the **Effect Controls** panel to display effects properties.

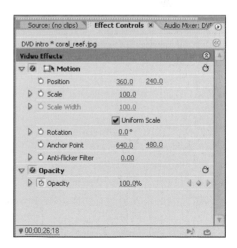

When using the **Effect Controls** panel, you'll notice next to each **property** is its **value**. Changing the value changes the property. Also, you'll notice the fixed effects are divided under two headings: **Motion** and **Opacity**. Within the **Motion** properties, you can see **Position**, **Scale**, **Rotation**, **Anchor Point**, and **Anti-flicker Filter**. For reasons unbeknownst to all, **Opacity** gets its own heading. Within the **Opacity** heading is one effect: **Opacity**.

The reason for these two groups being split up is most likely because the **Motion** properties used to appear in a separate **Motion** panel in older versions of Premiere. But, in reality, you modify all the properties in the same way.

The **Effect Controls** panel doesn't actually display what the fixed effect *looks like*—that's the job of the **Program Monitor**. Rather, you use the **Effect Controls** panel for viewing and modifying the property *values*. You can modify effect values in one of two ways. You can click the value and type a new number (shown in the illustration here on the left), or you can position your cursor over the number and click and drag left or right to lower or increase the value (shown in the illustration here on the right).

Once you modify the values, the changes will be reflected instantaneously in the **Program Monitor**.

Showing and Hiding the Effect Controls Timeline

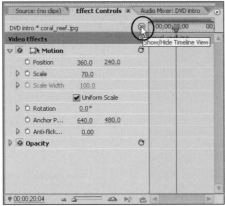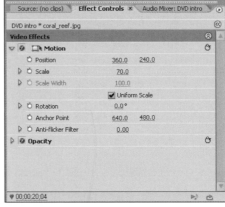

Mini-Timeline shown   *Mini-Timeline hidden*

By default, the **Effect Controls** panel also displays its own **mini-Timeline**. You can use this **mini-Timeline** for changing effect values over time (which you will learn about in Chapter 8, *"Animating Effects"*). For example, you can start an image on the left side of the screen and animate it so it moves across the screen to the right. If you are not animating the effect properties at this time, then you can safely hide the **mini-Timeline** by clicking the **Show/Hide Timeline View** toggle, circled in the illustration here on the left.

The **Timeline** panel at the bottom of your Premiere Pro 2 application shows you the entire sequence. The **mini-Timeline** in the **Effect Controls** panel shows you only the clip. The far left is the beginning of the currently selected clip, and the far right is its end.

(If you've previously closed this when working on projects outside this book, Premiere Pro 2 may remember your "preference" and automatically hide the **mini-Timeline**, so it may be hidden by default.)

In the next exercise, you will learn how to view and modify the values of different effect properties using both of the methods described here, and you will learn how to temporarily hide the **mini-Timeline** until you are ready to use it.

Modifying Fixed Effects in the Effect Controls Panel

Premiere Pro 2 gives you precise visual control over every graphic and video clip you use. You can change the position, scale, rotation, opacity, and more. You make all of these changes in the **Effect Controls** panel, which is for viewing and modifying the fixed effects of every type of clip. You can modify the values by clicking the number and entering a new one or by dragging the value higher or lower. In this exercise, you will learn how to view the fixed effects and modify them in a variety of ways.

---

1 On the **Welcome Screen**, click **Open Project**. In the **Open Project** dialog box, navigate to the **c:\exercise_files\chap_04** folder, click **exercise01.prproj** to select it, and click **Open**.

This project file begins where you left off at the end of Chapter 3, *"Assembling a Sequence."* So far, you have imported clips, created subclips, and assembled video, audio, and still images in a few sequences. If you're unsure of this process, review the exercises in Chapter 3.

---

2 Choose **File > Save As**. Navigate to the **c:\exercise_files\dutch_harbor** folder. Name the file **dutch harbor promo.prproj**, and click **Save**.

Note: If a previous version of dutch harbor promo.prproj already exists, you may be asked to replace it. Click **Yes**.

---

3 Choose **Window > Workspace > Effects**.

This workspace rearranges your panels so the Effect Controls panel is visible with plenty of room to work. Instead of the Source Monitor, you now see the Effect Controls panel.

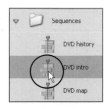

---

4 In the **Project** panel **Sequences** bin, double-click **DVD intro** to open it in the **Timeline**.

To modify a clip's fixed effects, you must first select the clip. If the Effect Controls panel is visible, it automatically displays the effect properties of the currently selected clip.

---

5 On Track **Video 1**, click the **coral_reef.jpg** image to select it and view its fixed effects in the **Effect Controls** panel.

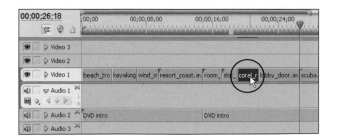

As soon as you select the clip, its fixed effect properties appear in the Effect Controls panel. By default, the Motion and Opacity headings are **collapsed**, meaning the properties within each heading are hidden until you click the arrow icons to expand them.

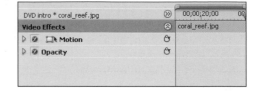

6 In the **Effect Controls** panel, click the **arrow** icon next to **Motion** to expand the fixed effects.

Within the Motion properties, you will see five of the six fixed effects. The sixth effect, Opacity, is listed by itself.

Note: Take care to *avoid* clicking the Effect Enable/Disable toggle, located next to the arrow icon (and shaped like a cursive letter *f* in a dark circle). Turning off this toggle hides any changes you make to the clip's properties. Luckily, because it *is* a toggle, you can always click it again to turn it back on.

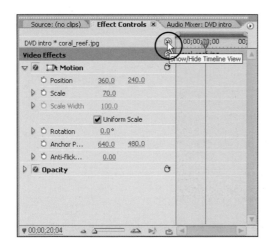

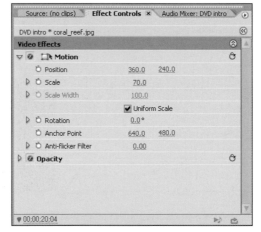

7 If the right side of your **Effect Controls** panel displays a **mini-Timeline**, click the **Show/Hide Timeline View** toggle to hide the **mini-Timeline**.

Clicking the Show/Hide Timeline View toggle hides the mini-Timeline in the Effect Controls panel. You'll use the mini-Timeline in Chapter 8, *"Animating Effects."* For now, it's just in the way.

8 With the **coral_reef.jpg** clip still selected in the **Timeline** panel, drag the **CTI** (**C**urrent **T**ime **I**ndicator), and move it left and right in the **Timeline** panel.

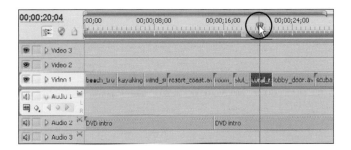

Notice as the Program Monitor changes to show the moving CTI, the Effect Controls panel doesn't change. This underscores an important fact: The Effect Controls panel always shows the properties of the *selected* clip, regardless of the CTI position.

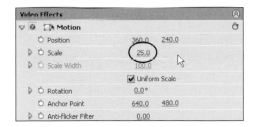

9 In the **Timeline** panel, drag the **CTI** to position the red line over any portion of **coral_reef.jpg**.

Now you can watch coral_reef.jpg in the Program Monitor as you make changes to it in the Effect Controls panel.

10 Locate the **Scale** property, click the value **100.0** to select it, type **25** to replace the existing value, and press **Enter**.

Clicking the value allows you to modify it by typing a new value. Notice the clip displays at 25 percent of its original size in the Program Monitor. This is a bit too small, so in the next step you will slowly increase the scale, but with a different method....

11 Position your cursor over the **Scale** value **25.0**. (Don't click yet!) When your cursor changes to a finger with a slide arrow, click and *slowly* drag the mouse to the right until the value is at (or near) **70.0**.

As you drag, the image slowly increases in size. Dragging a value in the Effect Controls panel is a fun way to visually adjust properties.

Tip: If you accidentally click instead of drag your mouse, Premiere Pro 2 will think you want to type the new value, like you did in Step 10. If that happens, press Enter, and try again.

Perhaps you'd like to see more of the mountain, which is cropped out of view in the Program Monitor. You'll learn how in the next steps.

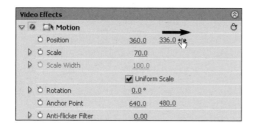

12 Position your cursor over the **Position** y value (the second value shown) until the cursor changes. Then drag your mouse to the right until the y value is about **336.0**.

It may seem counterintuitive to move the mouse to the right for the image to go down. But remember, you are *increasing* the y value, and dragging to the right always increases numbers. You can also move your mouse up to increase effect values.

13 Choose **File > Save**, or press **Ctrl+S**. Leave **dutch harbor promo.prproj** open for the next exercise.

In this exercise, you modified the Position and Scale properties using a few methods. A nice feature of Premiere Pro 2 is the ability to modify all clips and all values in the same way—so, you just learned a lot more than was shown because the same methods will work for all types of clips and all fixed effect properties.

Don't forget to use the Effects workspace to rearrange the panels for easy effects editing. Also remember, if you don't see a clip in the Effect Controls panel, you must select it in the Timeline first.

So far you have changed the clip's fixed effect properties using both the direct click method and the click-and-drag method. As they say on television, "But wait! There's more," because you can also modify a clip's properties *visually* in the Program Monitor, instead of working with the numerical values in the Effect Controls panel, as you are about to find out in the next exercise.

Scaling Clips to More Than 100 Percent

As described previously, scaling clips to more than 100 percent can cause noticeable blurriness and pixilation. You may not notice it at 105 percent, but at 150 percent your image may be downright ugly.

Which image size should you use? When in doubt, always start with a bigger image than you need and reduce the scale to fit your project. For example, perhaps you want to create a video montage of photographs from a vacation. Before you take any photos, make sure you set your digital camera to take pictures larger than 720 x 480 pixels, if possible. This allows you to play images full screen.

If you don't plan to animate the image, instead slowly zooming in or panning left and right like a documentary, then get as close as possible to 720 x 480 pixels at the time of taking the photograph. (Just don't go smaller than 720 pixels wide or 480 pixels tall.)

On the other hand, if you'd like to add motion and animation to your photographs, you should definitely take images *larger* than 720 x 480 pixels so you can zoom in on them without scaling to more than 100 percent. You will learn how to add motion to your images in Chapter 8, *"Animating Effects."*

Premiere Pro 2 does have a 4,096 x 4,096 pixel limit, so bigger is better only up to a point. Although Premiere Pro 2 is happy to display an immensely huge image, it can display and play back a 720 x 480 pixel image much quicker. So use restraint. Just because your camera *can* take images with 4,096 x 4,096 pixels, doesn't mean you always should.

Changing Fixed Effects Visually

Now that you understand the relationship between the fixed effect values, the **Effect Controls** panel, and the **Program Monitor**, it's time to let you in on a little secret: You can also modify three of the fixed effects directly in the **Program Monitor**: position, scale, and rotation.

Instead of clicking the numerical values, as you've done so far in the **Effect Controls** panel, you can directly click the still image or video clip in the **Program Monitor**. This can be a quicker method

of positioning your clips. After all, in the **Effect Controls** panel, it takes at least a couple of clicks to move the x and y coordinates individually. But in the **Program Monitor**, you can click and drag the clip exactly to where you want it to go. The downside is you may not get uniform, precise values.

To modify a clip visually in the **Program Monitor**, you must put the clip in direct select mode—a phrase that sounds imposing but truly isn't.

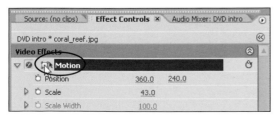

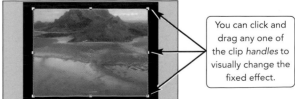

You can click and drag any one of the clip *handles* to visually change the fixed effect.

To place a clip in direct select mode, you can click the clip directly in the **Program Monitor** to select it, or you can click the **Motion** fixed effect heading, shown in the previous illustration. It's quicker to directly click the clip in the **Program Monitor**, but if you are working with multiple clips stacked on top of each other, Premiere Pro 2 tries to guess which clip you are attempting to select—and sometimes it guesses wrong. For this reason, it can be safer to explicitly click the fixed effect heading. That way, no confusion exists as to which clip you have selected and which one you want to move.

When you click the heading, the word is highlighted in black to indicate it is selected. In addition, in the **Program Monitor**, you can see eight **handles** (the solid squares) around the edges of the clip, which indicate it is selected and ready to be modified. When a clip is in direct select mode, you can position, scale, and rotate it.

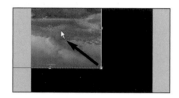 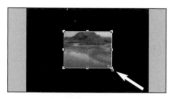 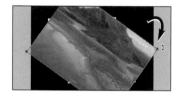

Depending on where you click the clip in direct select mode, as shown in the illustration here, you can position it (left), scale it (center), or rotate it (right):

Position: To modify a clip's **Position** fixed effect, click and drag anywhere *inside* the clip.

Scale: To modify a clip's **Scale** fixed effect, click and drag any one of the eight handles around the border of the clip. Note that the clip will always scale *centered on* the anchor point.

Rotation: To modify a clip's **Rotation** fixed effect, position your cursor just *outside* of any of the eight handles, until the cursor changes to a curved double arrow. Like Scale, the image will always rotate around the axis of the anchor point.

Keep in mind, these are the *only* three properties you can modify visually in the **Program Monitor**. You must modify all others in the **Effect Controls** panel.

 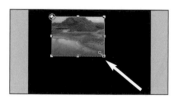 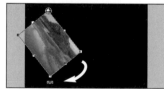

Speaking of anchor points, this is a perfect time to highlight the use of the **Anchor Point** fixed effect (even though you can modify the **Anchor Point** effect *only* in the **Effect Controls** panel). In the illustration shown here (left), the anchor point, indicated by a tiny crosshair, was moved to the upper-left corner of the clip.

When the clip is scaled (center), it is scaled to the anchor point. In other words, the upper-left corner of the clip *does not move*, but the rest of the clip shrinks toward the anchor point. If this clip were scaled as small as possible, it would eventually be a dot right at the anchor point.

When the clip is rotated (right), it is rotated around the axis of the anchor point. Again, the clip "hinges" like it is being held in the upper-left corner.

In both the scale and rotation examples, the upper-left corner of the clip does not move. It is...drumroll, please...**anchored** to the canvas.

In the next exercise, you will visually modify a clip's fixed effects in the **Program Monitor**.

EXERCISE
2 | Modifying Fixed Effects in the Program Monitor

If numbers don't float your boat, don't sweat it. Premiere Pro 2 allows you to modify a clip visually, rather than numerically, in the **Program Monitor**. This is useful for you creative types who aren't so hung up on precise values. Of course, some of us mathaholics can't live knowing our scale may be 49.5 percent instead of 50 percent. Modifying the values in the **Effect Controls** panel gives you precision; modifying the clip in the **Program Monitor** is better suited to eyeballing the effect to taste. In this exercise, you will learn how to visually modify an effect in the Program Monitor.

---

1 On the **Welcome Screen**, click **Open Project**. In the **Open Project** dialog box, navigate to the **c:\exercise_files\chap_04** folder, click **exercise02.prproj** to select it, and click **Open**.

This project file begins where you left off at the end of Chapter 3, *"Assembling a Sequence."* So far, you have imported clips, created subclips, and assembled video, audio, and still images in a few different sequences. If you're unsure of this process, review the exercises in Chapter 3.

---

2 Choose **File > Save As**. Navigate to the **c:\exercise_files\dutch_harbor** folder. Name the file **dutch harbor promo.prproj**, and click **Save**.

Note: If a previous version of dutch harbor promo.prproj already exists, you may be asked to replace it. Click Yes.

---

3 In the **Project** panel **Sequences** bin, double-click the **DVD map** sequence to open it in the **Timeline**.

You will practice another method for modifying fixed effects in the next few steps, but first you have to get your sequence ready.

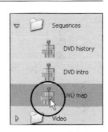

---

4 In the **Project** panel **Graphics** bin, drag **resort_map.ai** to the beginning of Track **Video 1** in the **Timeline**.

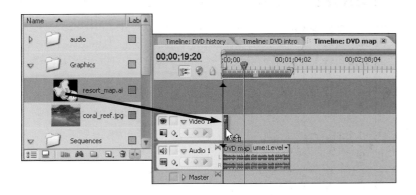

---

5 Press the **backslash** (\) key to quickly zoom in the **Timeline**.

Because the resort_map.ai clip is so short, it appears very thin compared to the audio clip already in the sequence. Zooming fixes this.

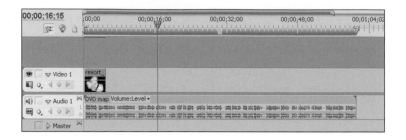

6 On Track **Video 1**, position your cursor over the **Out** point of the clip. When your mouse changes to the **Trim Out** cursor, snap the **Out** point of **resort_map.ai** to the **Out** point of **DVD map**.

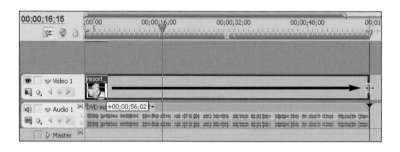

Here's an important fact you should remember about image clips: You can lengthen the duration of image clips to (almost) infinity. Video clips have a finite duration, however, and cannot be lengthened beyond their last frame. A still image, on the other hand, has no beginning and no end (how Zen!) and thus can play for as long as you need.

7 On Track **Video 1**, click **resort_map.ai** to select it and view its properties in the **Effect Controls** panel. Make sure the **CTI** is positioned somewhere over the clip so you can see it in the **Program Monitor**.

You can see in the Program Monitor the clip is too large to fit in the screen, so you need to scale it down. First you must put the clip in direct select mode.

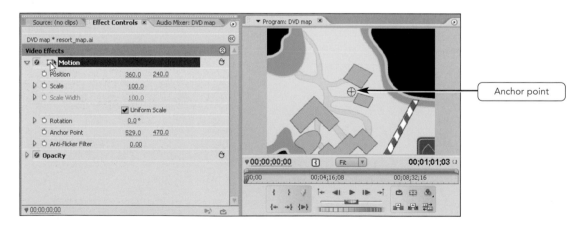

Anchor point

8 In the **Effect Controls** panel, click the **arrow** icon next to **Motion** to expand the fixed effects. Then click the word **Motion** to put the clip in direct select mode.

Direct select mode allows you to modify the clip visually in the Program Monitor, instead of modifying the values in the Effect Controls panel. When the clip is in direct select mode, you will see the anchor point and clip handles around the outsides of the clip.

Sometimes a clip is too large to fit within the Program Monitor canvas, and therefore you can't see its handles because they are outside the Program Monitor. To remedy this, you can change the zoom level of the Program Monitor to shrink the preview, which will allow you to see more of the area around the canvas.

9 In the **Program Monitor**, choose the **View Zoom Level** menu, and choose **10%** to change it.

This shrinks the Program Monitor canvas so you can work with clips falling outside the monitor. This is for viewing purposes only; it doesn't affect the real size of your sequence. Because the clip is so large, you cannot see all of its handles in the Program Monitor. Again, zooming fixes this.

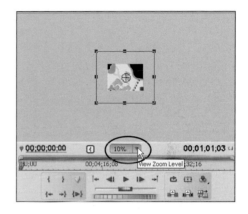

10 Position your cursor over any of the handles. When your mouse changes to a resize cursor, drag the handle until the clip fits well within the canvas of the **Program Monitor**.

Tip: No matter which handle you grab, the clip will always scale and rotate based on the anchor point.

11 In the **Program Monitor**, choose the **View Zoom Level** menu, and choose **Fit**.

The Fit choice resizes the canvas to fill the Program Monitor, and it depends on the height and width of your Program Monitor.

Sometimes you get to a point when you just want to start anew. Perhaps you've made so many modifications you can't remember what the image used to originally look like. Premiere Pro 2 provides a quick method to reset all of the fixed effect properties to their default values.

12 In the **Effect Controls** panel, click the **Reset** button.

Notice that Scale is returned to 100.0%. This resets all of the hard work you've

done to the clip's original properties. This button can be useful, especially when you want to start fresh.

New to Premiere Pro 2 is the Scale to Frame Size menu item, which automatically scales your image to fit inside the Program Monitor canvas, or **frame**. This option won't change the shape of your image (for example, it won't turn a circle into an egg), but it will shrink the image's width and height until *both* fit in the Program Monitor canvas.

This feature is useful only when dealing with oversized images. The larger the image, the more pixels you are "discarding" when shrinking to frame size, which results in quicker performance in Premiere Pro 2. (Having fewer pixels means Premiere Pro 2 doesn't have to do as much math, which speeds up effects, transitions, and so on.)

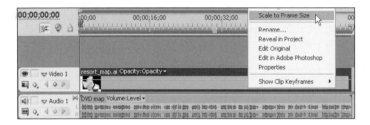

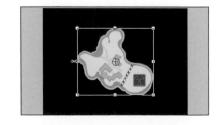

13 In the **Timeline** panel, right-click **resort_map.ai** on Track **Video 1**, and choose **Scale to Frame Size**.

This reduces the image so its largest dimension (width or height) fits inside the Program Monitor. You can see the handles around the clip are all visible now.

Also notice the Scale value in the Effect Controls panel *still* displays 100.0%, even though the image is clearly smaller. This is an important fact about the Scale to Frame Size menu item: It shrinks the image so 100 percent is the size of the Program Monitor. No matter how big the image used to be, 100 percent *now* represents the frame size of the Program Monitor.

Note: If you plan to zoom in on the clip later, you should *not* use Scale to Frame Size. Why? Instead of using the original pixels, you end up scaling to more than 100 percent. And you learned earlier that scaling to more than 100 percent is bad.

---

14 In the **Effect Controls** panel, click **Motion** to put the clip in direct select mode. In the **Program Monitor**, drag any of the clip's handles until the **Scale** value is approximately **65.0**.

Notice the following here: First, as you drag, the values change in small increments. You may not be able to get exactly 65.0. Second, as you drag, the clip becomes pixilated. Premiere Pro 2 lowers the resolution, allowing the screen to update quicker so you can see your changes in real time. When you release the mouse, Premiere Pro 2 increases the resolution back to full.

15 Choose **File > Save**, or press **Ctrl+S**. Leave **dutch harbor promo.prproj** open for the next exercise.

As with the previous exercise, you've learned the basics of modifying clips in direct select mode. Even though you modified only the Scale property, everything you've learned applies to rotation and position. Above all else, remember this: You should *always* move the Timeline CTI above the clip you have selected so you can see it *both* in the Effect Controls panel and in the Program Monitor.

Lastly, if you find yourself wanting to modify an anchor point, it's a good idea to make sure the anchor point changes *first*. Because the anchor point affects all other properties, all other properties depend on the location of the anchor point. Many, many editors have spent hours tweaking their scales and rotations to perfection only to have to redo their work after changing the anchor point.

NOTE:

Default Duration and Scale

In the previous exercise, you learned still images can play for an (almost) infinite duration. Even so, Premiere Pro 2 assigns the clips a duration of 5 seconds at the time you import them into the project. The developers of Premiere Pro 2 chose this number arbitrarily, and you can easily change it to your liking.

To change the default image duration, choose **Edit > Preferences > General**. In the **Preferences** dialog box, you will see the **Still Image Default Duration** option. Keep in mind the number is in frames, so 150 frames ÷ 30 frames per second = 5 seconds.

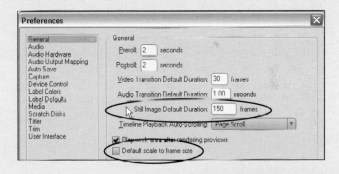

In the previous exercise, you used the **Scale to Frame Size** menu item to reduce the size of a clip to fit in the **Program Monitor**. Premiere Pro 2 provides an option to allow you to do this to *all* images at the time you import them. To automatically scale images upon importing them, turn on the **Default scale to frame size** check box.

This turns on resizing for *all* images that you import. However, if you want to turn off automatic resizing for a single image, you can right-click the individual clip on the Timeline and choose **Clip > Scale to Frame Size** until the check box is turned off. You would do this when you are scaling the clip more than 100 percent in order to prevent a loss in picture quality.

It's important to note that the **Default scale to frame size** option has no effect on items *already imported* into a project; it affects only items you will import in the future.

Understanding Alpha Channels and Render Order

Many types of images you work with in Premiere Pro 2 do not have transparency, such as photographs from a digital camera. However, another type of graphic file has transparency *within the clip*. Like looking through a hole in a fence, the transparent area of the clip allows any underlying video to show through. To do this, the graphic needs an alpha channel.

An **alpha channel** is an extra channel of information defining transparency in an image. Some images have alpha channels, and some don't. When you save an image with an alpha channel in a program such as Adobe Photoshop, the alpha channel information is embedded in the image. When you import the image as a clip into a Premiere Pro 2 project, Premiere Pro 2 automatically reads the alpha channel and creates a transparent area. When you place the clip on a track above a video clip, the video underneath shows through. (Unfortunately, you can't create an alpha channel in Premiere Pro 2; you must save the alpha channel with the software you used to create the image.)

Alpha channels are especially useful for logos, titles, and bugs. (A **bug** is a tiny icon, such as the CBS Eye or NBC Peacock in the lower-right corner of your television screen.) The illustration here demonstrates how an image with an alpha channel can make your finished product appear more professional.

Image without an alpha channel on top of video. No video shows through the image.

Image with an alpha channel on top of video. Video shows through the transparent regions.

So how exactly do you place an alpha channel image on top of a video clip? In reality, you're not placing it literally on top of the video. Instead, you are placing it on the video track *above* the image. Premiere Pro 2 renders from the top down, which means the clip in the topmost video track will display on top in the Program Monitor. If you place the alpha channel image on the top track, it will show on top of the video below it.

| 👁 | ▷ Video 2 | dutch_harbor_logo.psd |
| 👁 | ▷ Video 1 | beach_tropical.avi |

In the illustration shown here, the logo is on Track **Video 2**, so it displays on top of the video on Track **Video 1**, as shown in the Dutch Harbor Resort and Casino illustration above. If the logo had no alpha channel, it would look similar to that shown in the Dutch Harbor Resort and Casino illustration on the left.

Finally, you should know alpha channels are not restricted solely to images. Some video clips can have alpha channels. These types of clips are usually computer generated or modified by a computer in some way. Clips captured directly from your video camera *never, ever* have alpha channels.

In this next exercise, you will practice working with both still images and computer-generated video clips containing alpha channels.

Alpha Channel versus Opacity

Transparency is a tricky term to pin down. Earlier, you learned about **opacity**, which defines the amount of transparency when images are placed on top of each other. And now, you just learned about alpha channels, which also define transparency. So what exactly is the difference?

An **alpha channel** defines transparency for just a *portion* of a clip. Some pixels can be more transparent, and some can be **less**. In the illustration shown here on the left, some pixels are completely **opaque** (solid), and others are completely invisible. The video underneath shows through the invisible area, defined by the alpha channel.

Opacity defines the overall transparency of an *entire* clip. It's like a dimmer switch for a light bulb; you can make the entire room only more bright or less bright. The same is true of opacity. Opacity makes the entire image more transparent or less transparent. In the illustration shown here on the right, the clip's opacity has been lowered to 50 percent. You can see that every single pixel is now semitransparent, and the video underneath shows through each pixel.

3 | Using Graphics with Alpha Channels

Alpha channels allow you to place an image on top of a video and have the video show through the transparent regions of the image. Thankfully, you do not need to do anything in Premiere Pro 2 to "turn on" an alpha channel. If a clip has an alpha channel, Premiere Pro 2 should automatically detect it. All you have to do is place the clip above another clip to take advantage of the alpha channel. In this exercise, you will use still images and video clips with alpha channels. Because it is so easy to work with these types of clips, this exercise is jam-packed with other goodies as well, such as adding video tracks and pasting clips.

---

1 If you followed the previous exercise, **dutch harbor promo.prproj** should still be open in Premiere Pro 2. If it's not, click **Open Project** on the **Welcome Screen**. Navigate to the **c:\exercise_files\chap_04** folder, click **exercise03.prproj** to select it, and click **Open**.

---

2 Choose **File > Save As**. Navigate to the **c:\exercise_files\dutch_harbor** folder. Name the file **dutch harbor promo.prproj**, and click **Save**.

Note: If a previous version of dutch harbor promo.prproj already exists, you may be asked to replace it. Click Yes.

---

3 In the **Project** panel **Sequences** bin, double-click the **DVD map** sequence to open it in the **Timeline**.

You may not have realized it, but the resort_map.ai clip you worked with in Exercise 2 had an alpha channel around it. However, because there was no video clip below it, Premiere Pro 2 displayed the "empty" portion of the screen as black.

To take advantage of the alpha channel in a clip, you need to have it on any video track *above* another track. In this case, the clip is on Track 1, which means you need to move it to at least Track 2 if you plan to play some video below it.

---

4 From Track **Video 1**, drag the **resort_map.ai** clip to the gray area above the track. Make sure you stay snapped to the beginning (far left) of the sequence as you drag the clip upward.

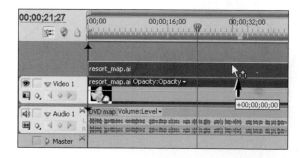

Dragging a clip to the empty gray area above the tracks in the Timeline panel creates a new video track. Now your clip should be on Track Video 2 (and Track Video 1 is empty).

5 In the **Project** panel, right-click the **Graphics** bin icon, and choose **Import**. Navigate to the **c:\exercise_files\media_files\graphics** folder, click **background_blue.avi** to select it, and click **Open**.

Tip: If you right-click a bin and choose Import, Premiere Pro 2 imports the clip into the bin. (This is just a reminder, since it has been a few chapters since you learned this.)

Once you have some empty track space below your alpha channel clip, you can place either a video or an image clip below.

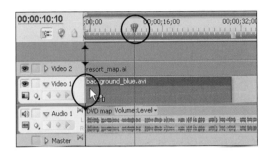

6 In the **Project** panel **Graphics** bin, drag the **background_blue.avi** clip, and snap it to the beginning of Track **Video 1** in the **Timeline**. Drag the **CTI**, and position it somewhere over both clips.

In the Program Monitor, you will see the blue background behind the map image—all thanks to your friend, Mr. Alpha Channel. And that's really all there is to using a clip with an alpha channel. You don't need to turn on anything or specify the channel—Premiere Pro 2 does all the work.

Sometimes your background video is too short, which can easily be remedied by dragging an additional copy of the background clip onto the track and snapping it to the end of the first instance of the clip. This is called **looping** because you can continue doing this over and over to create a never-ending loop.

7 In the **Project** panel **Graphics** bin, drag the **background_blue.avi** clip, and snap it to the end of the **background_blue.avi** clip already on Track **Video 1**.

Some clips, such as the *Jumpback* background video from Digital Juice, which you

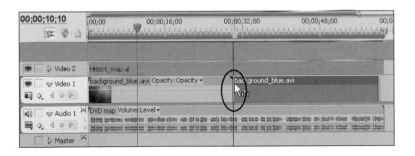

are using in this exercise, are designed to be looped so that the first and last frames match each other. Therefore, you can string it many times in a row, and to an audience member, it will look like a single, long, fluid clip.

8 In the **Program Monitor**, click the **Play** button to preview the sequence. As it plays, verify that you can see the background through the alpha channel and the background appears to be looping.

You will return to complete this sequence in Chapter 5, *"Adding Titles."*

Besides still images with alpha channels, Premiere Pro 2 can also handle video clips with alpha channels. If you watch any televised sporting event, you will see this all the time—swirling and animated boxes with stats, a player's bio, and so on. Anytime this box is animated, you can guarantee it's a video with an alpha channel.

In this exercise, you will work with a lower third that has an alpha channel.

Note: A **lower third** is video-geek terminology for a graphic appearing on the lower third of a screen. You can see this in documentaries, in interviews, and on the evening news (when it displays the reporter's name on the lower third of the screen).

---

9 In the **Project** panel **Sequences** bin, double-click **DVD history** to open it in the **Timeline**.

Because the lower third has not been imported yet, you must import it like any other video clip.

---

10 In the **Project** panel, right-click the **Graphics** bin icon, and choose **Import**. From the **Import** dialog box, navigate to the **c:\exercise_files\media_files\graphics** folder. Click **lower_third.mov** to select it, and click **Open**. In the **Project** panel, double-click **lower_third.mov** to open it in the **Source Monitor**.

In the Source Monitor, you see the lower third displays as a pink bar running across the screen, and the background displays as black. Keep in mind the background really isn't black; it's actually transparent, thanks to the alpha channel.

Currently you are looking at the **composite video** of this clip (that is to say, the final product of this clip, which combines the alpha channel and all of its color information). However, sometimes you might want to see just the alpha channel to better understand what the clip looks like. For example, it can be hard to distinguish between "empty" black and "painted" black, both of which *appear* black but are completely different.

---

11 In the **Source Monitor**, click the **wing menu**, and choose **Alpha**.

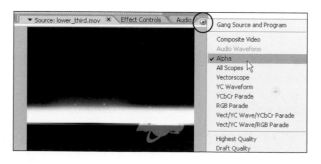

Instead of looking at the actual color channels, you are looking at only the alpha channel. Anything black is transparent, and anything white is opaque. And—here's where it gets *really exciting*—anything gray is semitransparent.

This is the power of alpha channels—because 256 shades of gray exist, you get 256 levels of transparency. Thus, you can have very smooth and soft gradients, from opaque to transparent. This may not get *you* excited, but to a video geek, this is titillating stuff!

12 In the **Source Monitor**, click the **wing menu**, and choose **Composite Video**.

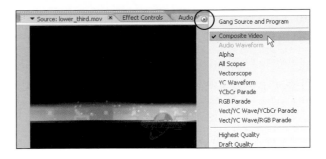

This returns the clip to its normal color mode.

Tip: Changing the view between Composite Video and Alpha does not affect the clip. This is merely for preview purposes so you can observe the clip in different ways.

You have now imported the clip into the Project panel, so you can place it above any existing video clip in a sequence.

---

13 In the **Source Monitor**, drag the clip to the beginning of the sequence on Track **Video 2**.

---

14 In the **Program Monitor**, drag the **CTI** to the beginning, and click the **Play** button.

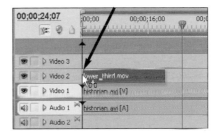

Not too shabby. Because of the many levels of transparency in the alpha channel, the lower third has a soft shadow at its upper and lower edges. Furthermore, because this is a movie clip, the alpha channel can also change shape over time.

A common technique in documentaries is to play the interviewer's dialogue for a second or two and then bring in the person's name at the upper edge of a lower third. To do this, all you need to do is move the lower-third video clip farther down the Timeline so it starts playing later in time.

---

15 In the upper-left corner of the **Timeline**, click the **blue time display**, type **300**, and press **Enter** to move your **CTI** to **00;00;03;00**.

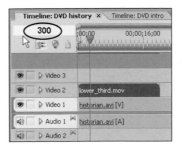

Premiere Pro 2 interprets typing 300 as 3 seconds and 00 frames. If you typed 3, that would be only three frames. If you typed 30, that would be 30 frames.

16 On Track **Video 2**, drag the **lower_third.mov** clip, and snap its **In** point to the **CTI**. Drag the **CTI** to the beginning of the sequence, and press the **spacebar** to play your sequence. After you've previewed the lower third, press the **spacebar** to stop the sequence.

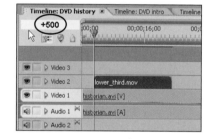

Later in this book, you learn how to gently fade in the lower third so it doesn't suddenly pop on the screen. But for now, you have other fish to fry.

When you use a lower third to display a person's name, it's a good idea to monitor the length of the lower third. For example, it doesn't take that long to read someone's name and their occupation. But some lower third clips can play for 10 or more seconds. Five seconds is usually ample time to display someone's name on the screen. And even that might be too long, depending on your time constraints.

This lower third is too long, so you will use an easy shortcut to make it only 5 seconds.

---

17 Hold down **Shift**, and snap the **Timeline CTI** to the **In** point of the **lower_third.mov** clip on Track **Video 2**. Click the **blue time display**, type **+500**, and press **Enter**.

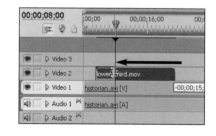

Adding + or – to the value moves the CTI relative to its initial point in time. In other words, its initial point was the In point of the lower third, and then you moved it to the right 5 seconds.

---

18 On Track **Video 2**, position your cursor over the end of the **lower_third.mov** clip, and use the **Trim Out** cursor to snap its **Out** point to the **CTI**.

The clip should now be 5 seconds long.

The last thing to fix on the lower third is its position on the screen. (It's a bit too high.) Luckily, you are a whiz with the Effect Controls panel, so this should be a piece of cake.

---

19 In the **Timeline**, click the **lower_third.mov** clip to select it. Choose **Window > Effect Controls**.

Tip: Because the Effect Controls panel and Source Monitor share the same space, you can lose one or the other easily. However, you can always "recover" lost panels by using the Window menu.

---

20 In the **Timeline** panel, drag the **CTI** to position it over the **lower_third.mov** clip.

This lets you see the lower third and the historian in the Program Monitor.

You can put videos into direct select mode just like images. For example, if you think the lower third video is too high on the screen (maybe it's cutting off the interviewee's chin), you can easily move the video clip down using direct select mode.

21 In the **Effect Controls** panel, click **Motion**. Hold down **Shift**, and drag the anchor point (in the center) of the **lower_third.mov** clip to the lower part of the screen, using the illustration shown here as a guide.

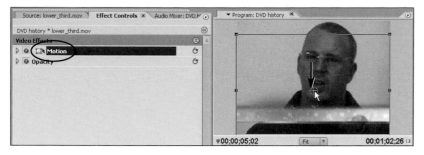

Holding down Shift constrains your movement to up and down *or* left and right. (This will seem familiar if you have used other Adobe products.)

Once you have your lower third just the way you like it, Premiere Pro 2 makes it easy to copy the fixed effects from one clip and paste them onto a second clip. This is called **pasting attributes**.

Before you can paste the attributes of the first clip, you need to place an additional copy of the lower third video on top of the next actor.

---

22 In the **Program Monitor**, click the **Play** button. Play the clip until the second actor says, "...they should never have built Dutch Harbor where they did," and then click the **Stop** button at **00;00;35;26**.

This is where you will snap an additional copy of the lower third movie from the Project panel.

---

23 In the **Project** panel **Graphics** bin, drag the **lower_third.mov** clip, and snap it to the **CTI** on Track **Video 2**.

As you did previously, you will shorten this clip because it is too long.

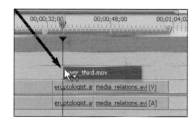

---

24 In the **Timeline**, click the **blue time display**, type **+500**, and press **Enter**.

This moves the CTI to the right 5 seconds from its original position. This is where you will snap the Out point to when trimming.

---

25 On Track **Video 2**, position your cursor over the **Out** point of the second **lower_third.mov** clip. When you see the **Trim Out** cursor, drag and snap the **Out** point to the **CTI**.

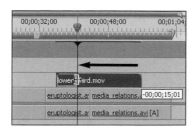

Just like before, your clip is now 5 seconds long.

You are now ready to paste the fixed effects from the first clip onto the second clip. First you copy the entire clip, and then you choose to paste only the attributes.

---

26 On Track **Video 2**, right-click the *first instance* of **lower_third.mov**—the one beginning at 03 seconds—and choose **Copy**.

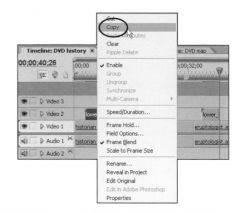

27 In the **Timeline**, right-click the second instance of **lower_third.mov** on Track **Video 2**, and choose **Paste Attributes**. Move the **Timeline CTI** to any point above the lower third you just modified so you can view it in the **Program Monitor**.

This pastes only the *attributes* from the first clip (such as its fixed effects, such as Position, Rotation, Scale, Opacity, and so on). The second clip is now lowered like the first clip.

Pasting attributes is handy when you want to quickly make a second clip look like the first clip. However, sometimes it's easier to just copy the *whole first clip*. After all, why bother doing all the work to place the clip in the sequence and shorten it when you can just duplicate the existing clip?

Premiere Pro 2 makes it easy to duplicate a clip anywhere in the Timeline. You can *always* perform a two-step tango when pasting a clip: First, move your CTI, and second, set your target track, which is where Premiere Pro 2 pastes the clip.

28 Move the **CTI** in the **Timeline** to where you want to the new clip to begin; in this example, that is **00;00;45;11**.

29 Set the target track by clicking Track **Video 2**.

When you click the track name, it should have a lighter background than the other video tracks.

30 Right-click the *first instance* of **lower_third.mov**, and choose **Copy**. Then, choose **Edit > Paste**, or press **Ctrl+V**.

The first clip is pasted in the target track, beginning at the CTI. This new, *third* clip has the same attributes and duration as the first clip. It is an exact duplicate.

31 Choose **File > Save**, or press **Ctrl+S**. Leave **dutch harbor promo.prproj** open for the next exercise.

During this exercise, you may have realized that working with clips containing alpha channels is the same as working with regular clips. Premiere Pro 2 treats them all the same, and you do not need to do anything special to turn on the alpha channel. Just remember to always place the alpha channel clip *on top of* the clip you want it to display above.

You also learned how to paste a clip and paste just the attributes. Pasting a clip is easiest when you want to duplicate an entire clip. Pasting the attributes is easier when a second clip already exists but you just want to position, scale, or rotate the second clip like the first clip.

Importing Photoshop Files as Sequences

Premiere Pro 2 imports Photoshop files in one of two ways: as regular images (called **footage**), like all of the other images you've been using, or as sequences.

If you decide to import a Photoshop file as footage, Premiere Pro 2 imports the Photoshop image as a single clip. When you choose to import as footage, you get to decide how Premiere Pro 2 should interpret the Photoshop layers. You can choose to merge all layers as a clip, or you can choose to import only one of the layers as a clip. (If you are unfamiliar with Photoshop, just smile and nod.)

If you import the Photoshop file as a sequence, every single layer of the Photoshop file becomes a separate clip in a new Premiere Pro 2 sequence. For example, if you have five Photoshop layers, you have five clips. The sequence is the same kind of sequence with which you've been working. Once you have a new sequence, you can nest the new sequence inside other sequences (like a Russian tea doll!).

Nesting Sequences

Nesting is the act of inserting one sequence inside another sequence. When you insert a nested sequence, you are inserting every clip, graphic, track—everything—from the nested sequence into the other sequence. However, the nested sequence displays and behaves like any other audio or video clip. You can select, move, trim, and apply effects to nested sequences just as you would any other clip.

Later in this book, you will work more in depth with nested sequences. For now, the next exercise gives you a basic introduction to nesting and importing Photoshop files.

When you import a Photoshop image into Premiere Pro 2, you have the choice of flattening the image into one clip or converting each layer as its own clip. Converting each layer is advantageous when you want to have individual control over each Photoshop layer, such as animating the letters of a word individually. When you import a Photoshop file as individual layers, it places each layer into a sequence. You can then place this sequence into *other* sequences—this is called **nesting**. In this exercise, you will learn how to import a Photoshop file as a sequence and how to nest it.

1 If you followed the previous exercise, **dutch harbor promo.prproj** should still be open in Premiere Pro 2. If it's not, click **Open Project** on the **Welcome Screen**. Navigate to the **c:\exercise_files\chap_04** folder, click **exercise04.prproj** to select it, and click **Open**.

2 Choose **File > Save As**. Navigate to the **c:\exercise_files\dutch_harbor** folder. Name the file **dutch harbor promo.prproj**, and click **Save**.

Note: If a previous version of dutch harbor promo.prproj already exists, you may be asked to replace it. Click Yes.

The first step when importing a Photoshop file is to import it like any other clip. Premiere Pro 2 will recognize it as a special type of file and ask you some specialized questions.

3 In the **Project** panel, right-click the **Graphics** bin, and choose **Import**. Navigate to the **c:\exercise_files\media_files\graphics** folder. Click **dutch_harbor_logo.psd** to select it, and click **Open**.

When importing a Photoshop file, you will see a special Premiere Pro 2 dialog box open. The Import Layered File dialog box asks you how to import the file.

4 In the **Import Layered File** dialog box, choose the **Import As** menu, and choose **Sequence**. Click **OK**.

After importing, Premiere Pro 2 creates a new bin just for the Photoshop sequence and its clips and also creates a sequence containing each clip shown in the bin.

5 Next to the **dutch_harbor_logo bin** icon, click the **arrow icon** (its name may be truncated in the **Project** panel) to view its contents. Scroll down to see all of the contents.

This Photoshop file has six layers, which are represented as six individual clips in the bin. At the bottom of the bin is the newly created sequence.

You can open this sequence like any other sequence you have worked with in this book. In fact, it *is* the same as any other sequence in this book.

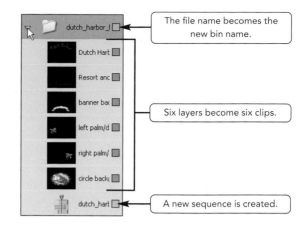

The file name becomes the new bin name.

Six layers become six clips.

A new sequence is created.

6 In the **Project** panel Graphics\dutch_harbor_ logo bin, double click the **dutch_harbor_logo** sequence to open it in the **Timeline**.

In the Timeline, notice the video tracks have been renamed to match the Photoshop layer. (Each layer becomes a track, so this sequence has six video

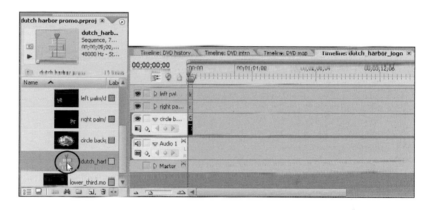

tracks.) Also notice the audio track. As you may remember from earlier in this book, every sequence must have *at least one* audio track. Although this Photoshop sequence has no audio, it still must have one audio track.

7 Zoom the **Timeline** by pressing the **backslash** (\) key.

Because this sequence contains so many tracks, you cannot see them all at once. Dragging allows you to see the video tracks.

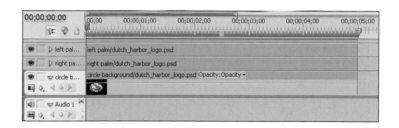

8 Drag the **vertical scroll bar** to the top of the **Timeline**.

You should be able to scroll up and down and count all six video tracks.

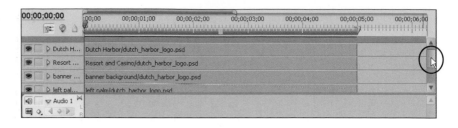

You may be thinking, "Since this is a Photoshop file, why does my new sequence have an audio track?" Good question. All sequences must have at least one audio track. That's just the rule in the Premiere Pro 2 universe. You have no way around that.

Although Premiere Pro 2 won't let you delete the audio track, you *can* move it out of view, which lets you see all the video tracks with ease.

---

9 Just above the track name **Audio 1**, position your cursor over the thin gray area. When your cursor changes to the separator cursor, drag your mouse to the bottom of the **Timeline**.

This moves the separator between audio and video tracks to the bottom of the Timeline, giving your video tracks more room to be seen. Now you should be able to see all of the video tracks in the Timeline without having to scroll.

When space is limited in the Timeline panel—especially when you have six video tracks—it's helpful to hide the options currently displayed in any video track because every inch of screen real estate counts.

---

10 Next to the **circle background** video track, click the **arrow** icon to hide its track options.

Once you have successfully imported a Photoshop file as a sequence, you can nest that sequence in other sequences. To do this, you must have the parent (container) sequence open in the Timeline panel. Then, you drag the child (nested) sequence into the Timeline.

11 At the top of the **Timeline**, select the **DVD intro** tab.

Tip: Opening a sequence this way is a shortcut for double-clicking it in the Project panel.

Before nesting the child sequence into the parent sequence, you can open the child in the Source Monitor—since, after all, it is about to become a regular clip like other source clips you've placed into sequences. Opening the child sequence in the Source Monitor allows you to set In and Out points if you want and even choose to ignore the audio or video portions of the sequence, as you did in the previous chapter with regular clips.

---

12 In the **Project** panel **Graphics\dutch_harbor_logo** bin, right-click the **dutch_harbor_logo** sequence, and choose **Open in Source Monitor**.

If you are going to open a sequence in the Source Monitor, it's best to do it this way. Why? Well, with normal clips, you simply double-click them to open them in the Source Monitor. But what happens when you double-click a sequence? It opens in the Timeline panel. So the method in this step provides an alternate method for getting the sequence to open in the Source Monitor.

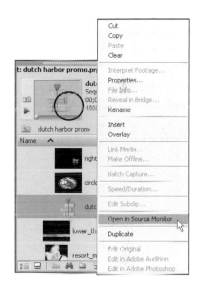

Remember that the sequence automatically created from the Photoshop file had one audio track? Since you won't be using it, you do not need to place it in the Timeline. Just as you did in the previous chapter, you will tell the Source Monitor to ignore the audio portion of this clip.

---

13 In the **Source Monitor**, click the **Toggle Take Audio and Video** toggle until only the **filmstrip** icon displays.

14 Drag the clip from the **Source Monitor** to Track **Video 2**, and snap it to the **In** point of **resort_coast.avi**.

Although this sequence comprises six video tracks and many clips, when you nest a sequence into another sequence, it shows as one clip.

You want this nested sequence to be the same length as resort_coast.avi (so they start and stop at the same time), but it is a tad too short. The next few steps will show you how to lengthen a nested sequence.

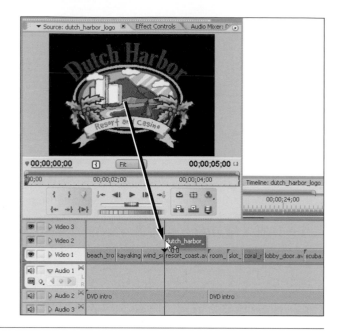

15 In the **Timeline**, double click the **dutch_harbor_logo** nested sequence on Track **Video 2**.

This opens the nested sequence for editing in the Timeline.

If you were a glutton for punishment, you could position your cursor over the end of each of the six clips in the logo sequence and use the Trim Out cursor to extend them one at a time. Or, you can use the **Multi-Track Select tool** to select *all* the clips so you can modify them all at once.

16 Select the **Track Select** tool from the **Tools** panel.

The Track Select tool becomes the Multi-Track Select tool when you hold down the Shift key. What's the difference? The Track Select tool chooses only one track. The Multi-Track Select tool chooses *all* tracks (that aren't locked).

17 Hold down **Shift**, and click in the center of any of the clips.

18 Select the **Selection** tool from the **Tools** panel.

Don't forget to select this tool after using any other tool. (Are you tired of being told that?)

All of the clips in the Timeline are still selected.

19 Position your cursor over the **Out** point of any one of the clips until you see the **Trim Out** cursor, and drag the clips to approximately **00;00;10;00**.

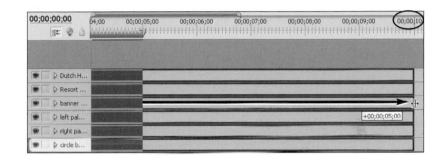

Tip: Use the Time Ruler as a guide. Because the default for images is 5 seconds, the yellow tool tip says you are increasing the length by another +00;00;05;00.

When all the clips are selected, you can manipulate them as one. Very handy!

20 Press the backslash (\) key to autozoom the **Timeline**.

Now that you have lengthened the individual clips *within* the nested sequence, you can return to the parent sequence and make the nested sequence longer. Keep in mind you cannot lengthen a nested sequence *until* you first lengthen its constituent clips.

21 At the top of the **Timeline**, select the **DVD intro** tab to open it.

22 Position your cursor over the **Out** point of the nested sequence on Track **Video 2**. Drag and snap it to the **Out** point of **resort_coast.avi**.

You don't have to drag very far, only about 11 frames.

This would not have been possible without Step 19. Remember, a nested sequence is only as long as the clips making up that sequence. In other words, if a sequence is 5 seconds long and you nest it in another sequence, the nested clip can be only 5 seconds long.

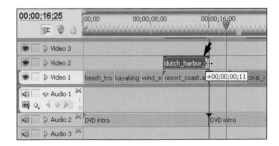

23 Choose **File > Save**, or press **Ctrl+S**. Leave **dutch harbor promo.prproj** open for the next exercise.

Premiere Pro 2 makes importing a Photoshop file extremely simple. With the click of a button you can choose whether to import the file as a single clip or as multiple tracks in a sequence.

Also remember, any changes to a nested sequence are updated automatically in the parent sequence. Although you have only touched the "nested sequences iceberg," you will discover a few more common uses of nested sequences as you progress through this book.

NOTE:

Playback Quality

During this chapter, you may have noticed the **Program Monitor** often becomes pixilated during playback of graphics and video clips containing alpha channels. At other times, when playback is stopped, the screen looks smooth. Why?

Premiere Pro 2 draws its speed, power, and memory from your computer. The faster and more powerful your computer, the more Premiere Pro 2 can do and juggle.

In addition, Premiere Pro 2 can display regular, run-of-the-mill DV clips without a problem. But when you add still images and other graphics on top of the DV clips, then things get more complex. If your system isn't up to snuff, Premiere Pro 2 has to make a compromise.

It's the age-old question: Do you want it good, or do you want it fast? Premiere Pro 2 strives to find a happy medium. To keep smooth playback so your video doesn't become jerky or jumpy, Premiere Pro 2 lowers the resolution during playback of complex alpha channels and still images. This lowers the burden on your computer system so Premiere Pro 2 can display the video with greater ease (shown in the illustration here on the left). However, lowering the resolution results in a lowered, pixilated video quality (shown in the illustration here on the right). When playback stops, however, Premiere Pro 2 isn't working very hard and can revert to the highest-quality image.

This issue becomes even more apparent in future chapters as you deal with titles, video filters, and transitions—all of which cause Premiere Pro 2 to work harder than it wants to work.

---

5 | Reducing Image Flicker

Twittering, flickering, fluttering, jumping, and jittering. These are all (very technical) words used to describe what happens to some titles, text, and images when displayed on a video screen. A graphic that looks good on your computer monitor may be quite ugly on a video monitor. Thin lines and horizontal lines especially tend to flicker on television screens. This exercise introduces you to the **Anti-flicker Filter** found in the **Effect Controls** panel.

---

1 If you followed the previous exercise, **dutch harbor promo.prproj** should still be open in Premiere Pro 2. If it's not, click **Open Project** on the **Welcome Screen**. Navigate to the **c:\exercise_files\chap_04** folder, click **exercise05.prproj** to select it, and click **Open**.

---

2 Choose **File > Save As**. Navigate to the **c:\exercise_files\dutch_harbor** folder. Name the file **dutch harbor promo.prproj**, and click **Save**.

Note: If a previous version of dutch harbor promo.prproj already exists, you may be asked to replace it. Click Yes.

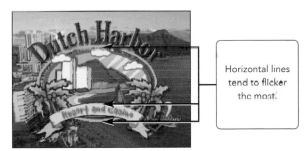

Horizontal lines tend to flicker the most.

3 At the top of the **Timeline**, select the **DVD intro** tab to bring that sequence to the foreground. If necessary, move the **CTI** to **00;00;12;00**.

It may not be apparent in the Program Monitor, but if you have a video monitor attached to your computer, you can detect a flicker near the edges of the logo's horizontal lines—most noticeably around the yellow ring and black outline of the banner. Flickering is usually caused by sharp, horizontal lines.

Adding the Anti-flicker Filter isn't hard. In fact, it's best to just eyeball it as you go. Increase the value *very* slowly, from 0 to 1. It goes in increments of 0.1, so you can choose from 10 incremental steps, each slightly more blurred than the last. As you slowly drag, at each increment along the way, look at your video monitor to see whether the flicker has stopped. Continue tweaking the value until you find a suitable amount.

---

4 In the **Timeline**, click the **dutch_harbor_logo** nested sequence to select it. Choose **Window > Effect Controls**. In the **Effect Controls** panel, click the **arrow** icon next to **Motion** to display the properties for this clip. Click and drag the **Anti-flicker Filter** to **0.80**. (If you have an attached video monitor, you can slowly increase from **0** to **0.80** and see whether you can detect when the flicker stops.)

The Anti-flicker Filter adds a *very* subtle blur to the graphic. In this case, 0.80 was just enough to soften the horizontal lines and nix the flicker. Again, it may take a true video monitor to detect the subtle difference.

If you have a computer monitor only, try turning the effect on and off (with the italic *f* next to the Motion property). When done comparing, make sure the effect is on.

Flicker tends to occur most on computer-generated graphics, especially logos and still images. Next, another image in your project could use some Anti-flicker Filter.

---

5 At the top of the **Timeline**, select the **DVD map** tab. Make sure the **Timeline CTI** is positioned anywhere above the **resort_map.ai** on Track **Video 2** so you can see it in the **Program Monitor**.

If you have a video monitor attached, you should notice flickering around the horizontal border of the red nuclear symbol.

---

6 On Track **Video 2**, click **resort_map.ai** to select it. In the **Effect Controls** panel, click the **arrow** icon next to **Motion** to display the properties. Click and drag the **Anti-flicker Filter** value to **0.40**.

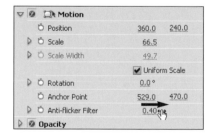

---

7 Choose **File > Save**, or press **Ctrl+S**. Choose **File > Close** to close this project.

That's the ease of using the Anti-flicker Filter. This property is available to every type of clip, but you will find it to be most useful with computer-generated graphics. To see this effect best, it is useful to have an attached video monitor.

If you *still* have a visible flicker at the maximum antiflicker amount of 1.0, you can take more drastic steps, such as adding the Fast Blur video effect to the clip, with vertical blur dimensions. (You'll learn how to add blur effects in Chapter 7, *"Adding Video Effects."* The blur can go from 0 to 100—so this can also be dangerous if you add too much blur. Like so many things in life, moderation is key!)

Right about now, you should be feeling pretty good. You reached the end of another chapter, and you imported every type of clip imaginable: video, audio, and a host of graphic clips. You learned how to use alpha channels and modify the fixed effects of clips. This is all becoming the foundation for the more advanced tips and tricks you get to experience in future chapters. In the next chapter, you will learn to create a title, which is a unique type of graphic because you create it from scratch within Premiere Pro 2.

5

Adding Titles

The next frontier to conquer is the art of adding titles to your program. Creating titles from scratch is one of the many nonediting tasks Adobe Premiere Pro 2 is designed to tackle. Instead of using another application to build titles, you can do it straight from within your Premiere Pro 2 project.

At its most basic, a **title** is text on a screen. A title can be one simple line, such as the subtitle of a foreign movie. Or a title can be a full screen of text, such as a Microsoft PowerPoint presentation. Titles can roll up and down like the end credits of movies, or they can scroll left and right to add visual interest. You can create titles in Premiere Pro 2 with ease by using existing templates or by creating them from scratch—and with great precision.

You treat titles as you do clips—just like the audio, video, and graphic clips you've worked with so far. Once you drag them to the **Timeline** panel, you can shorten and lengthen them, move them in time, and so on. Many of the tools and features you have practiced in this book also apply to title clips.

Using Titles in a Project

Everything you did to graphic clips in Chapter 4, "*Adding Graphics,*" you can do to titles. Both have alpha channels, and you can manipulate both as regular clips in the **Timeline**.

However, titles and graphics have one difference: where they exist. Titles are unique because you create them entirely in Premiere Pro 2. With other clips you've used so far, you have imported an external file from your hard drive into your project. Video, audio, and graphic clips are not saved inside the project file—rather, the project merely links to the external file.

Premiere Pro 2 titles, on the other hand, do not exist as separate files on your hard drive. They exist *only* in your project, and they are saved inside the project file. This is an important distinction to understand because a title differs from every other type of clip in this way. If you delete a project, you delete the title.

Working with the Titler Panel

When you double-click a sequence, it opens in the **Timeline** panel. When you double-click a clip, it opens in the **Source Monitor**. When you double-click a title, it opens in the...drumroll, please... **Titler** panel.

The **Titler** panel is a floating panel; when it's opened, it appears above the main application. At the heart of the **Titler** panel is the canvas area for creating your titles. You should think of the **Titler** panel as a group of panels, each contributing to the task of making titles.

Composition and Preview panel

Title Tools panel

Title Actions panel

Titler Styles panel

Title Properties panel

These are the main components of the **Titler** panel:

Composition and Preview panel: The primary **Titler** panel area is the canvas area where you build your titles. At the top of this panel, you may recognize some text and paragraph options, such as those you might see in a word-processing application.

Title Tools panel: This panel contains special tools used only in the **Titler** panel. The tools help you create text boxes, polygon shapes, and free-form objects.

Title Actions panel: This panel contains buttons to help you align and distribute titles and shapes in the **Composition and Preview** panel.

Titler Styles panel: This panel contains a collection of available styles. Just as you might find in

Microsoft Word, each style has a predefined font, size, color, shadow, and so on.

Title Properties panel: This is the real meat and potatoes of the **Titler** panel. This panel contains all the properties you can modify for each title. From the line spacing of paragraphs to drop shadows, every bit of fine-tuning takes place in this panel.

If you get a case of accidental clickitis and move one of the panels to somewhere else, you can always move it back by dragging and docking it into the **Titler** panel, as you learned to do in Chapter 1, *"Getting Started."* Or, if you accidentally close a panel in the **Titler** panel, you can access it from the **Window** menu.

You now know your way around the **Titler** panel, so why not take it for a test drive in the next exercise?

Title Safe Margins

Inside the **Titler** panel, you will see two thin rectangles. These rectangles represent the **action safe** and **title safe margins**, which are boundaries representing the area recognized by all television sets. Neither of these margins shows up in your final output; each exists only as a guide to help you place your titles on the screen.

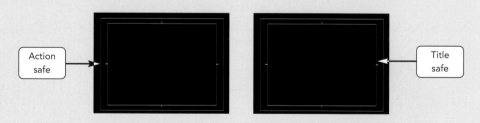

Specifically, the **action safe margins** represent the area most consumer television sets display. Any video (or **action**) occurring outside the margin is not guaranteed to be seen.

The **title safe margins** represent the boundaries for all titles and text on your screen. This ensures all television sets are able to clearly display any text you incorporate into your program.

Keep in mind, computer monitors work differently than television monitors. Whereas a television monitor may obscure the edges of a video beyond the action safe margins, computer monitors tend to show the *whole* video, which means you need to use the title and action safe margins only when creating a project for playback on televisions. If you intend to show your project on computer screens only, you can turn off these margins by choosing **Title > View > Safe Title Margin** and **Title > View > Safe Action Margin**. A margin is on when a check mark appears beside its name.

Creating and Modifying Titles

When you want to add text to a project, a title is the quickest way to go. Despite its name, a title can be *any* text you want displayed on the screen. Unlike other types of graphics you've used, titles are created and saved within the Premiere Pro 2 project. This means the title does not exist anywhere but inside your project file. In this exercise, you will design a title with Premiere Pro 2 to help label locations on a map and also learn how to modify the many title properties available in Premiere Pro 2.

---

1 On the **Welcome Screen**, click **Open Project**. In the **Open Project** dialog box, navigate to the **c:\exercise_files\chap_05** folder, click **exercise01.prproj** to select it, and click **Open**.

---

2 Choose **File > Save As**. Navigate to the **c:\exercise_files\dutch_harbor** folder. Name the file **dutch harbor promo.prproj**, and click **Save**.

Note: If a previous version of dutch harbor promo.prproj already exists, you may be asked to replace it. Click Yes.

---

3 Choose **Window > Workspace > HOT**.

Before creating a title, you should move the Timeline CTI (**C**urrent **T**ime **I**ndicator) to where you want the titles to start playing. This allows you to view the Timeline in the background while you create the title.

---

4 In the **Project** panel **Graphics** bin, double-click the **DVD map** sequence to open it in the **Timeline**. Drag the **CTI** to **00;00;18;26**.

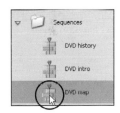

---

5 In the **Project** panel, click the **Graphics** bin to select it. At the bottom of the **Project** panel, click the **New Item** icon, and choose **Title** to open the **New Title** dialog box.

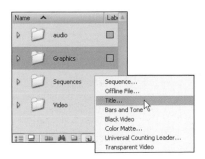

Premiere Pro 2 creates the title in whichever bin you selected. If no bin is selected, Premiere Pro 2 places the title in the root directory of the Project panel.

6 In the **New Title** dialog box, name the title **lobby**, and click **OK**.

The Titler panel opens automatically, and a snapshot of your sequence displays in the Composition and Preview panel. The frame shown correlates to the position of the CTI. You can use this video background as reference so you know where to place your titles in relation to the video behind it.

On some computer monitors, the floating Titler panel may be too large to fit entirely on the screen. To resolve this, you can reduce the Titler panel by clicking and dragging one of its four corners.

---

7 Position the **Titler** panel by clicking and dragging the top bar of the floating panel so you can see the entire panel on the screen. If necessary, click and drag any of the **Titler** panel corners inward to reduce its size.

You want the Titler panel centered and entirely visible on your screen.

Note: If you can already see the entire Titler panel, you do not need to make any adjustments.

Dragging any of the corners allows you to resize the panel.

Clicking and dragging this bar allows you to move the floating panel.

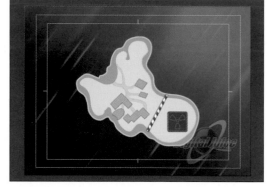

Before creating text, it's a good idea to make sure the title safe and action safe margins are visible so you know the safe boundaries for creating your title.

Composition and Preview panel with no margins visible

Composition and Preview panel with title and action safe margins visible

8 If you do not see the title safe and action safe margins in the **Composition and Preview** panel, choose **Title > View > Safe Title Margin** and **Title > View > Safe Action Margin**.

To add text to your title, you must select the Type tool. This is usually the first step in designing a title.

9 Select the **Type** tool in the **Title Tools** panel.

The Type tool allows you to make basic horizontal text. To its right, the Vertical Type tool allows you to make vertical text.

10 In the location where you want to place the title, click to create a text object.

In this case, click just inside the title safe margins in the lower-left corner of the Composition and Preview panel.

As soon as you click, a blinking cursor appears in the Composition and Preview panel, indicating the placement of the new text you are about to create.

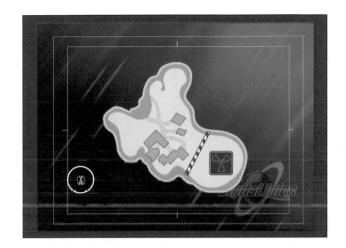

11 Type **Lobby**, and then select the **Selection** tool in the **Title Tools** panel.

Clicking the Selection tool when you are finished tells the Titler panel you are finished typing.

Note: Instead of being in text-edit mode, the text is placed in direct select mode—just as you experienced in Chapter 4, "Adding Graphics." You will even notice the same handles around the bounding box, just like when moving and scaling graphic clips.

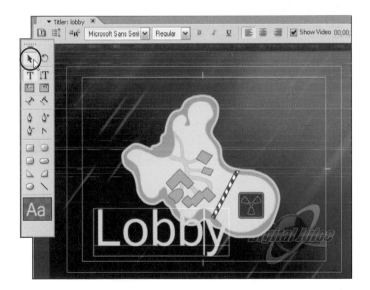

12 In the **Titler Styles** panel, select the third style from the upper-left corner to format the selected text.

Tip: If you want to experiment, you can click each style to see how it affects your text object. You can choose any style as many times as you want. Knock yourself out!

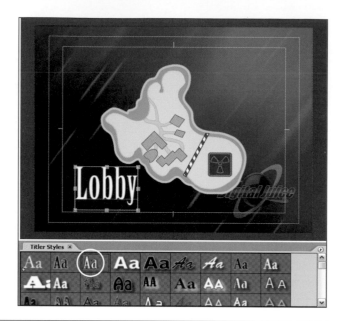

13 In the **Titler** panel, click the **Close** box to close the floating panel.

After designing a title, the next step is to place it in a sequence.

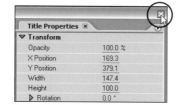

14 In the **Project** panel **Graphics** bin, drag the **lobby** title to the empty gray area at the top of the **Timeline**, and snap it to the **CTI**.

As soon as you release the mouse, a new track, labeled Video 3, appears. In the Program Monitor, notice the title overlays the existing video.

Next, you'll increase the lobby title duration (to match the narrator).

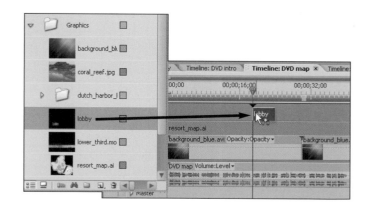

15 In the **Program Monitor**, click the **Play** button. Play the sequence until the narrator stops talking about the lobby, and click the **Stop** button at **00;00;24;18**.

16 In the **Timeline** panel, position your cursor over the **Out** point of the **lobby** title to display the **Trim Out** cursor. Drag and snap it to the **CTI**.

Once you've created the title, you can continually update it, such as changing its font, size, color, and so on. You can even open a title directly from the Timeline panel, and any changes to the title will be updated automatically, without having to save it.

---

17 In the **Timeline** panel, double-click the **lobby** title to open it in the **Titler** panel.

Tip: You can also double-click the title icon in the Project panel.

---

18 Select the **Selection** tool in the **Title Tools** panel.

This puts your text in direct select mode and places handles around its bounding box.

Note: The Titler panel always opens with the Type tool active. This is different from every other Adobe application, so be careful.

---

19 At the top of the **Composition and Preview** panel, click the **Font Browser** button to open the **Font Browser** dialog box.

---

20 In the **Font Browser** dialog box, scroll to **Adobe Garamond Pro Bold Italic**, click to select it, and click **OK**.

Tip: The Font Browser dialog box is helpful because it lets you try a variety of fonts before committing to any of them. When you click a font, you can preview the appearance of the font. If you don't like your font choice, you can click Cancel, and the text will return to its original font.

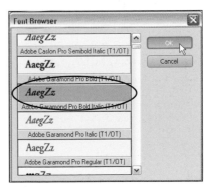

21 In the **Title Properties** panel, click the **arrow** icon next to **Properties** to expand its contents.

Note: The properties may already be visible.

You may notice the first property listed is Font. Yes, you can also change the font here, but the Font Browser dialog box is the only way to preview fonts before committing to them.

This font is a tad bigger than the previous font, so in the next step, you'll resize it. You can reduce the font size in the Titles Properties panel just like you did with the fixed effects in Chapter 4, *"Adding Graphics."*

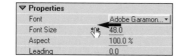

22 Position your cursor over the **Font Size** value of **100.0**, and then drag to the left until the value is **48.0**.

Tip: Font sizes less than 20 can be difficult to read on television monitors. Also, thicker or bold fonts work much better. Thin fonts can "flicker" and "jiggle" on the screen.

23 Position your cursor over the **Kerning** value of **0.0**, and then drag to the left until the value is **-3.0**.

As you drag, you will see the distance between the letters of your title contract in the Composition and Preview panel.

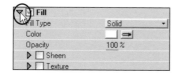

24 Next to the **Fill** property, click the **arrow** icon to expand its contents.

Fill refers to the color of the text. Right now, the Color property is white, represented by a white box.

25 To the right of the **Color** property, click the **Eyedropper** button.

The eyedropper will **sample**, or copy, whichever color you position your cursor over. Clicking a color will change the color of your text.

26 On the map of Dutch Harbor, click the yellow island to sample its color.

As you point to different colors, your text color changes. Your text now matches the yellow of the island.

Notice your text has a faint black stroke. A **stroke** is a colored outline around the text.

---

27 Next to **Strokes**, click the **arrow** icon to view the stroke properties, click the **arrow** icon next to **Outer Strokes**, and click the **arrow** icon next to **Outer Stroke**.

Text can have an inner stroke and an outer stroke. If you want to add a stroke, click Add. In this case, the text already has an outer stroke with a Size value of 15.0.

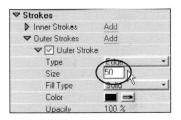

---

28 On the **Outer Stroke Size** value of **15.0**, click the value to select it, type **50**, and press **Enter**.

As you can see, just like with the fixed effects in the previous chapter, you can also type a value to change it.

---

29 Click the center of the text object and drag it within the lower-left corner of the title safe margins.

---

30 In the **Titler** panel, click the **Close** box to close the floating panel.

Note: Take care *not* to click the Close box in the upper-right corner of Premiere Pro 2. That will close the program. Yikes.

---

31 In the **Timeline**, drag the **CTI**, and position it over the **lobby** title.

In the Program Monitor, you will notice Premiere Pro 2 updates your changes automatically.

32 Choose **File > Save**, or press **Ctrl+S**. Leave **dutch harbor promo.prproj** open for the next exercise.

This exercise introduced the power of the Titler panel. Although you didn't modify every possible property of a title object, you have learned *how* to modify them—so in a way, you know how to modify them all. Then again, you may not know how each one affects your title object. The following table briefly explains each property:

Titler Text Properties	
Property	**Description**
Font	Controls the font face (such as Arial, Times New Roman, or Helvetica). Thicker or bold fonts display better on televisions and heavily compressed Web formats. In general, sans-serif fonts (no feet, like Arial) tend to work better than serif fonts (like Times New Roman).
Font Size	Controls the size of the font. For television, font sizes smaller than 20 can be difficult to read.
Aspect	Adjusts the width (%) of the font. Values less than 100% make the font narrower; values greater than 100% make it wider.
Leading	Adjusts the amount of space between horizontal lines of text. This property affects only text objects with more than one line.
Tracking	Adjusts the amount of space between letters. An amount less than 0 (zero) contracts the space between letters; more than 0 expands it.
Kerning	Adjusts the amount of space between certain pairs of letters. Kerning does not adjust uniformly like tracking; instead, it is meant to remedy uneven spacing between certain letter pairs. As shown in the illustration here, the upper line displays unkerned pairs, and the lower line displays kerned pairs: Ke To Ve Wo r, y, 115 Ke To Ve Wo r, y, 115
Baseline Shift	Adjusts the distance a character is raised or lowered, such as x^2 or H_2O.
Slant	Controls the *slant* of an object, in degrees.
Small Caps	Makes lowercase text APPEAR IN SMALL UPPERCASE.
Small Caps Size	Controls the size of the small cap (%) relative to its regular height.
Underline	Creates underlined text.

2 | Creating Shape Objects

Besides letting you add text to your titles, the **Titler** panel allows you to create custom shapes, such as lines, triangles, ellipses, and squares. Instead of text objects, they are called **shape objects**. You can modify shape objects in a title in much the same way you modified text objects in Exercise 1. Some common uses of shape objects include borders around text, boxes behind paragraphs, and other decorative elements. In this exercise, you will add some custom shapes behind the map label you created in Exercise 1.

---

1 If you followed the previous exercise, **dutch harbor promo.prproj** should still be open in Premiere Pro 2. If it's not, click **Open Project** on the **Welcome Screen**. Navigate to the **c:\exercise_files\chap_05** folder, click **exercise02.prproj** to select it, and click **Open**.

---

2 Choose **File > Save As**. Navigate to the **c:\exercise_files\dutch_harbor** folder. Name the file **dutch harbor promo.prproj**, and click **Save**.

Note: If a previous version of dutch harbor promo.prproj already exists, you may be asked to replace it. Click Yes.

---

3 In the **Project** panel **Sequences** bin, double-click the **DVD map** sequence to open it in the **Timeline** if necessary.

---

4 In the **Timeline**, double-click the **lobby** title on Track **Video 3** to open it in the **Titler** panel.

When you open a title, Premiere Pro 2 automatically selects the first text object. This can be helpful when you have only one object. However, to add another object, you must explicitly *deselect* the selected text object before creating a second object.

---

5 Select the **Selection** tool in the **Title Tools** panel. In the **Composition and Preview** panel, click anywhere outside the word **Lobby** to deselect the text.

When you deselect the text, the bounding box disappears.

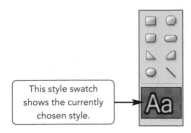
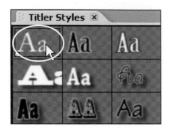

This style swatch shows the currently chosen style.

6 At the bottom of the **Title Tools** panel, notice the two-letter style swatch, as shown in the illustration here. In the upper-left corner of the **Titler Styles** panel, click the **default style** to change the style.

The Title Tools panel displays the currently chosen style, which means the next object you create will automatically be given this style. When you click a new style in the Titler Styles panel, the style swatch in the Title Tools panel changes, and the next text/object you create will be given this new style.

Tip: The default style, which is always the first style listed, is indicated with a (very tiny) white box and red slash in its lower-left corner, as shown in the illustration here. You can change the default style by right-clicking any style and choosing Set Style As Default.

---

7 Select the **Rounded Rectangle** tool in the **Title Tools** panel.

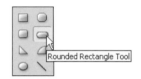

---

8 Position your cursor above and to the left of the **Lobby** text. Then, click and drag your mouse to the lower-right corner of the text, making sure you cover all the text, as shown in the illustration here. Release the mouse when you are satisfied with your finished position.

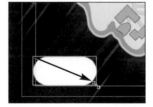

As you drag the mouse, a rounded rectangle containing the default style displays.

---

9 When you're done creating your rounded rectangle, select the **Selection** tool in the **Title Tools** panel.

Tip: In the Titler panel, as soon as you create a new object, it's safest to immediately select the Selection tool.

You can also change the properties of the title object as you did with the title text.

---

10 In the **Title Properties** panel, click the **arrow** icon next to **Fill** to expand its properties.

11 Next to the **Color** property, click the **Eyedropper** button. On the map of Dutch Harbor, click the **nuclear** symbol to sample the red color.

Tip: Remember, the eyedropper samples the *exact* pixel you click. Therefore, it's always nice to have a large swatch of color to choose from so that all the surrounding pixels are the same color.

---

12 Right-click the red object you created, and choose **Arrange > Send to Back**.

This places the red oval *behind* the **Lobby** text.

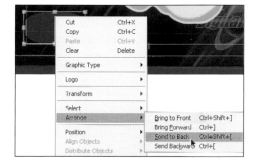

---

13 Hold down the **Shift** key, and click the yellow **Lobby** text to select all the objects. In the **Align and Distribute** panel, click the **Align Vertical Center** button.

Holding down the Shift key and clicking allows you to select both objects simultaneously.

---

14 In the **Align and Distribute** panel, click the **Align Horizontal Center** button.

The Align and Distribute panel is available only when you have two or more objects selected.

---

15 In the **Composition and Preview** panel, click anywhere outside the two objects to deselect them.

Before you create another object, deselect the current object(s) just to be safe. Is this absolutely necessary? Maybe not. However, it's better to be safe than sorry!

---

16 Select the **Line** tool in the **Title Tools** panel.

Pop quiz: What style will the newly created object be? **Answer:** The same red style as the oval. You can tell because of the red style swatch. Unless you manually change it, Premiere Pro 2 applies the style of the last object to the new object.

17 Position your cursor in the upper-right corner of the red oval. Click and drag a line extending to the semicircular building on the map. (The semicircle represents the lobby...obviously!)

Drawing lines in the Titler panel is simple. Just click where you want the line to start, and drag your mouse to where you want it to end.

18 In the **Titler** panel, click the **Close** box to close the floating panel.

When you return to the Timeline, you can see Premiere Pro 2 automatically reflects the changes in the Program Monitor.

19 Choose **File > Save**, or press **Ctrl+S**. Leave **dutch harbor promo.prproj** open for the next exercise.

The Titler panel allows you to create many types of objects, including text objects and custom shapes. The shapes can get quite intricate, with gradient colors, shadows, and multiple levels of transparency. In fact, all of the predesigned title templates built into Premiere Pro 2 are built exclusively with title shapes. In Exercise 5, you will learn more about title templates in Premiere Pro 2.

Quite often in your projects, you will want to copy a title in order to stay consistent with your design scheme. (Too many title "styles" is the calling card of an amateur!) Luckily, you don't have to reinvent the wheel with each title: Premiere Pro 2 provides a convenient method for duplicating titles so you can start your next title with the same look.

3 | Copying Titles

The **Titler** panel in Premiere Pro 2 makes it easy to duplicate titles, as well as save your favorite styles for future use. This comes in handy when you are working on a project with multiple titles similar in style. Instead of redesigning each title from scratch, you can copy the existing title as you start working on your next title. In this exercise, you will learn how to copy a single title to multiple titles of similar styles.

---

1 If you followed the previous exercise, **dutch harbor promo.prproj** should still be open in Premiere Pro 2. If it's not, click **Open Project** on the **Welcome Screen**. Navigate to the **c:\exercise_files\chap_05** folder, click **exercise03.prproj** to select it, and click **Open**.

---

2 Choose **File > Save As**. Navigate to the **c:\exercise_files\dutch_harbor** folder. Name the file **dutch harbor promo.prproj**, and click **Save**.

Note: If a previous version of dutch harbor promo.prproj already exists, you may be asked to replace it. Click Yes.

---

3 In the **Project** panel **Sequences** bin, double-click the **DVD map** sequence to open it in the **Timeline** if necessary.

Remember, before creating a title, move the CTI in the Timeline or Program Monitor to the position you want the title to start.

---

4 Move the **CTI** to **00;00;25;10**, which is where the narrator begins describing the next building.

---

5 In the **Project** panel **Graphics** bin, double-click the **lobby** title.

Although this title has multiple objects, notice the text object is still selected by default. Premiere Pro 2 always opens with the first text object selected.

---

6 At the top of the **Composition and Preview** panel, click the **New Title Based on Current Title** button.

Besides having a really long name, the New Title Based on Current Title button creates a copy of the existing title in the Project panel.

7 In the **New Title** dialog box, name the new title **west towers**, and click **OK**.

8 Double-click the **Lobby** text object to select the entire word.

A semiopaque highlight indicates the entire word is selected.

Tip: Selecting text in the Titler panel is similar to selecting text in a word-processing program, such as Word. You can highlight a single letter, an entire word, or multiple lines of text.

9 Type **West**, press **Enter**, and type **Towers**. Select the **Selection** tool in the **Title Tools** panel.

10 At the top of the **Composition and Preview** panel, click the **Center** button to center the text.

Note: Depending on the width you made the Titler panel when resizing, the Center button may be on the second line of menu buttons.

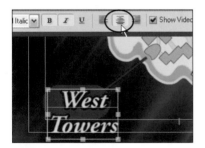

11 In the **Title Properties** panel, position your cursor over the **Leading** property. Slowly drag the value to the left to **-11.0**.

As you drag, the distance between the lines contracts.

Next, you want to increase the size of the red, rounded rectangle to match the new text size. However, because it is behind the text, selecting it may be challenging. You will remedy this in the next step.

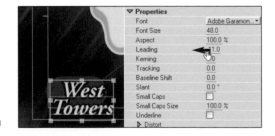

12 Choose **Title > Select > Next Object Below**.

Tip: When two or more objects are stacked in Premiere Pro 2, clicking the objects selects only the topmost item. The Select command allows you to choose objects below the topmost one.

13 Position your cursor over the lower-right handle until the cursor changes to a diagonal double arrow, as shown in the illustration here. Click and drag to the lower-right corner of the text.

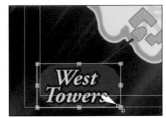

Note: Make sure you position your cursor directly over the handle, or else you may wind up accidentally selecting the text again. (Premiere Pro 2 doesn't know what you are trying to do, so it has to guess based on where you click your mouse!)

---

14 Hold down the **Shift** key, and click the **West Towers** text.

You should see a white bounding box around both objects. Just like last time, you can align your text and object so they are perfectly centered.

---

15 In the **Align and Distribute** panel, click the **Horizontal Center** button, and then click the **Vertical Center** button.

---

16 With both objects still selected, click in the middle of the objects, and drag them to the upper-left corner of the island, as shown in the illustration here.

---

17 Click the red line to select it. Click the upper-right handle of the red line, and drag it to the L-shaped building on the map.

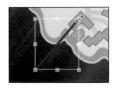

---

18 Drag the other end of the line—the lower-left handle—to the red, rounded rectangle.

---

19 In the **Titler** panel, click the **Close** box to close the title.

20 In the **Project** panel **Graphics** bin, drag the **west towers** title to Track **Video 3**, and snap it to the **CTI** in the **Timeline**.

The Timeline should still be at 00;00;25;10.

21 Move the **Timeline CTI** to **00;00;30;20**, and then snap the **Out** point of the **west tower** title to the **CTI**.

Now it's time to make your next title.

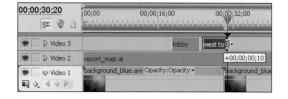

22 Move the **Timeline CTI** to **00;00;31;15**. In the **Project** panel **Graphics** bin, double-click the **west towers** title.

23 At the top of the **Composition and Preview** panel, click the **New Title Based on Current Title** button. In the **New Title** dialog box, name the new title **dining**, and click **OK**.

24 If necessary, select the **Type** tool. Click and drag your mouse over both words of the **West Towers** text.

A semiopaque highlight covers the text.

25 Replace the **West Towers** text with the word **Dining**. Select the **Selection** tool in the **Title Tools** panel.

26 Hold down the **Shift** key, and click the red, rounded rectangle. With both objects selected, in the **Align and Distribute** panel, click the **Horizontal Center** button, and then click the **Vertical Center** button.

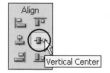

Instead of dragging your title objects with your mouse to position them, Premiere Pro 2 provides a quick menu command to automatically position the objects for you. You can choose to position them in the center of the screen or in the lower third. This is helpful when you want to precisely position an object quickly.

27 With both objects still selected, choose **Title > Position > Horizontal Center**.

This command positions the objects in the horizontal center (left and right) of the Composition and Preview panel.

28 With both objects still selected, choose **Title > Position > Lower Third**.

This command positions the objects in the vertical lower third of the screen.

29 Click the red line to select it. Click a handle, drag one end of the line to the rounded rectangle, and then drag the other end of the line to the stair-shaped building, as shown in the illustration here.

30 In the **Titler** panel, click the **Close** box to close the title.

31 In the **Project** panel **Graphics** bin, drag the **dining** title to Track **Video 3**, and snap it to the **Timeline** CTI at **00;00;31;15**.

32 Move the **Timeline CTI** to **00;00;40;00**, and then snap the **Out** point of the **dining** title to the **CTI**.

33 Choose **File > Save**, or press **Ctrl+S**. Choose **File > Close** to close this project.

The New Title Based on Current Title button is an extremely helpful feature to use when you want to duplicate a title *within the same project*. (This button copies only to the project you currently have open.) However, if you want to copy a title for use in a separate project, then you can export the title and import it into the separate project just like you would do with any other external graphic file.

Exporting Titles to Other Projects

When you create a title, it is saved inside the project, not as a separate file on your hard drive. However, if you want to save a title to your hard drive, Premiere Pro 2 provides a method to do so. For example, if you want to use Title A in Project B, you can export Title A from Project A and then import it into Project B. This allows you to share files between separate projects and saves you from re-creating your work over and over. In this exercise, you will export a title and then import it into a separate project.

1 On the **Welcome Screen**, click **Open Project**. In the **Open Project** dialog box, navigate to the **c:\exercise_files\chap_05** folder, click **titles.prproj** to select it, and click **Open**.

This project contains two titles. (In the real world, a project would also have a sequence and a handful of audio/video clips. But for the purposes of this exercise, it has only two titles.)

Premiere Pro 2 makes exporting a title from one project to another simple. All you have to do is select the title and then choose File > Export > Title. *Voila!*

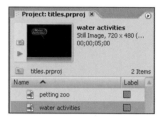

2 In the **Project** panel, click **petting zoo** to select it. Choose **File > Export > Title**. In the **Save Title** dialog box, navigate to **c:\exercise_files\chap_05** (it may already be navigated to this directory), and click **Save**.

3 In the **Project** panel, click **water activities** to select it. Choose **File > Export > Title**. In the **Save Title** dialog box, click **Save**.

You have just exported both titles to the same directory. Now they exist as two separate title files on your hard drive. Now you are ready to import them into a different project. To do this, you must first open the project into which you want to import them.

4 Choose **File > Close**. On the **Welcome Screen**, click **Open Project**. In the **Open Project** dialog box, navigate to the **c:\exercise_files\chap_05** folder, click **exercise04.prproj** to select it, and click **Open**.

5 Choose **File > Save As**. Navigate to the **c:\exercise_files\dutch_harbor** folder. Name the file **dutch harbor promo.prproj**, and click **Save**.

Note: If a previous version of **dutch harbor promo.prproj** already exists, you may be asked to replace it. Click Yes.

Since the titles exist as external files on your hard drive, you can import them like any other graphic clips.

6 In the **Project** panel, right-click the **Graphics** bin, and choose **Import**. In the **Import** dialog box, navigate to the **c:\exercise_files\chap_05** folder. Hold down the **Ctrl** key, and click both **petting zoo.prtl** and **water activities.prtl** to select them. Click **Open**.

This imports both titles and places them in your Graphics bin.

Tip: When you import an external title file, it is converted to an internal title file and saved as part of the project file, as if you had created the title within this project, which means you can delete the title files on the hard drive, and the titles inside the project will *not* be deleted.

It is important to note this is the opposite of how every other type of external clip behaves. If you delete a video, audio, or image clip from your hard drive, it will *also* be deleted from the project. Not so with titles.

---

7 In the **Project** panel **Sequences** bin, double-click the **DVD map** sequence to open it in the **Timeline** if necessary.

---

8 In the **Timeline**, move the **CTI** to **00;00;40;20**, which is where your next title will begin.

Before dragging the next title to its location, notice that *both* titles are selected in the Project panel. When multiple clips are selected, dragging one of the selected clips moves all of the selected clips. To prevent this type of accident, it's important you memorize how to quickly deselect objects.

---

9 Select the tab at the top of the **Project** panel to make it the active panel. Choose **Edit > Deselect All**.

Because you have deselected the clips, you can safely move one of them at a time.

---

10 In the **Project** panel **Graphics** bin, drag the **petting zoo** title to Track **Video 3**, and snap it to the **CTI** in the **Timeline**.

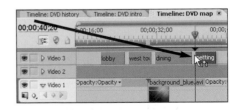

---

11 In the **Program Monitor**, position your cursor over the end of the **petting zoo** title on Track **Video 3**, and snap its **Out** point to the end of the first audio clip on Track **Audio 1**.

12 In the **Program Monitor**, click the **Play** button. Play the sequence until the narrator starts talking about the aquatic center, and click the **Stop** button at **00;00;46;15**.

---

13 In the **Project** panel **Graphics** bin, drag the **water activities** title to Track **Video 3**, and snap it to the **CTI** in the **Timeline**.

---

14 On Track **Video 3**, drag the **Out** point of the **water activities** title, and snap it to the **Out** point of the **background_blue.avi** clip on Track **Video 1**.

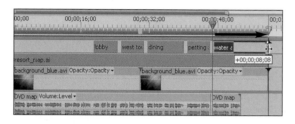

Tip: This may seem like a lot of excess footage at the end of your sequence. After all, the audio stops playing on Track Audio 1 way before the video stops, right? Then again, you can really never have too much excess at the end of a sequence. It's *much* easier to get rid of excess footage than it is to create more. Therefore, give yourself a good 4 or 5 seconds when you're creating your own sequences, just in case you need extra material for transitioning to another scene.

Whew. That's a lot of titles for one sequence.

---

15 In the **Program Monitor**, click the **Play In to Out** button to preview your sequence from the beginning.

Note: If you notice "blocky" or "fuzzy" image quality during playback (these are very technical terms, mind you), read the note following this exercise.

---

16 Choose **File > Save**, or press **Ctrl+S**. Leave **dutch harbor promo.prproj** open for the next exercise.

In this exercise, you used the export title feature to share a title (or two) from one project with another project. Creating a separate title file on your hard drive is also helpful when you want to share it with another user; for example, you can e-mail the selected file to someone else. How handy is that?

If you plan to use a title repeatedly, not just in one or two projects but over and over again in future projects, Premiere Pro 2 allows you to turn any title into a template. Instead of importing an external title file, you can use the always-available template, which Premiere Pro 2 remembers even if you deleted the original title file long ago. In the next exercise, you will learn how to transform your title into a template.

NOTE:

Clarity Versus Continuity

During playback in the previous exercise, you may have noticed the image quality in the **Program Monitor** seemed to degrade during playback. Why?

First things first: The **Program Monitor** is a **preview**, or approximation, of your final output. It's darn close to the real thing, but it is not the real thing. So the quality of the display has little effect on your final product.

Premiere Pro 2 is a whiz at playing regular DV (**D**igital **V**ideo) footage. It loves this kind of footage. When you have a sequence with *just* DV footage, Premiere Pro 2 breezes through it without any trouble.

However, when you load the **Timeline** with anything *not DV*—such as graphics, titles, high-definition video, or video clips with alpha channels—Premiere Pro 2 has to think a little harder, and it asks your computer for some extra *oomph* to juggle the clips.

Low resolution preview during playback   Maximum-resolution preview when stopped

If Premiere Pro 2 determines the sequence is demanding more than your system can deliver, it sacrifices image clarity for the sake of smooth playback. This is what you may have seen during playback: Premiere Pro 2 reduced the image quality in the **Program Monitor** to lighten the burden on your computer. (Low image resolution = less information = less data to process.)

When playback stops, Premiere Pro 2 doesn't have to think as hard, so the **Program Monitor** *easily* displays the preview at its maximum image quality.

5 | Making Title Templates

At its core, a title **template** is a predesigned title. You can save existing titles as templates for use in current and future projects. The advantage of a title template is that it always resides in the **Templates** area of the **Titler** panel, until you choose to remove it. For example, when you delete a project from your hard drive, all titles inside the project are also deleted. However, a template is not deleted and will still be available in the **Templates** area for use in future projects. In this exercise, you will learn how to turn an existing title into a template for usage in future projects.

---

1 On the **Welcome Screen**, click **Open Project**. In the **Open Project** dialog box, navigate to the **c:\exercise_files\chap_05** folder, click **exercise05.prproj** to select it, and click **Open**.

---

2 Choose **File > Save As**. Navigate to the **c:\exercise_files\dutch_harbor** folder. Name the file **dutch harbor promo.prproj**, and click **Save**.

Note: If a previous version of dutch harbor promo.prproj already exists, you may be asked to replace it. Click Yes.

---

3 In the **Project** panel **Sequences** bin, double-click the **DVD history** sequence to open it in the **Timeline**.

In this exercise, you will add names to the lower third above each actor.

---

4 In the **Timeline**, hold down the **Shift** key, and drag and snap the **CTI** to the **In** point of the *first* clip on Track **Video 2**.

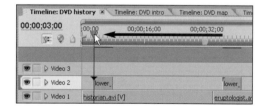

---

5 In the **Project** panel, click the **Graphics** bin to select it. At the bottom of the **Project** panel, click the **New Item** icon, and choose **Title**.

---

160 | Adobe Premiere Pro 2 : H·O·T

6 In the **New Title** dialog box, name the new title **historian**, and click **OK**.

7 Make sure the **Type** tool is selected in the **Title Tools** panel. In the **Composition and Preview** panel, click just inside the title safe margin and just above the pink lower third video clip.

It's time to give your actors some phony names.

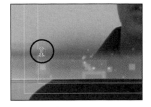

8 Type **Clay Potter**. Select the **Selection** tool in the **Title Tools** panel to put the title in direct select mode.

Remember, when in direct select mode, your text displays with handles around it.

9 Scroll to the bottom of the **Titler Styles** panel, and click the **MyriadPro LtBlue 30** style to select it.

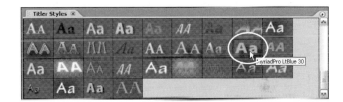

10 In the **Title Properties** panel, change the **Font Size** to **50.0** by clicking and dragging the **Font Size** value to the left.

Tip: Hold down the Ctrl key when dragging a value to change it in smaller increments. If you have trouble getting precisely 50.0, try the Ctrl key.

11 In the **Title Properties** panel, click the **arrow** icon next to **Shadow** to view its properties. Change the **Distance** value to **6.0**.

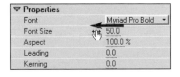

12 In the **Composition and Preview** panel, click in the middle of the title, and drag it so it's mostly over the lower third. And of course, make sure it is inside the title safe margin.

13 Select the **Type** tool in the **Title Tools** panel. Anywhere in the upper-left corner of the **Composition and Preview** panel, click once to create a text object, and type **Historian**. When done, select the **Selection** tool.

Note: It doesn't matter where you click. The point is, just don't click anywhere *near* the existing title. This is because you want two separate title objects. If you click too close to the original title, Premiere Pro 2 assumes you are trying to modify the existing title, rather than beginning a new title.

14 In the **Title Properties** panel, change the **Font Size** value to **40.0**.

15 In the **Shadow Properties**, change the **Distance** value to **4.0**. Change the **Spread** value to **20.0**.

If you have trouble dragging the value to 20.0, remember to hold down the Ctrl key as you drag. As you reduce the Spread value, the shadow becomes more in focus, with sharper edges.

Tip: The Shadow Spread property controls the shadow's blur amount.

16 Click in the middle of the **Historian** text, and drag it to the bottom of the pink lower third, just below the name.

You have finished the title, so you can save it to use as a template in future projects.

17 Choose **Title > Templates**. In the **Templates** dialog box, click the **wing menu**, and choose **Save historian as Template**.

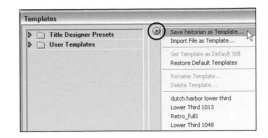

18 In the **Save As** dialog box, name your new template **dutch harbor lower third**, and click **OK**. Click **Close**.

19 In the **Titler** panel, click the **Close** box to close the floating panel.

20 In the **Project** panel **Graphics** bin, drag the **historian** title to Track **Video 3**, and snap it to the **CTI**.

21 In the **Timeline**, hold down the **Shift** key, and drag and snap the **CTI** to the **In** point of the *second* clip on Track **Video 2**.

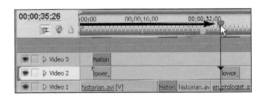

This is where your second title will start. Since you have turned the first title into a template, you can now use this template to create new titles.

22 In the **Project** panel, click the **Graphics** bin to select it. Press the **F9** key to create a new title. In the **New Title** dialog box, name the new title **eruptologist**, and click **OK**.

Ooh, fancy! You can use a keyboard shortcut for making titles.

23 Choose **Title > Templates**.

Tip: Speaking of keyboard shortcuts...next to Templates on the menu, you can see **Ctrl+J**. If a menu item has a keyboard shortcut, you will see it mentioned to the right of the command name.

24 In the **Templates** dialog box, click the **arrow** icon next to **User Templates** to view its contents. Click **dutch harbor lower third** to select it as the template, and click **Apply**.

In the Composition and Preview panel, you will see your template automatically applied.

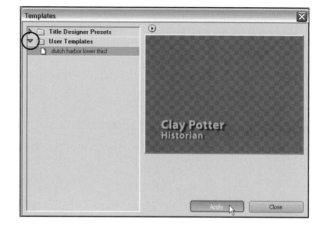

25 Select the **Type** tool, if necessary. Click and drag your mouse over the name **Clay Potter** to select that portion of the title.

26 Type **Rock Igneous**.

27 Position your cursor over the word **Historian** until the white bounding box appears. Click and drag your mouse over the word **Historian** to select it. Type **Eruptologist**. When done, select the **Selection** tool in the **Title Tools** panel.

Tip: When trying to highlight text that is close to another text box, Premiere Pro 2 tries to guess which text box you want to modify, based on the position of your cursor. Positioning your cursor until you see the white box appear around the text indicates which text box you are about to modify.

28 In the **Titler** panel, click the **Close** box to close the floating panel.

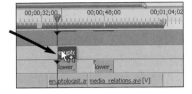

29 In the **Project** panel **Graphics** bin, drag the **eruptologist** title to Track **Video 3**, and snap it to the **CTI**.

You have only one last title to make....

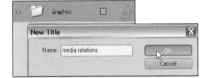

30 In the **Timeline**, hold down the **Shift** key, and drag and snap the **CTI** to the **In** point of the *third* clip on Track **Video 2**.

31 In the **Project** panel, click the **Graphics** bin to select it. Press the **F9** key to make a new title. In the **New Title** dialog box, name the new title **media relations**, and click **OK**.

32 Choose **Title > Templates**. In the **Templates** dialog box, click the **arrow** icon next to **User Templates** to view its contents. Click **dutch harbor lower third** to select the template, and click **Apply**.

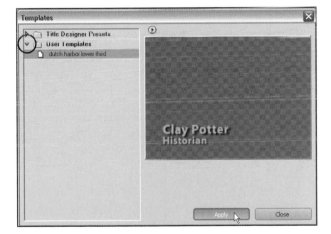

33 Select the **Type** tool, if necessary. Click and drag your mouse over the name **Clay Potter** to select that portion of the title. Type **Shirlee Cunning**.

34 With the **Type** tool selected, click and drag your mouse over the word **Historian**. Type **Media Relations**.

35 In the **Titler** panel, click the **Close** box to close the floating panel.

36 In the **Project** panel **Graphics** bin, drag the **media relations** title to Track **Video 3**, and **snap** it to the **CTI**.

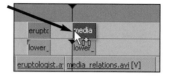

37 Choose **File > Save**, or press **Ctrl+S**. Leave **dutch harbor promo.prproj** open for the next exercise.

The goal of creating a template is to have a file that can be reused, over and over, in any project and be quickly found in the Templates dialog box in Premiere Pro 2. Templates are only a starting point when designing a title; they help ensure a consistent theme across multiple titles and projects, but you can then change any of the text to customize it to each project.

Tip: Igneous rocks are formed as molten lava cools. (And you thought you'd be learning only Premiere Pro 2 stuff!)

You have learned how to create a new title and how to reuse it about 1,000 different ways. You have yet to create one more type of title: the rolling and crawling titles. In the next exercise, you will create titles with motion.

NOTE:

Copying Versus Exporting Versus Using Templates

In the previous few exercises, you experienced many ways to create new titles from other titles. You copied titles within a project, you exported titles to an external file, and you created title templates. Since you now know how to do all this, you may be wondering, "*When* should I use one method over the other?" Here's a cheat sheet:

Title templates are probably the safest when reusing titles. Even if the original project has been deleted, the template will remain.

Copying titles can be done only within a project. If you don't plan to use that title for any other projects, copying is the quickest.

Exporting titles is the quickest when you want to have a separate file on your hard drive, especially if you're going to share it with someone. However, unlike templates, as soon as you delete the file on your hard drive, you can no longer import it into other projects.

6 | Adding Motion to Titles

Invariably, once someone learns how to makes titles in Premiere Pro 2, their first thought is, "Aha! I can make *credits*! Like at the end of movies." (Perhaps you too had this same idea.) Premiere Pro 2 makes it easy to add motion to your titles. You can create **rolling titles**, which move up the screen (like credits), or **crawling titles**, which move left to right across the screen (like a news bulletin). You can specify whether your title should start offscreen and finish onscreen, or vice versa, and whether the title should decelerate (like a car) as it comes to its final resting place on the screen. In this exercise, you will learn how to create rolling text at the beginning of a sequence while using many of the title motion features described previously.

---

1 On the **Welcome Screen**, click **Open Project**. In the **Open Project** dialog box, navigate to the c:\exercise_files\chap_05 folder, click **exercise06.prproj** to select it, and click **Open**.

---

2 Choose **File > Save As**. Navigate to the **c:\exercise_files\dutch_harbor** folder. Name the file **dutch harbor promo.prproj**, and click **Save**.

Note: If a previous version of dutch harbor promo.prproj already exists, you may be asked to replace it. Click Yes.

---

3 In the **Project** panel **Sequences** bin, double-click the **DVD history** sequence to open it in the **Timeline**.

---

4 In the **Project** panel **Graphics** bin, press the **F9** key to make a new title. In the **New Title** dialog box, name your new title **history**, and click **OK**.

---

5 In the **Composition and Preview** panel, turn off the **Show Video** check box.

The Show Video check box turns on or off the background preview. When it is off, the empty area of the title displays as a checkerboard. This title does not need any background video for positioning.

Instead of creating your title with the Type tool as you have been doing, in the next step you will use the Area Type tool to create a title.

---

6 Select the **Area Type** tool in the **Title Tools** panel.

The Area Type tool creates a defined text box, and when your typing extends beyond the borders of the box, your text wraps to the next line.

7 In the **Titler Styles** panel, double-click the style **GaramondProItalic OffWhite 35**. If you don't see this particular style listed, double-click any style of your choosing.

The style's name is in the format "Font Color Size," if you were wondering.

Note: Make sure you double-click the style. If you click only once, you do not get the font *size*. So give the style a nice and quick double click, just to be safe. Unfortunately, until you start typing your text, Premiere Pro 2 doesn't display the font size, so you find out only after you've typed text (an unfortunate design choice by Adobe).

---

8 With the **Area Type** tool, click the upper-left corner of the title safe margin, and drag your mouse to the lower-right corner.

The box you create by dragging your mouse is called the **text area**. A blinking cursor appears.

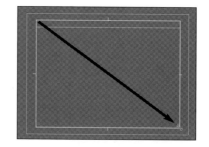

---

9 Type the following: **Dutch Harbor is a tropical paradise with a rich tapestry of customs and tradition. Join us as we take a look back at the geologic formation of Dutch Harbor.**

---

10 Select the **Selection** tool in the **Title Tools** panel.

---

11 In the **Composition and Preview** panel, click the **Center** button to center the text.

If you want to fill up the entire screen with text, you can quickly do this by increasing the font size. Because you drew the text area (boundary) already, as the text grows in size, it will wrap to the next line but still stay within the text area.

---

12 In the **Title Properties** panel, click the **arrow** icon next to **Properties** to expand its contents, if necessary. Change the **Font Size** value to **50.0**.

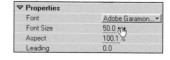

---

13 In the **Composition and Preview** panel, click the **Roll/Crawl Options** button.

14 In the **Roll/Crawl Options** dialog box, in the **Title Type** area, click the **Roll** radio button. In the **Timing (Frames)** area, turn on the **Start Off Screen** check box. Click **OK**.

Again, rolling titles move up the screen. Crawling titles move left or right.

15 In the **Titler** panel, click the **Close** box to close the floating panel.

16 Hold down the **Ctrl** key, and in the **Project** panel **Graphics** bin, drag the **history** title to the beginning of Track **Video 2** in the **Timeline**. Make sure to hold the **Ctrl** key down until you place the clip.

As you may recall from eons ago (Chapter 3, "*Assembling a Sequence*"), holding down the Ctrl key while dragging a clip to the Timeline *inserts* the clip and scoots everything else to the right.

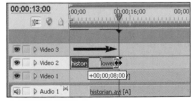

17 In the **Timeline**, snap the **CTI** to the beginning of the sequence. Press the **spacebar** to begin playback and watch the title scroll. After the title finishes, press the **spacebar** again to stop playback.

This title moves pretty quickly. After all, it's only 5 seconds long. For this title to move slower, you need to make the clip longer.

18 In the **Timeline**, drag the **CTI** to **00;00;13;00**. Position your cursor over the **Out** point of the **history** title to display the **Trim Out** cursor. Hold down the **Ctrl** key, and drag and snap it to the **CTI**. When you release the mouse, all of the other clips will slide to the right.

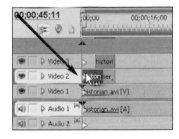

Tip: Holding down the Ctrl key turns the Trim Out cursor to the Ripple Trim Out cursor. You may recall that the Ripple Trim Out cursor slides all other clips to the left to close any gaps. Of course, in this case, if you *lengthen* a clip, the Ripple Trim Out cursor slides all clips to the right.

19 In the **Timeline**, snap the **CTI** to the beginning of the sequence. Press the **spacebar** to begin playback and watch the title scroll slower. After the title finishes, press the **spacebar** again to stop playback.

This time the title plays much slower. However, because the title ends up onscreen, it would be nice if it "sat" there a little while after moving into position.

20 On Track **Video 2**, double-click the **history** title to open it. In the **Titler** panel, click the **Roll/Crawl Options** button.

21 In the **Roll/Crawl Options** dialog box, in the **Timing (Frames)** area, change the **Postroll** value to **90** frames. Click **OK**.

The Postroll value determines how long the title "freezes" after it has reached its final position. In this case, the title scrolls up the screen and then freezes for 3 seconds. (Remember, 90 frames ÷ 30 frames per second = 3 seconds.)

22 In the **Titler** panel, click the **Close** box to close the floating panel.

23 In the **Timeline**, snap the **CTI** to the beginning of the sequence. Press the **spacebar** to begin playback and watch the title scroll. Press the **spacebar** again to stop playback.

Did you notice how the title held onscreen for 3 seconds before the clip ended? The last feature of this scrolling title you may want to fix is how the title suddenly freezes. It seems a bit jarring. Premiere Pro 2 provides you with the ability to decelerate the title as it comes to a stop.

24 On Track **Video 2**, double-click the **history** title to open it. In the **Titler** panel, click the **Roll/Crawl Options** button.

25 In the **Roll/Crawl Options** dialog box, in the **Timing (Frames)** area, change the **Ease-Out** value to **90** frames.

The Ease-Out value determines how long the title takes to decelerate and freeze. Think of it like a car coming to a stop at a red light. In this case, the clip decelerates for 3 seconds.

Here's a quick review of what your title is doing: The title is 13 seconds long. The last 3 seconds are "frozen" as part of the Postroll value. The 3 seconds before the Postroll effect takes place are used for decelerating as part of the Ease-Out value. This leaves 7 seconds for your title to scroll.

26 In **Titler** panel, click the **Close** box to close the floating panel.

27 In the **Timeline**, snap the **CTI** to the beginning of the sequence. Press the **spacebar** to begin playback and watch the title scroll. Press the **spacebar** again to stop playback.

Did you notice how the title slowed down and gently nudged into place? Adding an Ease-Out value makes the title movement much less distracting and gives a real-world sort of motion to your scroll.

28 Choose **File > Save**, or press **Ctrl+S**. Choose **File > Close** to close this project.

As you've discovered, Premiere Pro 2 makes it simple to create single lines of text or entire paragraphs. Just like other text objects, you can select the text in the paragraph and change its properties such as color, font size, shadow, and so on. Premiere Pro 2 also makes it quick and painless to add motion to your title, be it a rolling or crawling movement. Changing the duration of a roll/crawl is as easy as lengthening the title clip, and you can add deceleration to a clip with the click of a button or two.

Throughout this chapter, you learned how to build titles with simple text, objects, and paragraphs. You also learned how to save titles, modify text properties, and create rolling/crawling titles. In the next chapter, you'll learn how to add simple transitions to the beginning and end of your clips.

6

Adding Transitions

Transitions allow you to smoothly blend two clips together as the scene changes from Clip A to Clip B. So far in this book, all of your scene changes have been **straight cuts**, where one clip butts up against the next clip. Transitions provide another way for your scenes to change from one clip to another; they can dissolve, wipe, spin, and push one clip into the next. In this chapter, you will learn how to add, modify, and remove transitions.

Understanding Transitions

A **transition** smoothly blends the last few frames of Clip A with the first few frames of Clip B. You apply transitions at **edit points**, which are the points on the **Timeline** where the two clips meet. Think of transitions as "edit point spackle."

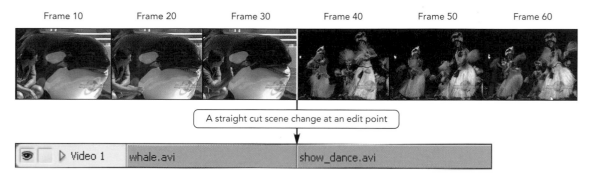

A straight cut scene change at an edit point

So far you've used only straight cuts, where one clip immediately follows, or butts up against, the preceding clip. As shown in the illustration here, the second clip doesn't start playing until the edit point at **Frame 40**. Another way to phrase this is that the **In** point of the second clip is at **Frame 40**. Simple so far, right?

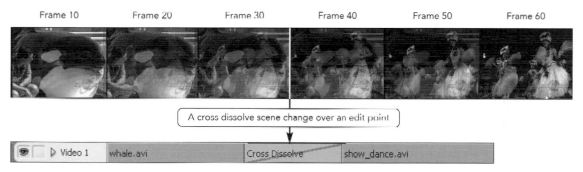

A cross dissolve scene change over an edit point

However, once you add a transition, you begin to see the second clip *before* the edit point and *before* its **In** point. If you carefully examine **Frame 20** as shown in the illustration here, you can see the first clip begins to disappear, or **dissolve**, as the second clip begins to appear. (This is called a **cross dissolve**.) So, this begs the question: If the **In** point of the second clip isn't until **Frame 40**, then what part of the clip do you see at **Frame 20**? Answer: the head material.

Using Heads and Tails

Head material

Tail material

The **head material** represents the unused portion of the video *before* a clip's **In** point. The unused video *after* the **Out** point is the **tail material**. Transitions rely on head and tail material in order to help blend the clips before and after the edit points. This underscores the importance of always having an extra second or two of video at the head and tail of every clip when shooting video.

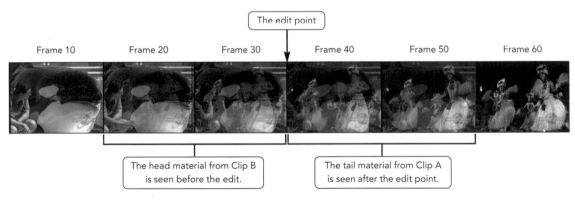

The edit point

Frame 10 Frame 20 Frame 30 Frame 40 Frame 50 Frame 60

The head material from Clip B is seen before the edit.

The tail material from Clip A is seen after the edit point.

The cross dissolve shown in the illustration here uses about 20 frames of head material from Clip A before the edit point. After the edit point, the cross dissolve uses about 20 frames of tail material from Clip B. In this example, the transition is perfectly centered on the edit point, and you are using 20 frames of head material and 20 frames of tail material. However, this is only one of three possible alignments for your transitions.

When you drag a transition over an edit point, depending on where you release the mouse, you have three possible alignments for the transition in relation to the edit point: **Center at Cut**, **End at Cut**, and **Start at Cut**. The following table illustrates a straight cut and each alignment option for transitions:

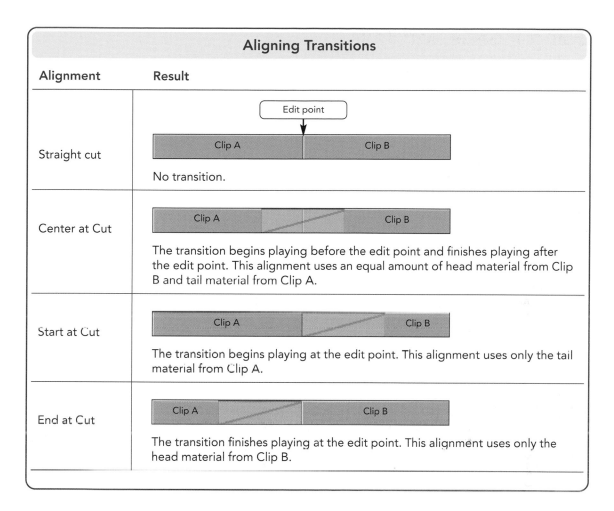

Aligning Transitions

Alignment	Result
Straight cut	Edit point Clip A | Clip B No transition.
Center at Cut	Clip A | Clip B The transition begins playing before the edit point and finishes playing after the edit point. This alignment uses an equal amount of head material from Clip B and tail material from Clip A.
Start at Cut	Clip A | Clip B The transition begins playing at the edit point. This alignment uses only the tail material from Clip A.
End at Cut	Clip A | Clip B The transition finishes playing at the edit point. This alignment uses only the head material from Clip B.

As with many functions in Adobe Premiere Pro 2, the alignment of the transition is determined by where you release the mouse as you drag the transition over the edit point. Each alignment option gives you a different look—and sometimes Premiere Pro 2 makes the alignment decision for you because you don't have enough head material of Clip B or enough tail material of Clip A. At other times, the decision may be an aesthetic one.

In the next exercise, you'll learn how to add, align, and remove transitions.

1 | Adding, Aligning, and Deleting Transitions

Transitions are one of the most essential components of any documentary, movie, video, commercial...you name it. You would be hard-pressed to watch television for more than 5 minutes and *not* see a transition. One of the strengths of editing video on a computer is the ability to add, modify, and remove transitions as many times as you want, without harming the original video. Premiere Pro 2 gives you precise control over a transition's alignment, duration, and sometimes direction. In this exercise, you will learn how to add transitions at the edit points between video clips and change the transition's alignment. You'll also learn how to remove a transition.

1   On the **Welcome Screen**, click **Open Project**. In the **Open Project** dialog box, navigate to the c:\exercise_files\chap_06 folder, click **exercise01.prproj** to select it, and click **Open**.

2   Choose **File > Save As**. Navigate to the **c:\exercise_files\dutch_harbor** folder. Name the file **dutch harbor promo.prproj**, and click **Save**.

Note: If a previous version of dutch harbor promo.prproj already exists, you may be asked to replace it. Click Yes.

3   Choose **Window > Workspace > Effects**.

4   In the **Timeline**, select the **DVD intro** tab to bring the sequence to the foreground. Press the **backslash** (\) key to zoom the sequence to fit in the **Timeline**.

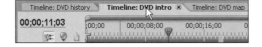

5   In the **Effects** panel, click the **arrow** icon next to the **Video Transitions** folder to view its contents, and then click the **arrow** icon next to the **Dissolve** folder.

Premiere Pro 2 organizes all transitions by type within the Video Transitions folder. The Dissolve folder, for example, contains all the dissolve transitions.

6 In the **Effects** panel, drag the **Cross Dissolve** transition, and drop it on the edit point between the first clip and the second clip on Track **Video 1**. Make sure to center the transition exactly on the edit point so it will align as **Center at Cut**.

Tip: The cursor changes to let you know which of the three alignments you are about to create. (See the cursor shown in the illustration here.)

---

7 Drag the **Timeline CTI** to the beginning of the sequence. Press the **spacebar** to play the sequence. After you watch the cross dissolve, press the **spacebar** to stop playback.

---

8 In the **Effects** panel, scroll to the **Wipe** folder in the **Video Transitions** folder. Click the **arrow** icon next to the **Wipe** folder to expand its contents.

---

9 Scroll to the **Wipe** transition in the **Wipe** folder. Drag the **Wipe** transition, and drop it on the edit point between the second clip and the third clip on Track **Video 1**. Just like last time, take care to center the transition on the edit point.

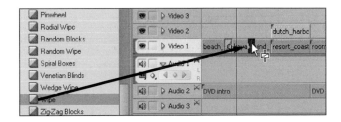

As you position the transition over the edit point, you may notice your cursor snapping to each of the three alignment options. In this case, you want Center at Cut alignment.

---

10 Drag the **Timeline CTI** to any point before the second transition. Press the **spacebar** to play the sequence. After you watch the wipe transition, press the **spacebar** to stop playback.

11 In the **Effects** panel **Video Transitions** folder, click the **arrow** icon next to the **Stretch** folder. Drag the **Funnel** transition, and drop it on

the right of the edit point between the third clip and the fourth clip on Track **Video 1**. Make sure to align the transition as **Start at Cut** so the transition begins at the edit point.

This time, as you drag the transition over the edit point, notice Premiere Pro 2 allows you only one alignment option: Start at Cut. That's because the clip to the right of the edit point has no unused head material, which means no additional frames are available for the transition to use on the left side of the edit point.

---

12 Drag the **Timeline CTI** to any point before the third transition. Press the **spacebar** to play the sequence. After you watch the **Funnel** transition, press the **spacebar** to stop playback.

You would be hard-pressed to find an uglier transition, so this is a good opportunity to learn how to remove a transition.

---

13 Right-click the **Funnel** transition (third transition) on Track **Video 1**, and choose **Clear** to remove the transition.

Tip: You can also select the transition and press Delete to remove a transition.

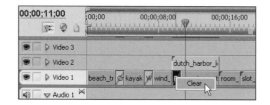

---

14 In the **Effects** panel **Video Transitions > Dissolve** folder, drag the **Cross Dissolve** transition onto the edit point between the third clip and the fourth clip on Track **Video 1**.

---

15 In the **Effects** panel **Video Transitions > Dissolve** folder, drag the **Cross Dissolve** transition to the edit point between the fourth clip and the fifth clip on Track **Video 1**.

---

16 Choose **File > Save**, or press **Ctrl+S**. Leave **dutch harbor promo.prproj** open for the next exercise.

As you can see, there's not too much to mastering the art of applying, removing, and aligning transitions. The real art to working with transitions is finding aesthetically pleasing ones. As you can see, some transitions are ugly. Very ugly. Limiting the "variety" of transitions you use will help your finished video appear more professional. In reality, 95 percent of the available transitions in Premiere Pro 2 will never see the light of day in any of your projects, simply because they are not aesthetically pleasing or useful.

NOTE:

Less Is More

Premiere Pro 2 and many other video-editing programs use their zillions of transitions as a selling point. And some companies sell nothing but extra transitions you can load into Premiere Pro 2. Are the transitions worth it? Or are they just marketing hype?

The next time you watch a movie, count how many different transitions you see. Odds are, you will see just one: a cross dissolve (unless it's an action or comedy, which may use a wipe with the requisite *whoosh* sound effect). You will rarely see more than a dissolve or wipe, unless there is a darn good reason. Watch the evening news, for example, and you will rarely see any transitions beyond dissolves, wipes, and slides. Why? Because the video should speak for itself, and the transition should not draw attention away from the content.

The moral here? Less is more. Be consistent with your transitions. Never mix and match just for the sake of variety. Any transition you use should be a conscious decision based on the theme of your project, and it should support—not detract from—the story.

---

2 | Modifying Transitions

You can modify transitions in two ways: duration and appearance. You can lengthen and shorten the duration of a transition, just like you would a regular clip in the **Timeline** panel—position your cursor over the end and drag. Very simple! In addition, some transitions can change direction, color, shape, and so on. In this exercise, you will learn how to modify transitions in the **Timeline** and in the **Effect Controls** panel.

1 If you followed the previous exercise, **dutch harbor promo.prproj** should still be open in Premiere Pro 2. If it's not, click **Open Project** on the **Welcome Screen**. Navigate to the **c:\exercise_files\chap_06** folder, click **exercise02.prproj** to select it, and click **Open**.

2 Choose **File > Save As**. Navigate to the **c:\exercise_files\dutch_harbor** folder. Name the file **dutch harbor promo.prproj**, and click **Save**.

Note: If a previous version of dutch harbor promo.prproj already exists, you may be asked to replace it. Click Yes.

3 In the **Effects** panel **Video Transitions > Dissolve** folder, drag the **Cross Dissolve** transition to the edit point between the fifth clip and the sixth clip on Track **Video 1**.

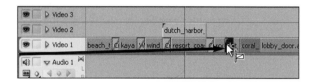

4 Drag the **Timeline CTI** to any point before the transition you just applied. Press the **spacebar** to play the sequence. After you watch the transition, press the **spacebar** to stop playback.

At the end of the transition, you can see the bellhop walk into the frame. Before you added the transition, he was not there, which means the transition is playing too long after the edit point. This is a good opportunity to shorten the duration of the transition.

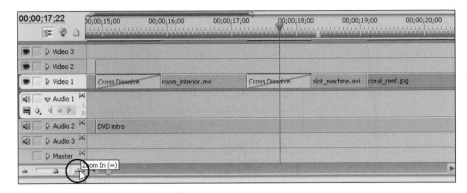

5 Drag the **Timeline CTI** over the center of the transition you just added, at **00;00;17;22**. In the lower-left corner of the **Timeline**, click the **Zoom In** button three times.

Tip: Remember, the Zoom In button zooms *centered on* the CTI. For this reason, when zooming in, it's helpful to first move the CTI to the region you want to zoom in so it will be centered in the Timeline.

6 Position your mouse over the end of the transition. When you see the **Trim Out** cursor, drag the end of the transition -23 frames to the left, at **00;00;00;23**.

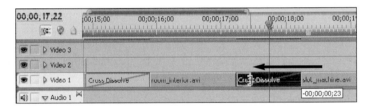

Tip: Look for the yellow tool tip to guide you.

Just like trimming clips in the Timeline, you can use the Trim In/Trim Out cursor for increasing or decreasing the duration of transitions.

7 Drag the **Timeline CTI** to any point before the transition you just modified. Press the **spacebar** to play the sequence. After you watch the transition, press the **spacebar** to stop playback.

8 While still zoomed in, drag the **Cross Dissolve** transition from the **Dissolve** folder onto the edit point between the sixth clip and the seventh clip on Track **Video 1**, positioning your cursor over the center of the edit point, to align as **Center at Cut**.

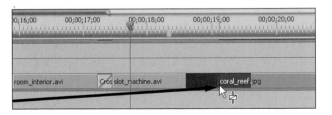

9 Drag the **Timeline CTI** to any point before the transition you just applied. Press the **spacebar** to play the sequence. After you watch the transition, press the **spacebar** to stop playback.

During the transition, the slot machine clip jumps to a close-up of the slot machine. This is another situation when you will want to modify the transition.

10 Click the **Cross Dissolve** transition at the end of the **slot_machine.avi** clip to open the transition in the **Effect Controls** panel.

Note: Don't confuse the Effects panel with the Effect Controls panel. The Effects panel is the library for all of the effects and transitions. The Effect Controls panel is where you modify those effects and transitions, once you've applied them.

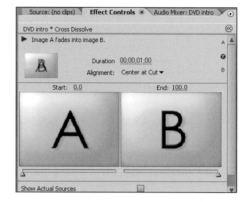

11 In the **Effect Controls** panel, turn on the **Show Actual Sources** check box.

12 In the **Effect Controls** panel, choose the **Center at Cut** alignment option. Change the **Alignment** pop-up menu to **End at Cut**.

Notice the selected transition in the Timeline shifts to the left so it ends at the edit point. This prevents the unwanted tail material of the first clip from being seen.

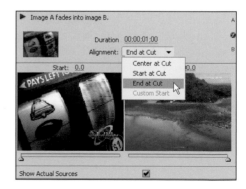

13 In the **Effect Controls** panel, position your cursor over the **Duration** value of **00;00;01;00**. Drag your mouse to the left until the **Duration** value is **00;00;00;15**.

In the Timeline panel, notice that the transition was shortened. This is another way to change the duration of a transition.

14 Press the **backslash** (\) key to zoom the sequence to fit in the **Timeline**.

15 In the **Effects** panel, scroll to the **Video Transitions > Wipe** folder. Drag the **Wipe** transition onto the edit point between the seventh clip and the eighth clip, positioning your cursor over the center of the edit point to align it as **Center at Cut**.

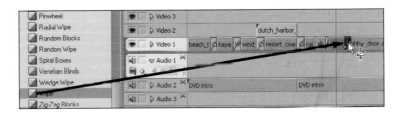

16 In the **Timeline**, click the **Wipe** transition you just applied to open it in the **Effect Controls** panel.

Some transitions start on one side of the screen and move across to the other side. These types of transitions have direction. Some of these transitions allow you to customize their direction. For example, you can change a wipe from traveling left to right to traveling from lower-left to upper-right. These types of transitions have arrows displayed around their preview in the Effect Controls panel.

17 In the **Effect Controls** panel, click the **Northwest to Southeast** direction arrow to change the direction of the wipe.

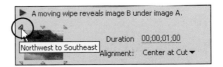

18 In the upper-left corner of the **Effect Controls** panel, click the **Play the transition** button to preview the new transition direction in the preview area. Click the button again to stop playback.

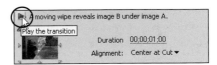

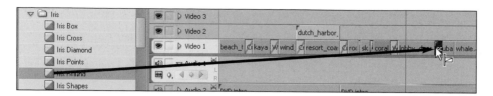

19 In the **Effects** panel **Video Transitions** folder, scroll to the **Iris** folder, and click the **arrow** icon to view its contents. Drag the **Iris Round** transition to the edit point between the eighth clip and the ninth clip (**lobby_door.avi** and **scuba.avi**).

Your only alignment option is Start at Cut because the scuba.avi clip has no head material.

---

20 In the **Timeline**, drag the **CTI** to **00;00;27;03** to position it over the **Iris Round** transition you applied so you can see it in the **Program Monitor**.

---

21 In the **Timeline**, click the **Iris Round** transition you just applied to open it in the **Effect Controls** panel.

Some transitions can be positioned to begin "appearing" from a certain location on the screen. These types of transitions display a white circle in the preview area (the left preview) of the Effect Controls panel.

22 In the **Effect Controls** panel preview area, drag the small white circle to the upper-left corner of the preview area.

In the Program Monitor, you will see the round transition now centered in the upper-left corner of the screen, which is the position of the white circle.

---

23 With the **Iris Round** transition still selected, change the **Anti-aliasing Quality** pop-up menu to **High** in the **Effect Controls** panel.

In the Program Monitor, notice the edges of the round transition appear much softer, almost blurred. **Anti-aliasing** controls how smoothly the edges of a transition blend with the video. If you don't detect a difference, try alternating the Anti-aliasing Quality between Off and High again.

24 In the **Effects** panel **Video Transitions** folder, scroll to the **Dissolve** folder. Drag the **Cross Dissolve** transition to the edit point between the ninth clip and the tenth clip (**scuba.avi** and **whale.avi**).

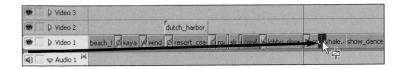

---

25 Click the **Cross Dissolve** transition you applied in the previous step once to view its options in the **Effect Controls** panel.

As you will see, not all transitions have options. The Cross Dissolve transition, for example, doesn't have a direction or a shape to change.

Next, it's time to apply one more transition—using an easy method you have yet to try.

---

26 In the **Program Monitor**, click the **Go to Next Edit Point (Page Down)** button until the **CTI** is between the **whale.avi** and **show_dance.avi** clips at **00;00;31;28**.

The Go to Next Edit Point (Page Down) and Go to Previous Edit Point (Page Up) buttons snap the CTI to edit points on the Timeline. You can also use the Page Up and Page Down keys on your keyboard.

---

27 Choose **Sequence > Apply Video Transition**, or press **Ctrl+D**.

The default transition has a red border.

The Apply Video Transition menu command automatically applies the *default* transition at the CTI edit point. The default transition is indicated with a red border in the Effects panel.

You can set *any* transition as the default transition by selecting it, then clicking the Effects panel wing menu, and finally choosing Set Selected as Default Transition.

---

28 Choose **File > Save**, or press **Ctrl+S**. Leave **dutch harbor promo.prproj** open for the next exercise.

In this exercise you applied a variety of transitions for the purpose of helping you learn the different options. In the real world, you would probably *not* want to apply so many types of transitions.

Variety aside, you also learned how to modify vital properties of each transition, such as duration and alignment. Furthermore, you worked with some transitions that have position and direction options. Keep in mind, a simple transition like a cross dissolve has no position or direction—it is applied to the entire screen.

NOTE:

First and Last Frame

In the previous two exercises, you saw Premiere Pro 2 limit your options when applying transitions, depending on the amount of available head and tail material. A nice feature of Premiere Pro 2 is that it designates the first and last frames of a clip with tiny dark notches in the upper corners of a clip.

A dark notch in the upper-left corner of a clip indicates the first frame of a clip. This tells you no head material is available because you are already using the first frame. Likewise, a dark notch in the upper-right corner of a clip indicates the last frame, and thus no tail material is available to use for transitioning.

Because many of the clips used throughout this book are pre-edited, you may see many of these dark notches. In the real world, however, it's best to see as few dark notches as possible because it limits your options when editing and when applying transitions.

EXERCISE

3 | Adding Transitions to Graphics

Beyond video clips, you can also apply video transitions to graphics and titles. This can be a quick and painless way to fade in or out of a title. In this exercise, you will add some visual interest by adding cross dissolves to many of your graphics and titles.

---

1 If you followed the previous exercise, **dutch harbor promo.prproj** should still be open in Premiere Pro 2. If it's not, click **Open Project** on the **Welcome Screen**. Navigate to the **c:\exercise_files\chap_06** folder, click **exercise03.prproj** to select it, and click **Open**.

---

2 Choose **File > Save As**. Navigate to the **c:\exercise_files\dutch_harbor** folder. Name the file **dutch harbor promo.prproj**, and click **Save**.

Note: If a previous version of dutch harbor promo.prproj already exists, you may be asked to replace it. Click Yes.

---

3 In the **Timeline**, select the **DVD history** tab to bring the sequence to the foreground.

---

4 In the **Effects** panel **Video Transitions > Dissolve** folder, drag the **Cross Dissolve** transition to the **In** point of the first clip on Track **Video 3**.

Video-geek lingo alert: You have just added a **single-sided transition**. It is single-sided because it applies to a single clip. Instead of cross dissolving two clips, which would be a **double-sided transition**, it is used to fade in a single clip from "nothing."

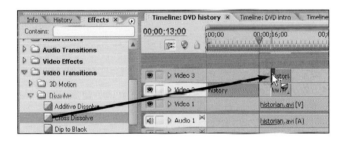

---

5 Repeat Step 4, but drag the **Cross Dissolve** transition to the **In** point of the second clip on Track **Video 2**.

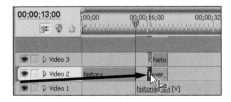

---

6 Drag the **Timeline CTI** to a point before the transitions you just added. Press the **spacebar** to play the sequence. When done, press the **spacebar** to stop playback.

You can also add transitions to animated titles, as in the next step.

7 In the **Dissolve** folder, drag the **Cross Dissolve** transition to the end of the rolling title on Track **Video 2**.

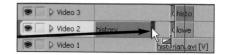

8 Drag the same **Cross Dissolve** transition to the beginning of the **historian.avi** clip on Track **Video 1**. Press the **spacebar** to play the sequence. When done, press the **spacebar** to stop playback.

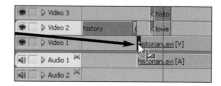

Tip: Adding two single-sided transitions, back to back, is an easy way to "dip to black" between two clips.

And before you mention it, I almost forgot to show how to fade out the historian lower third....

9 Drag the **Cross Dissolve** transition to the **Out** points of both the **historian** title and **lower_third.mov** on Tracks **Video 3** and **Video 2** above **historian.avi**.

You can find some useful and interesting ways to introduce titles and clips that have alpha channels by using different types of wipes.

10 In the **Effects** panel **Video Transitions > Wipe** folder, drag the **Wipe** transition to the **In** points of the **eruptologist** title and **lower_third.mov** on Tracks **Video 3** and **Video 2** above **eruptologist.avi**.

11 Press the **spacebar** to play the sequence. When done, press the **spacebar** to stop playback.

12 Drag the same **Wipe** transition to the **Out** points of the **eruptologist** title and **lower_third.mov** on Tracks **Video 3** and **Video 2** above **eruptologist.avi**.

13 In the **Effects** panel **Video Transitions > Slide** folder, drag the **Slide** transition to the **In** points of the **media relations** title and **lower_third.mov** on Tracks **Video 3** and **Video 2** above **media_relations.avi**.

14 In the **Effects** panel **Video Transitions > Slide** folder, drag the **Push** transition to the **Out** points of the **media relations** title and **lower_third.mov** on Tracks **Video 3** and **Video 2**.

15 Press the **spacebar** to play the sequence. When done, press the **spacebar** to stop playback.

Tip: A Wipe transition "reveals" the item. The clip itself doesn't move, but the wipe moves across the screen and reveals the existing clip. By contrast, a **Slide** transition moves the clip itself, to bring it on camera. A **Push** transition also moves like a slide, but it "pushes" (or shoves) any existing items out of the way, like a snowplow!

16 In the **Timeline**, select the **DVD map** tab to bring the sequence to the foreground.

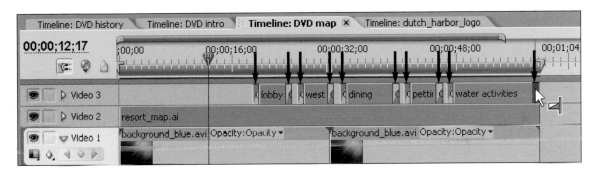

17 In the **Effects** panel **Video Transitions > Dissolve** folder, drag the **Cross Dissolve** transition to the **In** and **Out** points of each title on Track **Video 3**.

In this step, you are applying a total of ten transitions.

18 Press the **spacebar** to play the sequence. When done, press the **spacebar** to stop playback.

19 Choose **File > Save**, or press **Ctrl+S**. Choose **File > Close** to close this project.

By now, you should be an expert at applying transitions. Thankfully, in Premiere Pro 2, you can apply video transitions equally to all types of clips: videos, graphics, and titles. Also, remember that single-sided transitions "stick" to a single clip. Even if you move the clip, the transition sticks to it. On the other hand, double-sided transitions stick to edit points between two clips. But if you move one of the clips involved in the edit point, you will lose the edit point—and therefore you will lose the transition.

As you can see from this chapter, transitions are a piece of cake, and there's no mystery to adding and modifying them. In the next chapter, you'll modify the look of your video and graphic clips by adding video effects.

7

Adding Video Effects

If video editing is the meat and potatoes of Adobe Premiere Pro 2, then adding a video effect is the sweet, fruit filling that makes it all worthwhile. You can create thousands of "looks" in Premiere Pro 2. For example, you can make your video blurry, you can make it look black and white, and you can distort it like it's being shown through a kaleidoscope—just to name a few! It may sound like a cliché, but the only limit is your imagination. In fact, you can create many looks with a single effect; others require you to mix and match effects. In addition, you can create even more looks just by changing the order in which the effects are applied. In this chapter, you will learn how to add, modify, and remove video effects, as well as learn some of the more popular techniques you can use in the real world.

Understanding Video Effects

Strictly speaking, a **video effect** is a filter you apply to video clips or still images to change how a clip appears. The **Effect Controls** panel lists video effects, just like the video transitions covered in Chapter 6, *"Adding Transitions."* You apply video effects to clips the same way you apply transitions—simply select the effect you want, drag it from its **Effects** panel folder, and drop it on the clip you want to modify.

However, there's a lot more to video effects. In terms of this chapter, the phrase **video effect** describes anything affecting how a clip displays, including video effect filters (such as color correction, blurs, and 3D orientation), frame holds (also called **freeze frame**, as if the video is paused or "frozen"), and slow motion and fast motion.

In this chapter, you will learn how to create each of these types of video effects. Along the way, you will also learn some handy tricks for saving effect presets and copying effects from one clip to another.

NOTE:

Video Effects Versus Video Filters

So what's the difference between a video **effect** and a video **filter**? Your answer depends on whom at Adobe you ask.

In Premiere Pro 2, video filters are called **video effects**. Users who are migrating from earlier versions of Premiere Pro will recognize the word **filter**. (Isn't it odd Adobe calls them filters in every other program but Premiere Pro?)

To make this chapter confusion free, you will learn the techniques using the Premiere Pro 2 terminology. Just keep in mind, when you read **video effect**, it can mean the actual filter applied to a clip, or it can mean any effect that changes how a clip displays (such as slow motion or frame holds).

Changing Effect Render Order

In Chapter 4, *"Adding Graphics,"* you modified a clip's fixed effects, such as position, rotation, and so on. If you recall, you had to first select a clip and then modify its **Motion** properties in the **Effect Controls** panel. You can also use the **Effect Controls** panel for modifying and removing video effects.

The **Effect Controls** panel displays fixed effects, such as **Motion** and **Opacity**, and any applied video effects, such as **Gaussian Blur**.

Fixed effects and video effects have one difference: You can apply multiple video effects to a single clip. When you apply multiple effects, Premiere Pro 2 renders them in a specific order, known as **effect render order**.

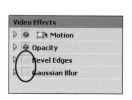

As shown in the illustration here, two effects were applied to the kayaking clip. However, both effects were turned off by clicking the effect toggles. Because the two video effects are temporarily turned off, the **Program Monitor** displays the original clip.

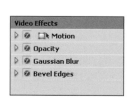

As shown in the illustration here, however, both video effects are turned on. Premiere Pro 2 renders the effects from the first listed to the last in the **Effect Controls** panel. First, the **Gaussian Blur** effect was applied, which created a blurry kayaking video. Next, the **Bevel Edges** effect was applied, which created a sharp bevel around the blurry video.

Notice what happens when you change the effect order. As shown in the illustration here, the **Bevel Edges** effect was moved *above* the **Gaussian Blur** in the **Effect Controls** panel. In this case, Premiere Pro 2 first created a beveled edge and then applied the blur. The result is a blurry, beveled edge because the blur was the last effect applied.

The lesson here is this: The order of effects does indeed matter. In the next exercise, you will learn how to apply and remove video effects, as well as change the render order of multiple effects in the **Effect Controls** panel.

EXERCISE

1 | Creating Sepia Photograph Effects

One of the most common requests for video effects is, "How do I make old-timey video or photographs?" You've probably seen this done before—a simple photograph is given a brown color (called **sepia**) to mimic old photographs. In this exercise, you will create a sepia tone on a video clip and then copy the effect attributes to a still image.

1 On the **Welcome Screen**, click **Open Project**. In the **Open Project** dialog box, navigate to the c:\exercise_files\chap_07 folder, click **exercise01.prproj** to select it, and click **Open**.

2 Choose **File > Save As**. Navigate to the **c:\exercise_files\dutch_harbor** folder. Name the file **dutch harbor promo.prproj**, and click **Save**.

Note: If a previous version of dutch harbor promo.prproj already exists, you may be asked to replace it. Click Yes.

3 Choose **Window > Workspace > Effects**.

4 In the **Timeline**, select the **DVD History** tab to bring the sequence to the foreground. Press the **backslash** (\) key to zoom the sequence to fit in the **Timeline**.

5 In the **Project** panel **Video** bin, drag the **beach_tropical.avi** clip, and snap it to the end of the first lower third (after the transition) on Track **Video 2**.

When you apply effects to a clip, you are able to see the results immediately. Therefore, it is helpful to position the CTI (Current Time Indicator) to somewhere over the clip so you can see it in the Program Monitor and preview your effects immediately.

6 Move the **Timeline CTI** to **00;00;23;00**.

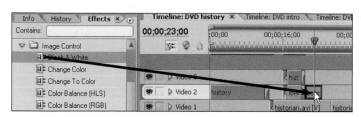 

7 In the **Effects** panel, click the **arrow** icon next to **Video Effects** to view its contents, and then expand the **Image Control** folder. Drag the **Black & White** video effect, and drop it on the **beach_tropical.avi** clip on Track **Video 2**.

As soon as you drop the Black & White effect on the beach_tropical.avi clip, the video turns black and white in the Program Monitor.

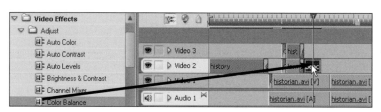 

8 In the **Effects** panel **Video Effects** folder, click the **arrow** icon next to **Adjust** to view its contents. Drag the **Color Balance** video effect, and drop it on the **beach_tropical.avi** clip.

This time, when you apply the Color Balance effect, nothing changes in the Program Monitor. This is because some effects, such as the Black & White effect, are automatically on; other effects, such as Color Balance, are set to 0 and won't do anything unless you change their values.

9 If you see a small **Timeline** in the right side of the **Effect Controls** panel, click the **Show/Hide Timeline View** toggle to hide the **Effect Controls Timeline**.

Note: The small Timeline in the Effect Controls panel may already be hidden. You can click the Show/Hide Timeline View toggle to switch between showing and hiding it.

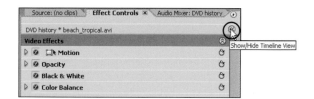

10 In the **Effect Controls** panel, click the **arrow** icon next to **Color Balance** to view its contents. Click the **Midtone Blue Balance** value to select it, and change the value to –**50.0**.

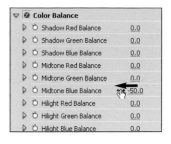

Your video displays in a sepia tone. Premiere Pro 2 first renders the Black & White effect and then colorizes it.

Tip: Premiere Pro 2 provides many other color-changing video effects for creating a sepia tone. You can create sepia by reducing the blue values or by increasing the reds and greens.

---

11 In the **Effect Controls** panel, click the **arrow** icon next to **Color Balance** to hide its contents.

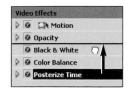

12 In the **Effects** panel, scroll to the **Time** folder, and expand its contents. Drag the **Posterize Time** effect, and drop it on the **beach_tropical.avi** clip on Track **Video 2**.

Did you notice your clip just turned back into color again? This is because some effects, such as Posterize Time, completely ignore effects previously applied. This highlights the importance of effect render order. In this case, you want to move the Posterize Time effect to the top of the list, so it renders first.

---

13 In the **Effect Controls** panel, click the **Posterize Time** effect, and drag it just above the **Black & White** effect. Release the mouse when you see a thick, black line above the Black & White effect, indicating where the Posterize Time effect will be placed.

When you release the mouse, the Posterize Time effect should be listed above the Black & White effect, and the video in the Program Monitor should again be sepia toned.

Tip: When dragging, be careful to drag *just slightly above* the Black & White effect until you see a thick, black line. If you move your mouse too far, the effect will not move when you release the mouse.

Note: You'll never be able to drag an effect above the Opacity and Motion fixed effects. Those are, as the name implies, fixed, and they'll never budge.

14 In the **Effect Controls** panel, click the **arrow** icon next to the **Posterize Time** effect to view its properties. Drag the **Frame Rate** value to **8.0**. Click the **Play** button to play the **Timeline** from the beginning of the **historian.avi** clip. After previewing the effect, click the **Stop** button (or press the **spacebar**).

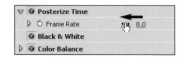

Tip: The Posterize Time effect changes the clip's existing frame rate to the value you specify. In this case, it makes the video appear "choppy," playing only eight frames in one second. (To use the flip book analogy, it's like flipping to every third picture and holding it longer before flipping to the next picture.) This look is reminiscent of an old-timey movie.

Bonus tip: Some editors apply a 24.0 frame rate to their videos to get a "film" look. Although it is next to impossible to get your video to look like real film, this is just one method editors employ to strive for the film look.

---

15 In the **Effects** panel **Video Effects** folder, scroll to the **Blur & Sharpen** folder, and click the **arrow** icon to view its effects. Drag the **Gaussian Blur** effect to the end of the list effects in the **Effect Controls** panel.

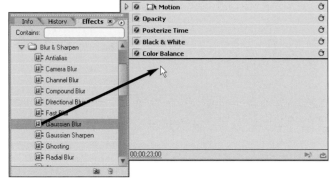

When you release the mouse, you will see the effect listed in the Effect Controls panel.

Dragging clips directly to the Effect Controls panel can be useful when applying an effect to a clip that is too "thin" to see (when the Timeline is zoomed out, for example).

---

16 In the **Effect Controls** panel, click the symbol next to **Gaussian Blur** to view its properties. Change the **Blurriness** value to **4.0**.

This subtle blur softens the crispness of the video and helps support the overall effect of old-timey footage.

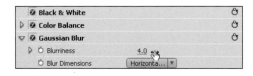

Tip: If you don't see a difference, click the effect toggle next to Gaussian Blur to turn the effect on and off. When finished, make sure the effect is turned on.

---

17 Drag the **Timeline CTI** to the beginning of the **historian.avi** clip on Track **Video 1**. Press the **space-bar** to play the sequence and preview your effect. Press the **spacebar** to stop playback after the historian finishes speaking.

Did you notice the cut in the middle of the historian's interview? This is because an entire sentence was removed. (Actors. You know how they are.) Unfortunately, in its current state, this would be obvious for an audience member to see. To mask this, you might consider using b-roll.

B-roll is additional footage related to what is being described on camera. You can place the b-roll clip on a track above the edit point. While the b-roll plays, the audience is unaware that an edit occurred underneath. B-roll is used everyday at news stations and does a wonderful job of hiding obvious edits, such as this one.

---

18 In the **Project** panel **Graphics** bin, drag the **mountain.jpg** clip, and snap it to the **Out** point of the **beach_tropical.avi** clip on Track **Video 2**.

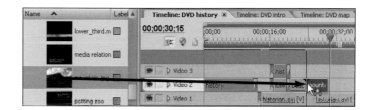

---

19 Drag the **Timeline CTI** to the beginning of the **beach_tropical.avi** clip on Track **Video 2**. Press the **spacebar** to play the sequence and watch the b-roll. When done, press the **spacebar** to stop.

You probably found the cut much less distracting. In fact, you probably didn't even *notice* that an edit was made to the actor's narration.

A quick way to re-create the look of an effect is to copy the effects from one clip and paste them to another. You can quickly do this using the Paste Attributes command, which pastes only the "look" of one clip to another.

---

20 On Track **Video 2**, right-click the **beach_tropical** clip, and choose **Copy**.

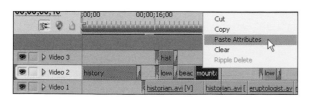

21 On Track **Video 2**, right-click the **mountain.jpg** clip, and choose **Paste Attributes**.

As soon as you choose the Paste Attributes command, you will see the mountain image tinted with sepia in the Program Monitor.

Removing a clip's effect in Premiere Pro 2 is equally as easy as applying it. Simply select the effect in the Effect Controls panel, and press the Delete key.

In this exercise, because mountain.jpg is a still image, you don't need the Posterize Time video effect (since the image has no frames of video to posterize!). Therefore, you can remove it.

22 If necessary, click the **mountain.jpg** clip on Track **Video 2** to select it. In the **Effect Controls** panel, click the **Posterize Time** effect to select it, and press the **Delete** key.

Tip: Even though the Posterize Time effect had no noticeable effect on the final video, it's still a good idea to remove any unnecessary effects. Each effect you add will add a bit more processing time and weigh down your computer just a tad more. The moral of this story is this: If an effect isn't doing anything, get rid of it!

23 Drag the **Timeline CTI** to the beginning of the **beach_tropical.avi** clip on Track **Video 1**. Press the **spacebar** to play the sequence and preview your effect. Press the **spacebar** to stop playback after the **mountain.jpg** b-roll.

24 Choose **File > Save**, or press **Ctrl+S**. Leave **dutch harbor promo.prproj** open for the next exercise.

In this exercise, you applied, reordered, and removed video effects to both video clips and still images. Premiere Pro 2 makes it easy to apply effects to all types of clips because all effects are applied in the same way. You can drag them to the desired clip or drag them to the Effect Controls panel (as long as the clip is first selected). In addition, reordering effects is as easy as clicking and dragging.

This exercise was an example of how you can create a custom "look" by combining multiple effects on one clip. There is no end to the number of looks you can create. In the next exercise, you will create another popular look by applying an effect and pasting a clip on top of itself.

EXERCISE

2 | Creating a Bloom Effect

The "bloom" look is a favorite of wedding videographers because it softens video and creates a soft haze around the subject. Imagine those slightly blurred, dreamy Hollywood close-ups of the 1950s. Brides go nuts for this effect. (Did I mention it tends to hide blemishes and wrinkles?) But Premiere Pro 2 has no effect called the "Bloom" effect; rather, you create this look by using the **Gaussian Blur** effect and compositing two clips together in a unique way, as you will soon learn.

1 If you followed the previous exercise, **dutch harbor promo.prproj** should still be open in Premiere Pro 2. If it's not, click **Open Project** on the **Welcome Screen**. Navigate to the **c:\exercise_files\chap_07** folder, click **exercise02.prproj** to select it, and click **Open**.

2 Choose **File > Save As**. Navigate to the **c:\exercise_files\dutch_harbor** folder. Name the file **dutch harbor promo.prproj**, and click **Save**.

Note: If a previous version of dutch harbor promo.prproj already exists, you may be asked to replace it. Click Yes.

3 At the top of the **Timeline**, select the **DVD intro** tab to bring the sequence to the foreground.

The first step in creating the bloom look is to copy and paste a clip directly on top of itself.

4 On Track **Video 1** of the **Timeline**, right-click the **show_dance.avi** clip, and choose **Copy**.

Before pasting this clip, you must move the CTI to the location you would like to paste the clip and also set the target track. For the bloom effect to work, the original clip and its copy must be *perfectly* aligned.

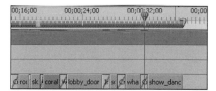

5 In the **Program Monitor**, click the **Go to Previous Edit Point** button to move the **CTI** to the start of the clip. The CTI should be at **00;00;31;28**.

This *guarantees* that the CTI is placed in the proper location—mostly because no human element is involved, which could result in accidentally moving the CTI to the wrong place.

Tip: Remember, the clip *starts* at the edit point, even though in the Timeline panel the edit point is obscured by a transition (as shown in the illustration here).

6 Click Track **Video 2** to highlight the track and set it as the target track.

When you click the track name, the track appears lighter than the other tracks.

You have now specified *where* you want to paste the clip (at the CTI) and on *which track* you want to paste the clip (the target track). All systems are go for pasting!

---

7 Choose **Edit > Paste**, or press **Ctrl+V**.

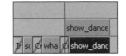

If all went according to plan, you should see a copy of the show_dance.avi clip directly above the original clip. Both the In point and the Out point of the upper clip should align with the lower clip. (As shown in the illustration here, a transition is obscuring the bottom clip's In point.)

---

8 Drag the Timeline **CTI** to **00;00;32;20**.

This frame of video, which is a close-up of the dancer, allows you to better see the effect as you apply it.

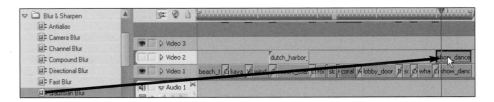

9 In the **Effects** panel **Video Effects > Blur & Sharpen** folder, drag the **Gaussian Blur** effect to the upper copy of **show_dance.avi**.

---

10 In the **Effect Controls** panel, click the **arrow** icon next to **Gaussian Blur** to view its properties. Change the **Blurriness** value to **15.0**.

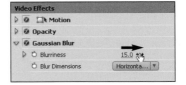

This heavily blurs the clip, as you can see in the Program Monitor.

11 In the **Effect Controls** panel, click the **arrow** icon next to **Opacity** to view its properties. Change the **Opacity** value to **40.0**.

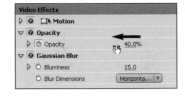

This is certainly a subtle effect, to say the least. That's the idea here, however; you don't want an *extreme* effect. You want just a subtle softening to remove blemishes, create a "dreamy" look, and so on. If you don't think you can see the results of applying this effect, try turning the **Gaussian Blur** effect off and on, and compare the before and after versions.

Original   With subtle bloom

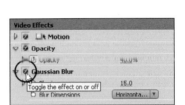

12 To easily see the effect, repeatedly click the effect toggle to turn it on and off. When finished, make sure to leave the toggle turned on.

13 Choose **File > Save**, or press **Ctrl+S**. Leave **dutch harbor promo.prproj** open for the next exercise.

You can vary this effect by increasing the opacity amount or increasing the blur amount. (Note: Blur amounts greater than 30 or 40 tend to have diminishing returns.) The trick to getting an effective bloom look is to make sure you have the clips perfectly aligned. And don't forget, when you paste a clip, Premiere Pro 2 always pastes it on the target track and at the CTI.

As you delve deep into the Blur and Sharpen effects folder, you will discover that Premiere Pro 2 comes with a variety of blurs. You may find equally good results, and faster rendering, with the Fast Blur effect. But if you're a stickler for quality, nothing beats the Gaussian Blur effect.

So far, the past two looks you have created have affected the entire image. However, you can also create some interesting looks by adding effects to clips that have alpha channels. These types of effects will alter only the "visible" portion of the clip and thus allow you to create drop shadows and bevels around your logos, images, and so on. You will do this in the next exercise.

3 | Creating Alpha Channel Effects

If I haven't sung the praises of alpha channels enough in this book, here's another reason to love them: Many video effects will apply themselves only to the "visible" area of a clip that has an alpha channel. In other words, the transparent area is left alone. This allows you to add some interesting looks around a logo, image, and so on. For example, you can add a drop shadow "behind" an image that has an alpha channel, or you can bevel the edges of your alpha channel to give the appearance of depth. These are just a couple of the many looks you can create. In this exercise, you will work with images containing alpha channels to add drop shadows and bevels around the alpha channel.

1 If you followed the previous exercise, **dutch harbor promo.prproj** should still be open in Premiere Pro 2. If it's not, click **Open Project** on the **Welcome Screen**. Navigate to the **c:\exercise_files\chap_07** folder, click **exercise03.prproj** to select it, and click **Open**.

2 Choose **File > Save As**. Navigate to the **c:\exercise_files\dutch_harbor** folder. Name the file **dutch harbor promo.prproj**, and click **Save**.

Note: If a previous version of dutch harbor promo.prproj already exists, you may be asked to replace it. Click Yes.

3 At the top of the **Timeline**, select the **dutch_harbor_logo** tab to bring the sequence to the foreground.

This sequence has six clips, which were converted from six layers of an Adobe Photoshop image. Each clip has its own alpha channel defining its shape.

4 In the **Contains** text box at the top of the **Effects** panel, type **shadow**.

This filters all of the effects and transitions and displays only those with the word **shadow** in their title.

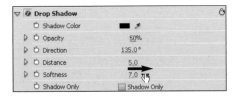

5 In the **Effects** panel **Video Effects > Perspective** folder, drag the **Drop Shadow** effect, and drop it on the **Resort and Casino** clip in the sequence.

Immediately upon placing this effect, you should see a slight drop shadow behind the green **Resort and Casino** text in the Program Monitor. Notice the shadow applies to the green text *only*.

6 In the **Effect Controls** panel, click the **arrow** icon next to the **Drop Shadow** effect to view its properties. Change the **Softness** value to **7.0** to blur the shadow.

Tip: Next to each effect name, you will see a Reset button, which you can use to reset the effect to its original state.

7 In the **Effect Controls** panel, right-click **Drop Shadow**, and choose **Copy**.

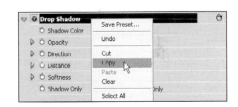

You will paste this effect onto another clip. This is similar to the Paste Attributes command you used in Exercise 1. However, Paste Attributes copies *all* effects from a clip. The method you used in this step copies only a single effect.

8 At the top of the **Timeline**, select the **DVD intro** tab to bring the sequence to the foreground. Drag the **Timeline CTI** to **00;00;12;00**.

9 On Track **Video 2**, click the **dutch_ harbor_logo** clip to select it. In the **Effect Controls** panel, right-click anywhere in the empty, gray area, and choose **Paste**.

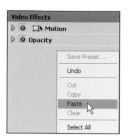

Premiere Pro 2 applies the Drop Shadow effect to the clip. If you don't see the effect, click the Drop Shadow toggle to turn the effect on and off.

Tip: Drop shadows are great for adding separation between graphics and underlying video. In this case, the drop shadow also helps to visually define the edges of the logo better so it's easier to read on top of the busy video underneath.

---

10 On Track **Video 2**, double-click the **dutch_harbor_logo** nested sequence to open the original **dutch_harbor_logo** sequence in the **Timeline**.

---

11 In the **Effects** panel, highlight the word **shadow** in the **Contains** text box, and press **Delete**.

Deleting the word removes the search filter. (If you didn't remove it, you wouldn't be able to find any other effects except those with **shadow** in the title.)

A Bevel Alpha effect is useful for beveling letters. This can help "raise" the letters of the flat screen and give the illusion of depth. In this next series of steps, you'll apply a Bevel Alpha effect to the words Dutch Harbor in the logo.

---

12 In the **Effects** panel **Video Effects** folder, click the **arrow** icon next to **Perspective** to view its effects. Drag the **Bevel Alpha** effect, and drop it on the **Dutch Harbor** clip in the **Timeline**.

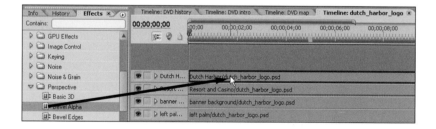

---

13 In the **Effect Controls** panel, click the **arrow** icon next to **Bevel Alpha** to view its properties. Change the **Edge Thickness** to 3.00 and the **Light Intensity** to 0.60.

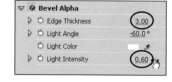

The Bevel Alpha effect works only on titles or clips with alpha channels. Also, it is best to use this effect on large, thick text.

---

14 At the top of the **Timeline**, select the **DVD intro** tab to see the finished effect.

15 Choose **File > Save**, or press **Ctrl+S**. Leave **dutch harbor promo.prproj** open for the next exercise.

You've just experienced two of the easiest and most common effects to apply to logos that have alpha channels. You also learned how to copy and paste just a single effect, rather than copying all effects from a clip. And lastly, if ever you're not happy with a look you've created, you can reset any effect with its Reset button. This is helpful when you want to start over from scratch.

NOTE:

Nested Sequences and Alpha Channels

In the previous exercise, you applied a drop shadow to a nested sequence. Because the nested sequence consisted of six clips, Premiere Pro 2 *composited* all six alpha channels and then applied the drop shadow to the overall composite. A **composite** is a blend of all visible clips combined. Confusing? The illustrations and explanations shown here should help.

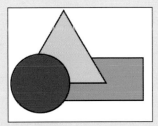 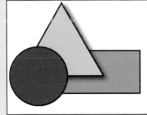 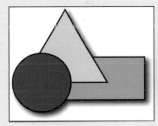

Figure 1   Figure 2   Figure 3

Figure 1 shows a sequence with three clips.

Figure 2 shows a drop shadow applied to a single clip in the sequence. As shown in the illustration here, you can see the drop shadow behind the triangle but in front of the rectangle.

Figure 3 shows a drop shadow applied to the nested sequence. Premiere Pro 2 composites the alpha channels of all the clips in the nested sequence before applying the effect. Remember, the composite is the shape of all three clips combined. The drop shadow appears only around the perimeter of all the clips, rather than behind each individual clip.

The moral of the story is this: Premiere Pro 2 treats nested sequences as one clip, and the alpha channel is composited by combining the shapes of all clips within the nested sequence.

4 | Creating Slow Motion and Frame Hold

Premiere Pro 2 makes it extremely easy to "mess with time." That is, you can alter the typical rate at which the video plays. For example, instead of playing 30 frames in a second, you can play 15 frames in a second—so the clip takes twice as long to play. You will recognize this by its common name, **slow motion**. Slow motion is used in every walk of video-editing life, from creating sports replays to heightening dramatic moments in movies. Beyond slow motion, Premiere Pro 2 provides a simple method to turn a video clip into a still image, also called a **freeze frame**. In the world of Premiere Pro 2, it's called a **frame hold**. In this exercise, you will learn how to create a slow-motion effect, as well as learn a useful technique for making a frame hold.

---

1 If you followed the previous exercise, **dutch harbor promo.prproj** should still be open in Premiere Pro 2. If it's not, click **Open Project** on the **Welcome Screen**. Navigate to the **c:\exercise_files\chap_07** folder, click **exercise04.prproj** to select it, and click **Open**.

---

2 Choose **File > Save As**. Navigate to the **c:\exercise_files\dutch_harbor** folder. Name the file **dutch harbor promo.prproj**, and click **Save**.

Note: If a previous version of dutch harbor promo.prproj already exists, you may be asked to replace it. Click Yes.

---

3 At the top of the **Timeline**, select the **DVD history** tab to bring the sequence to the foreground. Drag the **Timeline CTI** to the start of the sequence.

---

4 In the **Project** panel **Video** bin, double-click **show_fire.avi** to open it in the **Source Monitor**. Set an **In** point at **00;00;01;00** and an **Out** point at **00;00;04;00**.

Note: The Source In to Source Out is 3 seconds long. Remember that. You'll be quizzed in Step 9.

5 Drag the clip from the **Source Monitor**, and snap it to the beginning of Track **Video 1**.

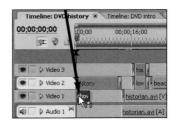

In this step, you put video underneath the scrolling title. To help make it less distracting, you will slow the video and blur it heavily.

6 On Track **Video 1**, right-click the clip, and choose **Speed/Duration**.

7 In the **Clip Speed / Duration** dialog box, change the **Speed** value to **50.00**, and click **OK**. Press the **spacebar** to play the sequence and preview the slow-motion clip. After the clip plays, press the **spacebar** to stop playback.

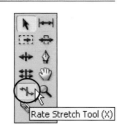

The clip on Track Video 1 is now twice as long. As you decrease the speed percentage, the duration of the clip gets longer. In the Clip Speed / Duration dialog box, you can specify speed *or* duration—both achieve the same result.

Although the clip was lengthened, it still is not long enough. No matter, because you can change the clip speed in an even better way, as you will see in the next step.

Tip: If you want the video to run at normal speed *but in reverse*, leave the speed at 100, and click Reverse Speed. (But don't do that in this step!)

8 Select the **Rate Stretch** tool from the **Tools** panel, or press the **X** key.

The Rate Stretch tool behaves a lot like the Trim Out/Trim In cursor you've come to know and love but with one major difference: The Rate Stretch tool does not change the In point or the Out point. Instead, it *stretches* a clip to get it to extend to the new Out point.

9 On Track **Video 1**, position your cursor over the **Out** point of the first clip. When the mouse changes to the **Rate Stretch** cursor, click and drag the **Out** point and **snap** it to the beginning of the first transition on Track **Video 1**.

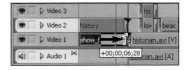

In this example, the Source In to Source Out is *still* only 3 seconds long. But instead of playing at 100 percent speed, the clip's *rate* was *stretched* to roughly 23 percent speed, so it takes much longer to play in the sequence.

10 Select the **Selection** tool from the **Tools** panel, or press **V**.

11 In the **Effects** panel **Video Effects > Blur & Sharpen** folder, drag the **Gaussian Blur** effect to the slow-motion clip on Track **Video 1**. In the **Source Monitor** panel, select the **Effect Controls** tab to bring it to the foreground.

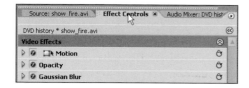

12 In the **Effect Controls** panel, click the **arrow** icon next to **Gaussian Blur** to display its properties. Change the **Blurriness** value to **40.0**. In the **Timeline**, drag the **CTI** to the beginning of the sequence. Press the **spacebar** to play the slow-motion clip. Press the **spacebar** to stop playback when it's done.

Tip: A heavy Gaussian Blur effect can help turn ordinary video into background video for text by smoothing it and making it less distracting. Also, it can help mask the jerkiness of slow-motion video.

Now it's time to create a frame hold (freeze frame). A common usage of a frame hold is to freeze the last frame of a clip after it finishes playing.

13 In the same sequence, at the end of Track **Video 1**, right-click the **media_relations.avi** clip, and choose **Copy**.

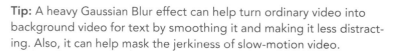

When you select the clip, the linked audio is also selected. That's OK.

In this clip, the actor didn't pause long before breaking character. (In other words, as soon as she stopped speaking, she smiled or did something you don't want the audience to catch.) You will freeze the video to give you ample time to fade out or cross dissolve.

14 Hold down the **Shift** key, and snap the Timeline CTI to the **Out** point of the selected clip. Click the name of Track **Video 1** to highlight it and set it as the target track.

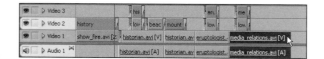
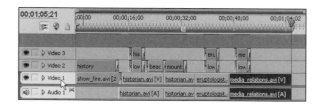

Time for another ARR (**A**nnoying **R**edundant **R**eminder): To paste a clip in the Timeline, you must first move the CTI and select the target track before pasting.

15 Choose Edit > Paste.

Now you have two identical clips, back to back. Next, you will freeze the second clip; the first clip will play back normally, and the second clip will be completely still, like an image.

---

16 Hold down the **Alt** key, and on Track **Audio 1** click the *audio portion* of the **media_relations.avi** clip. Press the **Delete** key to clear the audio clip from the sequence.

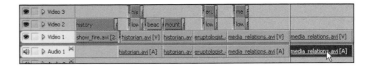

Tip: Holding down the Alt key when clicking a linked clip selects only the video *or* audio portion of a linked clip, but not both.

---

17 On Track **Video 1**, right-click the last **media_relations.avi** clip, and choose **Frame Hold**.

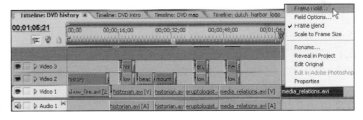

In the Frame Hold Options dialog box, Premiere Pro 2 gives you the option to hold (or freeze) your video on any one of several points. You can freeze the first frame—so the entire clip is a still image of the first frame. Or you can hold the last frame, or you can even hold a marker (if you've applied a marker to the video clip).

---

18 In the **Frame Hold Options** dialog box, turn on the **Hold On** check box. Change the pop-up menu to **Out Point**. Click **OK**.

---

19 In the **Timeline**, drag the **CTI** a few seconds to the left. Press the **spacebar** to play the hold effect you've just created. Press the **spacebar** to stop playback when it finishes.

---

20 Choose **File > Save**, or press **Ctrl+S**. Leave **dutch harbor promo.prproj** open for the next exercise.

I hope the frame hold you just created makes sense to you. Because you froze the last frame of Clip 2, the whole clip looked like the last frame. This happens to match the last frame of Clip 1 (because they are copies), so Clip 1 plays and appears to freeze.

The key to re-creating this effect is to have the *last frame* of the first clip be the frame you want to freeze. Then, simply make a copy, and freeze the copy. You can also do this to a clip's In point, such as if you want a clip to look frozen and then start playing after a few seconds.

Frame Hold Options

In the previous exercise, you were introduced to the **Frame Hold Options** dialog box. When you are creating a frame hold, you have a few options from which to choose. I briefly described them in the previous exercise, but here is a more in-depth look at each option:

Hold On: You must turn on the **Hold On** check box to activate the hold effect. The pop-up menu to the right lets you choose which frame to hold. **In Point** is the first frame of the clip, and **Out Point** is the last frame of the clip.

You are not limited to just those two points. You can also add a clip marker on *any* frame of video and choose to hold on **Marker 0**. To add a clip marker, move the **CTI** to the frame you want to mark, select the clip, and choose **Marker > Set Clip Marker > Next Available Numbered**. (Note: This works only for **Marker 0**, so it *has* to be the first marker you apply to the clip.)

Hold Filters: If the **Hold Filters** check box is on, any animated filters will be frozen. The filter will still be applied, but the filter values

will not change over time if you've added keyframes. (Notice the vestigial use of the word **filter**!)

Deinterlace: When the **Deinterlace** check box is on, one field of an interlaced video clip is doubled, and the other field is removed, which prevents **combing artifacts**. This sounds technical, but it's a fancy way of saying, "It prevents the video from flickering." That's oversimplifying things a bit, but you can always turn off this option and then turn it on again to see whether you notice a difference. The flicker will be most apparent in video clips displaying thin lines and fast movement.

You are left with this frame-hold caveat: Unlike still images, which can have a (nearly) infinite duration, frame holds can last only as long as the clip to which you apply them. If you create a frame hold on a 3-second clip, your frame hold can play for a maximum of 3 seconds.

If you need the frame hold to last *longer* than the original clip, you have two options: you can change the duration of the clip so it plays longer, or you can export the frame as a still image on your hard drive and then import the image into a sequence. You'll learn more about exporting to a still image in Chapter 13, *"Exporting to Files and Tape."*

Creating a Picture-in-Picture Effect

No doubt you've seen a picture-in-picture effect before, most likely on the evening news. A picture-in-picture effect is a small clip of video playing in the corner of the entire screen, such as a news clip playing above the shoulder of the news anchor. Like the other looks you have created, Premiere Pro 2 doesn't have a built-in picture-in-picture effect. Rather, you will make it from scratch. In this exercise, you too will partake in the sheer joy of creating a picture-in-picture effect.

---

1 If you followed the previous exercise, **dutch harbor promo.prproj** should still be open in Premiere Pro 2. If it's not, click **Open Project** on the **Welcome Screen**. Navigate to the **c:\exercise_files\chap_07** folder, click **exercise05.prproj** to select it, and click **Open**.

---

2 Choose **File > Save As**. Navigate to the **c:\exercise_files\dutch_harbor** folder. Name the file **dutch harbor promo.prproj**, and click **Save**.

Note: If a previous version of dutch harbor promo.prproj already exists, you may be asked to replace it. Click Yes.

---

3 At the top of the **Timeline**, select the **DVD map** tab to bring the sequence to the foreground.

You need to place the picture-in-picture effect on the topmost video track for it to show on top of the existing video. If you have used all your available tracks, Premiere Pro 2 makes it handy to quickly add more tracks.

---

4 On Track **Video 3**, right-click, and choose **Add Tracks**.

You can right-click any of the track names to add a track; this example just happens to use Track Video 3.

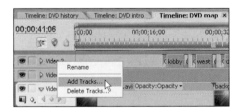

5 In the **Add Tracks** dialog box, make sure you have specified **Add 1 Video Track(s)**, and change **Audio Tracks** to **Add 0 Audio Track(s)**. Click **OK**.

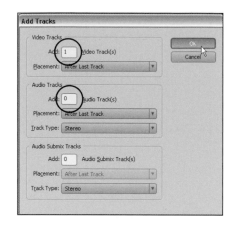

6 If necessary, scroll up in the **Timeline** to see the new Track **Video 4**. Right-click the track name **Video 4**, and choose **Rename**. Type **PiP**, and press **Enter** to accept the new track name.

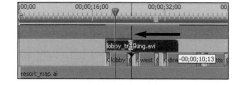

7 In the **Project** panel **Video** bin, drag the **lobby_tracking.avi** clip to Track **PiP**, and snap it to the start of the transition before the **lobby** title.

8 Position your cursor over the **Out** point of the **lobby_tracking.avi** clip in Track **PiP**, and snap the **Out** point to the end of the **lobby** title.

9 Drag the **Timeline CTI** to any position over the **lobby _tracking.avi** clip so you can see it in the **Program Monitor**. With the clip still selected, in the **Effect Controls** panel, expand the **Motion** properties. Change the **Scale** value to **50.0**.

10 In the **Program Monitor**, click the **Safe Margins** button to view the action and title safe margins, if they are not already showing.

11 In the **Program Monitor**, click in the middle of the **lobby_ tracking.avi** clip, and drag and drop it on the upper-right corner of the **Program Monitor**, just within the action safe margin.

Usually, the edges of a video clip are not visible on a video monitor. However, when scaling down for a picture in-picture effect, you may see black vertical lines on both sides of the clip. The Crop effect helps crop out these areas along the sides.

12 In the **Effects** panel **Video Effects** folder, scroll to the **Transform** folder, and click the arrow icon to expand its contents. On Track **PiP**, drag the **Crop** effect, and drop it on the **lobby_tracking.avi** clip.

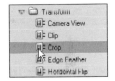

13 In the **Effect Controls** panel, click the **arrow** icon next to **Crop** to display its properties. Change the **Left** value to **2.0** and the **Right** value to **2.0**.

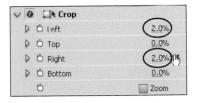

This should be enough to crop out the black areas of the clip in the Program Monitor.

14 In the **Project** panel **Video** bin, drag the **room_ interior.avi** clip to Track **PiP**, and snap it to the beginning of the transition before the **west towers** title.

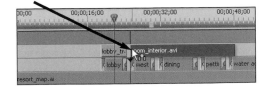

15 Position your mouse over the **Out** point of the **room_interior.avi** clip, and snap it to the end of the **west towers** title. Drag the **Timeline CTI** to any position above the clip.

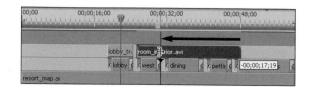

16 On Track **PiP**, right-click the **lobby_tracking.avi** clip, and choose **Copy**. Right-click the **room_interior.avi** clip, and choose **Paste Attributes**.

This applies all of the motion properties and effects from the lobby_tracking.avi clip to the room_interior.avi clip.

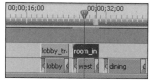

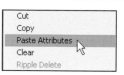

17 In the **Program Monitor**, click in the center of the **room_interior.avi** clip, and drag and drop it on the lower-right corner, just within the action safe margins.

A convenient feature of the Paste Attributes command is the ability to copy from a single clip and paste to multiple clips. In the next series of steps, you will insert three clips into the sequence, without changing their appearance. Then, once all three clips are in the sequence, you will paste attributes to all of them at once.

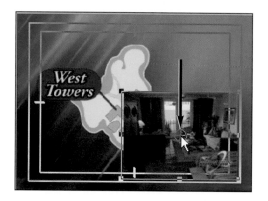

18 In the **Project** panel **Video** bin, drag the **restaurant_tracking.avi** clip to Track **PiP**, and snap it to the beginning of the transition before the **dining** title. Snap trim the **Out** point of **restaurant_tracking.avi** to the end of the **dining** title.

19 In the **Project** panel **Video** bin, drag the **tiger.avi** clip to Track **PiP**, and snap it to the beginning of the transition before **petting zoo** title. Snap trim the **Out** point of **tiger.avi** to the end of the **petting zoo** title.

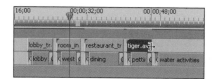

20 In the **Project** panel **Video** bin, drag the **scuba.avi** clip to Track **PiP**, and snap it to the beginning of the transition before **water activities** title.

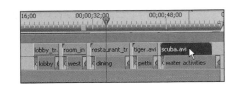

You can leave the Out point alone because the end of this sequence is just post-roll.

Video-geek vocab: Post-roll refers to any excess video after a clip or sequence. This can be handy to leave when you need extra video for transitioning, for example. You can always trim this later, but it's better to have it than need it and not have it.

Next, it's time to paste many attributes in one fell swoop.

---

21 On Track **PiP**, right-click **room_interior.avi**, and choose **Copy**. Click **restaurant_tracking.avi**. Hold down the **Shift** key, and click the **tiger.avi** and **scuba.avi** clips to select all three clips.

The restaurant_tracking.avi, tiger.avi, and scuba.avi clips should be selected.

---

22 Right-click any of the three selected clips, and choose **Paste Attributes**.

---

23 Choose **Edit > Deselect All**.

Tip: You can also click any blank spot of the Timeline to deselect the clips.

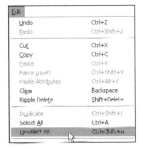

---

24 Drag the **Timeline CTI** to any position above the **restaurant_tracking.avi** clip on Track **PiP**.

---

25 In the **Program Monitor**, click and drag the center of the **restaurant_tracking.avi** clip, and drop it on the upper-left corner of the monitor, just inside the action safe margin.

---

26 Drag the **Timeline CTI** to any position above the tiger.avi clip on Track **PiP**. In the **Program Monitor**, click and drag the center of **tiger.avi**, and drop it on the *far* lower-left corner.

Be sure to drag the anchor point beyond the action safe margin because the map will otherwise be obstructed.

The scuba.avi clip is just fine where it is, so you don't need to drag that clip in the Program Monitor.

27 Drag the **Timeline CTI** to the beginning of the sequence. Press the **spacebar** to begin playback. After previewing all your hard work, press the **spacebar** to stop playback.

To add some visual interest to your picture-in-picture effect, you can easily apply a drop shadow and bevel. In addition, you can apply both of these effects to the same clip, tweak them to your liking, and then copy both effects to other clips in the sequence.

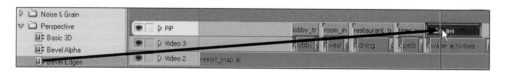

28 Position the **Timeline CTI** over the **scuba.avi** clip on Track **PiP**. In the **Effects** panel **Video Effects > Perspective** folder, drag the **Bevel Edges** effect, and drop it on **scuba.avi**.

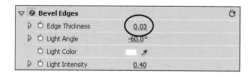

29 In the **Effect Controls** panel, click the triangle next to **Bevel Edges** to expand its properties. Click on the **Edge Thickness** value, and type a new value of **0.03**.

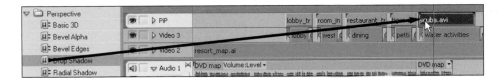

30 In the **Effects** panel **Video Effects > Perspective** folder, drag the **Drop Shadow** effect, and drop it on **scuba.avi**.

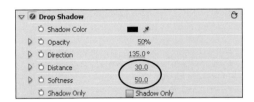

31 In the **Effect Controls** panel, click the triangle next to **Drop Shadow** to expand its properties. Click the **Distance** value, and type a new value of **30.0**. Click the **Softness** value, and type a new value of **50.0**.

Since you now have the two effects set up, you can copy both effects to other clips in the sequence. However, you do *not want* to use the Paste Attributes command—because that will paste *all* attributes, including position (which would cause you to lose all that positioning you did on each clip).

Instead, Premiere Pro 2 allows you to copy *just* the effects from a clip by selecting the desired effects in the Effect Controls panel and choosing Edit > Copy.

32 In the **Effect Controls** panel, click the effect name **Bevel Edges** to select it. Hold down the **Shift** key, and click the effect name **Drop Shadow** to select all the effects you want at once.

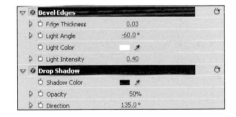

33 Choose **Edit > Copy**.

After copying the desired effects, the next step is to paste them onto different clips in the sequence. Luckily, Premiere Pro 2 lets you select multiple clips, so you can paste the effects onto many clips at one time.

34 In the **Timeline** panel, click **tiger.avi** on Track **PiP**. Next, hold down the **Shift** key, and click each of the three clips to the left: **restaurant_tracking.avi**, **room_interior.avi**, and **lobby_tracking.avi**.

You should have a total of four clips selected.

---

35 Choose **Edit > Paste**.

Voila! It is that simple. You just pasted the two copied effects onto all four clips at one time. To check out your handiwork, play the sequence.

Note: If you switch applications—for example, to check your e-mail (*tsk, tsk*)—then the effects copied to memory may be lost. Make sure you paste right away after copying.

---

36 Drag the **Timeline CTI** to the beginning of the sequence. Press the **spacebar** to begin playback. After previewing all your hard work, press the **spacebar** to stop playback.

---

37 Choose **File > Save**, or press **Ctrl+S**. Choose **File > Close** to close this project.

In this exercise, you used the Scale property of the Motion fixed effect to reduce your video, and then you applied a Crop effect to remove the black bands on both sides of the video clips. You will usually notice these bands when creating picture-in-picture effects using clips recorded by video cameras.

Usually, these bands are not seen because they are so far on the edges of the clips. However, when you reduce the entire clip, suddenly the "hidden" area is now visible, so you have to take care to clean up the edges.

So far, all the fixed effects you have modified and all of the video effects you have applied have been static. In other words, they don't change. They just sit there, doing their best to look pretty.

But what if you want a clip to *move* across the screen? What if you want an effect to gradually change over time, like a black-and-white clip that suddenly becomes colorized? Both of these actions require your effects to change over time. This is called **keyframing** and is the focus of the next chapter.

8

Animating Effects

In Adobe Premiere Pro 2, you can animate both fixed effects and video effects. No, you don't "animate" them like a cartoon; rather, the effects can change subtly over time. Perhaps you'd like a still image to slowly zoom out over time. Maybe you want to rotate a logo in a circle for about 5 seconds. Maybe you'd like to pixilate someone's face so you don't get involved in a nasty lawsuit. In this sense, animating refers to changing the values of an effect over time. To aid you in this process, it's time to learn about the wonderful world of keyframes.

Understanding Keyframes

So far, the fixed effects and video effects you have applied have been **static effects**. In other words, the effects haven't changed over time. When you changed an effect's value, such as blurriness, it applied equally to the entire clip, from start to finish. For example, a clip would begin with a blurriness of 4.0 and end with a blurriness of 4.0.

When you create **animated effects**, Premiere Pro 2 changes the value over time. For example, your clip could begin with a blurriness of 0.0 and end with a blurriness of 4.0. To achieve these animated effects, Premiere Pro 2 relies on **keyframes**, which are markers used to specify an effect's property, such as position, rotation, scale, etc.

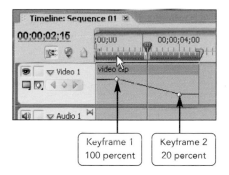

Keyframe 1
100 percent

Keyframe 2
20 percent

Each keyframe answers two vital questions:

1. What is the value?

2. When does the value occur?

As shown in the illustration here, the video clip on Track **Video 1** has two keyframes. You can ask the same two questions of both keyframes.

Keyframe #1:

1. What is the value? 100 percent.

2. When does the value occur? At 1 second.

Keyframe #2:

1. What is the value? 20 percent.

2. When does the value occur? At 4 seconds.

The amazing power of keyframes is that Premiere Pro 2 does the math to transition gradually from one keyframe value to the next. The solid, black line between the two keyframes represents the effect's value at every point in time. This line is called the **value graph** (although "solid, black line" is easier to remember).

In the same illustration, you can see Premiere Pro 2 slowly lowers the opacity from 100 percent to 20 percent over the course of 3 seconds. Also, notice the **Timeline CTI** (**C**urrent **T**ime **I**ndicator) is positioned halfway between the two keyframes. Can you guess what the value is at this point in time? (Hint: It's halfway between 100 percent and 20 percent.) Answer: 60 percent.

The value graph also informs you what happens before and after the keyframes. Before **Keyframe 1**, the value is constant at 100 percent. After **Keyframe 2** is reached, the value stays constant at 20 percent until the end of the clip.

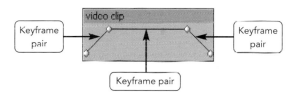

Keyframe pair

Keyframe pair

Keyframe pair

To change a value over time, Premiere Pro 2 requires a *pair* of keyframes. A clip can have as many keyframes as you want, but the work is frequently done in pairs. As shown in the illustration here, you have three pairs of keyframes:

First pair: The value increases from 0 percent to 100 percent.

Second pair: The value remains at 100 percent.

Third pair: The value changes from 100 percent to 0 percent.

The moral of keyframes is this: It takes two to tango. Premiere Pro 2 requires at least two keyframes in order to animate an effect.

Viewing Keyframes in the Effect Controls Panel

When creating and modifying keyframes, you will do much of your work in the **Effect Controls** panel, which can be overwhelming at first glance. The following introduction should help prevent any confusion.

A clip in the Timeline

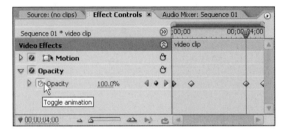

The same clip in the Effect Controls panel

First things first...to turn on keyframe mode for an effect, you must click the **Toggle animation** toggle. If this button is off, any changes you make apply to the entire clip (like the static effects you created in Chapter 7, *"Adding Video Effects"*). You can animate any effect parameter that has a stopwatch icon next to its name.

As shown in the illustration here, the **Effect Controls** panel displays all effects and keyframes

applied to a clip. The left side of the panel should look familiar; this is where you modify effect values. The right side is the **Effect Controls Timeline**, not to be confused with the regular **Timeline** you've been using thus far.

When you select a clip in the regular **Timeline**, the **Effect Controls Timeline** zooms to display only the selected clip. Each keyframe appears in a single row, next to its property. As shown in the previous illustration, the four **Opacity** keyframes appear in the row next to **Opacity**.

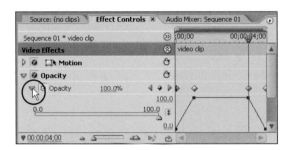

When you click the **arrow** icon to expand the effect's property, you will see the value graph in the **Effect Controls Timeline**. This is the same as the value graph dissected in the previous section.

In the following exercise, you learn how to create and modify keyframe values in the **Effect Controls** panel by animating the **Scale** and **Position** properties to create an image pan.

Animating Fixed Effects in the Effect Controls Panel

Technically speaking, an **image pan** is a camera movement left or right. However, in the world of video editing, image pan has come to mean any effect mimicking the action of a camera moving left, right, up, or down across an image. This is also called the **Ken Burns Effect**, in honor of documentary filmmaker Ken Burns. You create image pans by animating fixed effects, such as **Position** and **Scale**. In this exercise, you will create keyframes in the **Effect Controls** panel to produce an image pan.

1 On the **Welcome Screen**, click **Open Project**. In the **Open Project** dialog box, navigate to the **c:\exercise_files\chap_08** folder, click **exercise01.prproj** to select it, and click **Open**.

2 Choose **File > Save As**. Navigate to the **c:\exercise_files\dutch_harbor** folder. Name the file **dutch harbor promo.prproj**, and click **Save**.

Note: If a previous version of dutch harbor promo.prproj already exists, you may be asked to replace it. Click Yes.

3 At the top of the **Timeline**, select the **DVD history** tab to bring the sequence to the foreground. Hold down the **Shift** key, and snap the **Timeline CTI** to the **In** point of the **mountain.jpg** clip on Track **Video 2**.

4 Click the **mountain.jpg** clip to select it. If necessary, in the **Effect Controls** panel, click the **Show/Hide Timeline View** button to expand the **Effect Controls Timeline**.

This allows you to see keyframes as you create them.

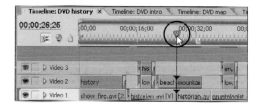

5 In the **Effect Controls** panel, click the **arrow** icon next to **Motion** to expand its properties.

In this exercise, you will create scale keyframes to slowly zoom in on the photograph. The first step you must perform when animating a property is to turn on keyframes for that property.

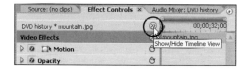

6 In the **Effect Controls** panel, click the **Toggle animation** toggle next to **Scale** to turn on the property.

Not only does this turn on keyframe mode for the Scale property, but it also creates your first keyframe. In the Effect Controls Timeline, to the right of the Scale property, you will see a black keyframe diamond.

Pop quiz: What is the value of this keyframe? Answer: 100.0. At what point in time is it found? Answer: at the beginning of the clip.

---

7 Change the **Scale** value to **55.0**.

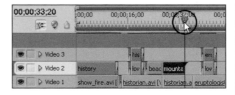

The value of your scale keyframe is now 55.0, and it is still at the beginning of the clip.

---

8 In the **Program Monitor**, click the **Play** button to preview the clip you modified.

Notice the clip doesn't do anything—the scale remains static. This is because you set only one keyframe. Remember, you need to set a *pair* of keyframes to create animation.

---

9 Hold down the **Shift** key, and snap the **Timeline CTI** to the last frame of the **mountain.jpg** clip on Track **Video 2**.

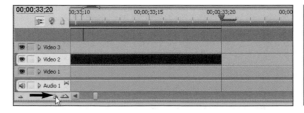

Although you snapped to the last frame of the mountain.jpg clip, notice the Program Monitor displays the *next* frame of the historian.avi clip. This highlights a primary frustration many editors have with Premiere Pro 2: When you snap to the end of a clip, you are actually snapping to the *first frame* of the next clip.

Does this make sense? No. Is there a workaround? Yes!

---

10 In the lower-left corner of the **Timeline,** drag the **Zoom Slider** as far to the right as it will go to zoom in as close as possible at the **CTI.**

This step underscores the point made earlier. When zoomed in as close as possible, you can see the red line of the Timeline CTI positioned immediately after the mountain.jpg clip on Track Video 2. The Program Monitor always displays the frame immediately *to the right* of the CTI.

---

11 Press the **left arrow** key once to move the **CTI** one frame to the left.

Now the frame immediately to the right of the CTI is the last frame of the mountain.jpg clip. In addition, the Program Monitor displays the mountain.jpg clip.

So…when you want to view the last frame of a clip, first snap to the end of the clip and then go one frame to the left. This is especially important when creating keyframes. If this concept seems foreign to you—don't worry. You will do it many (many) more times.

---

12 Press the **backslash** (\) key to zoom out to the entire sequence.

---

13 In the **Effect Controls** panel, change the **Scale** value to **70.0**.

Changing a value creates a new keyframe at the CTI.

Although it's partially obscured (because it's at the end of the clip), you can see you create a new keyframe when you change the Scale value. The value of this keyframe is 70.0, and its position is the last frame of the clip.

This is worth repeating, so chant the keyframe mantra three times a day: *Changing a value creates a new keyframe at the CTI.*

---

14 Drag the Timeline CTI to any point before the **mountain.jpg** clip. Press the **spacebar** to play the sequence and preview your animated scale. As it plays, watch the **Scale** value slowly increase by itself. When done previewing, press the **spacebar** to stop playback.

Way to go! You just completed your first keyframe pair. Time to practice some more.…

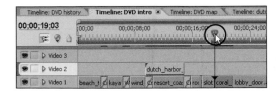

15 At the top of the **Timeline**, select the **DVD intro** tab to bring the sequence to the foreground. Hold down the **Shift** key, and snap the **Timeline CTI** to the beginning of the **coral_reef.avi** clip on Track **Video 1**.

16 Click the **coral_reef.avi** clip to select it. In the **Effect Controls** panel, click the **arrow** icon next to **Motion** to expand its properties.

Notice the Scale value, for the entire clip, is currently 70.0.

---

17 Next to **Scale**, click the **Toggle animation** toggle to turn on keyframe mode.

Premiere Pro 2 automatically creates an initial keyframe. The value of the keyframe is 70.0.

---

18 Hold down the **Shift** key, and snap the **Timeline CTI** to the end of the **coral_reef.avi** clip on Track **Video 1**. Press the **left arrow** key to move one frame to the left at **00;00;21;18**.

Remember, to make keyframes, first move the CTI and then change the value. You just moved the CTI to the end of the clip, so now it's time to change the value.

---

19 Change the **Scale** value to **100.0** to create a new keyframe at the **CTI**.

---

20 Drag the **Timeline CTI** to any spot before the selected clip. In the **Program Monitor**, click the **Play** button to preview your changes. After the clip plays, click the **Stop** button to stop playback.

Hmm, that zoom in moves a little too fast. It's not quite the calm, tranquil movement you want to see in a resort video. This quick movement is caused by the value increasing from 70 to 100, a difference of 30 percent. To slow down the zoom in, perhaps the value could instead increase from 70 to 80, which is a modest difference of only 10 percent.

To make this change, you need to change the value of the final keyframe from 100 to 80. When changing an *existing* keyframe, it is extremely important your CTI is positioned directly on the keyframe. This next step will explain why.

21 Drag the **Timeline CTI** to the middle of the **coral_reef.avi** clip at **00;00;20;07**. In the **Effect Controls** panel, change the **Scale** value to **80.0**.

You created the 80 percent keyframe you wanted, but unfortunately you did it at the wrong point in time. Instead of modifying the *existing* keyframe, you created a new one. Now you have three keyframes, and you wanted only two. Luckily, removing keyframes is as easy as adding them.

---

22 Click the **Add/Remove Keyframe** button to delete the existing keyframe at the **CTI**.

Clicking the Add/Remove Keyframe button *removes* an existing keyframe at the CTI. And, as the name implies, the Add/Remove Keyframe button *adds* a new keyframe if *none exists* at the CTI.

This concludes your lesson on why positioning the CTI is important.

OK, let's return to the task at hand. You want to change the value of the last keyframe from 100 percent to 80 percent. To modify an existing keyframe, the CTI *must* be positioned precisely on top of the keyframe.

To assist you in the task of positioning the CTI with precision, Premiere Pro 2 provides the Keyframe Navigator. This set of buttons appears when you put a property in keyframe mode.

The Go to Previous Keyframe button (the left arrow) of the Keyframe Navigator automatically snaps the CTI to any keyframes to the left. The Go to Next Keyframe button (the right arrow) snaps the CTI to any keyframes to the right of the CTI.

For example, right now your Timeline CTI is in the middle of the two keyframes at 00;00;20;07. To modify the *last* keyframe, which is to the right of the CTI, you should click the Go to Next Keyframe button in the Keyframe Navigator.

---

23 In the **Effect Controls** panel, click the **Go to Next Keyframe** button (the right arrow).

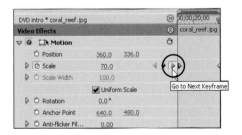

This snaps the Timeline CTI to the position of the next keyframe, at 00;00;21;18.

24 Change the **Scale** value to **80.0**. Drag the **Timeline CTI** to any point before the clip. In the **Program Monitor**, click the **Play** button to play the sequence to preview the animated effect. When done, click **Stop**.

Premiere Pro 2 doesn't limit the number of properties you can animate. In fact, you can animate every property on a single clip, if you feel like it.

In the next series of steps, you will add Position keyframes to the same clip.

---

25 In the **Effect Controls** panel, click the **Go to Previous Keyframe** button until the **CTI** is positioned at the first keyframe.

---

26 In the **Effect Controls** panel, click the **Toggle animation** toggle next to **Position** to turn on that property's keyframe mode.

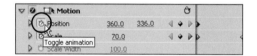

This creates a new Position keyframe at the CTI. In the Effect Controls Timeline, you can now see a total of three keyframes: two for Scale and one next to Position.

---

27 In the **Effect Controls** panel, click the **Go to Next Keyframe** button next to the **Scale** keyframe.

This ensures the Position keyframe you are about to create aligns with the existing Scale keyframe.

---

28 Change the **Position** y value to **291.0**.

Remember, changing the value creates a new Position keyframe, which happens to be aligned with the final Scale keyframe.

---

29 Drag the **Timeline CTI** before the current clip. In the **Program Monitor**, click the **Play** button to preview your animated effect. When done, click **Stop**.

Notice the "camera" tilts down as it zooms in.

---

30 Choose **File > Save**, or press **Ctrl+S**. Leave **dutch harbor promo.prproj** open for the next exercise.

Good work! You just completed one of the more difficult concepts in Premiere Pro 2. If it takes you some time to wrap your mind around keyframes, don't worry—it's far from an intuitive process. It just takes time and lots of practice.

Far be it from me to tell you what to do, but if you happen to have a highlighter handy, you might consider using it on these next few sentences. To animate an effect, begin by moving the CTI to where you want the first keyframe to be and set the initial value (if required). Next, turn on keyframe mode for the desired property.

After that, repeat the same process: Move the CTI to where you would like the next keyframe to be, and change the value of the property.

And, of course, don't forget your keyframe mantra: *Changing a value creates a new keyframe at the CTI.*

In this exercise, you animated fixed effects. Premiere Pro 2 also lets you modify video effects. Thankfully, the process is the same, so the next exercise may feel like review, since you already know how to make keyframes.

VIDEO: | **keyframe_basics.mov**

Creating, modifying, and removing keyframes may be the most challenging task you face in your Premiere Pro 2 education. To learn more about keyframes, check out **keyframe_basics.mov** in the **videos** folder on the **Premiere Pro 2 HOT DVD-ROM**.

Animating Video Effects in the Effect Controls Panel

You can animate any effect property that has the **Toggle animation** toggle (the stopwatch icon) next to it. This is good news because you can animate nearly all video effects. In this exercise, you will animate a blur to start at a value of 0.0 (no blur) and steadily get blurrier over time. So far, you have learned how to create keyframes from start to finish. However, the real power of keyframes is the ability to create them in any order you'd like. For example, sometimes you know where the effect should be *done* animating, but you're not so sure where it should start animating. This is a perfect opportunity to build the keyframes in reverse order, from finish to start.

---

1 If you followed the previous exercise, **dutch harbor promo.prproj** should still be open in Premiere Pro 2. If it's not, click **Open Project** on the **Welcome Screen**. Navigate to the **c:\exercise_files\chap_08** folder, click **exercise02.prproj** to select it, and click **Open**.

---

2 Choose **File > Save As**. Navigate to the **c:\exercise_files\dutch_harbor** folder. Name the file **dutch harbor promo.prproj**, and click **Save**.

Note: If a previous version of dutch harbor promo.prproj already exists, you may be asked to replace it. Click Yes.

---

3 At the top of the **Timeline**, select the **DVD history** tab to bring the sequence to the foreground. Drag the **Timeline CTI** to the beginning of the sequence. On Track **Video 1**, click the **show_fire.avi** clip to view its effects in the **Effect Controls** panel.

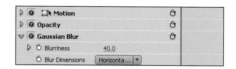

This clip has a Gaussian Blur video effect (with a value of 40.0), which you applied in Chapter 7, *"Adding Video Effects."* The goal in this exercise is to have the video start playing with no blur and then have it get really blurry before the rolling text appears.

---

4 Drag the **Timeline CTI** to **00;00;01;17**.

This marks the point in time where the blurriness should be at its maximum because the rolling text is beginning to appear in the Program Monitor. You want the background to be nice and soft by the time people need to start reading the rolling text.

5 Next to the **Blurriness** property of **Gaussian Blur**, click the **Toggle animation** toggle to turn on keyframe mode.

The keyframe initially created when you turn on keyframe mode takes on the current value of the effect. In this case, Blurriness was already set to 40.0, so the value of the initial keyframe is now 40.0.

Now it's time to work backward. In this step, you set your *end* keyframe. Next, you will specify the *beginning* keyframe value.

---

6 Drag the **Timeline CTI** to the first frame of the **show_fire.avi** clip. In the **Effect Controls** panel, change the **Blurriness** value to **0.0**.

---

7 In the **Program Monitor**, click the **Play** button to play the sequence to preview the effect. When done previewing the clip, click the **Stop** button.

It took only 1 second, but you should have noticed the effect start "sharp" and quickly blur.

Depending on the speed of your computer, the video may seem a tad choppy. This is because Premiere Pro 2 is trying to do the arithmetic for blurring the background video while displaying rolling text at the same time. This looks like a job for rendering.

Rendering is the act of combining effects and clips into a temporary file that Premiere Pro 2 can play back with ease. To learn more about rendering, see the sidebar immediately following this exercise.

---

8 Press the **backslash** (\) key to zoom the sequence to fit in the **Timeline** panel.

Whenever you ask Premiere Pro 2 to render, it always renders the section of the sequence below the work area bar. The work area bar can be shortened, which allows you to render just a small portion of the entire sequence. This can save time when rendering.

---

9 At the top of the **Timeline**, grab the right handle of the work area bar, and snap it to the end of the **show_fire.avi** clip.

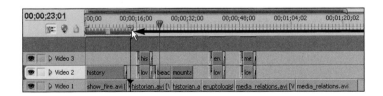

Notice the red strips below the Time Ruler. These indicate areas of the sequence that may require rendering in order to play back without compromise.

---

10 Choose **Sequence > Render Work Area**. Premiere Pro 2 displays the **Rendering** dialog box while it renders.

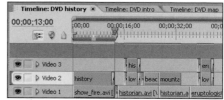

Depending on the speed of your computer, the rendering process may take up to 30 seconds. If Premiere Pro 2 does not automatically play the work area after rendering, press the Enter key. You should notice the background video plays much more smoothly.

Keep in mind you rendered only about 13 seconds of video. If you had rendered the entire sequence, it would have taken substantially longer. Instead of rendering the entire sequence, the work area bar helps you reduce the waiting time by rendering only a specific area.

Notice how the red render bar below the work area turned green. This indicates a portion of a sequence that has been rendered and can be played back at full quality.

---

11 Click the **Go to Previous Keyframe** or **Go to Next Keyframe** button until the **Timeline CTI** is positioned at the second keyframe, at **00;00;01;17**.

Right now, the Blurriness value starts at 0.0 and takes 1 second and 17 frames to get to 40.0. Perhaps it could take a little longer....

---

12 In the lower-left corner of the **Effect Controls** panel, click and drag the blue current time to the right until the **CTI** is at **00;00;03;14**.

---

13 Click and drag the second keyframe to the **CTI**.

Unfortunately, the keyframe does *not* snap, so just eyeball it as best you can.

A nice feature in Premiere Pro 2 is the ability to drag keyframes to new locations.

Also notice the green render line reverts to a red line. Because you changed the effect parameters, Premiere Pro 2 needs to render the area again.

---

14 In the **Effect Controls** panel, click the **arrow** icon next to **Blurriness** to view its value graph. (For now, ignore the velocity graph at the bottom of the panel.)

Remember the value graph from earlier in this chapter? This is a simple one to decipher; the first keyframe starts at 0.0, and the graph slowly increases until it reaches the second keyframe. After that, the value doesn't change (represented by a flat line).

Perhaps, instead of a gradual blur, you'd like the video to play without a blur for as long as possible and then heavily blur at the last second. To quickly achieve this, read on.

---

15 Grab the first keyframe, and drag it about halfway to the second keyframe.

Again, the position doesn't have to be perfect—releasing the mouse anywhere in the middle will suffice.

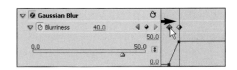

The value graph now describes what happens before the first keyframe; the value stays flat at 0.0 until it reaches the first keyframe.

---

16 Choose **Sequence > Render Work Area** to render and preview the clips below the work area bar.

Note: If playback doesn't automatically start, press the Enter key.

---

17 Choose **File > Save**, or press **Ctrl+S**. Leave **dutch harbor promo.prproj** open for the next exercise.

This exercise offered a potpourri of tips to better explain the nuances of creating keyframes. You learned how to access the value graph and how to drag keyframes to new points in time. You also learned how to use the work area bar to focus on a small section of a sequence in order to save time when rendering. The following sidebar contains a detailed explanation of the usage and benefits of rendering.

Rendering and the Red Render Bar

What is rendering? Rendering is the act of converting clips, or compositing effects, into a common format that is easier for Premiere Pro 2 to play. Any area of the **Timeline** that has been rendered appears with a green render bar.

What does the red render bar indicate? The red render bar displays above any clip needing to be rendered. This is the way Premiere Pro 2 alerts you that playback quality may suffer in the region below the red render bar.

Which clips need to be rendered? Titles and graphics need to be rendered. Any clip with an effect or a transition needs to be rendered. Any clip whose format does not match the project format needs to be rendered.

Why do clips need to be rendered? The types of clips mentioned in the previous paragraph cause Premiere Pro 2 to "think" harder than usual. If you don't render, Premiere Pro 2 does its best to display a "good enough" approximation of these clips during playback. But if you want to see the finished results at maximum quality, then you must render.

Why is rendering helpful? Premiere Pro 2 can play the rendered area at full quality because the compositing and converting has already been done.

How can I prevent rendering? To a certain extent, you'll always have clips that need to be rendered—whenever you add an effect or transition or make a title. When creating a new project, it is important to pick a project preset matching the format of your camera/source video. If the formats don't match, you will see a red render bar under every single clip!

3 | Creating 3D Motion with Light Reflection

Among the most popular effects in Premiere Pro 2 is the **Basic 3D** effect. This allows you to take a video clip, still image, or title and swivel it in three dimensions, like a revolving door. So far you have positioned and rotated your clips in only two dimensions, using the fixed effects. But the fixed effects lack *depth*. You can make clips look like they are very far away from the "camera" or like they are protruding into the camera. In addition, the **Basic 3D** effect has a light reflection capability, which allows you to add some shine to the surface of your clip.

1 If you followed the previous exercise, **dutch harbor promo.prproj** should still be open in Premiere Pro 2. If it's not, click **Open Project** on the **Welcome Screen**. Navigate to the **c:\exercise_files\chap_08** folder, click **exercise03.prproj** to select it, and click **Open**.

2 Choose **File > Save As**. Navigate to the **c:\exercise_files\dutch_harbor** folder. Name the file **dutch harbor promo.prproj**, and click **Save**.

Note: If a previous version of dutch harbor promo.prproj already exists, you may be asked to replace it. Click Yes.

3 At the top of the **Timeline**, select the **DVD map** tab to bring the sequence to the foreground. Select the **Razor** tool from the **Tools** panel.

In this exercise, you will apply the 3D effect to the resort map graphic. However, to save rendering time and processing, you won't apply it to the *entire* clip. Using the Razor tool allows you to "splice" the clip into multiple, shorter clips.

4 In the **Timeline**, position the **Razor** tool over the **resort_map.ai** clip on Track **Video 2**, below the **In** point of the **lobby** title. Click once to splice the clip into two clips.

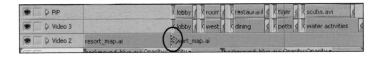

The **Razor** tool splices at the exact position of the razor cursor. This divides the clip into two segments.

5 Select the **Selection** tool from the **Tools** panel.

6 In the **Effects** panel **Video Effects > Perspective** folder, drag the **Basic 3D** effect to the *first* instance of the **resort_map.ai** clip on Track **Video 2**.

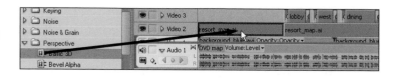

Because you spliced the resort_map.ai clip in two, you can modify one clip without affecting the other. In fact, as far as Premiere Pro 2 knows, these clips are completely separate.

This is helpful when adding a processor-intensive effect to a clip. In a way, razoring a clip is a quick way to apply an effect to only a segment of a clip. This saves on rendering time.

---

7 Drag the **Timeline CTI** to the beginning of the sequence.

Here's where keyframes come into play. You can set keyframes to automatically rotate the clip so it appears to swivel like a revolving door. In this case, you will set keyframes to swivel the image a quarter turn and then return to its starting point.

---

8 In the **Effect Controls** panel, click the **arrow** icon next to **Basic 3D** to expand its properties. Turn on keyframe mode for **Swivel**, **Tilt**, and **Distance to Image** by clicking the **Toggle animation** toggle for each property.

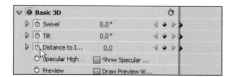

This creates three initial keyframes, one for each property. You have created your initial keyframes, so you should next move the CTI to the position of the next keyframes.

---

9 Hold down the **Shift** key, and snap the **Timeline CTI** to the end of the **resort_map.ai** clip. Press the **left arrow** key once.

This moves you to the last frame of the clip.

Here's where some brainpower is required: You want the graphic to start at 0.0, swivel a certain amount, and then return to 0.0. So, the end keyframes should also be 0.0, just like the start keyframes. Make sense?

So far you have learned to create new keyframes by changing the property value. However, in this case, the value is *already* 0.0! Therefore, you *don't* want to change anything.

Another method you can use to create keyframes is to click the Add/Remove Keyframe button. This adds a new keyframe with the current value displayed next to the property.

---

10 Click the **Add/Remove Keyframe** button for **Swivel**, **Tilt**, and **Distance to Image**.

This creates three new keyframes at the CTI. In addition, the value of each keyframe is 0.0, since that is what is displayed in the Effect Controls panel next to each property.

---

11 Drag the **Timeline CTI** to the beginning of the sequence. Click the **Play** button in the **Program Monitor** to preview the effect. After the first clip plays, click **Stop** to end playback.

Even though your Basic 3D effect has six keyframes (two for each property), nothing happened, right? This is because the first and last keyframes are identical in value, so the value changed from 0.0 to 0.0. In other words, the values didn't change, so the effect didn't animate.

Now that the effect starts and ends at the same point, you need to add a few more keyframes in the middle to get the clip to move in 3D.

---

12 Drag the **Timeline CTI** to the center of the **resort_map.ai** clip at **00;00;08;07**. Change the **Swivel** value to **33.0**.

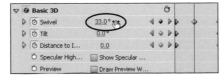

This creates a third Swivel keyframe, in between the original two. As you can see, the Swivel property of the Basic 3D effect rotates one side closer toward the camera and the other side farther away.

---

13 Change the **Tilt** value to **−25.0**. Change the **Distance to Image** value to **10.0**. In the **Program Monitor**, click the **Play** button to play the clip from the beginning and preview the animation.

---

14 Move the **Timeline CTI** back to the center of the clip. In the **Effect Controls** panel, turn on the **Show Specular Highlight** check box.

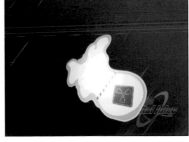

This adds a bright reflection, or highlight, to the graphic.

---

15 In the **Program Monitor**, click the **Play** button to play the clip from the beginning and preview the animation.

Did you notice during playback the specular highlight was missing? Some effects are so processor intensive that Premiere Pro 2 doesn't even try to show them during preview. To see them fully, you have to render the work area.

16 At the top of the **Timeline**, drag the right handle of the work area bar, and snap it to the end of the first **resort_map.avi** clip. Choose **Sequence > Render Work Area**.

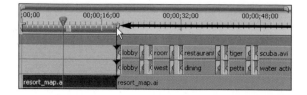

If Premiere Pro 2 does not automatically play the work area after rendering, press the Enter key.

Depending on the speed of your computer, this effect may take up to a few minutes to render. Yikes! It's a good thing you are rendering only a small section of the sequence.

---

17 Choose **File > Save**, or press **Ctrl+S**. Leave **dutch harbor promo.prproj** open for the next exercise.

The Basic 3D effect is a quick and easy way to add 3D depth to your logos, images, and even video clips, if you want. The Razor tool helps (literally) divide the task of processing so Premiere Pro 2 doesn't have to render the entire clip. In this case, you took a minute-long clip, and with the Razor tool, you applied the effect to just the first 19 seconds. Remember how long it took to render just the 19-second clip? If you had the work area bar over the entire minute-long clip, it would have been an unbearable render.

In this exercise, you added a reflective shine to your clip. However, if you really want to get detailed with lights, Premiere Pro 2 comes with an effect that allows you to add lights; you'll learn how to use it in the next exercise.

---

4 | Animating Lighting Effects

A great way to add some visual interest to a static logo is to add a **light sweep**, which creates a beam of light sweeping across the face of your logo. Watch for this on television, and you will see it used frequently on logos. In this exercise, you will get an introduction to one of the powerful new effects in Premiere Pro 2: **Lighting Effects**.

---

1 If you followed the previous exercise, **dutch harbor promo.prproj** should still be open in Premiere Pro 2. If it's not, click **Open Project** on the **Welcome Screen**. Navigate to the **c:\exercise_files\chap_08** folder, click **exercise04.prproj** to select it, and click **Open**.

---

2 Choose **File > Save As**. Navigate to the **c:\exercise_files\dutch_harbor** folder. Name the file **dutch harbor promo.prproj**, and click **Save**.

Note: If a previous version of dutch harbor promo.prproj already exists, you may be asked to replace it. Click Yes.

---

3 At the top of the **Timeline**, select the **dutch_harbor_logo** tab to bring the sequence to the fore-ground. Drag the **Timeline CTI** to the beginning of the sequence.

---

4 In the **Effects** panel, type **lighting** in the **Contains** text box.

This displays only the effects containing the word lighting.

5 In the **Effects** panel, drag the **Lighting Effects** video effect to the top clip in the sequence.

In the Program Monitor you can already see the dramatic styles you can create with the Lighting Effects effect. Also notice the effect is applied to the top clip, which is just the words Dutch Harbor. The clips on the track below are unaffected.

In this exercise, you will animate the light so it moves left to right across the letters. The first step in doing this is to get your "light" to look just right.

---

6 In the **Effect Controls** panel, click the **arrow** icon next to **Lighting Effects** to expand the effects and then expand **Light 1**. Choose **None** in the **Light Type** pop-up menu.

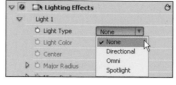

In the Program Monitor, you can see the light is turned off. In addition, the letters of Dutch Harbor are very dim.

---

7 Scroll to the end of the **Lighting Effects** properties, and change the **Ambience Intensity** to **50.0**.

This increases the ambient lighting to normal levels. The ambience properties affect the overall lighting level of the clip. Think of it like being in a room with a dimmer switch; when you increase the ambience, everything in the room gets brighter.

---

8 Scroll to the head of the **Light 1** properties. Choose **Spotlight** in the **Light Type** pop-up menu.

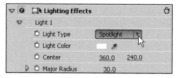

Compare this step with the illustration shown in Step 5. You can see the light is turned on again, but the ambient area "outside of the light" is definitely brighter.

Tip: The Spotlight effect casts an elliptical beam of light—like a flashlight pointing at the image. For a description of the other light types, see the sidebar following this exercise.

---

9 Click **Lighting Effects** to put the effect in direct select mode.

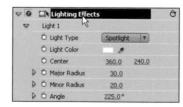

In the Program Monitor, you can see the Center property represented as a small crosshair. The light, which shines from the upper-left corner and points toward the center, is represented by a thin line leading to the center.

10 In the **Effect Controls** panel, change the **Minor Radius** value to **10.0**. Change **Major Radius** to **10.0**.

The Major Radius property specifies the length of the light, and the Minor Radius property controls the width of the light.

Now that you have your light look and ambient amount adjusted to your liking, the next step is to animate the light to move across the letters.

11 In the **Program Monitor**, drag the center of the **Light1** cone to the lower-left corner of the **Dutch Harbor** text.

The light cone now falls just outside the text. This is where your light will start.

12 Make sure the **Timeline CTI** is still at **00;00;00;00**. In the **Effect Controls** panel, click the **Toggle animation** toggle next to the **Center** property.

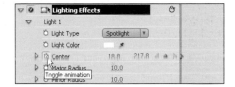

13 Move the **Timeline CTI** to **00;00;01;15**. In the **Program Monitor**, drag the center of the **Light1** cone to the top of the (imaginary) arch.

Two important things happened here: First, you dragged the light to a new position, which changed the Center property. Premiere Pro 2 created a new Center keyframe in the Effect Controls panel. (Remember, any time you change a value, a new keyframe is created; this includes dragging in the Program Monitor.)

Second, you can see the actual path the light is following, represented by a series of dots. This is visible only when the effect is in direct select mode.

14 Move the **Timeline CTI** to **00;00;03;00**. In the **Program Monitor**, drag the center of the **Light1** cone to the lower-right of the (imaginary) arch so the light cone falls just outside the text.

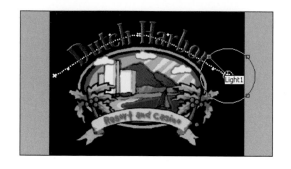

Did you notice that, as you dragged, the "path" of dots seemed to bend slightly? Instead of being a sharp angle, like a roof, the path follows a gentle curve, like the top of a hill. This is known as **keyframe interpolation** and will be discussed in detail after this exercise.

15 Drag the **Timeline CTI** to the beginning of the sequence. In the **Program Monitor**, click the **Play** button to play the sequence from the beginning and preview the effect.

To help reduce the light from looking computer generated, Premiere Pro 2 allows you to blur the edges of the light, which adds realism to your light.

16 In the **Effect Controls** panel, change **Focus** to **0.0**.

17 Drag the **Timeline CTI** to the beginning of the sequence. In the **Program Monitor**, click the **Play** button to play the sequence from the beginning and preview the effect.

Compared to the first time you previewed the effect, the light edges appear out of focus.

18 At the top of the **Timeline** panel, select the **DVD intro** tab to bring the sequence to the foreground.

19 On Track **Video 2**, drag the **Timeline CTI** to the beginning of the **dutch_harbor_logo** clip. In the **Program Monitor**, click the **Play** button to play the sequence and preview the effect. After previewing the effect, click **Stop**.

20 In the **Effects** panel, clear any text in the **Contains** text box.

Tip: This ensures you can see all of the available effects again. (Forgetting to clear this box can lead to frustration in the form of "Where did all of my effects go?!")

---

21 Choose **File > Save**, or press **Ctrl+S**. Leave **dutch harbor promo.prproj** open for the next exercise.

The Lighting Effects effect allows you to create artificial lights on your video clips and still images. The lighting effects have an endless number of uses; you can create light streaming through a window, you can make a desk lamp look like it is emitting real light, and you can catch a deer in your headlights (well, "spotlights" in this case). And don't forget, the Ambient property controls everything outside of the light. An Ambient value of 50.0 is neutral.

NOTE:

Lighting Effects

The previous exercise took you through a primer on the power of **Lighting Effects**. This is just the tip of the iceberg. Here are some of the advanced features for this effect:

Quantity: You can create up to five lights. Each light can be positioned by itself and can have a different light color, intensity, gloss, focus, angle, and so on.

Type: You can create three types of lights: spotlight, directional, and omni. In this exercise you used a spotlight. A **directional light** shines light from far away, like the sun. An **omni light** shines light directly from above, like a lightbulb over a piece of paper.

Texture: You can combine the light with textures to create 3D-like lighting and reflection. For example, the texture of a brick wall will reflect light much differently than a linoleum kitchen floor.

The Premiere Pro 2 Help file describes, in-depth, many of the effect's properties and is a great resource when you are ready to venture out on your own.

Changing Keyframe Interpolation

When you create a pair of keyframes, Premiere Pro 2 does the math to get from one value to the next. As you've experienced in this chapter, you need to create only two keyframes, and Premiere Pro 2 does the work of filling in the unknown data between the keyframes. The boring, technical term for this is **interpolation**. Adjusting interpolation allows you to fine-tune how your animation changes. For example, you can have a logo decelerate as it reaches its final destination. This is an example of **Bézier interpolation**.

Linear interpolation creates a uniform rate of change between keyframes (like a car traveling at a constant speed on the highway). **Bézier interpolation** allows the keyframe value to decelerate, like a car coming to a stop at a red light, or accelerate, like a car does when the red light turns green. Now, unless you're a high-school physics teacher, this may sound like gobbledygook. It's usually more helpful to look at a keyframe's value graph to really understand the difference.

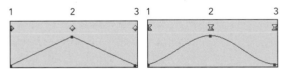

A value graph with linear interpolation (left) and Bézier interpolation (right)

As shown in the illustration here, you have three keyframes with linear interpolation (left). The value graph below the keyframes is in the form of a straight line. If it helps, remember that *linear* means *straight*. By default, most keyframes are created with linear interpolation.

You also can see the same three keyframes with Bézier interpolation (right). Rather than a linear line, the value graph is rounded and smooth. Also, instead of abruptly changing at the middle keyframe, the value slowly decelerates as it approaches the middle keyframe, creating the "mound" value graph. Notice Premiere Pro 2 changes the keyframe diamond icons to hourglass icons to signify Bézier interpolation.

Why is this so darn important? The ability to add Bézier interpolation to your keyframes adds a touch of realism to your effects. In the real world, you rarely see an object change direction or velocity in a linear fashion. For example, picture a baseball being thrown into the air. As it reaches the peak of its arc, it decelerates and for a split second is suspended in midair before gravity starts pulling it down. The value graph of the baseball's velocity would look like the Bézier curve in the illustration shown here.

Another common example is your car. When you come to a stop, your car doesn't automatically freeze. Instead, it gradually decelerates to a stop. Likewise, when the light turns green, your car doesn't suddenly zoom to 60 miles per hour instantaneously. Rather, you gradually speed up. In Premiere Pro 2, you can create this same type of deceleration and acceleration through Bézier keyframes.

Temporal Versus Spatial Interpolation

As already discussed, interpolation affects the way a keyframe changes over time. This is known as **temporal interpolation**. (*Temporal* is just a fancy word for *time*.) Examples of effects you have changed over time include **Opacity** and **Blur**.

In addition to being able to change effects temporally, you can also modify some effects spatially, known as **spatial interpolation**. This means you can modify the effects visually in the Program Monitor. Examples of effects also having a spatial quality include **Position**, **Rotation**, and **Scale**.

The dotted path in the Program Monitor represents spatial interpolation.

The value graph in the Effect Controls panel represents temporal interpolation.

You may recognize the illustration shown here from the previous exercise. The path you created for the spotlight traveling across the screen had a Bézier spatial interpolation (notice the path is gentle and curved). However, the spotlight's temporal interpolation is linear because its speed never changes. A straight line in the velocity graph represents this. To equate this to the real world—it's like a car going around a slight corner; the car takes the curve nice and gentle but doesn't change velocity as it turns.

Confused yet? Think of it like this: Temporal interpolation defines *how fast* the object travels, and spatial interpolation defines *where* the object travels. It's all about time versus space. (Einstein would have been a great video editor!)

Interpolation Methods

Premiere Pro 2 features a handful of different interpolation methods to help achieve different looks for your paths traveling across the screen. The following table describes each interpolation method and its associated keyframe icon:

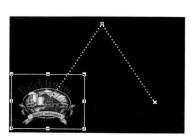

Linear spatial keyframe

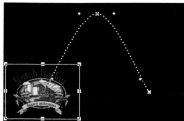

Auto Bézier interpolation

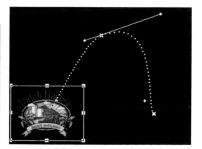

Continuous Bézier interpolation

Interpolation Methods

Keyframe icon	Description
◆	**Linear:** Spatially, the path is a straight line with sharp corners. Represented by a diamond.
●	**Auto Bezier:** Premiere Pro 2 automatically "bends" the path for the smoothest rate of change between keyframes. Represented by a circle.
⧗	**Bezier:** This interpolation method is similar to **Auto Bezier**; however, you can manually adjust the keyframe's handles to further bend the path. Represented by an hourglass.
⧗	**Continuous Bezier:** This interpolation method is similar to **Bezier**; however, when you manually adjust the path on one side of the keyframe, the path on the other side automatically adjusts to maintain a smooth transition. Represented by an hourglass.
◀	**Hold (Temporal only):** Instead of gradually changing the value over time, Premiere Pro 2 freezes the value until the next keyframe and then suddenly changes the value. Represented by a pentagon.
⧗	**Ease In (temporal only):** Gradually decelerates the value to a complete stop as it approaches a keyframe. Think of a car coming to a stop at a red light. Represented by an hourglass.
⧗	**Ease Out (temporal only):** Gradually accelerates the value leaving a keyframe. Think of a car speeding up after a green light. Represented by an hourglass.

In the next exercise, you will get to try a few of the interpolation methods and experience for yourself how they affect the keyframes in space and in time. (On the bright side, if your brain hasn't fizzled out, you are halfway toward a B.A. in physics.)

5 | Fine-Tuning Keyframes

When you're watching television, you may see a logo or text slowly come to a stop as it appears onscreen. This is an example of fine-tuning the clip's path. The ability to fine-tune keyframes by changing their interpolation methods is one of the most powerful features in Premiere Pro 2. This helps the paths appear less computer generated. In this exercise, you will "fly in" a logo with Bézier spatial interpolation to create a smooth spatial path and then use Bézier temporal interpolation to bring it to a smooth stop.

1 If you followed the previous exercise, **dutch harbor promo.prproj** should still be open in Premiere Pro 2. If it's not, click **Open Project** on the **Welcome Screen**. Navigate to the **c:\exercise_files\chap_08** folder, click **exercise05.prproj** to select it, and click **Open**.

2 Choose **File > Save As**. Navigate to the **c:\exercise_files\dutch_harbor** folder. Name the file **dutch harbor promo.prproj**, and click **Save**.

Note: If a previous version of dutch harbor promo.prproj already exists, you may be asked to replace it. Click Yes.

3 At the top of the **Timeline**, select the **DVD map** tab to bring the sequence to the foreground. Drag the **Timeline CTI** to the beginning of the sequence. In the **Project** panel **Graphics > dutch_harbor_logo** bin, drag the **dutch_harbor_logo** sequence to the beginning of Track **Video 3**.

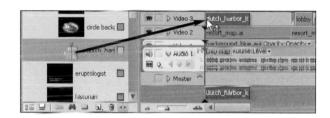

You've just nested the dutch_harbor_logo sequence on the DVD map sequence. By default, Premiere Pro 2 also includes the audio portion of the nested sequence, but the logo doesn't have any audio so you can safely remove just the audio portion.

4 Hold down the **Alt** key, and click the audio portion of the **dutch_harbor_logo** sequence on Track **Audio 2**. Press **Delete** to remove the audio.

5 On both Tracks **Video 1** and **Video 2**, click the **Toggle Track Output** toggle to temporarily turn them off.

Right now, you have a couple of effect-heavy clips on top of each other. The logo has the tracked lighting effect, and the resort_map.ai clip below has a 3D effect with reflection. Needless to say, your computer may choke while trying to play everything at once. Disabling other tracks while doing your effects work lightens your computer's load.

6 On Track **Video 3**, select the **dutch_harbor_logo** clip. In the **Effect Controls** panel, click **Motion** to put the clip in direct select mode. Click the **arrow** icon next to **Motion** to expand its properties, and change the **Anchor Point** values to **0.0** and **480.0**.

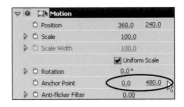 

In the Program Monitor, you can see the anchor point is now in the lower-left corner of the clip. Any rotation or scale changes you make will be based on this vertex.

Tip: You didn't have to put the clip in direct select mode to change the anchor point. Rather, you did this to see a visual representation of the anchor point while making the change.

7 In the **Effect Controls** panel, change **Scale** to **50.0**.

This should solidify the purpose of the anchor point—the item was scaled 50 percent, but everything was scaled relative to the anchor point in the lower-left corner. In other words, the lower-left corner of the clip stayed put.

8 In the **Program Monitor**, click the **View Zoom Level** pop-up menu, and change **Fit** to **25%**.

This reduces the project "screen" to 25 percent of its original size. Keep in mind, this doesn't affect output when creating the final movie. This affects only the preview while editing.

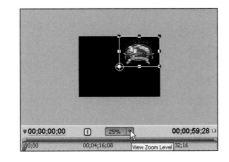

9 Click anywhere in the center of the logo, and drag it off camera to the upper-left corner of the screen.

As you move the logo to the empty part of the canvas, you will see only its handles.

The advantage of reducing the Program Monitor's zoom level is so you can move items to the empty canvas outside the screen. This allows you to start clips off camera.

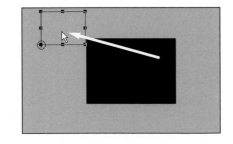

10 Make sure the **CTI** is still at **00;00;00;00**. In the **Effect Controls** panel, click the **Toggle animation** toggle next to **Position** to turn on keyframe mode.

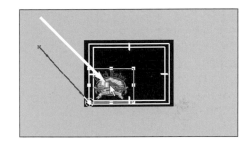

11 In the **Program Monitor**, click the **Safe Margins** button if necessary. Drag the **Timeline CTI** to **00;00;03;00**. In the **Program Monitor**, drag the clip to the lower-left corner of the screen, just inside of the title safe margins.

Here's where it gets tricky. Premiere Pro 2 provides a path handle so you can change the spatial path to a nice, soft curve. However, the handle is difficult to see. Zooming in closer may help you see the handle better.

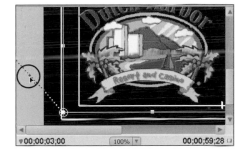

12 In the **Program Monitor**, change the **View Zoom Level** to **100%**. Scroll to the lower-left corner of the screen, and within the dotted lines of the spatial path, locate the dot that is markedly bigger than the others. Position your cursor over it.

If it is the Bézier handle, your cursor will change to an arrow with a hollow circle.

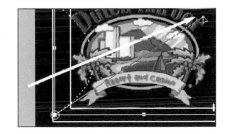

13 Make sure the **CTI** is still at **00;00;03;00**. Click and drag the Bézier handle to the upper-right corner of the **Program Monitor**.

As you drag, you can see the spatial path begin to curve. You have just changed the keyframe interpolation. Premiere Pro 2 allows you to change the Bézier curve at each keyframe. You just changed the Bézier handle of the second keyframe, but you can also drag the Bézier handle of the first keyframe to create a more rounded path.

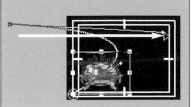

14 In the **Program Monitor**, change the **View Zoom Level** to **25%**. Click and drag the keyframe's first Bézier handle all the way across the **Program Monitor** to create a generous spatial curve.

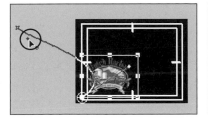

Before you drag, you should be able to see the first keyframe's Bézier handle floating by its lonesome.

15 In the **Program Monitor**, change **View Zoom Level** to **Fit**. Drag the **Timeline CTI** to the beginning of the sequence, and click the **Play** button to play the first few seconds. After the logo reaches its final destination, click the **Stop** button.

So far, so good. You just watched your clip fly in from the upper-left corner. But did you notice how the logo reached its end position and suddenly halted? If not, play the clip again and watch how quickly the logo stops. Next, you will change the temporal interpolation to fix this.

---

16 In the **Effect Controls** panel, click the **arrow** icon next to **Position** to view its velocity graph.

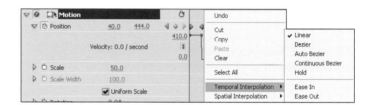

What does the velocity graph tell you? For starters, it shows the velocity is unchanged, traveling at a flat rate of 410.6 pixels per second (represented by the flat line between Keyframe 1 and Keyframe 2). After it reaches Keyframe 2, the velocity immediately drops to 0.0, which is the sudden halt you witnessed during playback.

Note: The exact values in your own project will be slightly different from the values shown throughout this exercise.

---

17 In the **Effect Controls Timeline**, right-click the second **Position** keyframe, and choose **Temporal Interpolation**.

You should see the interpolation method set to Linear (which jives with the straight line you see in the velocity graph, right?).

---

18 In the **Effect Controls Timeline**, right-click the second **Position** keyframe, and choose **Temporal Interpolation > Ease In**.

---

19 Drag the **Timeline CTI** to the beginning of the sequence. Click the **Play** button to preview the effect, and then click **Stop**.

Notice how the clip decelerates as it "eases in" to the final keyframe. In the Effect Controls Timeline, the second keyframe is now represented by an hourglass icon. The velocity graph starts at 551.6 pixels per second and gradually comes to a stop at 0.0. This is akin to a car coming to a stop at a red light (unless it is a yellow light, in which case the car would speed up!).

But maybe you'd like the clip to take longer to slow down. You can graphically change the Bézier velocity curve in the velocity graph, which you will do next.

20 In the **Effect Controls Timeline**, select the second keyframe. In the velocity graph, click and drag the Bézier handle as far to the left as it will go.

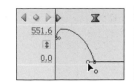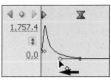

Notice the new velocity graph starts at a speed of 1,757.4 pixel per second (or similar in your own project), which is three times faster than the old velocity. This means the clip will travel much quicker at first and then take much longer to ease into place.

---

21 Drag the **Timeline CTI** to the beginning of the sequence. Click the **Play** button to preview the effect, and then click **Stop**.

Is your brain mush yet? If so, you can stop here. This is by far the most difficult concept you will face in Premiere Pro 2. For those of you who are gluttons for punishment, trudge on…. The last tweak you will make to this clip is to make it zoom out, which requires setting some Scale keyframes.

---

22 In the **Effect Controls** panel, use the **Keyframe Navigator** buttons to snap the **CTI** to the second keyframe at **00;00;03;00**.

---

23 In the **Effect Controls** panel, click the **Toggle animation** toggle next to the **Scale** property to turn on keyframe mode. Click the triangle next to **Scale** to view its value and velocity graphs.

Tip: The value graph shows you the value at any point in time. The velocity graph shows you how fast the scale changes (that is, how fast it reduces or enlarges).

---

24 Move the **CTI** to **00;00;06;00**, and change the **Scale** value to **0.0**.

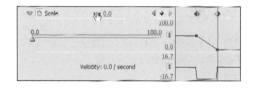

A few steps ago, you selected an individual keyframe and changed its interpolation. Premiere Pro 2 allows you to select multiple keyframes at once to make this same type of change. A quick way to do this is to click the property name. For example, clicking Scale selects all Scale keyframes.

---

25 Click **Scale** to select *all* keyframes of that property. Right-click either keyframe, and choose **Auto Bezier**.

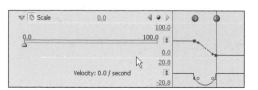

Notice the value graph (the top graph) is slightly curved with handles, as is the velocity graph (the bottom graph).

Next, you will set up the Scale effect to linger for a little while and then suddenly and quickly zoom away. (Imagine a marble rolling off a table.)

26 In the value graph, grab the handle of the first keyframe, and drag it slightly down and as far right as it will go.

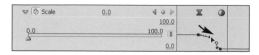

Notice the first keyframe changes from Auto to Continuous Bezier because you are manually changing the curve.

Comprehending the value graph may not happen overnight. Just remember these nuggets of wisdom: The closer the line is to horizontal, the slower it moves; and the closer the line is to vertical, the quicker it moves. So, in this situation, after the first keyframe, the line zooms slowly at first and then quickly zooms out as the graph gets more vertical.

---

27 Click and drag the second keyframe handle (the tiny dot to the left of the keyframe in the value graph) to just above the second keyframe in the value graph.

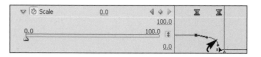

---

28 Drag the **Timeline CTI** to the beginning of the sequence. Click the **Play** button to preview the effect, and then click **Stop**.

---

29 In the **Timeline**, click the **Toggle Track Output** toggles for Tracks **Video 1** and **Video 2** to turn them on. Choose **Sequence > Render Work Area**. If necessary, click the **Play** button to play the clip if it does not automatically start after rendering.

Note: Depending on your system strength, these particular effect-loaded clips may take a few minutes to render.

---

30 Choose **File > Save**, or press **Ctrl+S**. Leave **dutch harbor promo.prproj** open for the next exercise.

This exercise was perhaps one of the more challenging ones you've tackled. You should walk away remembering these key points from this exercise: View Zoom Level allows you to see more of the canvas so clips can begin offscreen. In addition, when a clip is in direct select mode, you can drag its Bézier handles to modify the spatial interpolation to create a gentle, curved path.

VIDEO: | **interpolation.mov**

Video editing—at least it's not rocket science. Unfortunately, keyframe interpolation has a lot in common with rocket science. To learn more about keyframe interpolation, check out **interpolation.mov** in the **videos** folder on the **Premiere Pro 2 HOT DVD-ROM**.

6 | Creating a Track Matte

Have you ever watched a television show, such as *Cops*, and seen the face of a criminal blurred out while the rest of the video is untouched? Or, have you ever seen a sports highlight reel where the whole screen goes dim except for the player about to make a big play? These are both examples of mattes. In video-editing terms, a **matte** is a shape that can be used to isolate a portion of an image. The shape can be anything. When you animate the matte's position with keyframes, you have a **tracking matte**. In this exercise, you will create a track matte to pixilate a person's face so you can hide their true identity.

---

1 If you followed the previous exercise, **dutch harbor promo.prproj** should still be open in Premiere Pro 2. If it's not, click **Open Project** on the **Welcome Screen**. Navigate to the **c:\exercise_files\chap_08** folder, click **exercise06.prproj** to select it, and click **Open**.

---

2 Choose **File > Save As**. Navigate to the **c:\exercise_files\dutch_harbor** folder. Name the file **dutch harbor promo.prproj**, and click **Save**.

Note: If a previous version of dutch harbor promo.prproj already exists, you may be asked to replace it. Click Yes.

---

3 At the top of the **Timeline**, select the **DVD intro** tab to bring the sequence to the fore-ground. On Track **Video 1**, snap the **Timeline CTI** to the **In** point of **lobby_door.avi**.

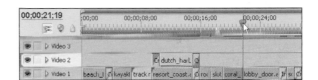

In this exercise, you will pixilate the face of the man walking through the door. (For example, say you forgot to get his signed release form to broadcast his likeness.)

To achieve the track matte, you will create a title object that is the shape of the man's head and then animate that shape to obscure the man's face as he walks.

---

4 On Track **Video 1**, click the **lobby_door.avi** clip to select it. Choose **Edit > Copy**. If neces-sary, click **Video 2** to set it as the target track. Choose **Edit > Paste**.

Remember, to paste a clip, you move the CTI and then set the target track.

Now you have two copies of the clip. You will use the top clip to pixilate the man's face, and the bottom clip will show the rest of the image that is left untouched.

Next, you will create a circle to place over the face of the actor you want to pixilate. You will do this with a polygon shape in a Premiere Pro 2 title.

5 Select the **Project** panel **Graphics** bin. Choose **File > New > Title**. In the **New Title** dialog box, type **matte shape** in the **Name** text box. Click **OK**.

Notice the floating Titler panel. If you don't see the video background in the main Titler panel, turn on the Show Video check box. Also, as you did in Chapter 5, *"Adding Titles,"* you may have to resize the Titler panel so it fits within your computer monitor.

---

6 If necessary, choose **Title > View > Safe Title Margin** to turn off the title safe margin, and choose **Title > View > Safe Action Margin** to turn off the action safe margin.

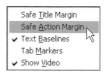

Because you are not creating text, you do not need to view the text margins, so you turned them off. When the margins are turned off, neither command should have a check mark next to its name.

Next, you will need to see the actor's face as a guide for creating your polygon shape.

---

7 In the upper-right corner of the main **Titler** panel, drag the **Background Video Timecode** to **00;00;25;26**.

Tip: If you have trouble getting to this exact timecode, you can hold down the Ctrl key and drag in more minute increments, or you can directly type a timecode of 2526. (Remember, you don't need to include the leading zeroes or semicolon delimiters.)

---

8 Select the **Pen** tool from the **Titler Tools** panel.

The Pen tool is the tool you use to draw custom shapes.

---

9 Click once below the actor's chin to create your first polygon handle, represented by a square. In the **Title Properties** panel, make sure the **Graphic Type** pop-up menu is set to **Open Bezier**.

Now it's time to play connect the dots. You will click dots around the perimeter of the actor's head. Each time you click the mouse, it creates a dot along the path, also called a **node**.

10 In the main **Titler** panel, click nodes around the perimeter of the actor's head until you end up where you started.

Tip: You don't have to do anything to "close" the loop as you do in other applications such as Adobe Illustrator. Just make sure your last node is relatively close to the first node.

 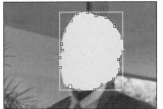

11 In the **Title Properties** panel, choose **Filled Bezier** in the **Graphic Type** pop-up menu.

In the Titler panel, you can see the shape filled with the default color. You now have your matte shape. The next step is to isolate the head from the rest of the video frame so that you can pixilate just the head.

12 In the upper-right corner of the **Titler** panel, click the **Close** box to close the title.

13 In the **Project** panel **Graphics** bin, drag the **matte shape** title to Track **Video 3**, and snap it to the **In** point of the **lobby_door.avi** clip.

14 In the **Effects** panel, type **matte** in the **Contains** text box. Drag the **Track Matte Key** video effect to the **lobby_door.avi** clip on Track **Video 2**.

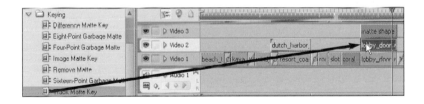

15 In the **Effect Controls** panel, click the **arrow** icon next to **Track Matte Key** to expand its properties. Choose **Video 3** in the **Matte** pop-up menu.

This tells the effect to "borrow" the shape of the clip on Track Video 3. In the Program Monitor, you probably didn't see anything change. This next step will tell you why.

16 In the **Timeline**, click the **Toggle Track Output** toggle next to track **Video 1** to turn it off.

Much better! This hides all clips on Track Video 1. Now you can see the matted video. Keep in mind you are seeing only the video from Track Video 2, matted with the shape from Track Video 3.

---

17 Drag the **Timeline CTI** before the **lobby_door.avi** clip, and click the **Play** button to play the sequence and preview your effect.

You have a slight problem: The matte shape is starting much too soon. You don't need it to appear until the actor appears, much later in the clip. Don't worry—you can easily rectify this by trimming the In point to start later.

---

18 In the **Effect Controls** panel, click the **Effect Toggle** toggle next to **Track Matte Key** to turn it off.

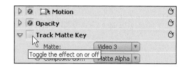

Temporarily turning off Track Matte Key allows you to see the original clip again.

---

19 Drag the **Timeline CTI** to the point when you *first* see the actor's face at **00;00;24;24**.

This is where the matte should start.

---

20 Using the **Trim In Pointer** cursor, snap-trim the **matte shape** clip's In point to the **CTI**.

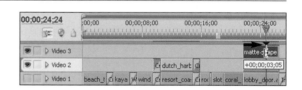

Now the matte shape doesn't start until the actor's face appears.

---

21 On Track **Video 2**, click the **lobby_door.avi** clip to select it. In the **Effect Controls** panel, click the **Effect Toggle** toggle next to **Track Matte Key** to turn on the effect.

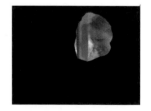

OK, you have successfully created the matte. Now it's time to add some motion keyframes and truly make this a *tracking* matte so it follows the man's face as he walks.

---

22 On Track **Video 3**, snap the **Timeline CTI** to the **In** point of the **matte shape.avi** clip. Click the **matte shape** clip to select it. In the **Effect Controls** panel, click the **arrow** icon next to **Motion** to expand its properties.

---

23 Click the **Toggle animation** toggle next to **Position** to turn on keyframe mode.

24 In the **Program Monitor**, drag the matte shape to the right to where the actor's face is about to appear.

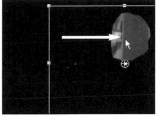

Remember, because you changed the Position value, you changed the value of the first Position keyframe.

25 Click the blue **Timeline Timecode** display, type **+15**, and press **Enter** to advance the **CTI** 15 frames. In the **Program Monitor**, drag the matte shape clip over the actor's face.

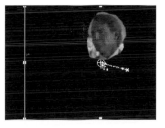

26 Again, click the blue **Timeline Timecode** display, type **+15**, and press **Enter** to advance the **CTI** 15 frames. In the **Program Monitor**, drag the **matte shape** clip over the actor's face.

27 For a third and final time, click the blue **Timeline Timecode** display, type **+15**, and press **Enter** to advance the **CTI** 15 frames. In the **Program Monitor**, drag the **matte shape** clip over the actor's face.

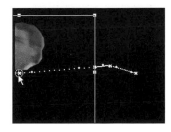

28 Snap the **Timeline CTI** to the **Out** point of the **matte shape** clip. Press the **left arrow** key once to move the **CTI** to the final frame of the matte. Drag the matte shape completely off the left of the screen.

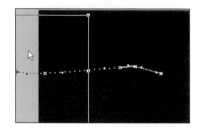

As you may notice, the "dots" path in the Program Monitor displays the position of each keyframe and the velocity. The farther apart the dots, the faster the clip moves.

---

29 Drag the **Timeline CTI** to the start of **lobby_door.avi**. In the **Program Monitor**, click the **Play** button to play that portion of the sequence to preview the position keyframes you created. After previewing, click **Stop**.

Now it's time to pixilate the matte.

---

30 Snap the **Timeline CTI** to the **In** point of the **matte shape** clip.

---

31 In the **Effects** panel, type **mosaic** in the **Contains** text box. Drag the **Mosaic** video effect to the **lobby_door.avi** clip on Track **Video 2**.

The effect takes place immediately. In the Program Monitor, you can see the matted video become heavily pixilated.

---

32 In the **Effect Controls** panel, click the **arrow** icon next to **Mosaic** to expand its properties. Change the **Horizontal Blocks** value to **20**. Change the **Vertical Blocks** value to **20**.

This divides the image into smaller blocks.

---

33 With the **Trim In Pointer** cursor, snap trim the **In** point of **lobby_door.avi** on Track **Video 2** to the **In** point of the **matte shape.avi** clip.

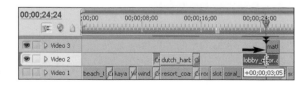

This is because you need the pixilated clip to start playing only when the man appears.

---

34 Click the **Toggle Track Output toggle** to turn on Track **Video 1**.

---

35 In the **Program Monitor**, click the **Play** button to play the clips and preview the sequence. When done, click **Stop**.

You are looking at three layers. The first layer is the matte shape. The second layer is just the man's face, heavily pixilated. The bottom layer is the original video.

---

36 Choose **File > Save**, or press **Ctrl+S**. Choose **File > Close** to close this project.

Way to go. Now you know how to create your own matte. Mattes have hundreds of uses. Even though you've applied only one type, the concept is similar no matter what the usage. Just remember, put the shape—be it a title or still image—on the top track, and put the video on the track below the shape. To turn the matte into a track matte, animate its position.

VIDEO: | **track_matte.mov**

Creating a track matte is not the most intuitive thing in the world. In fact, it can be downright difficult. To learn more about creating track mattes, check out **track_matte.mov** in the **videos** folder on the **Premiere Pro 2 HOT DVD-ROM**.

VIDEO: | **garbage_matte.mov**

A track matte is not the only type of matte effect you can create in Premiere Pro 2. You can also create something called a **garbage matte**. To learn more about garbage mattes, check out **garbage_matte.mov** in the **videos** folder on the **Premiere Pro 2 HOT DVD-ROM**.

Congratulations! You have animated your way through a variety of effects, motions, and mattes. In this chapter you sampled some techniques and learned how to animate some popular effects to achieve different results. You just used a few of the total number of effects shipping with Premiere Pro 2—but you apply and animate most if not all in the same manner. This next sentence is a bona fide "highlight me" sentence: Remember, when creating keyframes, first move the CTI and then change the value.

You have now animated fixed effects and video effects and also have applied a variety of different effects. You have yet to learn one more type of video effect, and that's color correction, which you'll get to experience as soon as you turn the page!

9

Correcting Color

Have you ever watched a "behind-the-scenes" feature on a DVD and noticed how drastically different the unprocessed film looked compared to the final version of the movie? That's because the final version has undergone color correction. Altering the look—be it color, brightness, or contrast—falls under the heading of color correction.

Color correction allows you to adjust the color and luminance of your video clips. (In video-editing terms, **luminance** is the measure of brightness in a clip.) In Adobe Premiere Pro 2, you can use color correction to eliminate a strong color in a clip, correct video that is too dark or too light, or change the overall hue of a clip to create a mood. You can also use color correction to match the "look" of different clips filmed under different lighting conditions. Premiere Pro 2 also provides professional tools to help conform your program to broadcast standards and assist you in making color adjustments.

Understanding Video and Light Color

Video cameras sometimes record colors very differently than what your eyes perceive. If you've ever shot video under fluorescent lights, like those in an office or school, you may notice a slight yellow-green tint on your video. At the time of shooting, your human eye might not have seen this.

| 1,800K | 4,000K | 5,500K | 8,000K | 16,000K |

As shown in the illustration here, the color of light changes at different temperatures (shown in kelvins). The list to the right illustrates the light temperature of common lighting conditions.

Incandescent lights (also called **tungsten**), such as those in your home, tend to cast a yellowish-orange tint on subjects. If you've ever shot someone outside on an overcast day, you probably noticed a blue tint on your video. This is all because your video camera picks up subtle color hues your human eyes cannot see.

Sometimes this affects the shadows of your video; other times it affects the highlights (the bright areas). Some color correction effects in Premiere Pro 2 allow you to independently adjust the highlights, shadows, and midtones.

Light Temperature	
Lighting Conditions	**Kelvins**
Candle	1,800K
Sunrise/sunset	2,000K
Indoor tungsten	3,000K
Indoor fluorescent	3,400K
Summer day sunlight	5,500K
Overcast sky	6,000K
Outdoor shade	8,000K

Correcting Color in Premiere Pro 2

Color correction is a catchall phrase including the following tasks:

Balancing color hues to neutralize a dominant color: Balancing can help eliminate a color cast from a lighting condition (such as those listed in the previous illustration).

Correcting the brightness or contrast of a video clip: This is especially useful for video shot under less-than-ideal lighting situations. Keep in mind, you can make subtle correction to brightness and contrast, but if the video quality is beyond repair, such as too dark or too bright (overblown areas of white), you may not get satisfactory results.

Altering the color to create a mood: The next time you watch a movie or drama on television, notice how much lighting plays a role in setting the mood. Family scenes are often bathed in a warm light. A detective interrogating a subject is often bathed in a cold, steely blue light.

Matching clips shot under different lighting conditions: Perhaps you have two people talking to each other in a scene, but you videotaped each person at a different time of day and therefore under different lighting conditions. You can use color correction to match the colors of one clip to those of the other so the clips appear identical.

Monitoring the luminosity and saturation levels to ensure broadcast compliance: Sometimes what is appealing to your eye may not be broadcast compliant according to the standards of your local television station.

Although Premiere Pro 2 has many, many ways to achieve these results, the tasks fall under two main types of effects: automated and manual.

Original video   *Auto Contrast*   *Auto Color*

As shown in the illustration here, the original image (left) is adjusted with an **Auto Contrast** effect (center) and an **Auto Color** effect (right). You can see the **Auto Contrast** effect brightens the image and reduces the contrast but doesn't improve the color. The **Auto Color** effect correctly removes the greenish tint of the original.

The automated color correction effects include **Auto Color, Auto Contrast,** and **Auto Levels**. When using these effects, Premiere Pro 2 analyzes the image and determines how to best apply the correction. The downside of these automated effects is that sometimes what is *technically accurate* to a computer may not represent well to the human eye.

Some effects allow you to manually set the white balance. Using the color picker, represented by an eyedropper, you sample the area that should be pure white.

Manual color correction effects are a tad trickier, but they can provide better results because you are at the helm. When manually performing color correction, you tell Premiere Pro 2, "This area of my image is really white, and this part of my image is really black." Premiere Pro 2 then analyzes the areas you've picked and responds, "OK, if that color is *supposed* to be white, then I will adjust the entire image until that area is white" (except Premiere Pro 2 doesn't really talk). This is called **white balancing**.

Becoming a good color corrector takes time and practice. Entire departments of people at movie studios are dedicated solely to color correction. The following exercises will serve as an introduction to applying the color correction effects and how to most effectively use them.

Using the Color Correction Workspace

Throughout most of the exercises in this book, you have been using a workspace that organizes the panels so they are most useful for the tasks of trimming and editing. However, when you're dealing with color correction, you may find you need more room in the **Effect Controls** panel, or you may decide you don't need the **Timeline** panel to be as big because you are no longer trimming and editing sequences. Luckily, Premiere Pro 2 provides a special **Color Correction** workspace for just such an occasion.

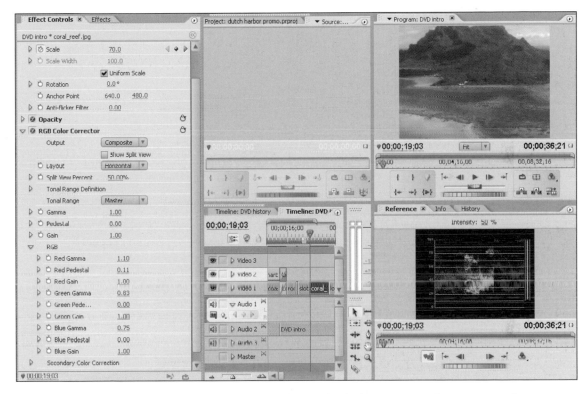

As shown in the illustration here, the **Effect Controls** panel, which you are used to seeing at the upper part of the screen, now appears on the far left of the workspace—and it's much larger. This is because many of the color correction video effects have a lengthy list of attributes and options needing to be viewed all at once.

You can find the **Project** panel as a tab behind the **Source Monitor**, in the upper-center part of the workspace. The **Timeline** panel has been heavily reduced because, at this point, you should primarily be done editing and trimming clips. Finally, you will find a new panel called the **Reference Monitor** residing where the **Timeline** panel used to be.

Viewing the Reference Monitors

The **Reference Monitor** panel acts like a secondary **Program Monitor**. You can use the **Reference Monitor** to compare different frames of a sequence, to display different color characteristics of your video, and to assess compliance with local broadcast standards.

Vectorscope

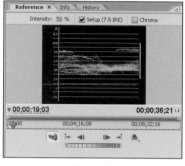

YC waveform

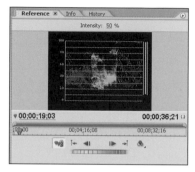

RGB parade

As shown in the illustration here, the **Reference Monitor** can show different viewing modes, such as the **Vectorscope** monitor (left), the **YC waveform** monitor (center), and the **RGB parade** (right).

The different viewing modes of the **Reference Monitor** help you output a video program that meets broadcast requirements and also assist you in gauging adjustments in color correction. The following list provides a basic overview of the purpose of each **Reference Monitor** mode:

Vectorscope: Measures the hue and saturation (the color) of a video signal and then maps that information to a circular chart. The vectorscope signal appears as a green "blob" (for lack of a better term) in the center of the circular chart. The more saturated (vivid) a color is, the further the green signal stretches to the outer ring of the chart.

The chart is divided, like a pie, into colors, with each slice of the chart representing a different color. Black-and-white video, which has no color information, displays as a dot at the center of the vectorscope. You can use the vectorscope mode to make sure your saturation levels don't extend beyond the limit of the chart ring.

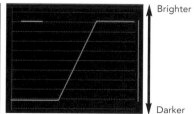

A video clip (left) as it appears in the YC waveform (right)

YC waveform: Displays a graph showing the luminance (brightness) information of a video signal, as shown in the illustration here. Bright objects produce a waveform pattern near the upper part of the graph; darker objects produce a waveform toward the lower part. The left side of the YC waveform corresponds to the left side of the original image, and the right side of the graph corresponds to the right side of the original image. For video in the United States, luminance levels should range from 7.5 to 100.

You can use a YC waveform to make sure the brightest areas of your video don't exceed 100 and the black areas don't dip to less than 7.5. Of course, if you're creating video for the Internet, none of this applies because you can use any luminance level that appeals to your eye.

RGB parade: Displays the RGB (**R**ed, **G**reen, and **B**lue) levels of a video signal. This waveform is useful for displaying the amount of each color in the video signal, graphed on a scale of 0 to 100. Why is it called **parade**? The three components—red, green, and blue—are lined up one after the other.

An important caveat about all of the **Reference Monitor** panels: As the name implies, the monitors are for *reference* only. In other words, you cannot do anything within the actual **Reference Monitor** to change your video. The monitors show you only different qualities of the video. If you want to change those qualities, you must do so with color correction effects.

Also, the vectorscope and waveform monitors are primarily for ensuring compliance for playback on a television. Although the monitors can provide insight when color correcting, if you are not concerned with ensuring broadcast standards—that is, if you are not going to take the finished product to your local television station—then you may not ever need to view the **Reference Monitor** panels.

In the following exercises, you will learn how to apply and modify a few of the most common color correction effects, as well as change the output modes of the **Reference Monitor** panels.

NOTE:

Fix It in Post

A common mantra in the videography world is, "Fix it in post." What this is really saying is, "Don't worry about mistakes at the time of videotaping; you can always fix them later in your video-editing software."

Well, this truth goes only so far. You can correct colors, sure. But if your video is way too bright, you will lose color **detail**. In other words, what was once a blue lake with a reflective highlight is now a sea of white because the whites are overblown. You will not be able to recover the detail of the lake, such as the subtle waves because it is one big blob of white.

Here's another example: If you are shooting in an area that is too dark, Premiere Pro 2 can do only so much to increase the brightness. But if the scene is too dark for your camera to see it, then all you are recording is black, and Premiere Pro 2 cannot fix that.

As a rule of thumb, you should invoke the "fix it in post" mantra only when you *have to* fix it in post. If you can get it right at the time of shooting, it's always better to do so. Here are a couple tasks you can perform to avoid later color correction:

Set the white balance: Many cameras allow you to zoom in on a white piece of paper (a white T-shirt will do in a pinch) and assign that color to be pure white. This color balances the entire shot based on the color you've specified as white. If your camera doesn't have a white balance function, then, at a minimum, record a white piece of paper before each shot. When you get your footage into Premiere Pro 2, you can perform white balancing based on the white piece of paper.

Set the correct light aperture: An **aperture** controls how much light is permitted through your camera's lens. Some cameras are able to allow more or less light into the lens, which prevents white "blowout" or dark "blackout." Some cameras even have "zebra bars" dancing across the camera's viewfinder to indicate any areas that may be too **hot** (bright). If you record too hot or too dark, you will lose detail in the video and won't be able to recover it in Premiere Pro 2.

1 | Applying Auto Effects

When you want to make the quickest possible color correction, Premiere Pro 2 offers three automated color correction effects: **Auto Color**, **Auto Contrast**, and **Auto Balance**. For example, if you want to quickly adjust the contrast of a clip without having to fiddle with anything, you can apply **Auto Contrast**, and Premiere Pro 2 will automatically determine the best correction. These automated effects can give you technically accurate results, but sometimes the final result is not as appealing to the eye as manually corrections can be. (After all, Premiere Pro 2 relies on numbers, while your human eye relies on overall aesthetic.) In this exercise, you will learn how to apply the automated effects.

1 On the **Welcome Screen**, click **Open Project**. In the **Open Project** dialog box, navigate to the **c:\exercise_files\chap_09** folder, click **exercise01.prproj** to select it, and click **Open**.

2 Choose **File > Save As**. Navigate to the **c:\exercise files\dutch_harbor** folder. Name the file **dutch harbor promo.prproj**, and click **Save**.

Note: If a previous version of dutch harbor promo.prproj already exists, you may be asked to replace it. Click Yes.

3 At the top of the **Timeline**, select the **DVD intro** tab to bring the sequence to the foreground. Hold down the **Shift** key, and snap the **Timeline CTI** (Current Time Indicator) to the **In** point of **coral_reef.jpg** on Track **Video 1**.

4 Choose **Window > Workspace > Color Correction**.

In the Color Correction workspace, the Reference Monitor appears below the Program Monitor. By default, the Reference Monitor outputs the same "composite" video as the Program Monitor.

An unfortunate side effect of switching to the Color Correction workspace is you may not be able to see the CTI in the Timeline panel.

5 In the **Timeline** panel, scroll to the right until you can see the CTI and the **coral_reef.jpg** clip.

6 In the **Reference Monitor**, click the **Output** button, and choose **RGB Parade**.

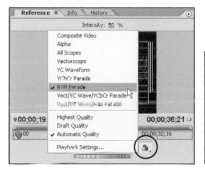

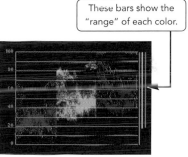

These bars show the "range" of each color.

The RGB parade waveform shows the percentage of red, green, and blue in the Program Monitor. You can see the current clip is heavily weighted toward greens and blues because the majority of the green and blue waveforms fall between 20 and 100 percent on the graph.

Notice also the three bars on the right of the Reference Monitor. These bars represent the range of each of their respective colors. For instance, the range of red in this clip is 0–100 percent (even though most of it falls between 20–40 percent).The range of green and blue is 20–100 percent. To translate that into layman's terms, "No pixels in this image have less than 20 percent green and 20 percent blue. Some pixels in the image have 0 percent red."

7 In the **Program Monitor**, click the **Output** button, and choose **Highest Quality** to change the output mode.

Highest Quality mode forces Premiere Pro 2 to output your video at its best quality at the expense of playback performance (smoothness). Despite the slow-down of processing, this mode is always the best to use with color correction since there is little need for frequent playback.

Tip: Premiere Pro 2 will remember the playback mode until you change it. When done color correcting, it is usually best to revert to Automatic Quality, which allows Premiere Pro 2 to find a nice compromise between picture quality and performance.

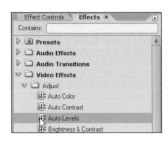  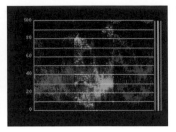

8 In the **Video Effects > Adjust** folder, drag the **Auto Levels** effect to the **coral_reef.jpg** clip on Track **Video 1**.

Yikes! In the Program Monitor, you can see the clip has more red (almost making the mountain look brown). The Reference Monitor shows the range of each color has been automatically expanded. Remember the three range bars described a few steps ago? Now they show each color has been maximized to a range of 0–100 percent.

Note: This underscores the problem with automatic color correction—although the automated effects are easier to apply, sometimes what is technically accurate is not as visually appealing.

---

9 Choose **Edit > Undo** to remove the effect you just applied.

---

10 In the **Effects** panel **Video Effects > Adjust** folder, drag the **Auto Color** effect to the **coral_reef.jpg** clip on Track **Video 1**.

---

11 Select the **Effect Controls** panel to bring it to the foreground. In the **Effect Controls** panel, click the effect toggle next to the **Auto Color** effect to turn the effect on and off so you can compare the before-and-after output.

 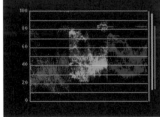

The clip still ends up a tad on the red side, but the RGB parade waveform shows the blue range is now 15–85 percent, instead of 0–100 percent, as it was with the Auto Levels effect. Also, notice the clip has less contrast (is a bit "hazier") than it was with the Auto Levels effect.

This highlights two important distinctions between the Auto Levels and Auto Color effects. First, the Auto Levels effect affects *both* color and contrast, whereas the Auto Color effect only changes the color. Second, the Auto Levels effect tweaks each color channel individually rather than balancing all colors together, like the Auto Color effect does.

---

12 In the **Effect Controls** panel, select the **Auto Color** effect, and press the **Delete** key to remove it.

---

13 In the **Effects** panel **Video Effects > Adjust** folder, drag the **Auto Contrast** effect to the **coral_reef.avi** clip on Track **Video 1**.

14 In the **Effect Controls** panel, click the effect toggle next to **Auto Contrast** to turn the effect off and on so you can compare the before and after output.

As you can see, the Auto Contrast effect does not change the color of the clip but instead automatically adjusts the contrast.

To understand better what the Auto Contrast effect is doing to your clip, it may be more useful to view the YC waveform.

15 In the **Reference Monitor**, click the **Output** button, and choose **YC Waveform**. If necessary, turn off the **Chroma** option in the upper part of the **Reference Monitor**.

The green waveform display shows you luminance (black and white) values. When Chroma is turned on, you see a blue waveform overlaid on top, which shows you chrominance (color) values. Although it may be interesting to see the chrominance values, the YC waveform is primarily needed only to view the luminance values.

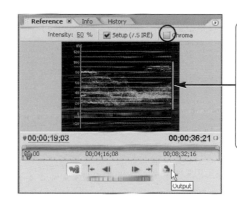

The range bar on the right shows the Auto Contrast effect maximizing the luminance (brightness) between 7.5 and 100 IRE.

16 In the **Effect Controls** panel, click the effect toggle next to **Auto Contrast** to turn off and on the effect so you can compare the before and after output.

If you watch the YC waveform while toggling the effect off and on, you can see the effect uses the maximum range of luminance (brightness/darkness).

Tip: At the top of the YC waveform, you will see the Setup (7.5 IRE) check box. Short of a lengthy explanation, just know you want this box turned on if you are monitoring luminance levels for output to television in the United States. The 7.5 IRE level is the lowest luminance level acceptable by broadcast standards (100 IRE is the maximum).

The Intensity value increases the glow brightness of the green waveform and does not affect the actual video.

17 In the **Effect Controls** panel, click the **arrow** icon next to **Auto Contrast** to view its properties. Change the **Temporal Smoothing** value to **1.0**.

The Temporal Smoothing value specifies how many seconds before the current frame Premiere Pro 2 analyzes to determine the amount of correction needed for each frame. For example, if you set a value of 1.0 (seconds), Premiere Pro 2 will "look" at each of the 30 frames before the current frame when factoring how much to autocorrect. If you set Temporal Smoothing to 0.0, Premiere Pro 2 analyzes each frame independently, without regard for the surrounding frames.

Temporal Smoothing can result in smoother-looking corrections over time. All of the automated color correction effects have a Temporal Smoothing option.

Perhaps the Auto Contrast effect is a bit *too* dark for your tastes. Fortunately, you can blend the effect with the original clip to soften the results.

---

18 In the **Effect Controls** panel, change the **Blend With Original** value to **25.0%**.

Now the image ought to look just about right. In the Program Monitor, you can see the effect lose a little bit of contrast, which is no longer technically maximized, but it is nonetheless more attractive.

---

19 Choose **File > Save**, or press **Ctrl+S**. Leave **dutch harbor promo.prproj** open for the next exercise.

This exercise served as an introduction to the world of the Reference Monitor. Please keep in mind, this is only to show you what is happening "under the hood" of your video clips when you're color correcting. By no means are you required to view these monitors. They serve only as guides and are completely optional.

As a famous movie character once said, "Life is like a box of chocolates...." Similarly, with the automated effects, you never know what you're going to get. Sometimes the best method for applying them is to add each one and see which suits your needs best. If the applied effect is too strong, you can water the results down by increasing the Blend With Original value.

Working with the Hue Color Wheel

Now that you have mastered the automated color correction effects, in the next two exercises you will learn how to work two manual color correction effects. Both manual color correction effects rely on the controls of the color wheel for balancing color in your video. **Color balancing**, as the name implies, balances the red, green, and blue components to produce a desired color. You can use the color wheel to make subtle changes to a clip's hue or to colorize a scene by adding, for example, a cool (bluish) color cast to a crime documentary.

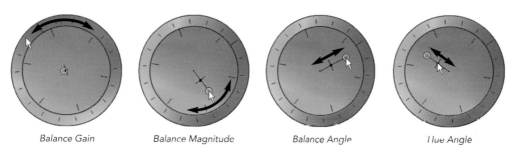

| Balance Gain | Balance Magnitude | Balance Angle | Hue Angle |

The color wheel is four tools in one. Depending on which part of the wheel you are changing, you can control and adjust a different color property, described next. The tools are split into the outer ring and the inner ring.

The Outer Ring

The **outer ring** of the color wheel is best for making subtle changes to the video hue. You can make only one adjustment to the outer ring, and that is **Hue Angle**.

Hue Angle: You can move the outer ring to make subtle changes to the hue of the video. Rotating the ring counterclockwise (to the left) rotates the colors toward green; rotating the outer ring clockwise (to the right) rotates the colors toward red.

The Inner Ring

The **inner ring** of the color wheel shifts the hue of the video in more intense or dramatic ways. You can use the following three controls for adjusting within the inner ring:

Balance Angle: As you drag the tiny, black circle within the inner ring, the hue shifts toward the target color.

Balance Magnitude: The farther you drag the tiny, black circle from the center the wheel, the more intense the hue shift.

Balance Gain: The perpendicular handle along the **Balance Magnitude** bar affects the subtlety of the magnitude. Moving the handle close to the center of the wheel makes the magnitude adjustment subtle; moving the handle away from the center makes the adjustment obvious.

To see how each of the color wheel adjustments affects your video, it is useful to view the vectorscope in the **Reference Monitor**. In the next exercise, you will use the **Hue Angle** adjustment (the outer ring) to subtly rotate the hue of your video.

2 | Using the Fast Color Corrector

The **Fast Color Corrector** effect changes a clip's color by providing you with manual hue and saturation controls. Use the **Fast Color Corrector** effect when you want to make simple (manual) color corrections and preview them in real time. The **Fast Color Corrector** is ideally suited for quickly white balancing a shot, using its built-in **White Balance** tool.

---

1 If you followed the previous exercise, **dutch harbor promo.prproj** should still be open in Premiere Pro 2. If it's not, click **Open Project** on the **Welcome Screen**. Navigate to the **c:\exercise_files\chap_09** folder, click **exercise02.prproj** to select it, and click **Open**.

---

2 Choose **File > Save As**. Navigate to the **c:\exercise files\dutch_harbor** folder. Name the file **dutch harbor promo.prproj**, and click **Save**.

Note: If a previous version of dutch harbor promo.prproj already exists, you may be asked to replace it. Click Yes.

---

3 At the top of the **Timeline**, select the **DVD history** tab to bring the sequence to the foreground. Move the **Timeline CTI** to **00;00;15;00**.

---

4 In the **Reference Monitor**, click the **Output** button, and choose **Vectorscope**.

Notice the vectorscope is in a circle? It's no coincidence the color wheel described earlier is also in a circle. In fact, you'll see a direct correlation between the **Hue Angle** adjustment (the outer ring) and the angle of the green waveform in the vectorscope.

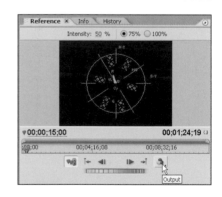

5 In the **Effects** panel **Video Effects > Color Correction** folder, drag the **Fast Color Corrector** effect to the **historian.avi** clip on Track **Video 1**.

With the manual color correction effects, you won't notice an immediate change upon applying the effect. You have to manually kick-start the effect to get it going.

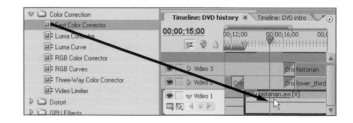

---

6 In the **Effect Controls** panel, click the **arrow** icon next to **Fast Color Corrector** to view its properties.

Yikes—this effect has so many properties that they don't all fit in the Effect Controls panel! Some of these properties are redundant, and some you won't use. In this exercise, you will walk through the most important properties.

7 In the **Fast Color Corrector** properties, click the **White Balance** eyedropper, and then click anywhere in the background of the **Program Monitor** to sample that color as the white point.

This manually white balances the clip. In essence, you are telling Premiere Pro 2, "This background color is supposed to be pure white." Premiere Pro 2 then adjusts the overall color of the clip so the background is white.

Tip: If your camera doesn't have white balance, this is a quick and easy way to white balance in Premiere Pro 2. You can either find something supposed to be white, as you did in this step, or get in the habit of holding up a white piece of paper at the beginning of every take and then sampling the paper as your white point.

Bonus tip: If you hold down the Ctrl key while using the color sample eyedropper, Premiere Pro 2 will sample a "group" of pixels, rather than sample an individual pixel.

Because the resulting hue is a tad too red, you will use the Hue Angle adjustment (the outer ring of the color wheel) to subtly rotate the hue away from the reds.

8 In the color wheel of the **Fast Color Corrector** effect, drag the outer ring slowly to the left until the **Hue Angle** value shows **-8.0°**. As you drag the color ring, watch the vectorscope waveform slowly rotate in a similar fashion.

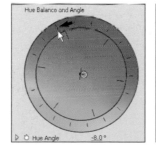 

Tip: The Hue Angle value, below the wheel, has the same effect as graphically rotating the outer ring.

9 In the **Fast Color Corrector** properties, turn on the **Show Split View** check box. From the **Layout** pop-up menu, choose **Vertical**.

This creates a split screen—the left shows you the corrected version, and the right shows you the original version.

10 Turn off the **Show Split View** check box to remove the split screen.

---

11 In the **Fast Color Corrector** properties, change the **Saturation** value to **125.00**. As you drag, notice the vectorscope waveform increases toward the outside of the chart.

In a vectorscope, the farther away from center the waveform extends, the more saturated the hue. Black-and-white video, which has zero saturation, would display as a dot at the center of the waveform.

So far you have white balanced the video and made subtle corrections to the hue and saturation. Lastly, you will change the contrast (luminosity) of the clip.

When viewing the Fast Color Corrector effect in the Effect Controls panel, it may help to mentally divide is like this: The upper properties, including the color wheel, are for making color adjustments. The properties in the lower part, including the Auto buttons, are for making brightness/contrast adjustments.

---

12 In the **Reference Monitor**, click the **Output** button, and choose **YC Waveform**.

---

13 In the **Fast Color Corrector** properties, click the **Auto Contrast** button.

Notice the YC waveform range expand, just like it did when using the Auto Contrast effect in the previous exercise.

The other two buttons available are Auto Black Level (expands the bottom range to 7.5 IRE) and Auto White Level (limits the white levels so they do not exceed 100 IRE). The Auto Contrast button applies both simultaneously.

You might think the result has a tad too much contrast. (For example, notice you lose detail in the actor's black T-shirt.) You can fix this by reducing the Output Levels values.

---

14 In the **Fast Color Corrector** properties, change the **Output Levels** values to **12.0** and **240.0**.

Tip: Alternatively, you can perform this by dragging the two small black-and-white tabs below the Output Levels bar.

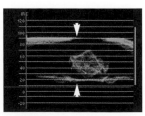

The actual values you use on your own clips are a matter of taste. Eyeball your video as you slowly drag the levels to reduce the amount of contrast. The black tab on the left reduces the black level (the lower range of the YC waveform), and the white tab on the right reduces the white level (the upper range of the YC waveform).

It's now time to compare the original to the final version.

15 Click the effect toggle next to **Fast Color Corrector** to turn the effect off and on so you can compare the before and after output. When done comparing, make sure the effect remains on.

I hope you agree the final result has less of a yellow tint, has realistic flesh tones, and has better contrast. The last task to perform in this exercise is to save the effect as a preset so you can easily apply it to the other actors in this sequence.

16 In the **Effect Controls** panel, right-click the **Fast Color Corrector** effect, and choose **Save Preset**. In the **Save Preset** dialog box, type **interviews corrected color** in the **Name** field. Click **OK**.

You've now saved the preset, so you can quickly apply it to the other clips. To see the results when applying, you will move the CTI. (Note that you don't need to place the CTI over each clip to which you want to apply an effect. This is just so you can preview the changes in the Program Monitor.)

17 Move the **Timeline CTI** to **00;00;33;20**.

This is the next interview clip in need of color correction.

18 In the **Effects** panel, click the **arrow** icon next to **Presets** to expand the folder and see the preset you saved in the previous step. Drag the **interviews corrected color** preset to **historian.avi** at the **CTI** on Track **Video 1**.

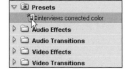

In the Program Monitor, you will see the clip automatically color corrected. Because these clips were shot in the same room, by the same camera, it is safe to apply the same color correction. However, if the clips were different, you would need to color correct from scratch.

19 Move the **Timeline CTI** to 00;00;45;13. In the **Effects** panel **Presets** folder, apply the same preset to **eruptologist.avi** at the **Timeline CTI** on Track **Video 1**.

20 Move the **Timeline CTI** to 00;01;04;15. In the **Effects** panel **Presets** folder, apply the same preset to **media_relations.avi** at the **Timeline CTI** on Track **Video 1**.

21 Move the **Timeline CTI** to **00;01;07;00**. In the **Effects** panel **Presets** folder, apply the same preset to **media_relations.avi** at the **Timeline CTI** on Track **Video 1**.

22 Choose **File > Save**, or press **Ctrl+S**. Leave **dutch harbor promo.prproj** open for the next exercise.

This exercise walked you through some of the most common features of the Fast Color Corrector effect. If you struggle with color correction, don't worry. It can take some time to become truly comfortable with the myriad options. At least now you understand the concepts, so you should be able to venture out on your own and practice, practice, practice. If you get lost, remember these key points: Use white balance to manually specify a target color of your clip as true white, rotate the outer ring of the color wheel to rotate the hues to remove a subtle tint to your video, and use the Output Levels values to manually tweak the results of the automated properties if they are not to your liking.

VIDEO: | **color_corrector.mov**

To learn more about the **Fast Color Corrector** effect, check out **color_corrector.mov** in the **videos** folder on the **Premiere Pro 2 HOT DVD-ROM**.

3 | Using the Three-Way Color Corrector

The **Three-Way Color Corrector** effect allows for subtler color correction by separating the adjustments into three tonal ranges. Instead of altering the entire clip, you can individually adjust certain ranges of color. For example, you can adjust only the dark areas, or **shadows**. On the other hand, you can choose to modify the brightest areas, also called **highlights**. In this exercise, you will adjust the shadows, midtones, and highlights, and you will apply the **Three-Way Color Corrector** effect to adjust each tonal range.

1 If you followed the previous exercise, **dutch harbor promo.prproj** should still be open in Premiere Pro 2. If it's not, click **Open Project** on the **Welcome Screen**. Navigate to the **c:\exercise_files\chap_09** folder, click **exercise03.prproj** to select it, and click **Open**.

2 Choose **File > Save As**. Navigate to the **c:\exercise files\dutch_harbor** folder. Name the file **dutch harbor promo.prproj**, and click **Save**.

Note: If a previous version of dutch harbor promo.prproj already exists, you may be asked to replace it. Click Yes.

3 At the top of the **Timeline**, select the **DVD intro** tab to bring the sequence to the foreground. Move the **Timeline CTI** to **00;00;09;05**. In the **Effects** panel **Video Effects > Color Correction** folder, apply the **Three-Way Color Corrector** effect to the **wind_surfing.avi** clip on Track **Video 1**.

4 In the **Effect Controls** panel, click the **arrow** icon next to **Three-Way Color Corrector** to expand its properties.

Instead of a single color wheel, the Three-Way Color Corrector effect uses three color wheels (which is how it gets its name). Each color wheel affects a different tonal range of the output—from left to right: shadows, midtones, and highlights.

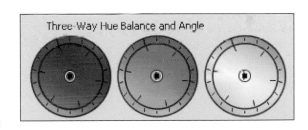

5 In the **Three-Way Color Corrector** properties, choose **Tonal Range** from the **Output** pop-up menu.

The Program Monitor now displays the three tonal ranges. Highlights appear as white, midtones appear as gray, and shadows appear as black.

 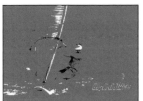

Each of the three tonal ranges corresponds to one of the three color wheels. Adjusting the Shadow wheel (far left) affects only the area of the clip represented by the black tonal range. Keep in mind you are not modifying the actual color black but the area of the video appearing as black.

Likewise, the Midtone wheel (middle) affects the area shown as gray, and the Highlight wheel (right) affects the area shown as white.

---

6 In the **Three-Way Color Corrector** properties, choose **Composite** from the **Output** pop-up menu to see the actual video again. Select the **White Balance** eyedropper, and then click the whitest portion of the man's visor.

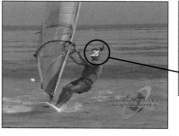

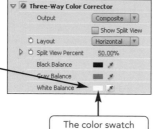

The color swatch updates as you position your cursor over different pixel colors in the images.

Tip: As you position the eyedropper cursor over different pixels, the pixel color updates in the color swatch next to the White Balance property. When you find the "whitest" color possible, carefully click the mouse. (You don't want to move the mouse and accidentally choose the wrong pixel.) For this reason, it's always best to find the largest, most uniform area of white possible when balancing color.

---

7 In the **Three-Way Color Corrector** properties, select the **Gray Balance** eyedropper, and then click the gray shadow on the underside of the surfboard.

After you click the mouse, you should see a subtle, yet noticeable, shift away from yellow and toward a more balanced, cooler color.

As you position your mouse with the eyedropper selected, you will see the Midtone color wheel (middle) adjust "on the fly." Once you click the mouse, Premiere Pro 2 applies the color balance. Notice the balance of the Midtone color wheel shifts to the upper right. Again, it's a subtle color shift, so the balance will remain close to the center of the wheel.

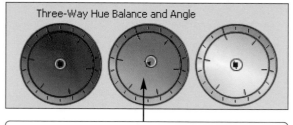

As you position the Gray Balance eyedropper over different pixels, the Midtone color wheel adjusts automatically.

8 In the **Three-Way Color Corrector** properties, select the **Black Balance** eyedropper, and click the darkest area of the image, which could be the dark shadow on the surfer's shorts or the black bar of the sail.

Did you notice that, temporarily, the original clip color returned while you were using the eyedropper? This is because Premiere Pro 2 allows you to select from the original colors of the image, rather than drawing from the already-processed colors. (Otherwise, you would accidentally balance the already balanced image.) After you click the mouse, Premiere Pro 2 reapplies the adjustments.

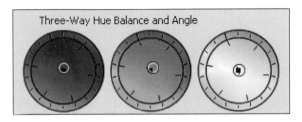

The midtone adjustment has the most impact on the image because most of the image falls within the midtone range, represented by the gray area.

You may also notice the Shadow color wheel (left), although it has been adjusted, had little effect on the final color. The Midtone color wheel (middle) had the biggest impact. Why? Well, remember the tonal range view? Ninety-eight percent of the image fell within the midtone range, represented by the gray area of the tonal range view. Hence, adjusting the midtone (Gray Balance) affected the image the most because it affects all of the area shown as gray. The Shadow color wheel affects only the area displayed as black.

---

9 Click the effect toggle next to **Three-Way Color Corrector** to turn the effect on and off and compare the effect's results. When done comparing, make sure the effect is on.

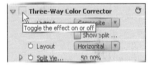

Although the hue balance is more neutral, the image seems a tad less saturated. The colors of the sail and water just don't "pop" as much as they did originally. You can adjust this by increasing the midtone saturation.

---

10 In the **Three-Way Color Corrector** properties, choose **Midtones** from the **Tonal Range** pop-up menu.

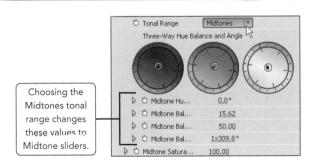

Choosing the Midtones tonal range changes these values to Midtone sliders.

This changes the value sliders below the color wheels to Midtone sliders. This does not affect the color wheels—they never change. But the values displayed below the color wheels are now only the midtone values. (Note: Your values may differ slightly depending on the exact pixel on which you set your Gray Balance property.)

11 In the **Three-Way Color Corrector** properties, change the **Midtone Saturation** value to **150.00**.

Now the colors of the sail, water, and surfer are more intense.

You are now finished with color correcting. Don't forget to return the Program Monitor playback mode to Automatic Quality.

12 In the **Program Monitor**, click the **Output** button, and choose **Automatic Quality**.

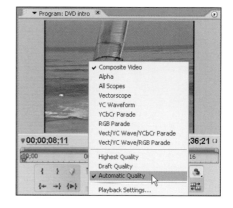

13 Choose **File > Save**, or press **Ctrl+S**. Choose **File > Close** to close this project.

As long as you understand the connection between the three tonal ranges and the three color wheels, grasping the Three-Way Color Corrector effect should be easy. Although the many options may be confusing, the basics, as you just discovered, are pretty simple. Viewing the tonal ranges shows you which areas of the image fall within which range; whites are highlights, grays are midtones, and blacks are shadows. Then, use the White Balance, Gray Balance, and Black Balance eyedroppers to specify the proper color for each range. This will automatically update the corresponding color wheel. And finally, if you want to modify a particular tonal range value, such as saturation, you must first choose it from the Tonal Range pop-up menu to display the values.

VIDEO:

three_way_color.mov

To learn more about the **Three-Way Color Corrector** effect, check out **three_way_color.mov** in the **videos** folder on the **Premiere Pro 2 HOT DVD-ROM**.

Throughout this chapter you applied three of the most common color correction effects. As you become more familiar with Premiere Pro 2, you will find a few more effects that provide useful results. The Premiere Pro 2 Help manual is a wealth of information and defines additional effects. Luckily, all of the concepts you learned in this chapter apply equally to most of the color correction effects. From using the eyedropper to understanding color wheels, these same tools and behaviors will pop up in other effects.

More than anything else in Premiere Pro 2, color correction is a subtle art form, requiring patience, skill, and sometimes even knowledge of broadcast standards. Although color correction is an important part of producing a finished program in Premiere Pro 2, you have experienced only the basics. (In fact, entire books are dedicated to color correction.) So don't get discouraged; keep experimenting until you find the right method for you.

At this point, you have learned how to do practically everything possible to video and still images, including editing video; adding transitions, effects, and keyframes; and correcting color. The final frontier to venture into in your Premiere Pro 2 education is the art of working with audio, as you will discover in the next chapter.

10

Working with Audio

Even though Adobe Premiere Pro 2 is known as a video-editing application, don't let the name fool you—audio is just as important to producing a high-quality product. On most prime-time dramas, rarely does a second go by without some sort of music underneath; it's ubiquitous. Audio can specify a mood, heighten tension, or underscore an important point. Being a good video editor is more than just editing video; it also involves understanding how to edit audio and improve the audio quality, such as removing the background hum of an air conditioner. Such attention to audio can elevate your product into the realm of professional. Premiere Pro 2 provides you with all the essential tools you need to adjust your audio. In fact, you apply audio effects to audio clips in the same way you apply video effects to video clips. The same is true for trimming audio in the **Source Monitor** and **Timeline** panels, as well as adding audio transitions. In this chapter, you will learn how to adjust the loudness of audio clips, apply audio effects and transitions, and even record your own voice-over as you narrate the action on the screen.

Displaying Audio

In Chapter 2, *"Importing and Editing,"* you worked with a few files containing audio. Some were clips with both audio and video—such as the actors in the history sequence—and others were files with audio only—such as the narrator's voice-over you turned into a subclip. You may recall viewing the waveform when editing those clips in the **Source Monitor**. As a reminder, a **waveform** is the visual representation of the sound within the audio clip.

Left

Right

Specifically, it is a graph of an audio's loudness—the louder the sound, the taller the wave (like a seismograph of an earthquake). Conversely, the shorter the waveform, the quieter the audio. A flat line represents silence. The waveform shown in the illustration here is a person talking. You can clearly see the silence between words when the actor is pausing or breathing. When a clip is in stereo, you will see two waveforms: one for the left stereo channel and one for the right stereo channel. When a clip is in mono, you will see only one waveform. (Note: Mono clips still play out of both speakers, even though they have only one waveform.)

Knowing how to read a waveform can help you understand where you should make edits, such as culling entire words, which are the big, black "chunks" between the silent points. Each waveform tells a story—whether it tells you how loud the audio is or whether it tells you how much silence you can find between words.

Understanding Clip Volume

You can use the **Volume** effect to change the loudness of a clip. All sound is measured in decibels (dB). The higher the decibel, the louder the sound. As an example, a jet engine 100 feet away measures about 150 dB, and someone whispering from 5 feet away measures 20 dB. The **Volume** effect increases or decreases the decibel level at which a clip plays.

Previously, you modified fixed effects of video clips and still images. These fixed effects included **Position, Scale**, and so on. Audio clips, however, have only one fixed effect: **Volume**. Because

volume is fixed, you can modify it and add keyframes, but you can never remove the **Volume** effect. (You can mute the volume, but the **Volume** effect remains.)

You can change the **Volume** fixed effect in one of two ways: in the **Timeline** panel or in the **Effect Controls** panel. In this chapter, you'll learn both methods. The **Volume** effect is animated with keyframes, in the same way you animated scale and opacity keyframes in previous chapters. Although you have yet to animate volume keyframes, you technically already know how to do it!

Changing Volume Versus Changing Gain

Now it's time to split hairs. The **Volume** effect doesn't *really* change the loudness of a clip. Technically speaking, volume changes how loud the sound *leaves* your computer speakers. However, another property of audio clips, the **Gain** effect, is responsible for changing the loudness of the clip itself. Confused yet?

In the music world, **volume** is the measure of the decibel level at which sound leaves the music device (such as a mixer, amplifier, and so on). **Gain** is the measure of the original sound coming into the device. An electric guitar, for example, has a much higher gain than a flute (unless it's an electric flute).

To translate that into the world of Premiere Pro 2, gain is the intrinsic "loudness" of a clip, whereas volume refers to the output level. Put yet another way, gain is the internal sound level before being touched by Premiere Pro 2; volume is an external effect applied to the clip.

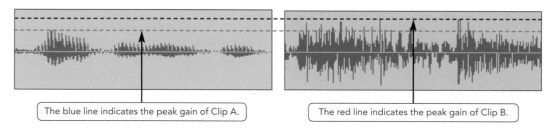

The blue line indicates the peak gain of Clip A.

The red line indicates the peak gain of Clip B.

Why is gain important, and why should you care? Here's a good example: Imagine you have a scene in which two actors are talking. You have two different shots—as shown in the illustration here, the audio on the left is the first actor talking, and the audio on the right is the second actor talking. The blue line represents the loudest point—or **peak**—of the first actor; the red line represents the peak of the second actor.

Without even listening to the clips, you can clearly see from the waveforms the second actor is talking much louder (perhaps her microphone was closer to her mouth). When you assemble these audio clips in a sequence, you will hear a noticeable difference in loudness every time you cut from the quiet actor to the loud actor.

It would be nice if you could match the two actors' "loudness" so the gain is equal and therefore less noticeable between shots. Luckily for you, Premiere Pro 2 provides a method—called **normalizing**—to take care of this very issue.

Normalizing Gain

Every single audio clip has a maximum threshold of how loud the sound can be before it begins to distort. This is called the **clipping threshold**. No matter the type of audio, this limit is the same.

When Premiere Pro 2 **normalizes** an audio clip, it scans the entire clip and calculates how many decibels it can increase or decrease the gain to reach the clipping threshold. Because the clipping threshold never changes, all clips that are normalized end up at the same gain level.

Keep in mind, when Premiere Pro 2 scans an audio clip, it scans for the *peak* level. In other words, it listens for the loudest point in the clip and then calculates how much the clip should be changed in order to reach the threshold.

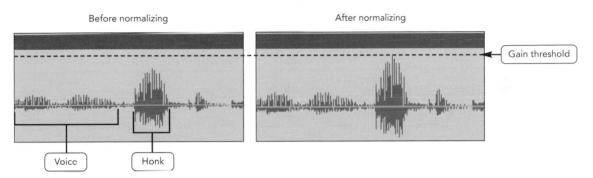

Before normalizing   After normalizing   Gain threshold   Voice   Honk

Why is this important to know? Imagine you have an audio clip of someone in a car talking on a cell phone. Suddenly, the car next to the actor honks. Because the honk is much louder than the actor's voice, the gain is loudest (it peaks) at the honk. When you normalize the audio clip, Premiere Pro 2 scans for the loudest point in the clip—which is the honk. So, your end result is a plenty loud car honk, but the voice is not as loud as it can be.

A workaround to this problem is to use the **Razor** tool to splice the audio clip into two separate clips: The first clip is the talking, and the second clip is the car honk. You can now normalize the voice as its own clip.

Warning: Normalizing very quiet audio will amplify everything in the clip, including background noise and hiss. For the best results, record source audio at the optimal levels with your camera and microphone. It's always better to decrease loud audio than it is to increase quiet audio.

In the next exercise, you will learn how to normalize the gain of multiple clips with ease.

1 | Changing Audio Gain

When working with audio, the first step is to normalize the gain. You should do this before adding effects or volume keyframes so all of your audio clips start at the same sound level. This helps prevent noticeable jumps between two people talking.

1 On the **Welcome Screen**, click **Open Project**. In the **Open Project** dialog box, navigate to the **c:\exercise_files\chap_10** folder, click **exercise01.prproj** to select it, and click **Open**.

2 Choose **File > Save As**. Navigate to the **c:\exercise_files\dutch_harbor** folder. Name the file **dutch harbor promo.prproj**, and click **Save**.

Note: If a previous version of dutch harbor promo.prproj already exists, you may be asked to replace it. Click Yes.

This exercise file is currently set to a custom workspace similar to the HOT workspace. When normalizing audio, you will be doing much of your work in the Timeline. You should use a workspace that allows you to see as much of the Timeline as possible.

3 In the **Timeline** panel, next to Track **Audio 1**, click the **arrow** icon next to **Collapse/Expand Track** to expand the audio track.

Because you are zoomed out and because the track is not very tall, it is hard to view the waveforms. When the audio track is expanded, you are able to see the waveforms.

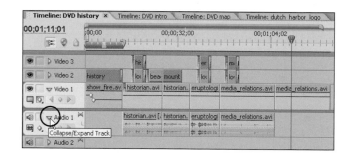

4 Position your cursor over the dividing line between Tracks **Audio 1** and **Audio 2**. When you see the track adjust pointer, click and drag to the bottom of the **Timeline** panel to increase the height of Track **Audio 1**.

With the track taller, you are better able to visualize the

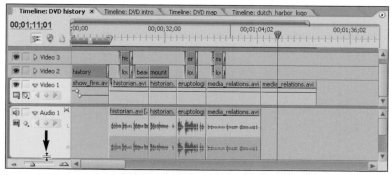

waveforms below each audio clip. You can see the third clip, eruptologist.avi, is much louder than the others, as indicated by the taller waveform. Normalizing will help even out the loudness.

5 On Track **Audio 1**, right-click the first **historian.avi** clip, and choose **Audio Gain**. In the **Clip Gain** dialog box, click the **Normalize** button, and click **OK**.

Based on the peak volume of this clip, Premiere Pro 2 calculates it can increase the gain by 3.8 dB before the clip's loudness reaches the clipping threshold.

---

6 Snap the **Timeline CTI (Current Time Indicator)** to the beginning of the first **historian.avi** clip at **00;00;13;00**. Press the **spacebar** to play the sequence. When Premiere Pro 2 reaches the end of the second **historian.avi** clip, press the **spacebar** to stop. The Timeline CTI should be at **00;00;36;10**.

As the sequence plays, listen for a difference in loudness between the first and second clips. The first clip sounds slightly louder (by about 3.8 dB). To fix this, you can normalize the second clip so they are equally loud.

---

7 On Track **Audio 1**, right-click the second **historian.avi** clip, and choose **Audio Gain**. In the **Clip Gain** dialog box, click the **Normalize** button, and click **OK**.

This time, Premiere Pro 2 calculates it can increase the gain by 6.2 dB.

---

8 Snap the **Timeline CTI** to the beginning of the first **historian.avi** clip at **00;00;13;00**. In the **Program Monitor**, click the **Play** button. Play the sequence until the clip reaches the end of the second **historian.avi** clip, and click the **Stop** button at **00;00;36;10**.

As the second audio clip begins playing, you can detect a noticeable jump in the loudness. This raises an interesting question: If these two audio clips originated from one long audio clip, why were they normalized by different amounts? Well, the actor must have been louder when emphasizing a certain word in the first clip.

So which normalizing amount is the correct one? Answer: It's usually better to err on the side of the lesser amount. When you normalize too much, you introduce artificial sounds and ambient noise. In other words, it's better to be slightly less loud than overly loud.

---

9 On Track **Audio 1**, right-click the second **historian.avi** clip, and choose **Audio Gain**. In the **Clip Gain** dialog box, drag the gain amount from **6.2** to **3.8**. Click **OK**.

Instead of letting Premiere Pro 2 determine the gain amount, you manually changed the gain by 3.8 dB, which is the same gain increase of the first clip. When you play the clip, you should not notice any change in loudness between the two clips.

---

10 On Track **Audio 1**, right-click the **eruptologist.avi** clip, and choose **Audio Gain**. In the **Clip Gain** dialog box, click the **Normalize** button, and click **OK**.

This time, Premiere Pro 2 suggested only a modest 0.9 dB increase—which isn't so surprising, considering how much "louder" the eruptologist.avi waveform appears.

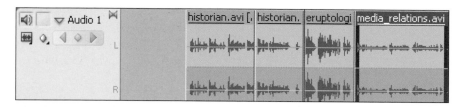

11 On Track **Audio 1**, right-click the **media_relations.avi** clip, and choose **Audio Gain**. In the **Clip Gain** dialog box, click the **Normalize** button, and click **OK**.

As the short waveform indicates, the actor in this clip is very quiet. Premiere Pro 2 increases the gain by about 10.5 dB to compensate. Unfortunately, when you make the voice louder, you also make every other noise louder, even the background hum. This can have the adverse effect of accenting less-than-ideal microphone noise.

To appreciate this problem, it may help to play both eruptologist.avi and media_relations.avi to compare the sound.

12 Snap the **Timeline CTI** to the beginning of the first **eruptologist.avi** clip, at **00;00;36;10**. Press the **spacebar** to play the sequence. At the end of **media_relations.avi**, press the **spacebar** to stop. The **Timeline** CTI should be at **00;01;05;21**.

This is a perfect example of the problem introduced by normalizing. Even though these two actors are now technically at the same gain level because the female actor had her gain increased by such a large amount, her audio sounds terrible because of the overwhelming background noise. (This actor's microphone was probably not close enough to her mouth.)

To fix this, Premiere Pro 2 offers an EQ audio effect that can help filter out unwanted background noise by removing sounds in specific ranges. You will do this in the next exercise.

13 Choose **File > Save**, or press **Ctrl+S**. Leave **dutch harbor promo.prproj** open for the next exercise.

Normalizing your audio helps your audio clips output at a consistent level. When normalizing, you have to sometimes override the gain amount suggested by Premiere Pro 2 to prevent unwanted background noises from becoming apparent.

Overnormalizing can also be a potential hazard when razoring clips into sections that are too small, such as by turning every word into its own clip. As humans, we naturally speak each word at a slightly different level for *emphasis*. If you normalize each word separately, not only do you run the chance of heightening the background noise but also the sentence won't sound natural. Normalizing gain works best when you can keep as much of a clip intact as possible so the overall loudness sounds more natural.

2 | Applying an EQ Audio Effect

After normalizing your audio, you may discover unwanted background noise in your audio clips. In these cases, the next step in your audio workflow is to apply audio effects. You apply audio effects the same way as their video counterparts—so you actually already know how to apply them. One of the most powerful audio effects is the **EQ** effect, which filters out unwanted noise. This helps isolate the "good" portion of the audio clip and ideally suppresses the unwanted, "bad" portion. The **EQ** effect can filter specific **frequencies**, or ranges of audio. For example, if you discover your unwanted background noise has a high pitch, you can suppress the high frequencies only. In this exercise, you will learn how to apply the **EQ** effect to your audio clips.

---

1 If you followed the previous exercise, **dutch harbor promo.prproj** should still be open in Premiere Pro 2. If it's not, click **Open Project** on the **Welcome Screen**. Navigate to the **c:\exercise_files\chap_10** folder, click **exercise02.prproj** to select it, and click **Open**.

---

2 Choose **File > Save As**. Navigate to the **c:\exercise_files\dutch_harbor** folder. Name the file **dutch harbor promo.prproj**, and click **Save**.

Note: If a previous version of dutch harbor promo.prproj already exists, you may be asked to replace it. Click Yes.

---

3 Choose **Window > Workspace > Effects**. Drag the **Timeline CTI** to **00;00;20;00**.

---

4 In the **Effects** panel, click the **arrow** icon next to **Audio Effects** to expand its effects.

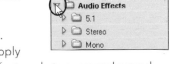

The Audio Effects folder contains three subfolders: 5.1, Stereo, and Mono. Most of the effects in each folder are the same, but you must be sure to apply the correct effect to the type of clip you have. You should apply the 5.1 effects only to surround-sound clips with 5.1 channels of audio (as opposed to stereo's two channels), you should apply the Mono effects only to mono audio clips, and you should apply the stereo effects only to stereo clips.

---

5 In the **Effects** panel **Audio Effects** folder, click the **arrow** icon next to the **Stereo** subfolder to expand its contents. Drag and drop the **EQ** audio effect on the first **historian.avi** clip on Track **Audio 1**.

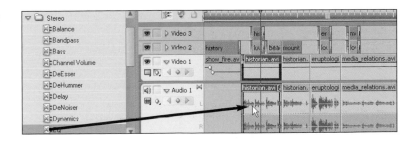

You can tell this clip is in stereo because it shows two waveforms (stereo left and stereo right). If it were mono, it would show only one waveform. This means you should apply effects from the Stereo subfolder only.

6 If your **Effect Controls** panel displays the **mini-Timeline**, click the **Show/Hide Timeline View** toggle in the upper-right corner to turn off the **mini-Timeline**.

7 Scroll down in the **Effect Controls** panel, and click the **arrow** icon next to **EQ** to expand its properties.

Audio effects are always listed under the Audio Effects heading and appear below any video effects in the Effect Controls panel.

8 Under **EQ**, click the **arrow** icon next to **Custom Setup** to expand its properties.

The EQ effect acts as a parametric equalizer—and who doesn't know what that is, right?

Basically, a **parametric equalizer** allows you to increase or decrease certain "portions" of the audio range. If you want to get rid of a loud bass sound, you can decrease the gain of the low frequencies. If you want to eliminate a high-pitched hiss, you can decrease the gain of just the high frequencies.

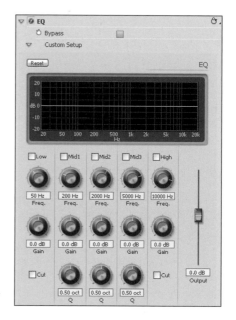

9 In the **Effect Controls** panel, click the **Toggle looping audio playback** toggle.

Turning on this option puts the audio playback in loop mode, which means once you start playing the audio as you make adjustments, it will loop over and over—until you stop playback.

Tip: Because looping audio may cause others around you to become violent after the tenth loop, you may want to put on some headphones.

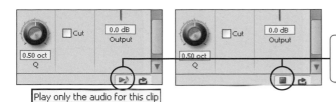

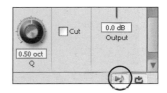

When looping audio for effects tweaking, always use these play and stop buttons, found in the lower-right corner of the Effect Controls panel.

Play only the audio for this clip

In the next few steps, you will tweak the audio EQ effect while listening to the looped playback. Because you might get sick of hearing the looped audio while reading this book, you can stop and restart the audio playback by clicking the **Play only the audio for this clip** button in the lower-right corner of the Effect Controls panel, as shown in the illustration here.

10 In the **Effect Controls** panel, click the **Play only the audio for this clip** button to begin playback. If you need to stop the looped playback, click the same button.

The audio playback feature in the Effect Controls panel plays only the audio of the selected clip. Don't be alarmed if the video appears frozen—this is by design. With the video frozen, Premiere Pro 2 is able to put all of its resources into accurately playing your audio clip.

As this clip plays, notice the high-pitched hiss, which is part of the ambient noise in the room where the actor was recorded. To remove this, you will use the EQ effect to filter out the sound falling in the high frequencies. The goal is to filter out the frequency range not normally found in a human's voice so you can successfully suppress all sound in that range.

11 In the **Effect Controls** panel, below the EQ graph, turn on the **High** check box to filter for the High values. While the audio is still looping, in the same **High** column, click the **High Gain** knob, and drag your mouse all the way to the left, until the gain is **–20.0 dB**.

As the audio loops, you should notice moving the High Gain knob to the left reduces the ambient noise found in the high frequency range.

Tip: If you want to test the audio, you can move the High Gain knob all the way to the right, in which case you will hear a very pronounced hiss. When done comparing, make sure you move the High Gain knob all the way to the left, at –20.0 dB.

Tip: Your natural reaction may be to try to *rotate* the knob, like a clock dial. Unfortunately, the knob shape is for looks only. To change the knob values, drag your mouse left or right in a straight line, just as you have done while changing other values in the Effect Controls panel.

12 Scroll to the top of the **EQ** effect. While the audio plays, turn on the **Bypass** check box to temporarily turn off the effect. Turn this check box on and off, several times, as the audio plays. When done, make sure the **Bypass** check box is turned off.

The effect is temporarily off when Bypass is on.

The effect is on when Bypass is off.

To compare the effect, you can turn on the Bypass check box of the EQ effect while it continuously plays. (It may seem counterintuitive, but turning *on* Bypass has the result of turning *off* the effect.)

When bypassing the audio effect, you should be able to hear the high-pitched room noise. When Bypass is turned off, the EQ effect is turned on, and the high frequencies are filtered out.

---

13 While the audio plays, drag the **High Frequency** knob slowly to the left, until the value is approximately **7151 Hz**.

By lowering the frequency value, you are increasing the range of frequencies caught in your net, so to speak. Instead of filtering out frequencies 10,000 Hz and greater, now you are filtering out frequencies 7,151 Hz and greater (or as close as you can get to 7,151 when dragging with your mouse).

In the EQ graph, you can see the green node (kind of like a keyframe) is acutely shifted to the left, at 7151 Hz.

Because all the actors were recorded in the same room, you can apply this effect to the other actors with the same effect parameters. To do this, it may be helpful to first save this effect as a preset, which you will do in the next step.

---

14 In the **Effect Controls** panel, scroll to the top of the **EQ** effect, and right-click the effect name **EQ**. In the **Save Preset** dialog box, click **OK** to save the preset with the default name of **EQ Preset**.

---

15 In the **Effects** panel, click the **arrow** icon next to **Presets** to expand the folder. Drag and drop the **EQ Preset** on the second **historian.avi** clip on Track **Audio 1**. Because the second clip is automatically selected when adding an effect, in the **Effect Controls** panel, click the **Play only the audio for this clip** button to listen to the effect on the second clip.

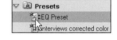

If you'd like to listen to before and after comparisons, you can scroll the Effect Controls panel to the top of the EQ effect and then turn on the Bypass check box during looped playback. When done, make sure the Bypass check box is turned off.

---

16 In the **Effects** panel, drag and drop the **EQ Preset** on **eruptologist.avi** on Track **Audio 1**. In the **Effect Controls** panel, click the **Play only the audio for this clip** button to listen to the effect.

As you did in the previous step, feel free to turn the Bypass check box on and off during looped playback for this clip. When done, make sure the Bypass check box is turned off.

17 In the **Effects** panel, drag and drop the **EQ Preset** on **media_relations.avi** on Track **Audio 1**. In the **Effect Controls** panel, click the **Play only the audio for this clip** button to listen to the effect.

This clip is slightly different from the other two. Because its gain was increased so much when normalizing, some other ambient noise is still noticeable. However, the remaining noise sounds like lower frequencies (such as a fan or air filter in the background). You can also filter out the low frequencies to remove this noise.

18 In the **Effect Controls** panel, scroll down to the **EQ knobs**. Turn on the **Low** check box. Drag the **Low Gain** knob all the way to the left, until the value is **–20.0 dB**.

19 While the audio plays, turn the **Low** check box on and off to compare what the effect sounds like with the low frequencies filtered out. When done, make sure the **Low** check box is turned on. Click the **Play only audio for this clip** button to stop looped playback.

It's a subtle difference, but you can definitely hear a low-frequency hum that is removed after applying the low frequency filter.

20 Choose **File > Save**, or press **Ctrl+S**. Leave **dutch harbor promo.prproj** open for the next exercise.

You could easily spend another few hours tweaking and adjusting the audio to get it just right. However, the equalization concepts you have learned here will help you understand how to set other audio effects in Premiere Pro 2, which often rely on frequency ranges and knobs.

When working with the EQ effect to clean a person's speech, it's helpful to start by reducing the High and Low frequencies. These ranges usually don't include human voices. If you still hear unwanted sound, you can try tweaking some of the other frequencies closer to the middle of the spectrum, but do this with care because you will definitely begin to suppress some of the "good" audio of the actor's voice.

In this exercise, you were told which ranges to use, but in the real world, you have to find out for yourself by testing each range.

VIDEO: | **eq_audio.mov**
To learn more about applying the **EQ** audio effect, check out **eq_audio.mov** in the **videos** folder on the **Premiere Pro 2 HOT DVD-ROM**.

3 | Applying a Reverb Effect

Sometimes filtering out too much of a sound's frequency can result in dry or unnatural sound, such as removing the natural echo of a room. You can restore the natural echo of a room by adding reverb. **Reverb**, in a general sense, is the reverberation of audio bouncing off of walls, floors, ceilings, and so on. The **Reverb** effect adds spatial properties to your sound, as if your sound was recorded in a large cathedral or a small room with shag carpet (or, better yet, a van with shag carpet!). Reverb can add a vocal presence to the audio, as if the person was in the room with you. In this exercise, you will apply a **Reverb** effect to restore some of the natural echo accidentally filtered out by the **EQ** effect in the previous exercise.

---

1 If you followed the previous exercise, **dutch harbor promo.prproj** should still be open in Premiere Pro 2. If it's not, click **Open Project** on the **Welcome Screen**. Navigate to the **c:\exercise_files\chap_10** folder, click **exercise03.prproj** to select it, and click **Open**.

---

2 Choose **File > Save As**. Navigate to the **c:\exercise_files\dutch_harbor** folder. Name the file **dutch harbor promo.prproj**, and click **Save**.

Note: If a previous version of dutch harbor promo.prproj already exists, you may be asked to replace it. Click Yes.

---

3 In the **Effects** panel **Audio Effects** folder, click the **arrow** icon next to the **Stereo** subfolder to expand its contents. Drag and drop the **Reverb** effect on the first **historian.avi** clip on Track **Audio 1**.

---

4 If your **Effect Controls** panel displays the **mini-Timeline**, click the **Show/Hide Timeline View** toggle in the upper-right corner to turn off the **mini-Timeline**.

---

5 If audio looping is turned off, in the lower-right corner of the **Effect Controls** panel, click the **Toggle looping audio playback** toggle to turn it on.

---

6 Scroll down in the **Effect Controls** panel, and click the **arrow** icon next to **Reverb** to expand the audio effect. Click the **arrow** icon next to **Custom Setup** to display its properties.

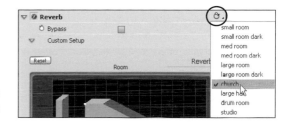

This Reverb effect has a 3D graph, providing a visual representation of the effect. But you do not need to understand the graph in order to use this effect. Even though the graph sure is pretty, you can basically ignore it if you'd like.

Some audio effects, such as Reverb, come equipped with presets you can use to achieve different results. Effects containing presets have a tiny arrow on their Reset/Preset buttons. To open the preset list, click the Reset/Preset button.

---

7 Next to the **Reverb** effect name, click the **Reset/ Preset** button, and choose **church**. At the bottom of the **Effect Controls** panel, click the **Play only audio for this clip** button.

You should be able to hear a noticeable reverberation effect, as if this actor was taped inside of a church. It's also important to note that many of these presets are applied *to the hilt*; in other words, you may not want to use them as is because they are so overwhelmingly fake. The idea is to apply them and then decrease the effect until it sounds a little more lifelike.

---

8 Next to the **Reverb** effect name, click the **Reset/Preset** button, and choose **small room**. At the bottom of the **Effect Controls** panel, click the **Play only audio for this clip** button.

The reverberation here is much subtler. The minor amount of reverberation/echo in this preset results in the sense that the actor is speaking in a small room.

Reverb vocabulary: The word **bright** indicates more of an echo, and its opposite is **dark**, which indicates less of an echo. In terms of different rooms, bright would be wooden or marble floors, and dark would be carpeted.

To really notice the Reverb effect, you can turn its Bypass check box on and off.

---

9 While the audio plays back, scroll to the top of the **Reverb** effect, and turn the **Bypass** check box on and off to compare the audio with and without the effect. When you are finished, make sure **Bypass** is off.

Some of the presets, although handy, can yield unrealistic results. After you choose a preset *close* to what you want, you can manually tweak it further.

10 In the **Effect Controls** panel, scroll down to the knobs below the reverb graph. As the audio plays back, drag the **Lo Damp** and **Hi Damp** knobs all the way to the left, at **–15.00 dB**.

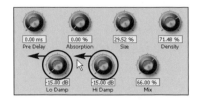

You should immediately notice a difference in the reverb. Lo Damp reduces the low frequencies of the effect, which prevents the reverb from rumbling or sounding muddy. Hi Damp reduces the high frequencies, which removes the metallic, tinny sound of the echo. (This is similar to the EQ effect you applied in the previous exercise, but the Lo and Hi Damp filter out only the echo frequencies created by the Reverb effect, not the actor's voice.)

Keep in mind it is hard to describe sound on the printed page. To fully appreciate the effect of each knob, you can drag the knobs as far left and right as they go during looped audio playback and then compare the resulting sound qualities.

---

11 As the audio plays, drag the **Size** knob slightly to the left, to **20.00 %** (or as close as you can get).

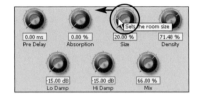

Size specifies the size of the room as a percentage. (A church is 100 percent.) Reducing the room size makes the room feel more intimate, which is appropriate in this sit-down interview clip with the historian.

---

12 As the audio plays, change the **Mix** knob to approximately **45.00 %**. Turn the **Bypass** check box on and off to compare the end result with the original audio clip. When you are finished, make sure **Bypass** is off.

Mix controls the amount of reverb applied to the clip. An amount of 00.00 % would have no reverb and would sound as if the effect was turned off.

Tip: For a complete description of each available property, the Adobe Help manual is a great resource.

---

13 In the **Effect Controls** panel, scroll to the top of the **Reverb** effect. Right-click the effect named **Reverb**, and choose **Save Preset**. In the **Save Preset** dialog box, click **OK**.

Tip: The preset's default name is the effect name plus the word Preset. In your own projects, you can make this more descriptive, such as "Brian's audio from day one," so you know to which clips you should apply it. You can also provide a description.

14 In the **Effects** panel, click the **arrow** icon next to **Presets** to expand the folder. Drag and drop the **Reverb Preset** on the second **historian.avi** clip on Track **Audio 1**. As you did previously, preview the effect by clicking the **Play only audio for this clip** button.

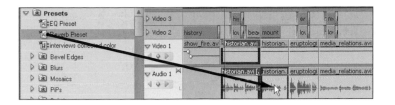

15 In the **Effects** panel, drag and drop the **Reverb Preset** on the **eruptologist.avi** clip on Track **Audio 1**.

16 Click the **Play only audio for this clip** button. While the audio plays back, scroll to the bottom of the **Reverb** effect, and change the **Mix** to **35.00 %**.

Because this speaker is naturally louder, it seemed like a 45 % Mix was giving a tad too much reverb. Lowering the mix to 35 % seems more natural.

17 In the **Effects** panel, drag and drop the **Reverb Preset** on the **media_relations.avi** clip on Track **Audio 1**.

18 As you did with the previous clip, click the **Play only audio for this clip** button. While audio plays back, scroll to the bottom of the **Reverb** effect, and change the **Mix** to **35.00 %**. When you are finished, click the **Stop** button to stop the audio playback.

19 Choose **File > Save**, or press **Ctrl+S**. Leave **dutch harbor promo.prproj** open for the next exercise.

You may be asking yourself, "Why did I have to remove all the background noise if I was going to put it right back in?" The EQ effect removed unwanted microphone hiss and ambient noise, but it also removed some of the good noise you wanted. The Reverb effect put some of that good noise back in to give your audio some presence and the feeling of being in the room with the speaker.

Don't forget, like many of the audio presets available in Premiere Pro 2, the preset may apply itself with unrealistic properties. It is up to you to tone the preset down until it sounds more realistic and you are happy with the results.

Reading the VU Meter

VU (**V**olume **U**nits) meters measure audio in terms of decibels. All of the audio meters in Premiere Pro 2 are VU meters because they measure the audio in decibels.

As shown in the illustration here, each bar of a VU meter represents a channel of audio. Stereo sequences have two channels: left and right. Mono sequences have one. Surround-sound 5.1 sequences have six bars—five audio channels plus one for bass.

As the sequence plays, the current volume level displays in the VU meter. The current level is continually on the move because the volume is always increasing and decreasing.

The **peak level** represents the maximum volume. When the VU meter peaks, a tiny bar remains for a few seconds to represent the peak level. As shown in the illustration here (left), the current level is at about –6 dB, but the peak level bars indicate a recent volume spike up to almost 0 dB.

The VU meters are color coded to represent the safe and dangerous volume levels. Anything less than –6 dB shows as green, which is a safe volume level. Anything from 0 dB to –6 dB is yellow and should be avoided unless absolutely necessary. When the volume spikes in the red, the volume has exceeded the clipping threshold and will result in digital distortion.

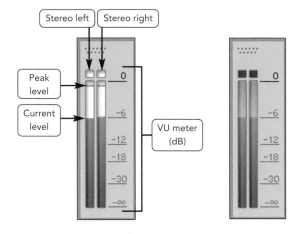

Anything greater than 0 dB will result in clipping. **Clipping** can best be described as loud, static, cacophonous noise. *Never, ever, ever* send out a finished product with audio greater than 0 dB. In fact, most DV camcorders normalize their audio to about –12 dB. As a rule of thumb, try to keep your projects from –12 dB to –6 dB. Many editors aim for an average level of –12 dB, and they never permit their levels to peak at greater than –6 dB.

In the following exercise, you will limit the volume of your clips to match the desired –12 dB to –6 dB.

4 | Modifying Clip Volume

As you learned earlier, **Volume** is a fixed effect of each audio clip. You cannot remove the **Volume** effect, but you can mute it by reducing its value to −∞. You can modify volume levels either by using the **Effect Controls** panel or by using the **Timeline** panel. In this exercise, you will practice lowering the volume of several clips to make sure they fall within the appropriate range of −12dB to −6dB on the VU meter.

1 If you followed the previous exercise, **dutch harbor promo.prproj** should still be open in Premiere Pro 2. If it's not, click **Open Project** on the **Welcome Screen**. Navigate to the **c:\exercise_files\chap_10** folder, click **exercise04.prproj** to select it, and click **Open**.

2 Choose **File > Save As**. Navigate to the **c:\exercise_files\dutch_harbor** folder. Name the file **dutch harbor promo.prproj**, and click **Save**.

Note: If a previous version of dutch harbor promo.prproj already exists, you may be asked to replace it. Click Yes

In this exercise, you will reduce the volume of several audio clips in different sequences to ensure they all fall within the safe range of −12 dB to −6 dB. To make volume changes in the Timeline, you need to change the track display.

3 In the **Timeline**, select the **DVD intro** tab to bring that sequence to the foreground. Click the **arrow** icon next to Track **Audio 2** to view the waveform. In the track options area for Track **Audio 2**, click the **Set Display Style** button, and choose **Show Name Only**.

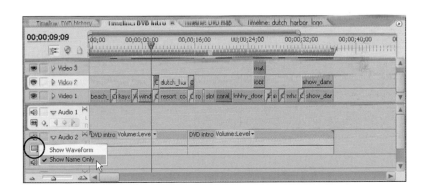

Because you will be editing the volume graph directly in the Timeline panel, it is helpful to hide the waveform, which allows you to see the volume graph better.

4 In the track options area for Track **Audio 2**, click the **Show Keyframes** button, and choose **Show Clip Volume**.

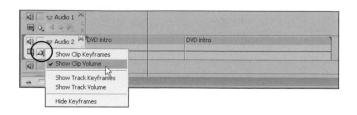

This displays the keyframes for *only* the audio volume. The thin black line you see in the middle of the audio clips represents the volume. Currently, the value is at 0.0 dB.

Note: You might think a volume of 0.0 dB is no sound, or **mute**. Alas, volume does not behave this way—0.0 dB means you have changed the volume by zero decibels. All clips start with a default volume of 0.0 dB.

To determine how much to change the volume for a clip, you should first monitor its volume level in the VU meters. Watch for any peak greater than –6 dB.

---

5 Drag the **Timeline CTI** to the beginning of the sequence, or press the **Home** key. Press the **spacebar** to play the sequence. Watch the VU meters during playback. After you have listened to several seconds, click the **spacebar** to stop.

While the clip plays, the VU meter is jumping up and down. Overall, you will notice most of the levels play at or about –6 dB, although you will see an occasional peak up to 0.0 dB. The goal of adjusting the volume is to reduce the audio so it plays from –12 dB to –6 dB and rarely peaks at greater than –6 dB.

---

6 In the **Timeline** panel, position your cursor over the audio graph of the first clip on Track **Audio 2**. As slowly as you can, click and drag anywhere in the value graph and then lower the value to approximately **–5.37 dB** (or as close as you can get).

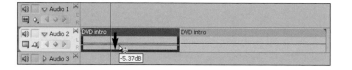

You have just lowered the overall value of the clip's volume—from start to finish. You will also notice, based on the height of the audio track and your computer monitor, you may be unable to get the exact value you'd like.

---

7 To verify the audio of the first clip is indeed lower, press the **Home** key, and press the **spacebar** to play the sequence. Monitor the VU meters during playback. At the beginning of the second clip, click the **Stop** button to stop playback.

This time, the VU meters tend to level out between –12 and –6 dB and peak at –6 dB.

A quick way to copy the volume level of one clip to another is to copy and paste attributes, a shortcut you have used in previous chapters.

---

8 On Track **Audio 2**, right-click the first audio clip, and choose **Copy**. On Track **Audio 2**, right-click the second audio clip, and choose **Paste Attributes**.

After pasting the attributes, you should notice the volume graphs of both clips are even with each other. If you'd like to verify the lowered volume level, you can play the sequence while monitoring the VU meters.

9 Snap the **Timeline CTI** to the beginning of **dutch_harbor_logo** on Track **Video 2**. Press the **spacebar** to play the sequence. Monitor the VU meters during playback, and compare the first and second audio clips. After you have compared enough, you can press the **spacebar** to stop playback.

You have just learned the quickest and easiest way to modify the volume of an entire clip. You can also perform this action in the Effect Controls panel.

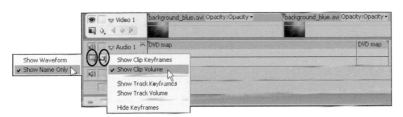

10 At the top of the **Timeline** panel, select the **DVD map** tab to bring that sequence to the foreground. If Track **Audio 1** is not expanded, click the **arrow** icon next to its name to expand it. On Track **Audio 1**, in the track options area, click the **Set Display Style** button, and choose **Show Name Only**. Click the **Show Keyframes** button, and choose **Show Clip Volume**.

Even though you will be doing your work in the Effect Controls panel, this technique allows you to watch how the volume graph in the Timeline is affected by your changes.

11 On Track **Audio 1**, click the first clip to select it. In the **Effect Controls** panel, click the **arrow** icon next to **Volume** to expand the fixed audio effect.

12 Drag the **Timeline CTI** to 00;00;11;25 to see what is happening concurrently in the **Timeline**. In the **Effect Controls** panel, change the **Level** value to –5.3 dB.

Changing the Level value in the Effect Controls panel has the same effect as changing it in the Timeline. Both methods lower the volume graph.

Why did you have to move the Timeline CTI? This highlights one major difference between the two methods—changing volume levels in the Audio Effects panel creates a keyframe! Notice the keyframe on the value graph in the Timeline, created at the CTI? This next step should help focus the issue.

13 Move the **Timeline CTI** to **00;00;03;11**. In the **Effect Controls** panel, change **Level** to **+6.0 dB**.

Yikes—did you notice what happened in the Timeline? A new keyframe was created at the CTI. Now the clip has two keyframes. The volume starts at +6.0 dB and lowers to –5.3 dB. This is not exactly what you wanted.

This underscores an important point about some effects, such as Level. By default, their keyframe mode is turned on. (Notice the stopwatch icons next to Level.) With other effects you've used, you had to explicitly turn *on* keyframe mode. This is not so with volume. It's on from the get-go!

Because creating a volume "fade" was not exactly what you wanted to do, you can quickly remove all keyframes by turning *off* keyframe mode.

---

14 In the **Effect Controls** panel **Volume** effect, click the **Toggle Animation** toggle next to the **Level** property to turn off keyframe mode. In the **Warning** dialog box, click **OK** to delete all existing keyframes. In the **Effect Controls** panel, change **Level** back to **–5.3 dB**.

Because keyframe mode is off, changing the volume level does *not* create a keyframe, and the change applies to the entire clip.

---

15 On Track **Audio 1**, select the second audio clip. In the **Effect Controls** panel, click the **arrow** icon next to **Volume** to expand the effect. Next to **Level**, click the **Toggle Animation** toggle to turn off keyframe mode for this property. Change **Level** to **–3.7 dB**.

Tip: If you do not need to change the volume level over time, then it is safest to turn off the Level property keyframe mode. This prevents accidental keyframes from being created.

---

16 Choose **File > Save**, or press **Ctrl+S**. Leave **dutch harbor promo.prproj** open for the next exercise.

You probably noticed changing value graphs in the Timeline is easier when you want to adjust an entire clip quickly. However, when using the Timeline, you lose the ability to fine-tune the values, like you can do with the Effect Controls. Changing the volume level in the Effect Controls gives you fine value adjustments, but you may have to first disable keyframe mode.

No matter the method, the goal is the same: Use the volume adjustments to monitor the levels of your clips in the VU meter. Strive for –12 dB to –6 dB.

In the next exercise, you will use volume keyframes to change the level over time.

NOTE:

VU Meter Versus Volume

Your head may be spinning with all this talk of decibels, VU meters, and volume graphs. It's easy to confuse the concepts behind VU meters and volume because both measure audio in terms of decibels. But there is an important difference:

VU meters: The meters tell you the final audio output level of your sound in decibels. You do not want your VU meters to ever peak at greater than 0.0 dB, or else you will get distortion.

Volume: This is also measured in terms of decibels, but volume measures how much the clip is being adjusted. That is, if you decrease volume to –12 dB, this does *not* mean the VU meters will read –12 dB; rather, this means you are lowering the existing clip by –12 dB.

Also, it's important to note volume is *relative* to each clip. If Clip A is louder than Clip B, changing the level by –12 dB on both clips will lower the levels, but Clip A will still be louder than Clip B because it started out louder.

Although it is helpful to know how to lower the volume of an entire clip, more often than not you want to lower the volume of just a particular section, say in the middle of a clip. This helps eliminate an unwanted word, breath, sound, or anything else you don't want the audience to hear. Conversely, you can increase the volume of a particular section to emphasize a word, sound, and so on. You achieve this by setting keyframes in the **Effect Controls** panel or **Timeline** panel. The keyframes are the same as the keyframes you've set before. This exercise will walk you through how to set keyframes for the **Volume** effect to mute a portion of an audio track you don't want.

1 If you followed the previous exercise, **dutch harbor promo.prproj** should still be open in Premiere Pro 2. If it's not, click **Open Project** on the **Welcome Screen**. Navigate to the **c:\exercise_files\chap_10** folder, click **exercise05.prproj** to select it, and click **Open**.

2 Choose **File > Save As**. Navigate to the **c:\exercise_files\dutch_harbor** folder. Name the file **dutch harbor promo.prproj**, and click **Save**.

Note: If a previous version of dutch harbor promo.prproj already exists, you may be asked to replace it. Click Yes.

3 At the top of the **Timeline** panel, select the **DVD history** tab to bring it to the foreground. Drag the **Timeline CTI** to **00;00;38;21**.

It can be much easier to mute a small section of audio if you zoom in on just the portion of audio to which you want to listen. When zoomed in, the waveforms appear much bigger, and you can easily view the "spaces" between each word.

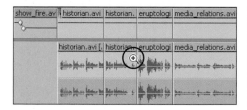 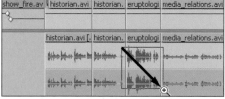

4 In the **Tools** panel, select the **Zoom** tool. On Track **Audio 1**, click and drag the **Zoom** tool from the upper-left corner to the lower-right corner of the **eruptologist.avi** waveform.

When you release the mouse after dragging, the Timeline panel automatically zooms to the area you specified.

Note: Unlike other Adobe applications, the Zoom tool zooms in only to the width you specified when dragging. However, the height you drag has no bearing on the final zoom amount.

5 In the **Tools** panel, choose the **Selection** tool. On Track **Audio 1**, click the **eruptologist.avi** clip to select it. If the mini-Timeline is not visible in the **Effect Controls** panel, click the **Show/Hide Timeline View** toggle to turn it on.

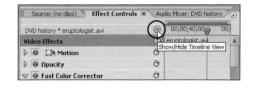

In this case, you want to get rid of the word high when the actor says, "...being buried in a massive landslide of molten lava are *high*. Very, very *high*." (After all, why would Dutch Harbor want to let potential tourists know this ominous fact?)

The first step is to position the CTI at the start of the section you want to mute.

---

6 In the **Program Monitor**, click the **Play** button. Play the sequence until the actor says, "...being buried in a massive landslide of molten lava are," and then click the **Stop** button at **00;00;42;26**.

In this case, you want the volume to begin fading out at 00;00;42;26.

---

7 In the **Effect Controls** panel, scroll down to the **Volume** audio effect and expand it. In the **Keyframe Navigator** next to the **Level** property, click the **Add/Remove Keyframe** button to create a new keyframe with the value of **0.0 dB** at **00;00;42;26**.

Before creating the next keyframe, you should move the CTI to where you would like it to finish fading to mute. In this case, you want to move the CTI right before the actor says "high."

---

8 Press the **right arrow** key to advance the **CTI** one frame at a time—until you hear the actor start to say "high"—at **00;00;43;01**.

---

9 In the **Effect Controls** panel, click and drag the **Level** value all the way to the left, until it is at its minimum of **–287.5 dB**.

 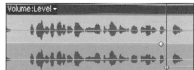

This creates a new keyframe. This step is an excellent example of how keyframe durations appear differently in the Effect Controls panel and the Timeline panel. In the Effect Controls panel, the two keyframes appear to be almost on top of each other—it's hard to discern how far apart they occur. However, because the Timeline is so much wider, you can clearly see the distance between the two keyframes.

The moral of this tiny story is this: Even when creating keyframes in the Effect Controls panel, you may find it useful to view them in the Timeline panel to get a spatial idea of where they are.

Next you want to move the CTI to where the volume should start fading back up. This is tricky because you have the volume completely turned off! Luckily, you can see the waveforms in the Timeline panel. (Aren't you clever?)

---

10 Press the **right arrow** key to advance the **Timeline CTI** to the point when the waveform ends at 00;00;43;16.

This waveform indicates where the actor finishes speaking the word "high."

---

11 In the **Effect Controls** panel, click the **Add/Remove Keyframe** button in the **Keyframe Navigator** next to the **Level** property.

This creates a third keyframe with the existing value of –287.5 dB.

Next, you should advance the CTI to where the volume finishes fading back up.

---

12 Press the **right arrow** key to advance the **Timeline CTI** to the point before the next waveform at **00;00;44;02**. In the **Effect Controls** panel, click the **Level** value, and type a new value of **0**. Press **Enter** to accept the value.

---

13 To preview this volume effect, in the **Program Monitor**, slowly drag the **Jog Wheel** left and right to listen to the group of keyframes.

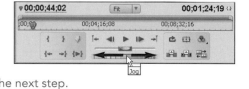

Note: Be careful not to jog the CTI outside the existing Timeline view because you need to return to this location in the next step.

You have successfully faded volume out and in using keyframes in the Effect Controls panel. Next, you perform the same task using the Timeline panel. The first step, as last time, is to move the Timeline CTI to where you want the volume to begin to fade out.

---

14 Move the **Timeline CTI** to where the first keyframe volume should be created, as the actor says "Very, very...," at **00;00;45;02**.

Because the keyframes you will create will be close together, it will be helpful to zoom in.

---

15 In the **Zoom Controls** of the **Timeline** panel, click the **Zoom in** button three times—or until you can see just the last few waveforms in the **Timeline** panel.

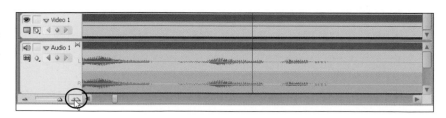

16 Position your cursor at the intersection of the **CTI** and the yellow volume graph. Hold down the **Ctrl** key, and click the mouse to create your first keyframe.

When creating keyframes in the Timeline panel, you should avoid two common pitfalls. First, because your cursor will not snap to anything, it's up to you to place the keyframe at the right point in time. Avoid moving the mouse too far left or right when creating the keyframe.

Second, the value of the keyframe may change based on where you release the mouse. Avoid moving the mouse too far up or down when creating the keyframe.

17 Hold down the **Ctrl** key, and click the yellow volume graph just to the left of the final waveform representing the word **high**.

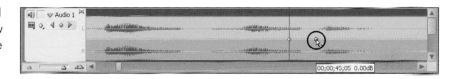

18 Click and drag the second keyframe directly down to the bottom of the waveform. Avoid moving the mouse left and right so the keyframe will not move in time.

Tip: If you hold down the Shift key *after* you begin dragging, you can constrain your movements up or down (so the position in time doesn't change), or you can constrain them left to right (so the value doesn't change).

19 Hold down the **Ctrl** key, and click the yellow volume graph just to the right of the final waveform representing the word **high**.

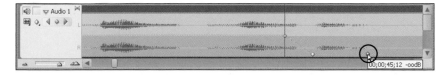

This is where the volume graph will begin to fade back in.

In the next step, you will move your mouse up as you create the new keyframe. This allows you to specify *both* the position in time and the value of the keyframe.

20 Hold down the **Ctrl** key, and click the yellow volume graph at just a handful of frames to the right of the last keyframe. As you click, hold down the mouse, and drag

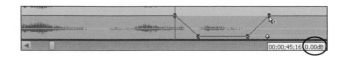

the keyframe straight up until the yellow tool tip reads approximately **0.0dB** (or as close as you can get).

Remember, the biggest downside of creating keyframes in the Timeline is the inability to fine-tune the value, so you may have to settle on *almost* 0.0dB.

---

21 Press the **backslash** (\) key to zoom the sequence out to automatically fit in the **Timeline** panel.

---

22 Drag the **Timeline CTI** to the beginning of **eruptologist.avi**. In the **Program Monitor**, click the **Play** button. Play the sequence so you can listen to the volume keyframe results, and click the **Stop** button after listening to **eruptologist.avi**.

---

23 Choose **File > Save**, or press **Ctrl+S**. Leave **dutch harbor promo.prproj** open for the next exercise.

No matter whether you create keyframes in the Timeline panel or the Effect Controls panel, they're equal. A keyframe is a keyframe is a keyframe. No matter what property or effect you are animating, the process is the same.

When creating keyframes in the Timeline panel, you may take additional measures to avoid moving the mouse too far up or down and too far left or right. This isn't a problem in the Effect Controls panel; however, you don't get to see the visual representation of the volume level as easily as you do in the Timeline panel.

You have now learned the hard way to go about muting a section of audio, so you may be thrilled (or quite upset) to learn a much simpler way exists—you can use audio transitions to fade in or fade out audio, in the same way you used a Cross Dissolve transition to fade video. You'll get to try this for yourself in the next exercise.

VIDEO:

volume.mov

After you've muted a clip, sometimes the silent "vacuum" is very noticeable. One trick is to fill in the silent area with natural sound, or as it is called at your local television station, natsot.

Natsot is nothing more than the natural sound of an environment—no actors, no interruptions...just ambient noises. Imagine the natsot of a babbling brook in an empty forest. Now contrast that with the natsot of downtown Manhattan at rush hour.

Whenever you shoot video, it's always a wonderful idea to roll for a minute of natsot. It may come in handy if you need to "fill in" the muted area of an actor's dialogue.

To learn more about creating volume keyframes and filling in muted areas with natsot, check out **volume.mov** in the **videos** folder on the **Premiere Pro 2 HOT DVD-ROM**.

6 | Adding Audio Transitions

Just as you added video transitions to video clips, you can add audio transitions to audio clips. Audio transitions can help you introduce an audio sound smoothly or fade out a sound smoothly (such as the end of a song slowly fading out). You can also use audio transitions between audio clips to subtly blend one audio sound to another. The true benefit to using an audio transition is you can quickly fade out or in an audio clip without having to fiddle with keyframes. In addition, you can quickly make the fade-in longer by stretching the duration of the transition, just as you did with video transitions. In this exercise, you will learn how to apply audio transitions.

1 If you followed the previous exercise, **dutch harbor promo.prproj** should still be open in Premiere Pro 2. If it's not, click **Open Project** on the **Welcome Screen**. Navigate to the **c:\exercise_files\chap_10** folder, click **exercise06.prproj** to select it, and click **Open**.

2 Choose **File > Save As**. Navigate to the **c:\exercise_files\dutch harbor** folder. Name the file **dutch harbor promo.prproj**, and click **Save**.

Note: If a previous version of dutch harbor promo.prproj already exists, you may be asked to replace it. Click Yes.

3 In the **Effects** panel, click the **arrow** icon next to **Audio Transitions** to expand the folder, and then expand the **Crossfade** folder.

Premiere Pro 2 comes with a whopping two audio transitions. (This is fine because a crossfade is really the only effect you can apply to audio.) The Constant Gain audio transition fades at a mathematically constant rate but may sound abrupt. The Constant Power audio transition fades at a nonlinear rate but sounds smoother to the human ear.

The moral of the audio transition story is this: Use Constant Power—unless you are editing for animals and aliens.

4 Drag and drop the **Constant Power** audio transition on the beginning of the first **historian.avi** clip on Track **Audio 1**.

Tip: The first audio clip of any sequence deserves an audio transition. This helps "sneak in" the audio and masks that the audience just heard 10 seconds of nothing.

Because the track options are expanded and because this particular track appears tall, the transition appears very tiny in the upper-left corner of the clip. To help visualize it better, you can collapse the track options.

5 Next to the Track **Audio 1**, click the **arrow** icon next to **Collapse/Expand Track** to collapse the track options.

After applying an audio transition, the next step is to verify whether it should be longer or shorter.

---

6 Move the **Timeline CTI** to the first frame where you hear the actor begin to speak, at approximately **00;00;13;22**. Press the **equals** (=) key twice to zoom in closer on the transition.

---

7 If the **mini-Timeline** is not visible in the **Effect Controls** panel, click the **Show/Hide Timeline View** toggle to turn it on. On Track **Audio 1**, click the transition you applied to view its duration in the **Effect Controls** panel.

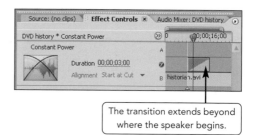

The Effect Controls panel shows you the transition extends well beyond the CTI, which means while the speaker is still talking, the transition is still fading in.

The transition extends beyond where the speaker begins.

---

8 To shorten the transition, in the **Effect Controls** panel, position your cursor over the end of the transition. Click and drag it so the **Out** point aligns with the **CTI**.

Note: Unfortunately, the mouse won't snap to the CTI in the Effect Controls panel, so you'll have to eyeball this one and hope it's "good enough."

Instead of dragging the CTI a few seconds back and previewing—as you probably have been doing throughout this book—it's time you are rewarded with the handy-dandy new Play Around button to do this all for you.

---

9 Hold down the **Alt** key, and in the **Program Monitor**, click the **Play Around** button.

The Play Around button "backs up" the CTI 2 seconds from its current position and then plays for the next 4 seconds. But wait, it gets better! The Play Around button even *returns* the CTI to its original position for you.

To access the top-secret Play Around button, you must hold down the Alt key. Otherwise, you will see its mild-mannered alter ego, the Play In to Out button.

While previewing the transition, you may have heard the actor breathe at the top of the audio clip. (Repeat Step 9 if you didn't hear it.) The next series of steps will show you how to eliminate sounds like this at the start of your audio clip.

---

10 Pressing the **left arrow** and **right arrow** keys, move the **CTI** to the point when you first hear the actor breathe, at approximately **00;00;13;06**. Hold down the **Alt** key, and click the **historian.avi** audio clip on Track **Audio 1**.

Tip: The Alt key allows you to select only the audio, or only the video, of a clip with both audio and video.

11 Repeatedly press the **equals** (=) key to zoom in around the **CTI**, until the audio transition takes up about one-fifth of the **Timeline** panel.

Now you are zoomed in very closely, which helps when making edits of only a frame or two.

12 With only the audio portion of the **historian.avi** clip still selected, position your cursor over the **In** point of the audio until you see the **Trim In** cursor. Snap the **In** point to the **CTI**.

As long as you have only the audio portion of the clip selected, you can trim the audio independently of the video (and vice versa).

13 Hold down the **Alt** key, and in the **Program Monitor**, click the **Play Around** button to preview your audio change. When you are finished previewing, press the **backslash** (\) key to zoom back out.

Before you add a transition to the last clip in the sequence, it's a good idea to check whether the audio needs to be trimmed.

14 Snap the **CTI** to the **Out** point of the **media_relations.avi** audio on Track **Audio 1**. Hold down the **Alt** key, and in the **Program Monitor**, click the **Play Around** button to preview the end of the audio.

You will notice two problems here. First, the microphone picks up clothing rustling. Second, the audio cuts out very abruptly. Time to trim!

15 Press the **left arrow** and **right arrow** keys to move the **CTI** to the right before the microphone picks up the clothing rustle, at approximately **00;01;05;05**.

You can trim everything to the right of the CTI.

16 Press the **equals** (=) key several times to zoom in closer so you can better visualize the small amount you are about to trim. Hold down the **Alt** key to select only the audio portion of

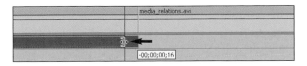

the **media_relations.avi** clip. Use the **Trim Out** cursor to snap-trim the **Out** point of the audio clip to the CTI. When you are finished, press the **backslash** (\) key to zoom back out.

After you have trimmed the audio to your liking, it is time to apply a transition to fade out.

17 In the **Effects** panel **Audio Transitions > Crossfade** folder, drag and drop the **Constant Power** audio transition on the end of the **media_relations.avi** audio clip on Track **Audio 1**.

It's time to take stock of what you just did. The transition you just applied ends at the spot at which you'd like it to end. (You made sure of that in Step 16.) Next, you want to make sure the transition *starts* no earlier than it should. In this case, you don't want it to start before the actor has finished speaking.

18 Slowly drag the **Jog Wheel** in the **Program Monitor** to where the audio should begin to fade out—when the actor finishes speaking, at approximately **00;01;04;09**.

Your CTI is positioned where the actor finishes speaking. This is where the transition should *start*.

19 Select the transition you just applied to view it in the **Effect Controls** panel. In the **Effect Controls** panel, position your cursor over the start of the transition, and trim it to the **CTI**.

Remember, the transition won't snap to the CTI in the Effect Controls panel, so get it as close as you can.

20 Hold down the **Alt** key, and click the **Play Around** button to listen to the transition you've just created.

Now you can add audio transitions between clips to smooth out the sudden differences in the audio.

21 Snap the **Timeline CTI** to the edit point between the **historian.avi** and **eruptologist.avi** clips, at approximately **00;00;36;10**. Hold down the **Alt** key, click the **Play Around** button, and listen for differences in ambient noise in the background.

Ideally, you should hear little difference between these two clips, thanks to all the hard EQ work you did earlier. Nonetheless, a subtle audio difference exists.

22 In the **Effects** panel, drag and drop the **Constant Power** audio transition on the edit point below the **Timeline CTI** on Track **Audio 1**. Hold down the **Alt** key, and click the **Play Around** button to see whether you can still detect a difference.

If you close your eyes, it's extremely difficult to guess where one audio clip finishes and the other starts. This is the idea behind transitioning between audio clips.

23 Snap the **Timeline CTI** to the edit point between the **eruptologist.avi** and **media_relations.avi** clips, at approximately **00;00;46;21**. In the **Effects** panel, drag the **Constant Power** audio transition to the edit point below the **Timeline CTI** on Track **Audio 1**. Hold down the **Alt** key, and click the **Play Around** button to listen to the transition.

As the edit plays, listen for a difference in audio between eruptologist.avi and media_relations.avi. Ideally, the transition is smooth.

24 Choose **File > Save**, or press **Ctrl+S**. Leave **dutch harbor promo.prproj** open for the next exercise.

Audio transitions are especially useful when combining several takes of an actor or combining two actors into a single scene. Many editors concentrate so much on video, they forget to focus on their audio. A noticeable "cut" in audio will be just as jarring to an audience, even if you've added a video transition. Successful editing requires attention to both video transitions *and* audio transitions.

In this exercise, you also learned the secret weapon of the Play Around button. This is extremely helpful when you want to "back up" the CTI just a couple of seconds to watch a change you've made. Plus, the CTI automatically return to its previous position. What's not to love about the Play Around button? (OK, its name *is* a bit silly.)

Displaying Timebase Versus Audio Units

All of the editing you have done throughout this book has been with a timebase of 30. The **timebase** is the ruler you use to measure the number of frames per second. Just as there are 12 one-inch hash marks on a ruler per every foot, there are 30 one-frame hash marks per every second of video. This means when editing video in this book, the smallest increment you can trim or move the CTI is one frame, which is $\frac{1}{30}$ of a second. This is true of every video file from a regular DV (**D**igital **V**ideo) camera ($\frac{1}{25}$th of a second in PAL countries).

Truth be told, in standard NTSC video, like in the United States, there are 29.97 frames of video flashing before your eyes every second. But trying to do long division while editing is hard, so Premiere Pro 2 rounds up to a timebase of 30 frames per second to make life easy.

Audio, on the other hand, may have as many as 48,000 "units" per one second. The number of

audio units per second is called the **audio sampling rate**, and it can be different for every audio file. CDs, for example, have an audio sampling rate of 44,100 units per second whereas a DV camera is capable of 32,000 or 48,000 units per second.

So why is this important to know? When you edit audio, especially music, sometimes the beats don't fall perfectly on every $\frac{1}{30}$ of a second. Sometimes, the beats fall *between* frames, which is why, when you try to edit the music on the beat, you can't. You can get within $\frac{1}{30}$ of the beat, but you can't truly set your **In** point on the exact beat.

Thankfully, Premiere Pro 2 lets you display the timebase of audio clips in audio sampling units instead of frames per second. This means your ruler now has 48,000 hash marks, instead of video's 30. This way, you can zoom in a *lot* further and be sure to accurately edit your music files on the beat—which you will get to do in the next exercise.

Audio Sampling Units

So what exactly are the units my audio is sampling? And why do I always see my camera's audio written as **48KHz, 16 bit**?

The **sampling units** refer to how many times the microphone "listens" to the environment around it. Your DV camera listens 48,000 times per second, which is a Hertz. One Hertz (Hz) equals one time per second. Thus, 48,000 Hz can be shortened to 48 KHz.

Imagine your camera's microphone is listening to the outside world. It then tells the camera what it hears, and the camera writes that down on a videotape. This happens 48,000 times per second.

Each time the microphone describes the outside world to the camera, it can choose to describe the sound with a lot of detail or with just a little bit of information. The more detail the microphone provides to the camera, the more accurate the reproduction on videotape.

The amount of detail passed along by the microphone is the **bit depth**. Most, if not all, DV cameras tend to record in either 12-bit or a deeper 16-bit.

Higher sampling rates and deeper bit depths equate to better sound reproduction. Many DV camera owners never realize they can change their camera setting to 48KHz 16-bit mode. If you haven't already, refer to your camera's instruction manual to learn how to do this.

Looping Audio

Let's say you want to add some music to underscore one of your sequences in order to heighten the dramatic tension of your movie's climactic moment. You find a perfect 30-second audio clip. Unfortunately, the sequence is 1-minute long. Your music is too short. What can you do?

Music clip is too short

Copied back to back

You could copy the clip, back to back, so the two 30-second music clips total 1 minute in duration. However, if the end of the first clip doesn't match the start of the second clip, it will be very noticeable during playback, like a record skip.

Audio looping to the rescue! The goal of looping audio is to edit the music clip so the end of the first clip matches the start of the second clip, allowing them to fit together like a jigsaw puzzle. When played, the looped audio will be seamless to the listener.

When editing a music clip for looping, make sure the **In** and **Out** points match, and make sure the rhythm is kept intact. (People will notice if suddenly the toe-tapping music is no longer tapping at the right time.) The best way to do this is to edit *on the beat*.

Beats provide great places to create your edit points because they are frequently repeated. Beats help keep the rhythm intact and provide distinct and recognizable sounds such as a drum thump or a cymbal clash. You can easily find these sounds when setting **In** and **Out** points.

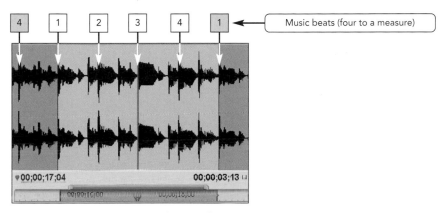

This music clip has an In point set at the start of the measure. The Out point is set right before the start of the next measure.

As shown in the illustration here, a music clip is ready to be looped. The **In** point is set at the start of Beat 1. It's not set before the beat, not after the beat, but at the exact instant you hear the beat—such as with a drum hit. The **Out** point is set right before the *next* Beat 1. Again, it is not set on the beat but as darn close to it as possible.

In the next exercise, you will experience for yourself how to loop a music clip.

7 | Looping Music with Audio Units

Looping allows you to seamlessly repeat your music over and over, so the audience doesn't realize that the song has restarted. To successfully loop, it is helpful to edit on the beat—so the audio matches perfectly and the overall tempo is maintained. To edit the beats, you can switch from the video timebase of 30 frames per second to the audio units (possibly 48,000 units per second). Using audio units gives you much more precise control when specifying **In** and **Out** points so you can keep in sync with the music beat. Being able to find the exact start of a beat is important when looping audio. In this exercise, you will use audio units to loop an audio clip that is too short in duration.

1 If you followed the previous exercise, **dutch harbor promo.prproj** should still be open in Premiere Pro 2. If it's not, click **Open Project** on the **Welcome Screen**. Navigate to the **c:\exercise_files\chap_10** folder, click **exercise07.prproj** to select it, and click **Open**.

2 Choose **File > Save As**. Navigate to the **c:\exercise_files\dutch_harbor** folder. Name the file **dutch harbor promo.prproj**, and click **Save**.

Note: If a previous version of dutch harbor promo.prproj already exists, you may be asked to replace it. Click Yes.

You will begin looping your audio by setting In and Out points in the Source Monitor. For this reason, you may find it helpful to return to the custom HOT workspace you created, which allows you to easily see the Source Monitor.

3 Choose **Window > Workspace > HOT**. At the top of the **Timeline** panel, select the **DVD map** tab to bring the sequence to the foreground.

4 In the **Project** panel **Audio** bin, double-click **DaReggaeMon_30.mp3** to open it in the **Source Monitor**.

5 Drag and drop the audio clip from the **Source Monitor** on the beginning of the sequence on Track **Audio 2**.

This audio clip is too short to play during the entire sequence. This is a perfect opportunity to edit the audio on the beat so you can make it loop.

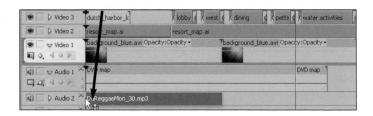

6 In the **Timeline**, select **DaReggaeMon_30.mp3** on Track **Audio 2**, and press the **Delete** key to remove it.

Instead of editing the clip in the Timeline, it's easier to edit the original in the Source Monitor.

First you should listen to your music and identify a beat to use as the Out point. Ideally, the beat should be at the *end* of a measure (because your In point will be the *start* of a measure).

---

7 In the **Source Monitor**, click the **Play** button. Play the entire clip, beginning to end.

Listen for a spot at the end of the song to set as the Out point. As the music plays, see whether you can find the beat—tap your toe if it helps!

This song ends with a measure of four beats, followed by a single beat of a new measure. The end of the four beats is a prime candidate for setting an Out point.

---

8 Move the **Source Monitor CTI** to the frame right before the last beat in this song, at approximately **00;00;29;02**.

Tip: As you get close to the last beat, advancing one frame at a time may help.

Note: Remember, in the Source Monitor, the top waveform is stereo left, and the bottom waveform is stereo right.

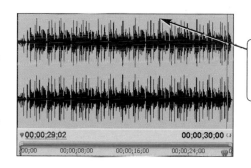

The tall spikes in the waveform can help you determine where a beat starts.

---

9 In the **Source Monitor**, click the left handle of the viewing area bar, and drag as far right as it will go to zoom in as close as possible on the **CTI**.

Viewing the Source Monitor like this highlights the problem: The CTI can't get you any closer to the beat because it is bound by the timebase of 30 divisions per second.

To resolve this problem, it's time to turn on Audio Units.

The CTI is here.

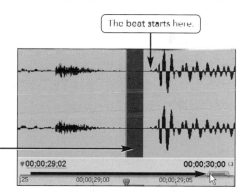

The beat starts here.

10 In the upper-right corner of the Source Monitor, click the **wing menu**, and choose **Audio Units**.

Notice how the time display changed in the lower-left corner? Instead of showing 00;00;29;02, it shows 00:00:29:04595.

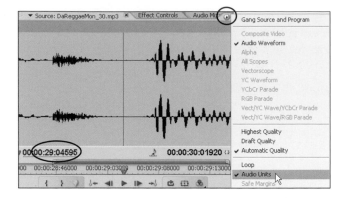

11 In the **Source Monitor**, click the **Step Forward (Right)** button to move one unit ahead.

Now the time display reads 00:00:29:04596.

Normally this button moves one frame ahead—but this time, you moved only one unit. You probably didn't see the CTI move; that's because there are 48,000 units per second of audio, so you just moved it $\frac{1}{48000}$th of a second, or .00002083 seconds (or 2.083×10^{-5}). Fun with numbers!

As you can see, audio units give you much, much, much more precise time control.

12 In the **Source Monitor**, drag and drop the blue **CTI** tab on the spot immediately before you hear the audio get louder, at approximately **00:00:29:06019**. Click the **Set Out** button to set your **Out** point.

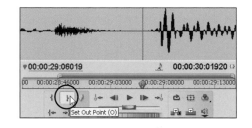

To recap what just happened, you are setting the Out point as darn close as you possibly can, before the unwanted beat starts.

Before setting the In point, you are ready to place the first music clip in the sequence. However, you must also turn on Audio Units in the Timeline panel.

13 In the **Timeline** panel, click the **wing menu**, and choose **Audio Units**.

14 Drag and drop **DaReggaeMon_30.mp3** from the **Source Monitor** on the beginning of the sequence on Track **Audio 2**.

The next step is to set an In point to match the Out point you've already set.

15 In the **Source Monitor**, click and drag the left handle of the viewing area bar as far left as it will go to zoom all the way out. Move the **Source Monitor CTI** to the beginning of the clip. Click the **Play** button. Play the sequence until you hear the first beat of the song, and click the **Stop** button at approximately **00:00:01:36816**.

Note: This song has a steel drum introduction, which obviously doesn't match the rest of the song, meaning the steel drum introduction would not be good for looping. Instead, you want to use the first beat right after the introduction.

---

16 In the **Source Monitor**, click and drag the right handle of the viewing area bar *slowly* to the left, until you can easily see the beginning of the beat's waveform.

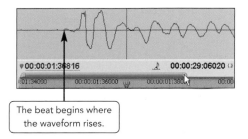

Oops. It looks like the placement of the CTI was a little bit off. As you can see, the beat begins slightly to the left of the current CTI position.

The beat begins where the waveform rises.

---

17 Drag and drop the blue tab of the **Source Monitor CTI** on the exact starting spot of the beat's waveform, at approximately **00:00:01:35122**. Click the **Set In point** button.

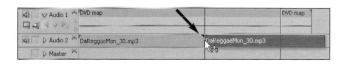

You have just set an In point at the start of the first beat.

It's time to take stock of what you have: You have an Out point, which is set *right before* a beat. And now you have an In point, which is set right *at* a beat. You hope, like a toy train track, the end of one clip fits perfectly into the beginning of the next clip.

---

18 Drag and drop DaReggaeMon_30.mp3 from the **Source Monitor** on the **Timeline** panel, and snap it to the end of DaReggaeMon_30.mp3 on Track **Audio 2**.

You have place the two clips back to back in the Timeline panel. Next, it is time to listen to your edit to see whether it worked.

---

19 In the **Timeline** panel, next to the track name **Audio 1**, click the **Toggle Track Output** toggle to temporarily mute the narrator on that track.

20 Snap the **Timeline CTI** to the edit point between the two **DaReggaeMon_30.mp3** clips on Track **Audio 2**. Hold down the **Alt** key, and click the **Play Around** button in the **Program Monitor**.

That is a job well done—the audio edit point should be imperceptible. (Go ahead—invite friends or family in. Make them listen to it, and see whether they can "hear" the edit.)

After you've placed all the looping clips in the sequence, the last task is to "unloop" the end of the last clip. Otherwise, the last music clip will end abruptly.

---

21 In the **Timeline** panel, on Track **Audio 2**, position your cursor over the end of the last clip until you see the **Trim Out** cursor. Click and drag all the way to the right.

Note: The Trim Out cursor won't drag very far because you edited out only a single beat.

After looping, remember to turn off Audio Units.

---

22 In the **Timeline** panel, click the **wing menu**, and choose **Audio Units** to unselect this option.

This places the Timeline panel back into its regular timebase of 30 frames per second. Unless you are doing more audio editing, it's good practice to turn off Audio Units right away, so you don't forget they are on.

---

23 In the **Source Monitor**, click the **wing menu**, and choose **Audio Units** to unselect this option.

Yes, you have to turn Audio Units off in *both* the Timeline panel and the Source Monitor.

---

24 Choose **File > Save**, or press **Ctrl+S**. Choose **File > Close** to close this project.

Technically speaking, setting In and Out points for looping is easy; you've done that dozens of times. However, finding the right spot to loop—now *that's* where you really have to work. It all begins by finding the beat at which you want to end. Once you find the last beat, set an Out point before the next beat starts.

Then, find the beat at the beginning of the song to which you want to "loop back." Once you find the first beat, set an In point right as the beat starts.

Following these steps should give you successful looping.

VIDEO: | **looping.mov**

This book provides two other music clips with which you can practice looping. You can watch the demonstration first and then try it by yourself. To practice looping, check out **looping.mov** in the **videos** folder on the **Premiere Pro 2 HOT DVD-ROM**.

This chapter was all about adding effects, adding transitions, and editing audio *clips*. Premiere Pro 2 also gives you the ability to modify entire audio *tracks* at once. In the next chapter, you will learn how to apply effects to audio tracks, as well as record your own audio.

11

Using the Audio Mixer

Eons ago, in Chapter 10, *"Working with Audio,"* you learned how to add audio effects, tweak gain, and create volume keyframes to alter the sound of a clip. Adobe Premiere Pro 2 provides a powerful feature to apply these types of effects to multiple clips at once: the **Audio Mixer**. This can be an incredible timesaving device since you are able to apply a single effect to every clip on a track, all at once. In addition, you can lower the volume of not just a single clip but of every clip on a track with the click of a single button. The **Audio Mixer** also allows you to monitor and adjust the overall output of each track in a sequence, as well as record narration from a microphone attached to your computer. In this chapter, you will learn about the most common functions of the **Audio Mixer**.

Understanding the Audio Mixer

The Premiere Pro 2 **Audio Mixer** provides one-stop shopping for all of your volume control needs. You can lower an entire track's volume or modify just a few seconds of a single track. Similar to a mixing board you would find in a recording studio, you can use sliders, knobs, and faders to adjust the sound of an entire track. Instead of affecting individual clips, the **Audio Mixer** affects every clip on a track. The primary functions of the **Audio Mixer** are as follows: applying one or more audio effects to an entire track of clips, monitoring and adjusting the volume and balance of individual tracks or multiple tracks at once, and recording your voice from your own microphone.

This chapter will cover each of these functions.

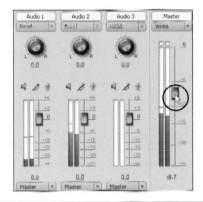

Each of the three audio tracks and master track appear in the Audio Mixer with their own balance knobs and volume faders.

The **Audio Mixer** is divided into tracks. As shown in the illustration here, the **Audio Mixer** has three audio tracks and one master track—for a total of four tracks. Each audio track of the sequence you are viewing appears in the **Audio Mixer** and includes its own balance knob and volume fader. In the **Audio Mixer** (left), you can see how each track appears. (A **volume fader**, by the way, is the slider you can move up and down to control the volume levels; it is circled in the illustration shown here.)

The **Audio Mixer** is best used after you have tweaked all of your clips and applied all effects. As the last step in your audio workflow, you can use the **Audio Mixer** to reduce or increase the overall volume of a track. You can also control how loud a track is in relation to other tracks. Combining all the tracks together is called **mixing**. You then output the final "mix" of all the audio tracks through the **master track**. It may help to think of the master track as the funnel where *all* audio must pass before playing to your speakers. In the **Audio Mixer**, you can also increase or decrease the volume of *all* tracks by dragging the **Master** volume fader.

For example, in Chapter 10, "*Working with Audio,*" you learned to monitor the output of individual clips, tweak their gain and volume accordingly, and make sure each clip doesn't spike into the red. But when you group the sounds of *all* tracks in a sequence, the final sound may be at dangerously high levels. After all, the loudness is the sum of its parts.

The goal of mixing is to combine all the tracks so the volume stays in an acceptable, safe range and so the overall mix is appropriate to the project. (Sure, the wedding music you used during the groom's vows may *technically* fall in a safe range, but if the music is mixed twice as loud as his speech, you'll have one angry bride.)

This is but one use of the **Audio Mixer**. Another use is applying effects to multiple clips at once. For example, perhaps you have an audio track comprised of 20 clips from the same speaker. Instead of applying 20 different audio effects, you can apply a single effect to the entire track at once. Or, instead of tweaking the volume of each clip, you can alter the volume of every clip in a track at once. This is a huge time-saver!

Yet another use of the **Audio Mixer** is to record your voice from a microphone attached to your computer. You can monitor your input levels as you speak and direct the results to automatically display as a clip in any track you choose.

Automating Volume and Balance

As you learned in Chapter 10, *"Working with Audio,"* you can change the volume of a clip by using keyframes. This was a manual and time-intensive process by which you moved the CTI (**C**urrent **T**ime **I**ndicator), created a keyframe, moved the CTI, created a keyframe, and so on. One of the best features of the **Audio Mixer** is the capability to change the volume and balance of a clip *as it plays*. Instead of creating keyframes one at a time, you can play your sequence and then drag the track's volume fader up and down to change the volume of anything on that track. This is called **automating** because keyframes are automatically created behind the scenes, so to speak, as you drag the volume fader up and down. Premiere Pro 2 records every movement your mouse makes when dragging the volume fader up or down or when dragging the balance knob left and right.

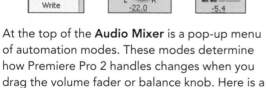

The automation options determine how Premiere Pro 2 handles changes to the volume and balance.

At the top of the **Audio Mixer** is a pop-up menu of automation modes. These modes determine how Premiere Pro 2 handles changes when you drag the volume fader or balance knob. Here is a description of each automation option:

Off: This option ignores any volume and balance changes you previously made.

Read: This option reads the volume and balance changes you previously made. You cannot make any new changes, but you can listen to your existing changes at least.

Latch: This option records only *changes* you make during playback. If you don't make any changes during playback, no new keyframes are recorded. If you do make a volume or balance change, Premiere Pro 2 records every movement of your mouse and turns those movements into keyframes. When you release the mouse after making changes, the volume fader and balance knob stay *latched* at their current positions and don't move.

Touch: This option is the same as **Latch**, with one notable exception. When you release the mouse after making changes, the fader or knob *slides* gradually to its previous position.

Write: This option records the current position of the volume fader and balance knob no matter what (even when you aren't making changes).

To summarize, only the last three automation options—**Latch**, **Touch**, and **Write**—actually create keyframes. Of these three, **Latch** and **Touch** create keyframes only when you are moving the volume fader or balance knob. (Otherwise, they keep the existing value.) **Write** doesn't care whether you are moving the volume or fader balance knob because it creates new keyframes *every time* you play a sequence.

The nuances of **Latch**, **Touch**, and **Write** can be confusing—even to longtime users of Premiere Pro. The next exercise will help clear up any confusion.

Altering the volume and balance of every clip on a track, all at once, is one of the key timesaving features of the **Audio Mixer**. This is especially useful when you have many clips from the same audio source on a single track. For example, you may have all of an actor's dialogue, divided into 20 clips, on a single track. Instead of modifying each clip one at a time, you can modify every clip on the track. In this exercise, you will learn how to use the track automation options to change track volume and balance all at once, as well as make changes "on the fly" as the sequence plays.

---

1 On the **Welcome Screen**, click **Open Project**. In the **Open Project** dialog box, navigate to the **c:\exercise_files\chap_11** folder, click **exercise01.prproj** to select it, and click **Open**.

---

2 Choose **File > Save As**. Navigate to the **c:\exercise_files\dutch_harbor** folder. Name the file **dutch harbor promo.prproj**, and click **Save**.

Note: If a previous version of dutch harbor promo.prproj already exists, you may be asked to replace it. Click Yes.

---

3 Choose **Window > Workspace > Audio**. Make sure the **DVD intro** sequence appears in the **Timeline** panel.

The Audio workspace is the best workspace for audio mixing. The Audio Mixer is smack-dab in the center of the workspace—and it takes up quite a bit of room. Both the Timeline panel and the Program Monitor are smaller than usual to make room for the mammoth Audio Mixer.

---

4 If the **Effects** and **Sends** areas appear in your **Audio Mixer**, as shown in the illustration here, click the **Show/Hide Effects and Sends** toggle at the left side of the **Audio Mixer**.

 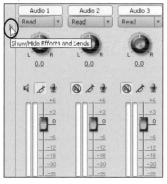

You need the Effects and Sends areas only when you are applying track-based effects (which you will do later in this chapter). Hiding this panel allows you to easily view the track VU meters and volume faders.

5 In the **Audio Mixer**, click the **Solo Track** toggle for Track **Audio 1**.

The Solo Track toggle mutes all other tracks. Notice the **Mute Track** toggles for Tracks Audio 2 and Audio 3 have slashes through them, indicating they are muted. By isolating a track, you can focus better on its sound.

The first step in monitoring and adjusting track volume is to make sure the track volume falls within acceptable ranges. Remember, the goal should be levels that peak at about –6 dB on the VU meter, just to be safe. True, you can take the output levels all the way up to 0.0 dB, but that's risky. With digital audio, it is better to play it safe; audio on the quiet side is infinitely more acceptable than audio on the loud, distorted side.

---

6 In the **Audio Mixer**, be sure the automation mode below Track **Audio 1** is set to **Read**.

---

7 In the **Audio Mixer**, click the **Play In to Out** button to listen to the isolated audio track from the beginning. During playback, lower the **Audio 1** volume fader until the sound peaks are at approximately **–6 dB**. In this exercise, a **Volume** value of **–4.6 dB** is being used.

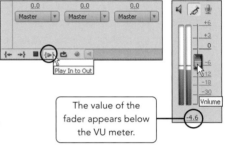

The value of the fader appears below the VU meter.

It may be confusing when dealing with two different volumes, one of –6 dB and the other of –4.6 dB. This should help clear up the mystery: The loudness at which the track plays, shown in the VU meter, should not peak at greater than –6 dB. This decibel level describes the overall volume of the track, or **track volume**.

However, to achieve a –6 dB level, you need to lower the volume fader by –4.6 dB. Even though both properties are described as volume, it is important to understand the distinction.

As you make changes to the track volume in the Audio Mixer, you are making changes to the track in the Timeline panel. They are one and the same. When moving faders in the Audio Mixer, it can be helpful to view the track volume in the Timeline panel at the same time and watch how the changes in one panel affect the other.

---

8 In the **Timeline** panel, below Track **Audio 1**, click the **Show Keyframes** button, and choose **Show Track Volume**.

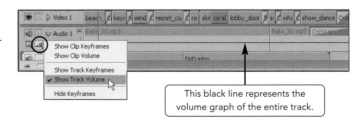

This black line represents the volume graph of the entire track.

The thin, black line represents the volume of the entire track, also called the **track volume graph**. As you make volume and balance changes in the Audio Mixer, Premiere Pro 2 moves the track volume graph up or down to reflect your changes.

When playback stops, each change of the volume fader corresponds to a change in the track volume graph. In the next step, watch how the track volume graph in the Timeline panel updates each time you drag the volume fader to a new position.

---

9 While playback stops, drag the Track **Audio 1** volume fader up, and release the mouse. Drag the volume fader to the bottom of the VU meter, and release the mouse. When done, drag the volume fader back to **–4.6 dB**.

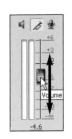

The Audio Mixer is capable of changing volume in two ways. It can change the volume of an entire track, or it can create keyframes and change just a tiny section of volume on a track.

This may sound confusing, but it's no different from the effects you've applied in previous chapters. You've already learned that when keyframe mode is off, any tweak to an effect value changes the value for the *entire* clip, right? And when keyframe mode is on, changing the value creates a keyframe at the CTI.

Well, the Audio Mixer behaves in a similar fashion. If no track keyframes exist on the Timeline, changing the volume fader in the Audio Mixer changes the volume of the entire track.

In this step, you verified your isolated audio track does not peak at greater than –6 dB, which is the technical side of monitoring audio. However, it's equally important to listen to the combined sound of all the audio tracks to make sure the mix balance is appropriate. For example, you don't want the music track to completely overpower the narrator track.

---

10 In the **Audio Mixer**, click the **Solo Track** toggle on Track **Audio 1** to unmute the other tracks.

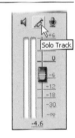

---

11 In the **Audio Mixer**, below track name **Audio 1**, make sure the automation mode is still set to **Read**. Click the **Play In to Out** button. During playback, lower the **Audio 1** volume fader until it does not overpower the narrator, at approximately **–15.0 dB**.

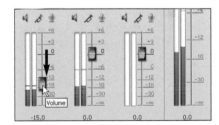

Tip: The Master VU meters on the far right of the Audio Mixer show the combined levels of all the individual VU meters. It's helpful to keep an eye on the Master VU meters to watch for dangerous peak levels when all audio tracks are playing at once.

Having monitored your track volume as well as the overall mix of all the tracks, it's time to start using the automation modes to tweak just a small portion of the sequence. In this case, you will use the Latch automation mode to fade in the audio at the end of the sequence, after the narrator finishes speaking.

Note: The next step requires a bit of fancy mouse work. Immediately after the narrator finishes speaking, you will grab the mouse and drag it up to its previous level of –4.6 dB. Because you are doing this during playback, you have to be prepared for it—it happens quickly.

---

12 In the **Audio Mixer**, below Track **Audio 1**, choose **Latch** for the automation mode.

13 Click the **Play In to Out** button. When the narrator finishes speaking, at approximately **00;00;36;00**, drag the volume fader to the previous level at approximately **–4.6 dB**.

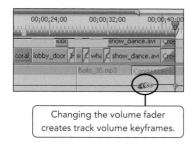

Changing the volume fader creates track volume keyframes.

Tip: Try to do this in about 2 seconds. If you want to try again, choose Edit > Undo, and repeat this step until you are satisfied with the results. If you don't hit –4.6 exactly, don't worry. (It can be hard to do it on the fly, especially when you have only a couple of seconds to get it right!)

When you are finished, you will see keyframes created along the track volume graph. More important, because you are in Latch mode, keyframes were created only when you moved the volume fader.

14 Click the **Play In to Out** button again to listen to the results.

During playback, you will see the volume fader "magically" move by itself; Premiere Pro 2 is playing back your mouse movements as well. (Show this to a friend, and tell them your system is possessed!) As long as you don't touch the volume fader, no keyframes will be created during playback.

Next, you will use the Audio Mixer to perform the same task on another sequence in your project. Whichever sequence is open in the Timeline panel appears in the Audio Mixer.

15 At the top of the **Timeline** panel, select the **DVD history** tab to bring the sequence to the foreground.

In the next series of steps, you will first set an appropriate mix level for the music so it doesn't overwhelm the actor's dialogue—just as you did in the previous steps. Then, you will use the Touch mode to change the volume of a small portion of the track.

16 On Track **Audio 2**, choose **Read** for the automation mode, and click the **Play In to Out** button. During playback, lower the volume fader of Track **Audio 2** until you are happy with the mix level, at approximately **–17.9 dB**.

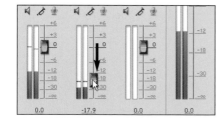

You should reserve judgment on the mix level until you hear both the actor's dialogue and the music, some time after 13;00. Also, because you haven't created any keyframes for this audio track yet, changing the volume fader in Read mode changed the volume of the entire track.

With the mix level set, you will use the Touch mode to increase the volume at the start of the sequence, then fade it back out as the scrolling text fades away, and finally have it return to –17.9 dB by the time the actor begins speaking.

17 Press the **Home** key to move the **Timeline CTI** to the start of the sequence. On Track **Audio 2**, choose **Touch** for the automation mode.

Note: The next step also requires deft mouse handling. Be sure to refer to the illustration here so you are prepared when playback begins. (Because the audio changes are at the beginning of the sequence, you don't get any time to think about it!)

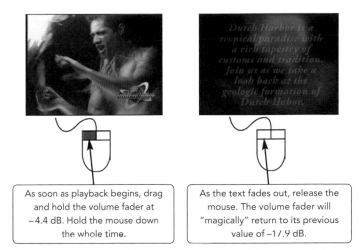

As soon as playback begins, drag and hold the volume fader at −4.4 dB. Hold the mouse down the whole time.

As the text fades out, release the mouse. The volume fader will "magically" return to its previous value of −17.9 dB.

18 In the **Audio Mixer**, click the **Play In to Out** button, and *immediately* drag and hold the **Audio 2** volume fader up to approximately **−4.4 dB**. Release the mouse as the text fades out.

When you release the mouse, the fader automatically slides to its previous value of −17.9 dB.

This highlights the difference between Touch and Latch. In Touch mode when you release the volume fader—that is, when you're not "touching it"—the fader returns to its previous position. But in Latch mode, the volume fader stays *latched* at its current position, even after you release the mouse.

A good rule of thumb is to use Touch to "touch up" a small portion of a track.

19 Click the **Play In to Out** button to preview the volume changes.

During playback, the volume fader replays your previous mouse movements. First the fader moves up, and then it automatically moves back down, coinciding with when you released the mouse.

The last mode to experiment with is Write mode. In the next series of steps, you will use the Write automation mode to mix the volume of a different sequence. Keep in mind, in Write mode, the position of the volume fader is recorded, whether or not you're moving it.

20 At the top of the **Timeline**, select the **DVD map** tab to bring the sequence to the foreground. Scroll down the **Timeline** panel until you can see

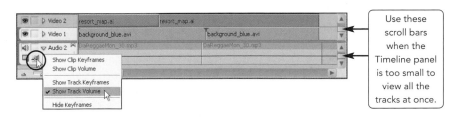

Use these scroll bars when the Timeline panel is too small to view all the tracks at once.

Track **Audio 2**. On Track **Audio 2**, click the **Show Keyframe** button, and choose **Show Track Volume**.

Note: Because the Timeline panel has been reduced, you cannot view all the tracks at once. When this happens, you will see two scroll bars to the far right of the Timeline. The top scroll bar is for the video tracks, and the bottom scrolls the audio tracks.

21 In the **Audio Mixer**, on Track **Audio 2**, choose **Write** for the automation mode. Click the **Audio Mixer** wing menu, and make sure a check mark appears next to **Switch to Touch after Write**.

Tip: The Switch to Touch after Write option changes the automation mode to Touch as soon as playback stops. Why? Well, Premiere Pro 2 is assuming as soon as you finish playing the track in Write mode, you'll want only to make small "touch-ups" to tiny sections of the audio track, using Touch mode.

Next, you will create keyframes in Write mode. You will use Write mode to fade out the volume at the beginning of the sequence and then fade it in at the end. Unlike Touch or Latch mode, you don't have to "touch" the volume fader to make changes. In Write mode, Premiere Pro 2 records the volume fader position even if you are in another room, nowhere *near* the mouse.

22 In the **Audio Mixer**, click the **Play In to Out** button. As playback begins, drag the **Audio 2** volume fader to an appropriate mix level, at approximately **–4.9 dB**. At the end of the sequence, when the narrator finishes, drag the fader back to **0.0 dB**.

When playback stops, the track volume graph in the Timeline displays the keyframes you've created.

Note: When playback is done, notice the Write mode switches to Touch mode. This is so you can pre-view your volume keyframes when done, without overwriting them.

If you had left the automation mode set to Write, however, every time you played the sequence, you would overwrite any existing keyframes. This would make it difficult to preview your changes because you would be erasing them each time you previewed the clip! This underscores the purpose of the Switch to Touch after Write command.

23 Choose **File > Save**, or press **Ctrl+S**. Choose **File > Close** to close this project.

Whew! This is one of the harder exercises—and techniques—in Premiere Pro 2 you will encounter. The Audio Mixer takes some time to master. At a minimum, just remember these basic rules when changing track volume in the Audio Mixer: If no keyframes have been created, changing the volume fader in Read mode will change the volume of the entire track.

If keyframes *have* been created, Latch and Touch modes will record only new changes you make to the volume. In other words, if you play back your audio but don't move the volume fader, then no new keyframes will be made.

On the other hand, Write mode is like a runaway locomotive. It barrels down the track destroying everything in its way, including existing keyframes. The Write mode records the position of the volume fader regardless of whether you're touching the volume fader. Be careful when in Write mode because new keyframes are written every time you play the sequence.

Recording from a Microphone

The next feature of the **Audio Mixer** you will learn about is the capability to record narration directly from a microphone attached to your computer. You can use this to record **voice-overs** (dubbing over one actor's speech with new speech) and to record narration over still images or video. When you record your microphone through the **Audio Mixer**, an audio clip appears directly on the audio track in the **Timeline** panel. Your voice is saved to a file on your computer, but the clip is automatically imported into your project and placed in the **Timeline** for you. (What service!)

One important point to keep in mind about recording the microphone is this: The recording will overwrite any existing audio on the track to which you record. Therefore, it is always a good idea to record your voice to an empty audio track so you don't lose any of your existing audio.

Before recording with your microphone, it is important to make sure your system is properly set up.

Preparing Your System for Recording

Premiere Pro 2 records sound from your microphone via the microphone port of your computer. However, Premiere Pro 2 does not know how to properly configure your sound card's input, so it is up to you to specify the correct hardware settings. In Windows XP, verify your settings by going to the **Control Panel** and selecting the **Sounds and Audio Devices** option. Use the documentation

bundled with your computer or sound card to set up your system. It's impossible to list settings for every system, but this section offers some general rules of thumb.

Your microphone should be attached to the microphone port of your computer or sound card. Newer systems have color-coded input ports, and the microphone port is often pink.

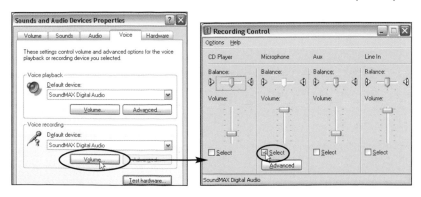

The options displayed vary depending on your system.

You need to configure your sound card to select the microphone port. Many Windows XP users will find this by choosing **Start > Control Panel > Sounds, Speech, and Audio Devices > Sounds and Audio Devices**. This opens the **Sounds and Audio Devices Properties** dialog box, as shown in the illustration here. Most users will see a **Voice** panel, which contains options for specifying which sound device input you'd like to use. If you have a second audio input device on your computer, such as a USB (**U**niversal **S**erial **B**us) microphone, you can select which device to record from by using the **Voice recording Default device** pop-up menu. If you have only one audio input device, such as a basic microphone attached to your primary sound card, you will see only the sound card device listed.

Clicking the **Volume** button under **Voice playback** opens the **Recording Control** panel, which lists available ports for the chosen audio device. (Some sound cards have multiple input ports, such as microphone, line, auxiliary, and so on). Make sure you have the proper port selected. Again, for the majority of Windows XP users, odds are the microphone will be plugged into the microphone port of your sound card, so make sure the **Microphone Select** check box is turned on.

Above the **Select** check box, you will see a **Volume** slider, which allows you to adjust your input volume. Unfortunately, sometimes the only way to learn the microphone level is by trial and error. For example, you may record your voice in Premiere Pro 2, realize it's too low, and then return to this panel to change the input level.

In the **Sounds and Audio Device Properties** dialog box, at the bottom of the **Voice** panel, you may see a **Test hardware** button. You can click this button to walk through a series of steps to troubleshoot any Windows problems with your microphone and also set your microphone at an appropriate level.

Note: Remember, this section does not apply to all Windows XP users and is meant as a general guide. Your system may have different options than those covered here. Refer to the documentation bundled with your computer and sound card.

Before you begin the next exercise, make sure you've specified your computer's audio settings and tested your microphone.

NOTE:

Avoiding Feedback

When recording via microphone to your computer, be careful to avoid a feedback loop. **Feedback** is when your microphone records its own sound as it plays out of speakers, creating an infinite loop and resulting in all sorts of nasty sounds.

Premiere Pro 2 comes with a handy new option to prevent feedback. Choose **Edit > Preferences > Audio** to open the **Preferences** dialog box. In the **Audio** panel, turn on the **Mute input during timeline recording** check box. This option still records your microphone at regular volume, but it doesn't play the sound from the microphone out through your speakers during the recording process.

Then again, nothing beats the old-fashioned method for preventing feedback: headphones! This way, *you* can still hear the audio, but the microphone picks up only your voice. You get the best of both worlds.

2 | Recording Narration in the Audio Mixer

Premiere Pro 2 makes it easy to add your own narration to sequences by recording audio from a microphone directly in the **Audio Mixer**. As you play the sequence, you can record narration into a microphone attached to your computer. This allows you to watch the playback as you speak so you can be sure the audio matches the video. The audio you record is captured to your hard drive and automatically inserted into the selected audio track in the sequence. In this exercise, you will learn how to use the **Audio Mixer** to record your voice from a microphone directly to an audio track.

Note: If you do not have a microphone, you can read along or skip to Exercise 3.

---

1 On the **Welcome Screen**, click **Open Project**. In the **Open Project** dialog box, navigate to the **c:\exercise_files\chap_11** folder, click **exercise02.prproj** to select it, and click **Open**.

---

2 Choose **File > Save As**. Navigate to the **c:\exercise_files\dutch_harbor** folder. Name the file **dutch harbor promo.prproj**, and click **Save**.

Note: If a previous version of dutch harbor promo.prproj already exists, you may be asked to replace it. Click Yes.

---

3 At the top of the **Timeline**, select the **DVD history** tab to bring the sequence to the foreground. In the **Timeline** panel, next to Track **Audio 2**, click the **Collapse/Expand Track** toggle to turn off the track options.

Scroll the lower half of the **Timeline** panel down so you can fully see Track **Audio 3**.

Before you begin recording, you need to make sure your audio hardware preferences are correctly set. In the next step, you will make sure you are properly suppressing feedback, as described previously.

---

4 Choose **Edit > Preferences > Audio**. If you do not have headphones during the recording process, turn on the **Mute input during timeline recording** check box in the **Preferences** dialog box. If you plan to use headphones during the recording process, you can leave this option turned off.

Tip: Even if you plan to use headphones, you may find it useful to mute input during Timeline recording. Have you ever had a phone conversation where you can hear yourself speaking? It can be quite disconcerting and makes it difficult to concentrate. Muting the input while recording will ensure you don't hear your own voice while talking into the microphone.

Next, you want to make sure Premiere Pro 2 is "listening" to the correct input device. This step applies only if you have additional audio devices beyond your regular sound card. A prime example of this is a USB microphone. Unless you tell Premiere Pro 2 otherwise, it won't know which device it should listen to when recording.

5 In the left side of the **Preferences** dialog box, click **Audio Hardware**. Click the **ASIO Settings** button.

ASIO (**A**udio **S**tream **I**nput **O**utput) is a universal standard allowing a wide variety of audio devices to communicate with a wide variety of computers. The ASIO settings let you choose which devices, attached to your system, you would like to use for input and output.

Note: If your audio device is ASIO compliant, you may see it listed in the Default Device pop-up menu. If you have no ASIO-compliant audio devices, then you should leave the pop-menu set to Premiere Pro Windows Sound, which defaults to whichever audio device you chose in the Windows XP Control Panel (as described previously in this chapter).

6 In the **ASIO Direct Sound Full Duplex Setup** dialog box, if you have more than one direct sound output or input port listed, turn on the check box next to the device you'd like to use. When done, click **OK** to return to the **Preferences** dialog box.

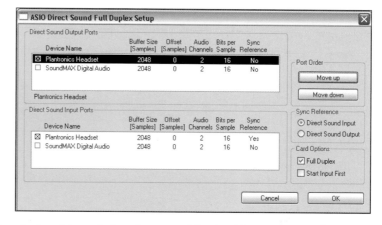

For the vast majority of users, you will see only one device listed for both output and input. As shown in the illustration here, the computer has two audio devices—a regular soundcard (SoundMAX Digital Audio) and a headphone/microphone combination (Plantronics Headset).

In this case, Premiere Pro 2 has been configured to play sound out to the headset (output port) and also capture sound from the microphone on the headset (input port).

Note: Your own options may differ from those shown here. In addition, if you have only one device listed, then you do not need to make any changes because Premiere Pro 2 defaults to the first device it finds.

7 In the **Preferences** dialog box, click **OK** to return to the project.

You have just configured your audio hardware, so Premiere Pro 2 should be "listening" and "speaking" to the correct device. Next, you want to prepare the Audio Mixer for recording.

8 In the **Audio Mixer**, above the VU meter of Track **Audio 3**, click the **Enable track for recording** button.

This step tells Premiere Pro 2 that anything you record from the chosen audio device will go into Track Audio 3.

It may not seem like it, but right now Premiere Pro 2 is "listening" to the chosen device. However, the VU meters, by default, display only what is playing *out* of the Timeline. You need to tell Premiere Pro 2 to display the VU meters for what is coming *into* the Timeline.

---

9 Click the **Audio Mixer** wing menu, and choose **Meter Input(s) Only**. Read and speak this step into your microphone to verify your levels are properly set.

As soon as you select this option, the VU meter for Track Audio 3 should show signs of life. In fact, if you speak into your microphone, you should see the VU meters jump up and down. Nothing is being recorded yet; Premiere Pro 2 is only listening.

Note: Your microphone level should be peaking, as usual, at about –6 dB—never at greater than 0 dB. Return to your Windows XP Control Panel if you need to adjust the input level of your microphone, as described previously in this chapter, or simply adjust how close you are speaking into the microphone.

Note: If you don't have headphones, then it is important to mute the other audio tracks—otherwise, they will play through your speakers while you are recording. In turn, this will cause your microphone to record the sound from the speakers, which will result in a feedback loop.

---

10 In the **Audio Mixer**, on Track **Audio 3**, click the **Solo Track** toggle.

This turns on the mute feature on the other two tracks. Notice those Mute Track toggles now contain slashes.

Tip: If you are using headphones during recording, you do *not* need to click the Solo Track toggle (unless you find the other tracks distracting while you're speaking).

Everything is prepared for takeoff. The next step is to record your voice as you read the scrolling text at the beginning of this sequence. Keep in mind, Premiere Pro 2 doesn't actually record anything until you begin playback.

---

11 At the bottom of the **Audio Mixer**, click the **Record** button.

The Record button might be misleading. This buttons tells Premiere Pro 2, "I'm *about to* record." Unlike the record button on your video camera, which starts recording right away, the Audio Mixer Record button doesn't actually *start* recording your narration until you begin playback. You can leave this Record button on all day, and nothing will happen or be recorded until you play the sequence.

In the next step, you will begin recording your voice immediately after playing the sequence. For this reason, be prepared to start your narration as soon as you click Play In to Out.

---

12 At the bottom of the Audio Mixer, click the **Play In to Out** button. Speak the scrolling text on the screen into your microphone. When the text fades out, click the **Stop** button to stop playback.

As soon as you click the Stop button, you will see a new audio clip on Track Audio 3. This is an audio clip of your microphone recording.

Note: Premiere Pro 2 will continue to record your microphone *until* you stop playback.

---

13 At the bottom of the **Audio Mixer**, click the **Play In to Out** button to listen to your recording. After you verify your microphone recording is working, click the **Stop** button to stop playback.

Tip: If you'd like to try again, you can repeat Steps 11 and 12. Your new audio will overwrite any existing audio. However, sometimes it's best to first delete the unwanted clip in the Timeline panel, just to be safe.

Now that you're done recording this section, you can check out the overall mix level in comparison to the other tracks.

---

14 In the **Audio Mixer**, click the **Solo Track** toggle of Track **Audio 3** to "unmute" the other audio tracks.

---

15 At the bottom of the **Audio Mixer**, click the **Play In to Out** button to listen to your recording. After you verify your microphone recording is working, click the **Stop** button to stop playback.

Your first reaction (besides "Is that *really* what I sound like?") may be the music score on Track Audio 2 is too loud. This is another opportunity to use the Touch automation mode, as you did in the previous exercise, on the music clip on Track Audio 2.

In the next step, you will lower the volume of the music track, Audio 2, during your narration. Since you will be using Touch mode, be sure to keep holding down the mouse. When your narration finishes, you can release the mouse, and the track will gradually slide to its previous volume.

16 In the **Audio Mixer**, on Track **Audio 2**, choose **Touch** for the automation mode.

---

17 Click the **Play In to Out** button. During playback of your voice, drag the volume fader of Track **Audio 2** to lower it to an appropriate mix level. As soon as your voice is done, release the volume fader. Once the volume fader returns to its previous position, click the **Stop** button to stop playback.

You can never get enough practice of the automation modes, right?

Another popular use of recording your voice is to dub over an actor's dialogue. This is akin to lip-syncing. For example, you may want to replace a single word. To ensure you don't record over the "good" part of the dialogue (the part you want to keep), you can set In and Out points in the Timeline panel. When these points are set, Premiere Pro 2 will insert your microphone recording only at the desired section, between the In and Out points.

In the next series of steps, you will use sequence In and Out points to make sure you record over the desired section only. You will also create a new audio track exclusively for this new audio.

---

18 Choose **Sequence > Add Tracks**. In the **Add Tracks** dialog box, be sure the **Add X Audio Track(s)** field is set to **1** and all others are set to **0**. Click **OK**. In the **Timeline** panel, scroll down so you can see the newly created audio track.

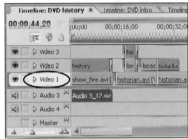

This creates a new track, Audio 4, in the Timeline panel. You should also be able to see the new track in the Audio Mixer.

Next, you will specify the In and Out points in the sequence so you don't accidentally record in the wrong section of the Timeline panel.

---

19 In the **Timeline** panel, drag the **CTI** to **00;00;43;00**. Press the **I** key on your keyboard to set a sequence **In** point. Drag the **CTI** to **00;00;43;25**. Press the **O** key on your keyboard to set a sequence **Out** point.

You have just set sequence In and Out points around the section of audio where the eruptologist says "high." You will record yourself saying "low." (After all, this is a blatantly biased advertisement for Dutch Harbor!)

---

20 In the **Audio Mixer**, on Track **Audio 4**, click the **Enable Track for Recording** button. On Track **Audio 3**, click the **Enable Track for Recording** button to turn off recording to that track. If you don't have headphones, click the **Solo Track** toggle on Track **Audio 4**.

Note: When dubbing, headphones are *highly* encouraged so you can hear the actor's original dialogue, without worrying about creating a feedback loop. If you *don't* have headphones available, then be sure to click the Solo Track toggle in the Audio Mixer for Track Audio 4.

---

21 At the bottom of the **Audio Mixer**, click the **Record** button.

The Audio Mixer is now ready to record only to track Audio 4 and only between the sequence In and Out points you set. In the next step, you will actually begin playback a few seconds before your In and Out points. This is so you can read aloud, into your microphone, to dub over the actor as accurately as possible (sort of like getting a running start).

---

22 Snap the **Timeline CTI** to the beginning of the **eruptologist.avi** clip on Track **Video 1**.

It's time to do a preflight check. Is only Audio 4 in record mode? Check. Is the Record button blinking? Check. If you don't have headphones, is the Solo Track toggle on for Track 4? Check. All right, prepare for takeoff!

---

23 In the **Audio Mixer**, click the (regular) **Play** button. Read aloud along with the eruptologist as you dub his voice, saying this instead: "The odds of Dutch Harbor being buried in a massive landslide of molten lava are *low*." When done, click the **Stop** button to stop playback.

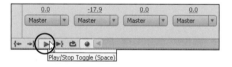

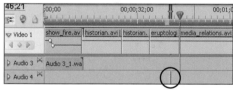

If everything went according to plan, you should see a thin audio clip on Track Audio 4, only between the In and Out points. If you want to try the dub again for accuracy, repeat Steps 21, 22, and 23.

This should underscore the added benefit of setting sequence In and Out points. This technique allows you to talk all you want into your microphone with only the vital section (between the In and Out points) being recorded.

Hold on. You have one more "high" to dub over. You will set new Sequence In and Out points, basically repeating the previous process.

---

24 Move the **Timeline CTI** to **00;00;45;02**, and press **I** to set a sequence **In** point. Move the **Timeline CTI** to **00;00;45;26**, and press **O** to set a sequence **Out** point. When done, snap the **Timeline CTI** to the start of the **eruptologist.avi** clip on Track **Video 1**.

---

25 In the **Audio Mixer**, click the **Record** button, and then click the **Play** button. Read aloud along with actor, saying this instead: "Very, very *low*." When you are finished, click the **Stop** button to stop playback.

---

26 Snap the **Timeline CTI** to the beginning of the **eruptologist.avi** clip, and click the **Play** button to play it.

If you are happy with the dub, keep reading. If not, you can repeat Step 25.

When you are done recording narrations and voice-over dubs, it's important to put away your toys, so to speak. In other words, you need to return the Audio Mixer to its normal, nonrecording state.

---

27 In the **Audio Mixer**, on Track **Audio 4**, click the **Enable Track Recording** button. In the **Audio Mixer** wing menu, click the **Meter Input(s) Only** toggle to turn it off. Choose **Marker > Clear Sequence Marker > In and Out**. If you had the **Solo Track** toggle turned on for Track **Audio 4**, click it again to turn it off.

This step turned off all the special buttons and modes you turned on for track recording. It's a good (and safe) habit to get into so you don't accidentally record anything else to the Timeline panel.

---

28 Choose **File > Save**, or press **Ctrl+S**. Leave **dutch harbor promo.prproj** open for the next exercise.

You should have found the process of recording with your own microphone quite easy. Just remember to set your audio input in the Windows XP Control Panel and then turn on track recording for the desired track. Click Record, and click Play—that's it!

Once you have recorded your audio, you can clean up the sound using the same audio effects, such as EQ and Reverb, you learned to use in Chapter 10, "*Working with Audio*." But instead of applying them to each clip, you can use the Audio Mixer to apply them to the entire track, all at once.

Using Submix Tracks

Submix tracks allow you to group two or more audio tracks and treat them as one. Just like a regular audio track, you can use the automation modes to alter the volume level of submix tracks. However, unlike regular audio tracks, you cannot place any audio clips into a submix track. A submix track exists only to help you group multiple audio tracks in one. Any changes you make to a submix track affect all the clip tracks assigned to that submix.

A popular use of submix is to apply a similar type of effect to multiple tracks. For example, if you have dialogue on more than one audio track, you can funnel these tracks into a single submix track. This allows you to apply a single audio effect to the submix track, which will alter the sound of every clip and every track being funneled to the submix track.

In the next exercise, you will learn how to send multiple audio tracks to a submix, as well as add an audio effect to the entire submix track.

3 | Applying Track-Based Effects to a Submix

As mentioned, submixes allow you to funnel multiple audio tracks into a single submix track. You can then add an audio effect to the submix, which affects all the audio tracks being routed to the submix. The primary benefit to submixes is saving time. Instead of adding effects to individual tracks, or individual clips, you can add effects to multiple tracks at once. In this exercise, you will learn how to create a submix, route tracks to the submix, and apply a track-based effect.

1 If you followed the previous exercise, **dutch harbor promo.prproj** should still be open in Premiere Pro 2. If it's not, click **Open Project** on the **Welcome Screen**. Navigate to the **c:\exercise_files\chap_11** folder, click **exercise03.prproj** to select it, and click **Open**.

2 Choose **File > Save As**. Navigate to the **c:\exercise_files\dutch_harbor** folder. Name the file **dutch harbor promo.prproj**, and click **Save**.

Note: If a previous version of dutch harbor promo.prproj already exists, you may be asked to replace it. Click Yes.

The first step of using submixes is to create a new submix track.

3 In the **Timeline** panel, be sure the **DVD history** sequence is open. Choose **Sequence > Add Tracks**. In the **Add Tracks** dialog box, be sure the **Add X Audio Submix Track(s)** field is set to **1** and all others are set to **0**. Click **OK**.

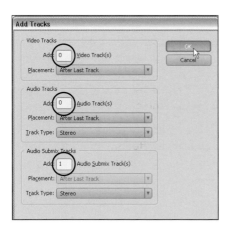

This creates a new track named Submix 1 in the Audio Mixer. A submix track is similar to the other tracks—except you cannot record your microphone to it or place other clips in a submix track.

After you create a submix track, you can redirect any audio track by assigning it to the submix track. Normally, the output goes directly to the master track, but when you output a track to a submix, the audio funnels through the submix before being output to the master track.

In this exercise, you will route your microphone tracks (Audio 3 and Audio 4) so you can process both tracks through a single submix track.

4 In the **Audio Mixer**, below the audio VU meters, choose **Submix 1** from the **Track Output Assignment** pop-up menus for Tracks **Audio 3** and **Audio 4**.

With tracks assigned to a submix, you can apply an effect to the submix track, which will affect tracks Audio 3 and Audio 4. But first, you must display the Audio Mixer Effects and Sends areas, which are the areas in which you will apply audio effects.

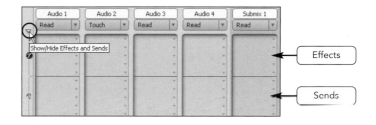

Audio 3 and Audio 4 output to Submix 1, which then outputs to the master track.

5 At the left side of the **Audio Mixer**, click the **Show/Hide Effects and Sends** toggle to turn on the **Effects** and **Sends** areas.

Each audio track, including the submix track, can hold up to five effects. Until now, you've done all of your effects work in the Effect Controls panel. However, you can apply and modify track effects only in the Audio Mixer.

Note: Sends are for sending a track to a submix for effects processing only. Any changes to the volume or balance in the submix have no effect on the track being sent.

Instead, if you *assign* a track to a submix, as you did in the previous step, any changes to the volume or balance in the submix indeed affect the tracks being assigned.

Next, you will apply an effect to the submix. It's easy to apply, but it is quite different from the Effect Controls panel you have grown accustomed to using, so it may seem odd at first.

6 In the **Effects** area, choose **EQ** from the top **Effect Selection** pop-up menu below the name **Submix 1**.

Unlike other effects you've applied, which you can find in the Effects panel, track effects in the Audio Mixer are contained inside the Effect Selection pop-up menu.

To access an effect's properties, the easiest step to perform is to double-click the effect name in the Audio Mixer. When you double-click, a floating panel opens for that effect. You will do this in the next step.

7 Double-click the effect name **EQ** to open a floating panel. Click in the top bar of the floating panel, and drag the panel to one side so you can see both the floating panel and the **Submix 1** track in the **Audio Mixer** at the same time.

This is where screen real estate gets very tight. Unless you have the luxury of two computer monitors, you may find yourself constantly moving the floating panel to access a button obscured by it.

Tip: Because this panel is floating, you can resize it by dragging the lower-right corner. In addition, you can move it by dragging the top bar of the panel.

To tweak Submix 1, it may be easier for you to mute the music and actors on Tracks Audio 1 and 2.

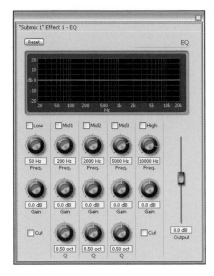

---

8 In the **Audio Mixer**, click the **Mute Track** toggle for Tracks **Audio 1** and **Audio 2**.

In the next series of steps, you will loop the audio of dialogue recorded by your microphone. But you will do it in the Audio Mixer, instead of looping it in the Effect Controls panel as you did when using the EQ effect in Chapter 10, *"Working with Audio."*

However, looping in the Effect Controls panel is smart enough to loop only the selected clip. When you are looping audio on a track, you have to manually specify how much of the track you'd like Premiere Pro 2 to loop.

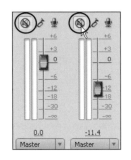

To specify the portion you'd like to loop in the Audio Mixer, you must set sequence In and Out points.

---

9 Close the floating **EQ** panel by clicking the **Close** box in the upper-right corner.

---

10 In the **Timeline** panel, drag the **CTI** to the start of the sequence, and press **I** to set a sequence **In** point. Drag the **Timeline CTI** to the last frame of your recorded narration on Track **Audio 3**, and press the **O** key to set a sequence **Out** point.

---

11 In the **Audio Mixer**, click the **Loop** toggle to turn on looping, and click **Play In to Out**.

Because you set In and Out points, the Play In to Out button will play back only the portion between the In and Out points. In addition, because you clicked the Loop toggle, the In to Out section will loop indefinitely.

Once you've got your audio looping, it is time to return to EQ and modify its effect properties.

12 With the audio still looping, double-click the **EQ** effect on Track **Submix 1**.

This opens the floating EQ panel again while the audio continues to loop.

13 Using what you learned in Chapter 10, *"Working with Audio,"* adjust the **EQ** effect properties on your own to improve the sound of the recorded microphone audio playing through **Submix 1**.

As a reminder, start by turning on the High check box to turn on the high frequency filter. Then lower the gain in the High frequency column. Once you're happy with that, turn on the Low check box to turn on the low frequency filter. Lower the gain in the Low frequency column.

When you are finished, close the EQ panel by clicking the Close box in the upper-right corner.

Note: The values shown in the illustration here are for example only.

Remember, start by selecting the High frequencies and reduce the high gain. This may help knock out any high-pitched ambient noises. Similarly, experiment with removing any low frequencies.

Tip: If an audio effect has presets, you can access the effects by right-clicking the effect name after you've applied it.

14 In the **Effects** area, below the **EQ** effect, choose **PitchShifter** from the second **Effect Selection** pop-up menu.

The PitchShifter effect raises or lowers the pitch of your voice. However, as with many effects in Premiere Pro 2, the effect is best in moderation. Choosing the highest and lowest values can sound downright horrible.

15 With the **Loop** toggle still turned on, click the **Play In to Out** button again. During playback, right-click the **PitchShifter** effect, and choose **Female becomes secret agent** from the available presets.

Note: While the audio loops, feel free to choose other presets to hear their results. When done, make sure you choose the same option as in the previous step: Female becomes secret agent.

Tip: Like many other effects in Premiere Pro 2, it's best to start with a preset and then tweak it from there.

16 While the audio is still looping, double-click the **PitchShifter** effect to open it in a floating panel. Make sure the **Formant Preserve** check box is turned off. Change the **Pitch** value to **–3 semi-t** (semitones).

By the way, a **semitone** is the small interval between two notes. This raises or lowers the overall sound pitch. Also, there are 100 cents in a semitone, so fine-tuning –50 cents or +50 cents will increase or decrease the pitch by half a semitone. (Do you need to know this to edit video? No. Will this impress your friends? Depends on your friends.)

Notice the Pitch control knob at the bottom of the Effects and Sends areas. Clicking the property name opens a pop-up menu, which allows you to choose a different property. These are the same properties as in the floating panel.

Changing a property in the floating effect panel is the same as changing the property in the track area.

The advantage of the floating panel is being able to see all the properties at once. The advantage of the single property in the Audio Mixer is you don't have to deal with a floating panel.

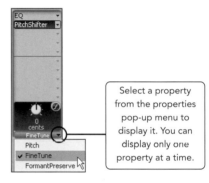

Let's return to reality. In real life, you probably wouldn't really be applying this effect in this situation. But at least you are learning to use this effect. Furthermore, it's equally important to learn how to remove an unwanted effect (and this one is *definitely* unwanted!).

Select a property from the properties pop-up menu to display it. You can display only one property at a time.

17 In the **Effects** area, next to the **PitchShifter** effect, choose **None** from the second **Effect Selection** pop-up menu.

You are done applying track-based effects. Before finishing, don't forget to remove any In and Out points, and be sure to "unmute" all the tracks.

18 For Tracks **Audio 1** and **Audio 2**, click the **Mute Track** toggles to "unmute" both tracks. Choose **Marker > Clear Sequence Marker > In and Out**. At the bottom of the **Audio Mixer**, click the **Loop** toggle to turn off loop mode.

19 Choose **File > Save**, or press **Ctrl+S**. Leave **dutch harbor promo.prproj** open for the next exercise.

Once you are comfortable with navigating track effects in the Audio Mixer, you will see the track effects are the same as regular audio effects. The only difference is figuring out where to find each property in the Audio Mixer, since they appear in a different layout. Sure, they have some additional nuances, such as muting other tracks or setting sequence In and Out points, but in the end, it's the same workflow you learned in Chapter 10, *"Working with Audio."*

Monitoring the Master Track

The last step in your audio workflow, when you are absolutely, 100 percent, positively done tweaking your audio, is to monitor and adjust the master track's volume levels. Sometimes you've added extra sound, and you want to take one last preventative measure to make sure your audio doesn't peak at greater than 0.0 dB. Think of the master track as the last double check you have before you send the client's commercial off to the television station!

The goal of monitoring the master levels is to make sure the entire sequence peaks at an acceptable level (–6 dB), even when all tracks are playing at the same time. And, lucky for you, this may be the easiest exercise in the entire book! Adjusting audio in the master track is the same as doing it for any other audio track. So, in reality, you already know how to do this.

1 If you followed the previous exercise, **dutch harbor promo.prproj** should still be open in Premiere Pro 2. If it's not, click **Open Project** on the **Welcome Screen**. Navigate to the **c:\exercise_files\chap_11** folder, click **exercise04.prproj** to select it, and click **Open**.

2 Choose **File > Save As**. Navigate to the **c:\exercise_files\dutch_harbor** folder. Name the file **dutch harbor promo.prproj**, and click **Save**.

Note: If a previous version of dutch harbor promo.prproj already exists, you may be asked to replace it. Click Yes.

3 In the **Timeline** panel, make sure the **DVD history** sequence is in the foreground.

4 In the **Audio Mixer**, make sure the master track automation mode is set to **Read**.

If the master track is set to Latch, Touch, or Write, any changes you make will create new keyframes; furthermore, those changes will affect only a specific section of the sequence. And that's not what you want.

Instead, keeping the master track in Read mode lets you modify the sequence volume from the beginning to end with the click of a single button. If you change the automation mode, you lose this unique ability.

5 Click the **Play In to Out** button. During playback, lower the **Master** volume fader to an appropriate level (such as **–3.4 dB**) so the audio peaks at approximately **–6.0 dB** in the VU meter.

While the audio plays, you can see the peak levels for yourself in the master track VU meter. You'll probably agree that –3.4 dB is an appropriate amount to reduce the volume of this track so the peaks don't exceed –6.0 dB.

This sequence is now ready to be exported. Before you call it a day, don't forget to monitor the other sequences in your project.

6 At the top of the **Timeline** panel, select the **DVD intro** tab to bring the sequence to the foreground.

---

7 In the **Audio Mixer**, make sure the master track automation mode is set to **Read**.

---

8 Click the **Play In to Out** button. As the sequence plays, lower the **Master** volume fader to an appropriate level (such as **–1.1 dB**) so the audio peaks at approximately **–6.0 dB**.

---

9 At the top of the **Timeline** panel, select the **DVD map** tab to bring the sequence to the foreground.

---

10 In the **Audio Mixer**, make sure the master track automation mode is set to **Read**.

---

11 Click the **Play In to Out** button. During playback, lower the **Master** volume fader to an appropriate level (such as **–4.0 dB**) so the audio peaks at approximately **–6.0 dB**.

---

12 Choose **File > Save**, or press **Ctrl+S**. Choose **File > Close** to close this project.

Premiere Pro 2 lets you do much more to the master audio track. Just like any other track, you can add effects to, and change the automation mode of, the master track.

Then again, there's something to be said for being able to alter the volume of an entire sequence with the click of a button. This is why we prefer to use the master track in this fashion. To be fair, not all editors you meet will use the master track in the method taught in this exercise. There's no right or wrong way to edit, of course. It's all a matter of personal taste and of finding the workflow that is most efficient for your editing style.

Well, you did it. You are ready to export your project. You've done everything possible to the Timeline, the Effect Controls panel, and the Audio Mixer. At this point, you should feel pretty comfortable that you have the tools to create your own Premiere Pro 2 project.

However, now that you've done all this work on your project, you have one task left to perform—and that's to export it from Premiere Pro 2 so other people can see it.

12

Authoring DVDs

One of the most touted and highly anticipated new features of Adobe Premiere Pro 2 is the ability to author and burn a DVD containing a menu and a submenu. In previous versions of Premiere Pro, you could always burn a movie to DVD, but it was more like making a videotape—when you put it in your home DVD player, the movie started playing right away. It offered no menus and no interaction. Premiere Pro 2 now lets you author a DVD with a main menu and a scene selection submenu. **Authoring** describes the process of creating a DVD video to be played on a home DVD player. You can choose from a variety of templates, add thumbnail images to your menu buttons, and even add video and audio to further customize your menu. In this chapter, you will walk through a typical workflow for creating simple DVDs and for creating complex DVDs with menus.

Understanding the DVD Workflow

When authoring a DVD in Premiere Pro 2, the most efficient workflow is as follows:

1. Assemble all your sequences into a single sequence: Premiere Pro 2 will export only *one* sequence as a DVD movie. If your project is divided into multiple sequences, then you should first nest all your sequences into a single sequence. The single sequence, containing the nested sequences, is often referred to as the **master sequence**.

2. Decide which type of DVD you plan to create: Premiere Pro 2 is capable of creating DVDs with and without menus. Do you want your DVD to have menus? If so, do you want someone to be able to jump to certain "scenes" in the DVD? Answering these questions will help you determine which type of DVD you will create.

3. Add DVD markers to your sequence: DVD markers act as chapter points (like tracks on a music CD) so you can use your remote control to quickly jump to the previous or next scene. In addition, each DVD marker equates to a button on the DVD menu. If you have four menu markers, your DVD will have four buttons you can choose from when navigating the DVD with your remote control.

4. Choose and customize a DVD template: Premiere Pro 2 comes with many predesigned templates to use as backgrounds for your DVD menus. Once you select a template, you can further customize it by adding your own video background and music for playing while the menu displays.

5. Burn the DVD to disc, or export to a file on your hard drive: Typically, the final stage in DVD authoring is to burn your DVD to disc. However, Premiere Pro 2 also provides the capability to save the DVD as a file on your hard drive so you can quickly burn multiple copies without having to reauthor the entire DVD each time.

Throughout this chapter, you will walk through each step of the authoring process. Your first pit stop, in the Authoring 500, is to decide which type of DVD to create.

Choosing from Three DVD Types

Premiere Pro 2 allows you to burn a DVD *with* a menu or *without* a menu. If you choose to make a DVD containing a menu, you further get to decide whether it should have only one menu or two menus. The following sections provide a brief summary of each type of DVD.

Choosing an Autoplay DVD

These are the most basic type of DVD. **Autoplay DVDs** have no menus and no interactive buttons. When you put an autoplay DVD into your home DVD player, the movie starts playing immediately. The only items you can add to autoplay DVDs are DVD markers to create chapter points (to quickly navigate ahead or back, like music tracks on a CD).

Choosing a Main Menu DVD

Premiere Pro 2 is capable of authoring a DVD with a main menu, known as a **main menu DVD**. When the user places the DVD in a home DVD player, the first screen to display is the main menu. From this menu, users can choose to play the entire movie or instead jump to another movie on the DVD.

For example, you know that blockbuster movie you have at home—the one set a long, long time ago in a galaxy far, far away? At its main menu, you can choose to play the movie, or you can view any number of additional "goodies" (more movies) on the DVD. Such goodies might include a "making of" documentary, deleted scenes, and so on. You would create these choices, in Premiere Pro 2, by using main menu markers.

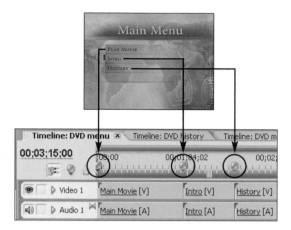

As shown in the illustration here, the user sees a main menu containing three choices. You create each choice with a DVD marker in the Timeline. In the Timeline, three sequences have been nested (inserted like clips) into a master sequence. Adding a DVD marker at the beginning of each sequence allows it to appear as a choice on the main menu.

Choosing a Scene Selection DVD

The last type of DVD you can author in Premiere Pro 2 is a scene selection DVD. A **scene selection DVD** is the same as the main menu DVD described previously, but it has one additional menu. Therefore, you get two menus: a main menu plus a scene selection submenu. The scene selection submenu allows a user to jump to a specific scene in a movie. You will recognize this feature on the DVDs of Hollywood movies.

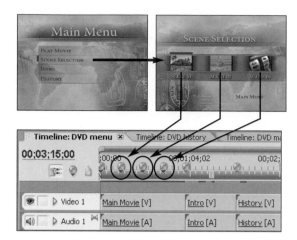

As shown in the illustration here, choosing **Scene Selection** from the main menu (upper-left) takes you to the Scene Selection submenu (upper-right). This is why it is called a **submenu**, or child, of the parent main menu.

Notice in the illustration that the sequence in the Timeline is the same as the sequence shown in the previous illustration—except it has three additional scene markers, which created three scene selection choices.

It's important to note that if a sequence does *not* have any scene markers, then the DVD will *not* have a scene selection submenu. So remember, no scene markers = no scene menu. Got it? Good.

Before diving in-depth into the wonderful and fascinating world of DVD markers, you will create an autoplay DVD with no menus. This will introduce you to the simple tasks of prepping your sequence for authoring, selecting a DVD type, and previewing your DVD. Only upon mastering these tasks may you progress to DVD markers, Grasshopper.

EXERCISE

1 | Building an Autoplay DVD

Autoplay DVDs have no menus. You pop the DVD into your home DVD player, and the movie starts playing. Autoplay DVDs are the most basic type of DVDs you can create, and they require little work. Autoplay DVDs are perfect for kiosks, where you want a movie to play repeatedly, without ever presenting the user with a menu choice. In addition, autoplay DVDs are useful when you just want to quickly burn your sequence to DVD, without spending a lot of time planning and arranging menus.

In this exercise, you will get your first taste of creating DVDs. You will learn how to prep your sequence for authoring, choose the type of DVD you want to author, and preview your DVD via the **DVD Layout** panel.

---

1 On the **Welcome Screen**, click **Open Project**. In the **Open Project** dialog box, navigate to the c:\exercise_files\chap_12 folder, click **exercise01.prproj** to select it, and click **Open**.

---

2 Choose **File > Save As**. Navigate to the **c:\exercise_files\dutch_harbor** folder. Name the file **dutch_harbor_promo.prproj**, and click **Save**.

Note: If a previous version of dutch_harbor_promo.prproj already exists, you may be asked to replace it. Click Yes.

The first step in authoring a DVD, no matter what type of DVD, is to nest all the sequences into a single sequence. Remember, Premiere Pro 2 will author only one sequence at a time. In other words, one sequence = one DVD.

For example, if you've divided your project into multiple sequences (such as Scene 1, Scene 2, and so on), you must nest all the sequences you want to export into a single sequence.

---

3 In the **Project** panel **Sequences** bin, choose **File > New > Sequence**. In the **New Sequence** dialog box, type **Autoplay** in the **Sequence Name** field. Click **OK**.

A new sequence, named Autoplay, appears in the Sequences bin and opens in the Timeline panel. This is the sequence you will export as an autoplay DVD.

Now that you have a sequence, it's time to fill it with the sequences you want to put on the DVD. Remember, placing one sequence inside of another is called **nesting**.

---

4 In the **Project** panel **Sequences** bin, click and drag **DVD intro** to the beginning of Track **Video 1**.

Here's a quick review on nesting: The DVD intro sequence is nested inside the Autoplay sequence. The *nested* sequence displays as a single clip (with video and audio) inside the *master* sequence.

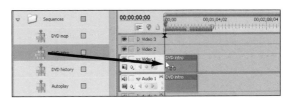

5 In the **Project** panel **Sequences** bin, click and drag **DVD map** to the end of **DVD intro** on Track **Video 1**. Make sure to snap the two clips together as you drag.

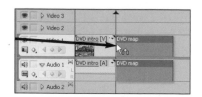

6 In the **Project** panel **Sequences** bin, click and drag **DVD history** to the end of **DVD map** on Track **Video 1**. Make sure to snap the two clips together as you drag.

You have nested three sequences inside the Autoplay sequence. Because you've already monitored all of your audio levels, you don't have to do anymore work. However, you could trim the In and Out points of these nested clips as you would any regular clip.

The next step in creating an autoplay DVD is to preview the DVD via the DVD Layout panel.

7 Choose **Window > DVD Layout** to open the **DVD Layout** panel.

You'll primarily use the DVD Layout panel to organize the layout of your DVD menus. In Exercise 4 you will learn how to use this panel to customize your menus.

For now, because autoplay DVDs contain no menus, the DVD Layout panel is empty. The only reason to open this panel for autoplay DVDs is to access the Preview DVD button, which lets you watch your movie as it will appear on the DVD.

8 In the **DVD Layout** panel, click the **Preview DVD** button.

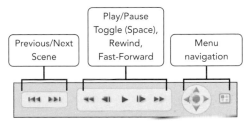

This opens the Preview DVD panel, which displays a preview of what the finished DVD will look like. In the lower part of this dialog box, you will see navigation buttons similar to those found on your DVD remote control (as shown in the illustration here).

The DVD remote control contains three groups of buttons. The center set of buttons should be familiar because they are the same as the playback buttons in Premiere Pro 2.

The Previous Scene and Next Scene buttons jump to different DVD chapters. You'll use these only when you've created DVD markers in the Timeline panel.

The menu navigation buttons are similar to those found on your DVD remote for moving between menu choices and returning to the main menu. These buttons are currently unavailable because your autoplay DVD has no menus.

---

9 In the navigation controls of the **Preview DVD** panel, click the **Play/Pause Toggle (Space)** toggle to start playback. During playback, click the **Play/Pause Toggle (Space)** toggle again to pause playback.

If you would like to experiment with any of the navigation buttons, knock yourself out. Nothing you do in the Preview DVD panel will harm your project or DVD.

---

10 In the upper-right corner of the **Preview DVD** panel, click the **Close** box. In the **DVD Layout** panel, click the **Close** box.

You've seen how easy it is to create and preview an autoplay DVD. In addition, if you would like to quickly be able to navigate between each clip in your sequence, Premiere Pro 2 makes it equally as easy to place markers at each edit point with the Auto-Generate DVD Markers command.

---

11 At the top of the **Timeline** panel, select the **Autoplay** tab to ensure the sequence is selected. Choose **Marker > Auto-Generate DVD Markers**.

This opens the Automatically Set DVD Scene Markers dialog box. Premiere Pro 2 lets you specify where you would like to automatically create DVD markers. The most common choice is to place markers at the beginning of each scene, although you can also choose to place markers at regular intervals of *X* minutes or create *X* markers spaced evenly throughout the DVD.

12 In the **Automatically Set DVD Scene Markers** dialog box, make sure the **At Each Scene** radio button is selected, and turn on the **Clear Existing DVD Markers** check box. Click **OK**.

This creates three DVD markers at the top of the sequence in the Timeline panel, although the first one may be obscured behind the CTI (**C**urrent **T**ime **I**ndicator). Each marker aligns with the beginning of a clip on Track Video 1.

The Clear Existing DVD Markers check box removes any existing DVD markers in a sequence. (This was a safety measure just in case any markers were already created accidentally.)

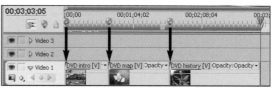

13 Choose **Window > DVD Layout**. Click the **Preview DVD** button.

With several DVD markers added, you can use the Next Scene and Previous Scene buttons to jump between scenes.

14 In the **Preview DVD** panel navigation controls, click the **Play** button. During playback, click the **Next Scene** button to jump to the next chapter.

Tip: In this usage, **chapter** and **scene** have the same meaning. If this were a music CD, they would be called **tracks**.

15 In the upper-right corner of the **Preview DVD** panel, click the **Close** box. In the **DVD Layout** panel, click the **Close** box.

---

16 Choose **File > Save**, or press **Ctrl+S**. Leave **dutch harbor promo.prproj** open for the next exercise.

You have successfully prepped the autoplay sequence for authoring to DVD. The last step in authoring the DVD is to burn the sequence to DVD or save it to your hard drive. However, you have to consider many factors when deciding how to export your DVD, so we won't cover this topic until Exercise 5.

This exercise also served as an introduction to DVD markers. Premiere Pro 2 provides two ways of creating DVD markers: You can autogenerate them, or you can manually create them. Even though autogeneration can be the quickest method, if your sequence is somewhat complex, then you may find better results by manually creating your own markers.

Now that you understand how DVD markers work, it's time to venture into the wonderful world of manually creating them.

WARNING:

Chapter Points May Not Work As Expected

In the previous exercise, you learned how to generate DVD markers automatically to create an autoplay DVD with chapter points. Unfortunately, due to an issue in the Premiere Pro 2 application, autoplay DVDs will burn *without* chapter points (despite information to the contrary in the online help file for Premiere Pro 2).

As a result, the DVD will still play in your home DVD player, but the next and previous scene buttons on your remote control won't work with this DVD. Adobe outlines the problem in the following technical support document: **www.adobe.com/support/techdocs/332415.html**.

Adobe's current solution is for you to add a quick menu to your DVD in order to make the chapter points work—luckily, you'll learn how to add menus in the next exercises.

At the time of this book's publication, Adobe has not yet released a patch or update to fix this acknowledged issue. Hopefully in the near future this problem will be addressed. You can check the Adobe site for updates at the following URL: **www.adobe.com/support/downloads**.

Understanding DVD Markers

DVD markers are the unsung heroes of the DVD authoring process. Oh, sure, the menus get all the glitz and glamour, but without markers, you would have no DVD menu choices, no chapter points to jump between, and no scene selection submenu. These features can exist *only* when a sequence has DVD markers.

DVD markers perform the following functions: They allow users to jump between chapters on the DVD, they display as menu buttons on the main menu, and they create scene selection submenus and display as menu buttons on the scene selection submenu.

You've already learned how to create markers to move between chapters. However, you're just scratching the surface of DVD markers. Next, you will focus on the relationship between DVD markers and DVD menus.

As described in Exercise 1, Premiere Pro 2 has two types of menus: main menus and scene selection submenus. Likewise, Premiere Pro 2 has two types of menu markers: main menu markers and scene markers. (Notice a pattern?) Each marker displays as a "button" an audience member can choose on the DVD menu. The following sections briefly describe each type of marker.

Understanding Main Menu Markers

All main menus come with a **Play Movie** option. However, unless you have created some **main menu markers**, the menu won't contain any other options. As shown in the illustration here, the sequence on the left has no markers. Its main menu has only the default **Play Movie** option.

The sequence on the right has two main menu markers; therefore, it has two additional menu choices. These markers are given names, which display as the text next to the button. In this case, the markers are named **Outtakes** and **Deleted Scenes**.

Understanding Scene Markers

A DVD without scene markers

A DVD with scene markers

When a DVD has no **scene markers**, it won't have any scene selection submenu, plain and simple. On the other hand, if you have *too many* scene markers, Premiere Pro 2 will automatically create additional "pages" of submenus for the overflow buttons. As shown in the illustration here, the scene selection submenu (bottom) has an arrow at the bottom of its submenu, which a user can select to navigate to the next page of scene selection buttons. Premiere Pro 2 will create as many scene selection pages as needed.

Understanding Stop Markers

OK, we lied. One more type of marker exists, but it is not linked to any type of menu. **Stop markers** designate the end of a movie. When the DVD player reaches a stop marker, it automatically stops playing and returns to the main menu. During playback, the user cannot jump to the next chapter point. A stop marker is like a brick wall—or better yet, an invisible force field (like in the movie about the wars amongst the stars!).

Stop markers are useful when you want to include separate movies in your DVD—such as deleted scenes or a "making of" documentary—and you don't want them to play right after one another. For example, usually after Premiere Pro 2 finishes playing one scene, it happily proceeds to playing the next scene. And because all your DVD scenes are placed in a single sequence, Premiere Pro 2 thinks they are all part of the same movie, so it continues playing.

A stop marker is a way of telling Premiere Pro 2, "No, the next scene is a separate movie from the scene you are currently playing. Do not play the **Timeline** from start to finish. Go home!" (Only it's nicer than that.)

Creating DVD Markers

The process for creating DVD markers is similar to the process for creating keyframes: First, move the **CTI** to the point in time where you would like the marker; and second, click the **Set DVD Marker** button. Simple! But once you click the **Set DVD Marker** button, you have to make some decisions about the marker you are creating.

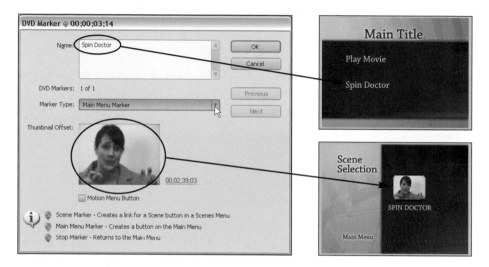

When you manually add a DVD marker, Premiere Pro 2 displays the **DVD Marker** dialog box, as shown in the illustration here. The following are the options you can specify:

Name: The name of the marker you choose appears as the label for a button in the main menu or scene selection submenu.

Marker Type: This is the type of marker to create: main menu, scene selection, or stop.

Thumbnail Offset: On some menu templates, the menu buttons include thumbnail images of the video to which they are linked. You can also specify to use a snippet of video as the thumbnail instead of a static, still image.

Keep in mind, the thumbnail display depends on the DVD template you choose. In other words, even if you specify a thumbnail, it will not appear unless the template is designed to do so. Of all the templates in Premiere Pro 2, only the scene selection submenus display thumbnail icons.

In addition to creating DVD markers, the **DVD Marker** dialog box provides controls for navigating between markers. You can jump to the previous or next DVD marker in a sequence by clicking the **Previous** or **Next** button. The **DVD Marker** dialog box also has a **Delete** button, which is an aptly named button because it deletes the existing marker.

Once you've created a marker and specified options in the **DVD Marker** dialog box, you are not stuck with those options. You can double-click a marker in the **Timeline**, and the **DVD Marker** dialog box will reappear.

Enough talk! We hope you are excited to create some DVD markers. In the next exercise, you will start by building a sequence with main menu markers.

2 | Creating Main Menu and Stop Markers

After nesting all your sequences into a single sequence, the next step in authoring a DVD with menus is to create your markers (because the DVD will have no menus until you create menu markers!). In the workflow of creating DVDs in Premiere Pro 2, it's best to specify your markers *before* choosing a DVD menu template. After all, if you don't have any markers, the menu is pretty much useless. You will begin this process by creating main menu markers, which create buttons on the main menu. In addition, you will create stop markers, which return the DVD player to the main menu.

1 If you followed the previous exercise, **dutch_harbor_promo.prproj** should still be open in Premiere Pro 2. If it's not, click **Open Project** on the **Welcome Screen**. Navigate to the **c:\exercise_files\chap_12** folder, click **exercise02.prproj** to select it, and click **Open**.

2 Choose **File > Save As**. Navigate to the **c:\exercise_files\dutch_harbor** folder. Name the file **dutch_harbor_promo.prproj**, and click **Save**.

Note: If a previous version of dutch_harbor_promo.prproj already exists, you may be asked to replace it. Click Yes.

In the previous exercise, you created a sequence for an autoplay DVD. Because you have done all of the work of nesting sequences in a single sequence, you'll start this exercise by duplicating the Autoplay sequence.

3 In the **Project** panel **Sequences** bin, select the **Autoplay** sequence, and choose **Edit > Duplicate**.

This creates a duplicate copy named Autoplay Copy.

4 In the **Project** panel **Sequences** bin, right-click the **Autoplay Copy** sequence, and choose **Rename**. When the sequence name is highlighted, type **Menu DVD**, and press **Enter** to rename the sequence.

5 In the **Project** panel **Sequences** bin, double-click the **Menu DVD** sequence to open it in the **Timeline** panel.

At the top of the Timeline panel, you can see this sequence already has three DVD markers. These are leftovers from the previous exercise because you duplicated the Autoplay sequence. Before creating DVD markers manually, you may find it easiest to remove any existing DVD markers.

6 At the top of the **Timeline** panel, click the **Menu DVD** tab to make sure the sequence is selected. Choose **Marker > Clear DVD Marker > All DVD Markers**.

Tip: You can also right-click at the top of the Time Ruler and choose Clear All DVD Markers.

Now it's time to manually create your main menu markers. The most logical place to create markers is at the beginning of each nested sequence. The steps for creating a DVD marker are to move the Timeline CTI and then to click the Set DVD Marker button.

7 Snap the **Timeline CTI** to the beginning of the **Menu DVD** sequence. In the upper-left corner of the **Timeline** panel, click the **Set DVD Marker** button.

This opens the DVD Marker dialog box. It is important to note that no marker is created until you click OK. If you click Cancel, the process is aborted.

In the DVD Marker dialog box, you can specify the type of marker and the name. You can also specify the thumbnail frame; however, you won't use this until Exercise 3, when you create a scene selection submenu.

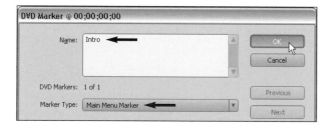

8 In the **DVD Marker** dialog box, change **Marker Type** to **Main Menu Marker**. In the **Name** text box, type **Intro**. Click **OK** to set the marker.

Note: The Previous and Next buttons are dimmed because you have no other DVD markers in this sequence.

9 In the **Program Monitor**, click the **Go to Next Edit Point** button. Alternatively, press the **Page Down** key.

Both of these methods quickly advance the CTI to the start of the next clip. The CTI should be at 00;00;39;26.

10 In the **Timeline** panel, click the **Set DVD Marker** button. In the **DVD Marker** dialog box, change **Marker Type** to **Main Menu Marker**. In the **Name** text box, type **Map**. Click **OK**.

You now have two main menu markers—Intro and Map—so your DVD menu will have the default Play Movie option, as well as two additional options.

In the next series of steps, you will add a stop marker to force the DVD player to return to the main menu. You create stop markers in the same way as main menu markers. However, instead of placing them at the beginning of each clip, it's best to place them *at the end* of a clip.

---

11 In the **Program Monitor**, click the **Go to Next Edit Point** button to advance the **CTI** to the start of the third clip. Press the **left arrow** key once to back up one frame. The **CTI** should be at **00;01;37;04**.

Essentially, you moved the CTI to the start of the next clip, but then you backed it up one frame so it is positioned on the last frame of the previous clip.

12 In the **Timeline** panel, click the **Set DVD Marker** button. In the **DVD Marker** dialog box, change **Marker Type** to **Stop Marker**. Click **OK**.

As soon as you choose Stop Marker, the other options in the DVD Marker dialog box become dimmed or completely disappear. The stop marker's sole purpose in life is to stop playback, so it doesn't get all the bells and whistles of the other DVD markers. In fact, it doesn't even get a name...poor stop marker!

Once you have created your markers, the next step is to choose a menu template.

13 Choose **Window > DVD Layout**. In the **DVD Layout** panel, click the **Change Template** button.

This opens the DVD Templates dialog box.

Tip: Even though you will eventually create a menu DVD, all sequences default to the autoplay DVD when you first open the DVD Layout panel. Unless you specify a DVD template, Premiere Pro 2 assumes your sequence is an autoplay DVD.

14 In the **DVD Templates** dialog box, click the **Apply a Template for a DVD with Menus** radio button, which is currently unselected.

In the DVD Templates dialog box, you can choose from one of several themes. Within each theme, you can choose from a handful of individual templates. For each template choice, you'll see two images. The image on the left is the main menu, and the image on the right is the scene selection submenu.

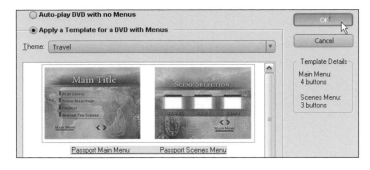

15 In the **Theme** pop-up menu, choose **Travel**. Click **Passport Main Menu** to select the template, and click **OK**.

Tip: The Template Details area to the right of the template preview displays vital stats for the currently selected template. Because the templates vary, it's helpful to know how many main menu and scene menu buttons are available for a particular template. This may be a factor when deciding which template to use.

---

16 In the **DVD Layout** panel, click the **Preview DVD** button.

In the Preview DVD panel, you can see the DVD navigation buttons are now ready to be clicked. These buttons mimic the controls found on your DVD remote.

Tip: In the Preview DVD panel, you can click your mouse directly in the menu, or you can use the DVD navigation buttons to make menu choices.

---

17 In the **Preview DVD** panel, click the **Map** button to begin playback from that marker. Let the preview play to the end of the scene.

Note two important issues here: First, the preview should return to the main menu as soon as it reaches the end of the scene. This is because of your friend, the stop marker. Second, you may notice the preview quality is pretty lousy. This is because Premiere Pro 2 is doing its best to display the video in real time without rendering. Rest assured, your finished product will be *much* higher quality.

---

18 In the **Preview DVD** panel, click the **Close** box. In the **DVD Layout** panel, click the **Close** box.

---

19 Choose **File > Save**, or press **Ctrl+S**. Leave **dutch harbor promo.prproj** open for the next exercise.

Way to go! You just built a DVD menu. You can still do much more to the menu, such as changing the text font and sizes, renaming buttons and titles, and adding motion backgrounds and music. You'll get to experience all of this in Exercise 4.

But first, before you can finish authoring the DVD, you will add some scene markers, as well as learn some of the additional features for displaying thumbnails next to the menu buttons.

NOTE: | **Advanced DVD Authoring**

The new DVD authoring options in Premiere Pro 2 are light years beyond what was offered in previous versions. In fact, you couldn't *ever* create DVDs with menus directly before Premiere Pro 2. Even so, you may someday reach the boundaries of what Premiere Pro 2 is designed to do when authoring DVDs. When you reach this point, it's time to take your DVD-authoring skills to Adobe Encore DVD. This application is Adobe's high-end DVD-authoring software. Encore DVD begins where Premiere Pro 2 leaves off.

Encore DVD offers an unlimited number of menus, which either can be based on an existing template or can be designed from scratch. You can specify how menus behave when they reach the end of their scenes—rather than returning to the main menu, like in Premiere Pro 2. In addition, you can specify what should happen when the user pushes any given button on the DVD player's remote control. Encore DVD even provides detailed flowcharts to help you create complex routing of DVD chapters and menus.

This merely touches on what Encore DVD can do. In the end, there's little a block-buster Hollywood movie DVD can do that you can't do using Encore DVD.

3 | Creating Scene Markers

You can include the scene selection templates bundled with Premiere Pro 2 in a DVD only after you create scene markers. You create these markers in the same way as you created the main menu markers in Exercise 2. In addition to showing the marker name, the scene selection templates also display a thumbnail picture associated with each marker. Premiere Pro 2 allows you to change the frame shown and even turn the thumbnail image into a tiny movie loop instead of a still image. In this exercise, you will create a handful of scene markers and explore the options for creating different types of menu thumbnails.

---

1 If you followed the previous exercise, **dutch_harbor_promo.prproj** should still be open in Premiere Pro 2. If it's not, click **Open Project** on the **Welcome Screen**. Navigate to **c:\exercise_files\chap_12** folder, click **exercise03.prproj** to select it, and click **Open**.

---

2 Choose **File > Save As**. Navigate to the **c:\exercise_files\dutch_harbor** folder. Name the file **dutch_harbor_promo.prproj**, and click **Save**.

Note: If a previous version of dutch_harbor_promo.prproj already exists, you may be asked to replace it. Click Yes.

In the previous exercise, you created a sequence to be eventually authored as a DVD with menus. You have already specified main menu markers, and now you will follow the same steps to create scene markers.

---

3 In the **Program Monitor**, click the **Go to Next** or **Go to Previous Edit Point** button until the **CTI** is positioned at the beginning of the **DVD history** clip on Track **Video 1** at **00;01;37;05**.

This is where you will create the first scene marker.

---

4 In the **Timeline** panel, click the **Set DVD Marker** button. In the **DVD Marker** dialog box, change **Marker Type** to **Scene Marker**. In the **Name** text box, type **Welcome**. Click **OK**.

Next, you will advance the Timeline CTI to the start of the historian scene so you can place another scene marker.

---

5 Drag the **Timeline CTI** to **00;01;50;07**. Click the **Set DVD Marker** button. In the **DVD Marker** dialog box, change **Marker Type** to **Scene Marker**. In the **Name** text box, type **Historian**. Do *not* click **OK**.

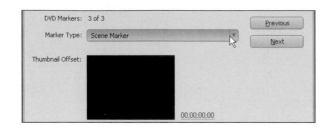

Before you click OK, you first need to fix the thumbnail because the current thumbnail frame is mostly black. This is a common problem when the beginning of your scene starts as a cross dissolve from black. Premiere Pro 2 allows you to resolve this problem by offsetting the frame timecode. In less technical terms, you can change the frame used as the thumbnail. (For example, if you want to use a frame that is 2 seconds away, you "offset" the timecode by 2 seconds.)

The best way to do this is to slowly drag the timecode to the right until you find a frame to better represent the scene.

---

6 In the **DVD Marker** dialog box, drag the **Thumbnail Offset** timecode to **00;00;01;22**. Click **OK**.

This tells Premiere Pro 2 to use the frame of video that is 1 second and 22 frames to the *right* of the DVD marker. (Note: You are not allowed to use an offset frame to the left of the marker.)

---

7 Drag the **Timeline CTI** to the start of the **Eruptologist** scene, at **00;02;13;17**. Click the **Set DVD Marker** button.

---

8 In the **DVD Marker** dialog box, change **Marker Type** to **Scene Marker**. In the **Name** text box, type **Eruptologist**. Drag the **Thumbnail Offset** timecode to **00;00;02;00**. Click **OK**.

This is an example where the first frame was representative, but the actor was smiling, so it was useful to find a more appropriate thumbnail. (The lesson here is to never let your friends be in your book.)

For this last thumbnail, you will create a Motion Menu button. When you preview the menu, a short snippet of video will play, instead of a static image such as a photograph.

---

9 Drag the **Timeline CTI** to the start of the **Media Relations** scene, at **00;02;23;28**. Click the **Set DVD Marker** button.

10 In the **DVD Marker** dialog box, change **Marker Type** to **Scene Marker**. In the **Name** text box, type **Media Relations**. Below the thumbnail, turn on the **Motion Menu Button** check box. Click **OK**.

You have now created all your scene markers, so it is time to preview and adjust the scene selection submenu.

11 Choose **Window > DVD Layout**.

Even though the DVD now has two menus, the DVD Layout panel opens, displaying the main menu by default. You can view the layout of other menus by clicking the menu thumbnail in the DVD Menus box in the lower portion of the panel.

Note: If your DVD layout preview does not display the title safe and action safe margins, you can turn them on by clicking the DVD Layout wing menu and choosing Show Safe Margins (so a check mark displays next to the name). These are useful guides when you need to make sure your DVD menu text will display on a standard television screen.

12 In the **DVD Layout** panel, in the **DVD Menus** box, click **Scenes Menu 1** to preview its layout.

Note two important issues about this menu: First, the Eruptologist text is so long it spills into the "unsafe for text" nether region. (It's a good thing you just learned how to turn on the safe margins!) Also, did you notice the Media Relations scene does not display? This is because this menu template allows for only three buttons. Because you created four scene markers, the fourth marker appears on a separate page.

13 In the **DVD Layout** panel **DVD Menus** box, click **Scenes Menu 2**. (You may need to scroll.)

There she is, all by her lonesome. Unfortunately, you have no way to move this thumbnail to the previous menu because the number of thumbnails is built into the template.

At this point, you have one of two choices: Either change your menu template to a template containing at least four buttons or delete one of your scene selection menus. In this case, however, you'll choose a third option: *Do nothing!*

14 In the **DVD Layout** panel, click the **Preview DVD** button. In the **Preview DVD** panel, click the **Scene Selection** link. In the scene selection submenu, click the **>** icon to navigate to the second scene page.

On the second page, you will notice the Media Relations thumbnail is actually a movie, rather than a still image.

15 In the **Preview DVD** panel, click the **Close** box. In the **DVD Layout** panel, click the **Close** box.

The nice feature of DVD markers is they can be modified at any time. If you want to convert one of the static thumbnails to a motion-movie thumbnail, it's as easy as double-clicking the marker and changing its thumbnail option.

16 In the **Timeline** panel, double-click the **DVD Marker** icon aligned with the start of the **DVD history** clip.

Because the scene marker at the beginning of the clip is right next to the stop marker from the previous clip, Premiere Pro 2 tries to guess which marker you are actually clicking. Unfortunately, it probably guessed wrong. Odds are, the DVD Marker dialog box opens with the stop marker instead of the marker you really wanted to modify.

17 If the **DVD Marker** dialog box displays the stop marker at **00;01;37;04**, click the **Next** button to jump to the scene marker at **00;01;37;05**. Below the thumbnail, turn on the **Motion Menu Button** check box. Click **OK**.

---

18 Choose **Window > DVD Layout**. Click the **Preview DVD** button. In the **Preview DVD** panel, click the **Scene Selection** link to view its submenu.

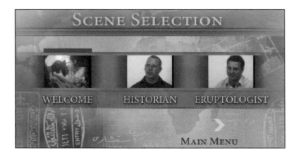 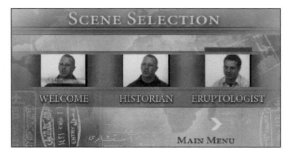

One minor problem remains. The button is now a movie; however, it doesn't stop playing. Instead of showing only the Welcome scene, the movie thumbnail continues to play the entire scene (as shown in the illustration here). No sweat! This is an easy fix, and you'll learn how to do it in Exercise 4.

---

19 In the **Preview DVD** panel, click the **Close** button. In the **DVD Layout** panel, click the **Close** button.

---

20 Choose **File > Save**, or press **Ctrl+S**. Leave **dutch harbor promo.prproj** open for the next exercise.

By now you should be an ace at creating DVD markers. There's no mystery to creating scene markers because you create them in the same way as other DVD markers. This exercise left a couple of loose ends, though. Namely, one of the menu button labels is displaying too far beyond the title safe margin, and also the movie button needs to loop instead of continually playing. You will learn how to tie up these loose ends in the next exercise.

Modifying DVD Templates

When you choose a DVD menu template, you can either leave the template as is or use it as a launching pad to build your own template. You can change the appearance of any text on the menu, as well as the labels for each button. You can position the objects in any arrangement you like. In addition, you can add background video and background audio to any menu. You can make some of these changes only in the **DVD Layout** panel, and you can make others only in the **Effect Controls** panel.

Making Template Changes in the DVD Layout Panel

So far, you have basically used the **DVD Layout** button as a means of previewing your DVD. Now it's time to get a bit more interactive with your menus. In the **DVD Layout** panel, you can select menu "objects," in the same way you can select text objects when creating your titles (as you did in Chapter 5, *"Adding Titles"*). Menu objects include the main title of the menu and the individual buttons.

In the **DVD Layout** panel, you can rename, resize, or reposition any title or button object. As its apt name implies, the **DVD Layout** panel is primarily for changing the layout of any menu. To modify a title object (as shown in the illustration here on the left) or a menu object (as shown in the illustration here on the right), simply click the object. Once the object is selected, you can drag it to a new position or drag its handles to resize the object.

Making Template Changes in the Effect Controls Panel

You may find it odd that you can make some changes only in the **DVD Layout** panel whereas you can make others only in the **Effect Controls** panel. You're right; it *is* odd. It's also confusing. If it helps, think of it like this: When you want to modify the *layout* of an object, the **DVD *Layout*** panel is the way to go. For everything else, change it in the **Effect Controls** panel.

The **Effect Controls** panel gives you control over the appearance of menu objects and menu backgrounds. You can modify the font, text size, and color of any object. You can also modify the thumbnail of any object containing a thumbnail. In addition, you can modify how long the thumbnail should play, and you can add any still image or video clip as a background of a menu. Finally, you can add an audio clip to a menu.

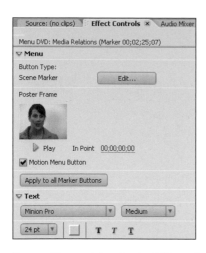

To modify an object in the **Effect Controls** panel, you must first select it in the **DVD Layout** panel. This can be somewhat daunting, especially if you are low on screen real estate. Because the **DVD Layout** panel floats above the **Effect Controls** panel, you may find yourself constantly dragging the **DVD Layout** panel "out of the way" so you can access the **Effect Controls** panel below it. If no object is selected, you will see options for modifying the menu background (as shown in the illustration here on the right).

Looking at Changes You *Can't* Make

Now that you know what you *can* do in the **DVD Layout** and **Effect Controls** panels, we'll talk about what you *can't* do to a DVD template in Premiere Pro 2. You can't change the number of title or menu objects. In other words, you can't add or delete buttons or titles. You can't add or remove a thumbnail icon next to a menu object. You can't remove the main menu. Likewise, if your DVD has a scene marker, then you cannot remove the scene selection submenu. Finally, you can't change what happens when you position your cursor over a button. (For example, some menus have bars and colored objects that appear when the menu button is selected.)

4 | Customizing DVD Menus

You perform all DVD template changes in Premiere Pro 2 in either the **DVD Layout** panel or the **Effect Controls** panel. Premiere Pro 2 allows you to customize the DVD layout by changing the font, text size, color, position, and scale of the menu titles and buttons. In addition, you can add audio and video backgrounds to your menus. In this exercise, you will learn how to use the **DVD Layout** panel and **Effect Controls** panel to customize your DVD menus.

---

1 If you followed the previous exercise, **dutch_harbor_promo.prproj** should still be open in Premiere Pro 2. If it's not, click **Open Project** on the **Welcome Screen**. Navigate to the **c:\exercise_files\chap_12** folder, click **exercise04.prproj** to select it, and click **Open**.

---

2 Choose **File > Save As**. Navigate to the **c:\exercise_files\dutch_harbor** folder. Name the file **dutch_harbor_promo.prproj**, and click **Save**.

Note: If a previous version of dutch_harbor_promo.prproj already exists, you may be asked to replace it. Click Yes.

Because you can modify some of the DVD layout options only in the Effect Controls panel, it's helpful to use the Effects workspace. This ensures the Effect Controls panel is nice and big, which will help you modify the DVD menu.

---

3 Choose **Window > Workspace > Effects**.

In Premiere Pro 2, the title of every main menu defaults to Main Menu. (How descriptive!) The first customization you will usually make is to change the title of the menu in the DVD Layout panel.

---

4 Choose **Window > DVD Layout**. Make sure the **Main Menu 1** thumbnail is selected in the **DVD Menus** box of the panel. Double-click the **Main Title** object. In the **Change Text** dialog box, type **Dutch Harbor** in the **Change Text** text box. Click **OK**.

Another nice feature of Premiere Pro 2 is the ability to change the label of *any* button. This is a great way to *cheat* the menu limitation of Premiere Pro 2. You can rename the scene selection submenu and turn it into any menu you'd like!

5 In the **DVD Layout** panel, double-click the **Scene Selection** object. In the **Change Text** dialog box, type **History** in the **Change Text** text box. Click **OK**.

After you have all your labels renamed as you'd like, you might want to rearrange them to help guide the viewer to watch them in a particular order. (Granted, viewers can still watch them in any order they want, but more often than not, they will watch them "in order.")

6 In the **DVD Layout** panel, click and drag the center of the **History** object below the **Map** object. Click and drag the **Intro** object into the empty row above it. Click and drag the **Map** object to the row above it. Click and drag the **History** object into the empty row above it.

Alas, you have no way to select multiple objects in the DVD Layout panel. You have to make due with simply dragging each object one at a time.

Now you have the main menu layout the way you'd like it. You can also do the same to the scene selection submenu(s).

7 In the **DVD Layout** panel **DVD Menus** box, click the **Scenes Menu 1** thumbnail to select it. In the layout area, double-click the **Scene Selection** object to rename it. In the **Change Text** dialog box, type **Dutch Harbor History** in the **Change Text** text box. Click **OK**.

Tip: Premiere Pro 2 also allows you to grab any of the handles around an object in order to resize the object. This is helpful if you want to quickly increase or decrease the size.

8 Click and drag the leftmost-center handle of the **Dutch Harbor History** object to the right until the title falls within the boundaries of the title safe margin.

In addition, besides dragging objects, you can move them in tinier increments by using the arrow keys on your keyboard. This is useful for fine-tuning position.

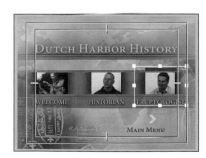

9 In the **DVD Layout** panel, click the **Eruptologist** thumbnail to select it. Press the **left arrow** key until most of the label falls within the title safe margin.

It's important to prevent DVD buttons from overlapping when repositioning your objects. In the DVD Layout panel, if you have chosen Show Overlapping Menu Buttons, then any overlapping buttons will display with a red border as a warning, as shown in the illustration in Step 9. If you do not see the red overlapping boundaries, click the wing menu in the DVD Layout panel, and choose Show Overlapping Menu Buttons.

---

10 In the **DVD Layout** panel, click the **Historian** thumbnail to select it. Press the **left arrow** key until the menu buttons no longer overlap.

You may have to reposition all three menu buttons until none of them overlaps.

---

11 In the **DVD Layout** panel **DVD Menus** box, click the **Scenes Menu 2** thumbnail to select it.

Even though you changed the title of the first scene selection submenu, this change is not reflected in the second scene selection submenu. It's important to note that you must modify each scene selection submenu independently.

---

12 In the **DVD Layout** panel, double-click the **Scene Selection** object to rename it. In the **Change Text** dialog box, type **Dutch Harbor History** in the **Change Text** text box. Click **OK**. As you did in Step 8, click and drag the leftmost-center handle to the right until the title falls within the boundaries of the title safe margin.

A convenient feature of thumbnails is they automatically move with their label, and vice versa. This prevents the thumbnail from becoming separated from its label.

---

13 In the **DVD Layout** panel, click and drag the **Media Relations** thumbnail to the center of the menu.

You can make the next series of changes only in the Effect Controls panel. The first change you may want to make is to adjust the length of time a video thumbnail plays. To do so, you must select the menu in the DVD Layout panel. In addition, you must have no other objects selected. To unselect all objects, you have to click an "empty" area of the menu template.

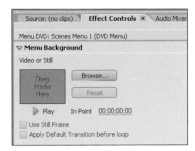

14 In the **DVD Layout** panel **DVD Menus** box, click the **Scenes Menu 1** thumbnail to select it. Click the background to unselect all objects.

When *no* objects are selected in the DVD Layout panel, the menu's background properties appear in the Effect Controls panel.

Tip: You may have to drag the floating DVD Layout panel out of the way if it is obscuring the Effect Controls panel.

15 At the bottom of the **Effect Controls** panel, under **Motion Menu Buttons**, change the **Duration** setting to **00;00;13;00**.

This will cause *any* video thumbnail on this menu to loop after 13 seconds. This also happens to the exact point in the DVD history sequence when the scrolling text fades to black, which prevents the thumbnail from playing the next scene.

The last change you will make to the menu template is to add a video background and an audio file to play while the menu plays. Premiere Pro 2 lets you use any imported still image or video clip for the menu background.

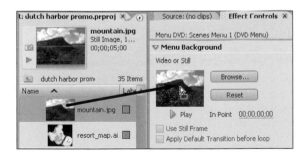

16 In the **Project** panel **Graphics** bin, drag the **mountain.jpg** still image to the **Drag Media Here** box in the **Menu Background > Video Or Still** section of the **Effect Controls** panel.

The background in the DVD Layout panel will immediately update to reflect the still image you've just applied. Because each menu is modified separately, you can add different backgrounds to subsequent menus.

17 In the **DVD Layout** panel **DVD Menus** box, click the **Scenes Menu 2** thumbnail to select it. Click the background to unselect all objects.

18 In the **Project** panel **Graphics** bin, drag the **tiki.jpg** still image to the **Drag Media Here** box in the **Menu Background> Video or Still** section of the **Effect Controls** panel.

19 In the **DVD Layout** panel **DVD Menus** box, click the **Main Menu 1** thumbnail to select it. Click the background to unselect all objects.

20 In the **Project** panel **Graphics** bin, drag **background_pink.avi** to the **Drag Media Here** box in the **Menu Background > Video or Still** section of the **Effect Controls** panel.

Tip: Animated backgrounds, such as those from Digital Juice (**www.DigitalJuice.com**), are a great way to give your DVD some visual interest. In addition, the backgrounds from Digital Juice are designed to loop seamlessly, so an audience member won't notice when the background "restarts."

Speaking of looping, when you add audio and video clips to your menu backgrounds, Premiere Pro 2 will respect any In and Out points you have specified. For example, you can create a manual audio loop with In and Out points (as you did in Chapter 10, *"Working with Audio"*), which will help your audio background loop seamlessly.

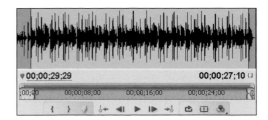

21 In the **Project** panel **Audio** bin, double-click **DaReggaeMon_30.mp3** to open it in the **Source Monitor**.

You may recall previously setting In and Out points around this clip in order to make it loop. Notice the total duration of In to Out is 00;00;27;10.

22 Choose **Window > Effect Controls** to bring the panel to the foreground. In the **DVD Layout** panel **DVD Menus** box, click the **Scenes Menu 1** thumbnail to select it, and click any empty region of the background to unselect all objects.

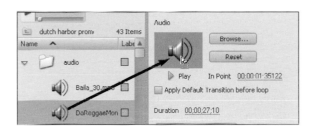

23 In the **Project** panel **Audio** bin, drag **DaReggaeMon_30.mp3** to the **Drag Media Here** box in the **Menu Background > Audio** section of the **Effect Controls** panel.

Notice the Duration in the Effect Controls panel displays 00;00;27;10. That's right—it's the In and Out duration from Step 21. The Duration timecode controls how long the audio and video background will play until they loop. In this case, Premiere Pro 2 automatically changes the duration to match the In to Out duration of your audio clip.

Now that you have finished adding still and video backgrounds, as well as audio accompaniment, you can preview your DVD.

24 In the **DVD Layout** panel, click the **Preview DVD** button. Watch the looping video background in the main menu, and then click the **History** button to view the submenu and listen for its audio looping.

Watch for a few features here. First, your video background in the main menu should loop seamlessly. Second, the first video thumbnail in the Dutch Harbor History submenu should loop only for 13 seconds. And lastly, your audio background should loop as well.

25 In the **Preview DVD** panels, click the **Close** box. In the **DVD Layout** panel, click the **Close** box.

26 Choose **File > Save**, or press **Ctrl+S**. Leave **dutch harbor promo.prproj** open for the next exercise.

Premiere Pro 2 lets you modify your menus in many ways. In fact, by the time you're done, the finished menu may look *nothing* like the original template.

As discussed previously, even though you can change the font, text size, color, and background of the menus, you *cannot* change the number of buttons on each menu. It's unfortunate, but "them's the breaks." Of course, nothing is stopping you from designing your *own* templates! (Shhh! Don't tell. See the following sidebar.)

NOTE:

Designing Your Own Templates

When editors first got their hands on the DVD templates in Premiere Pro 2, their initial response was, "Great!" Their second response was, "Can we make our own?" The online Help file is conspicuously silent on the matter. Before you learn the truth, you must first swear a vow of secrecy.

What you are about to read is top secret. If Adobe finds out you are being given this information, they might come after you, your family, and your pets. Many beta testers risked their lives to bring you this information.

Can it be done? Yes, most certainly. **Is it easy?** No, most certainly not.

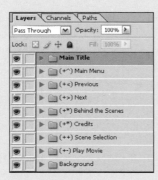 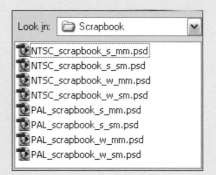

The DVD templates in Premiere Pro 2 are nothing more than layered Photoshop files. Granted, you may need a cryptologist to decipher the naming convention for each layer, as shown in the illustration here on the left.

You can find the templates in the **c:\Program Files\Adobe\Adobe Premiere Pro 2\DVD Templates** folder, assuming you installed Premiere Pro 2 to the default location. Each template has its own folder, and within the folder are eight Photoshop (.psd) files. Each file name represents a combination of video format (**NTSC** or **PAL**), screen size (**s**tandard or **w**idescreen), and menu type (**m**ain **m**enu or **s**cene **m**enu.)

Keep in mind, you should *not attempt this* unless you are proficient with Photoshop. In addition, it is wise to make copies of the template files before working on them.

If you do not know Photoshop, you can always beg a friend for help or purchase the *Adobe Photoshop CS 2 Hands-On Training* book. (Shameless plug!)

Exporting DVDs

It's time for all of your hard preparations to finally pay off. After you have created your markers, modified your templates, and previewed your DVD, you can finally get to the task of exporting your DVD. Premiere Pro 2 provides three methods for exporting:

Burn directly to DVD: This requires a DVD±R burner.

Copy the DVD architecture to a folder on your hard drive: This is like "burning" to your hard drive; every folder that would have been created on the DVD is instead created on your hard drive in a directory of your choosing.

Create an ISO image on your hard drive: An ISO image is like a snapshot of the DVD, all packed into a single file. Instead of a file that you can open, the ISO file is a series of binary 1s and 0s. Only burning software can use it. (If you're curious to know, ISO is an acronym for International Standards Organization.)

Each method has advantages and disadvantages, as described in the next section.

Burning Directly to DVD

To burn a DVD movie to disc, Premiere Pro 2 takes the following steps:

1. Premiere Pro 2 **encodes** (converts) the DV (Digital Video) clips, still images, titles, and audio clips into the DVD format. The DVD format is **MPEG-2**, which is a type of movie file, such as AVI or QuickTime. During the conversion process, the DVD files are stored temporarily on your hard drive. Approximately 95 percent of the time it takes to create a finished DVD is spent in this encoding step because it is very processor intensive. Depending on the complexity and length of your sequence and the speed of your computer, this step can take 1 to 4 hours.

2. After the sequence has been encoded into the DVD format, the temporary files on your hard drive are burned to disc—just like burning a music CD. This step is relatively quick, compared to encoding, and can take less than 20 minutes. The length of time depends on the size of the finished files and the speed at which your burner is capable of writing to disc.

If you want to burn multiple copies during the same burning "session," then Premiere Pro 2 does not reencode. Rather, it uses the temporary files already encoded on the hard drive and simply burns an additional copy.

The disadvantage of this method is that all encoded work is only *temporary*. Once you close the project, you lose all those hours of encoding. So, if you close the project and decide you want an extra copy—too bad! You'll have to start at Step 1.

Copying the DVD Files to a Folder

This method performs only Step 1 of the previous process. When copied, the files are encoded, but instead of burning to disc, the files are stored permanently on your hard drive—until you erase them. Even if you close the project, the files remain on your hard drive. The files on your hard drive are identical copies of what you would see on the DVD.

The copy method is useful when you want to do a "test run" and make sure the files encode correctly or when you do not have an attached DVD burner. In addition, if your computer has DVD-playing software, then you can open the DVD movie from your hard drive, and the software will treat it as if it were a real DVD. You can then preview the navigation and movies just as the user would see them in their DVD player.

The disadvantages of this method are that Premiere Pro 2 will not burn these files to disc (not now and not ever) and that you will need to use your own burning software. This is a minor problem because nearly all DVD burners are sold with burning software.

Creating an ISO Image on Your Hard Drive

This method performs Step 1 of the previous process and *sort of* performs Step 2. Once the files are encoded, instead of burning to disc, an ISO image of the disc is created. The ISO image is a snapshot of the entire DVD in a single file. However, you can't "view" the ISO image any more than you can view an EXE file. It's all binary 1s and 0s.

An ISO image has two advantages. First, if you don't have a DVD burner, you can take this image to *any* computer (Linux, Mac, and so on) to burn to DVD. A prime example of this is creating an ISO image on an external hard drive and then taking it to a workstation with a DVD burner.

The second advantage ISO images offer is the capability to quickly burn multiple copies without having to reencode. For instance, if you close the Premiere Pro 2 project, the ISO file remains until you delete it. If you want to burn an additional copy a year from now, you don't have to spend hours encoding; all that work has been done. Instead, you just use the existing software bundled with your DVD burner and burn the ISO image—in probably 20 minutes or less. (ISO is a standardized format any burning software can accept!)

The disadvantages of this method are the same as the previous method; Premiere Pro 2 will not burn these files to disc, and you need your own burning software.

Specifying Encoding Settings

At the time of encoding your DVD—whether the final destination is a disc, folder, or ISO image—you must specify the encoding settings. When you specify encoding settings, you are looking for a happy compromise between quality and file size. For example, a typical DVD may hold about 4.7 GB of data (truth be told, it's closer to 4.3 GB), but if you encode at too high of a quality, then your entire movie will not fit on the DVD. Then again, if you lower quality too much, even though it will fit, your video will suffer from pixilation and other artifacts. You can specify all these settings in the **Export Settings** dialog box.

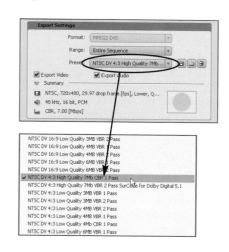

Anytime you want to export a movie, even for the Web, Premiere Pro 2 displays the **Export Settings** dialog box. However, this chapter will focus solely on DVD exporting options. In Chapter 13, "*Exporting to Files and Tape,*" you will focus on many other formats for other uses.

When you encode a DVD movie, Premiere Pro 2 allows you to encode only to the MPEG-2 format. And this is for good reason: it's the official standard of all DVD movie discs. As shown in the illustration here at the top, the **Format** pop-up

menu of the **Export Settings** dialog box is dimmed—you can select only **MPEG2-DVD**.

Premiere Pro 2 allows you to specify the range (work area or entire sequence) and also choose from one of more than 50 presets. A sample of the dizzying array of preset options is shown in the illustration here on the right. The preset choices are written in a video-geek sleight of hand. The following example should help translate this into English:

Preset:
NTSC DV 4:3 High Quality 7MB CBR 1 Pass

Let's take this one setting at a time.

NTSC: This is the video format in North America, parts of Central America, Japan, South Korea, and some islands in the South Pacific. (NTSC stands for **N**ational **T**elevision **S**ystems **C**ommittee.) The other format is PAL (**P**hase **A**lternating **L**ine), which is supported just about everywhere else in the world. (There's also SÉCAM in France and areas controlled by the former Soviet Union.)

DV: Premiere Pro 2 assumes your source video is from DV, which has a defined frame size of 720 x 480 pixels. Because DV is so omnipresent in the world of Premiere Pro 2, this is the only source format choice available.

4:3: This defines the frame of the finished DVD. You can choose from a final DVD with **4:3** (like a standard television) or widescreen with **16:9**.

High Quality: This specifies the encoding quality. Generally, higher values increase rendering time and file size.

7Mb. This value refers to the bitrate and is expressed as megabits per second. A higher **bitrate** increases the file size because you are packing in more information per second of video.

CBR: Speaking of bitrate, Premiere Pro 2 can have a CBR (**C**onstant **B**it **R**ate), where every single second has the same bitrate, or it can use a VBR (**V**ariable

Bit Rate). In variable bitrate, Premiere Pro 2 scrutinizes each frame a bit more; simple frames have a lower than normal bitrate, and more complex frames, such as those with lots of motion, are given a higher than normal bitrate. A variable bitrate can be more efficient but takes longer to encode. Then again, a constant bitrate is much less taxing on a player and your computer processor, so a constant bitrate may result in better compatibility.

1 Pass: This specifies the number of "render passes" Premiere Pro 2 makes. With each pass, Premiere Pro 2 learns a little bit more about your video. Using 2 Pass takes much longer than one pass, but the resulting video may be slightly better or more efficiently encoded (smaller file size). Only VBR encoding can use two passes.

In the end, the easiest step you can take is to simply use a preset, which specifies more than 20 settings for you. However, adventurous souls can also customize each preset to further meet their needs, and you will find these options in the same **Export Settings** dialog box.

Now that you know all the primary encoding settings, it's time to try exporting your own DVD.

Note: Adobe Premiere Pro 2 detects only those DVD drives connected to your computer and turned on at the time you started Premiere Pro 2. If you connected and turned on any DVD-burning drives after that point, they will not be recognized until you restart Premiere Pro 2.

NOTE:

Bits Versus Bytes

When speaking of DVD quality, you'll often see the word **bit**, as in megabits per second. When speaking of a file size on a computer, you'll see the word **byte**, as in megabyte. What's the difference?

A **bit** is a single character of data (a zero or a one). A **byte** is 8 characters of data. Therefore, 8 bits equal 1 byte. Easy, right?

Bits are written with a lowercase b. Bytes are written with an uppercase B. For example, 8 megabits is written as 8 Mb. This is the same as 1 megabyte, or 1 MB. Likewise, 8 gigabits (Gb) is the same as 1 gigabyte (1 GB).

When editors speak in terms of how much data is playing at any given time, they typically express this in bits. When they talk of file sizes on computer hard drives, they use bytes.

Once you've set up all your markers and menus in Premiere Pro 2, the final step is to burn to disc. As described previously, you can also choose to export to a file on your hard drive. No matter which export method you choose, you will have to specify your encoding settings at the time of exporting the DVD. These encoding settings specify the quality and length of your finished DVD. The best workflow is to encode at the highest quality, unless the finished movie is too big to fit on disc, in which case you should lower the quality until you find a happy compromise between quality and size. In this exercise, you will learn how to burn your DVD movie to disc and specify encoding settings.

1 If you followed the previous exercise, **dutch_harbor_promo.prproj** should still be open in Premiere Pro 2. If it's not, click **Open Project** on the **Welcome Screen**. Navigate to **c:\exercise_files\chap_12** folder, click **exercise05.prproj** to select it, and click **Open**.

2 Choose **File > Save As**. Navigate to the **c:\exercise_files\dutch_harbor** folder. Name the file **dutch_harbor_promo.prproj**, and click **Save**.

Note: If a previous version of dutch_harbor_promo.prproj already exists, you may be asked to replace it. Click Yes.

Because you can modify some of the DVD layout options only in the Effect Controls panel, it will be helpful to use the Effects workspace. This ensures the Effect Controls panel is nice and big, which will help you modify the DVD menu.

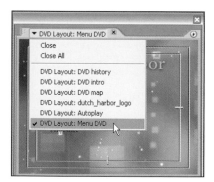

3 If necessary, open the **DVD Layout** panel by selecting the **Menu DVD** tab in the **Timeline** panel and choosing **Window > DVD Layout**.

4 In the **DVD Layout** panel, click the **Burn DVD** button.

Tip: Even if you plan to create a DVD folder or ISO image on your hard drive, you must still access these options via the Burn DVD button.

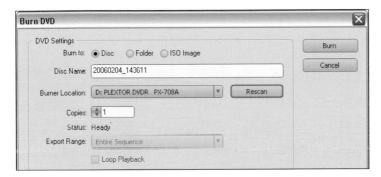

Clicking the Burn DVD button opens the Burn DVD dialog box. The first DVD settings are to choose to burn a disc, folder, or ISO image. This dialog box also allows you to specify the number of copies to burn.

If you have more than one DVD burner connected (lucky you), you can specify the proper drive in the Burner Location pop-up menu. If no media is present in the selected drive, the Status setting displays Media not present, and the Burn button is dimmed. To rectify this, place a blank DVD into the drive and click the Rescan button; the Status should display as Ready, and the Burn button should be ready to be clicked.

Note: The Export Range and Loop Playback options are available only for autoplay DVDs—such as if you are making a movie to loop all day in a kiosk, for example.

5 In the **Burn DVD** dialog box, make sure **Burn to** is set to **Disc**. In the **Disc Name** box, type **Dutch_Harbor**. If necessary, set **Copies** to **1** by clicking the up or down arrow next to **Copies**.

Note: If you don't have a DVD burner, you can still play along by setting the Burn setting to Folder to create a DVD on your hard drive. In addition, you can click the Browse button to specify the folder location; Premiere Pro 2 defaults to the My Documents folder.

The lower portion of the Burn DVD dialog box displays the current encoding settings. In this case, Premiere Pro 2 defaults to the preset shown in the illustration here. The Summary scrolling box displays the individual settings specified by the preset.

Before burning, you might want to customize the Encoding preset.

6 In the **Burn DVD** dialog box, click the **Settings** button to open the **Export Settings** dialog box.

As described previously, the Export Settings dialog box allows you to choose a new preset or customize a preset to your liking. Even though you have many, many options, it's easiest to digest this dialog box from the upper to the lower portion. First make sure the Range and Preset settings are correct.

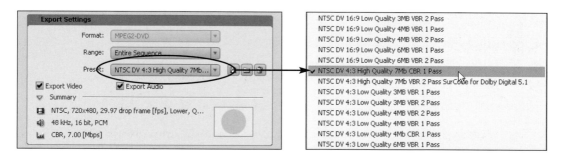

7 In the **Export Settings** dialog box, make sure **Range** is set to **Entire Sequence**. Click the **Preset** pop-up menu, and choose **NTSC DV 4:3 High Quality 7MBb CBR 1 Pass**.

After you've specified the Range and Preset settings, you can click OK and burn your disc. However, some editors like to use the preset as a starting point and then further customize some of the quality options to fit their needs. That's what you'll do here.

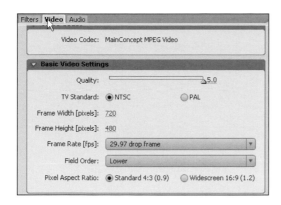

8 In the **Export Settings** dialog box, select the **Video** tab to bring the video settings to the foreground. Scroll down until you can see all of the **Basic Video Settings** area.

The basic video settings specify the television standard and associated settings. All of these settings are specified by the chosen preset.

Note: The DVD format is picky. The only basic video setting you should ever change is the Quality setting. This setting has a direct impact on quality and render time; the higher the quality, the more Premiere Pro 2 "thinks about" each frame as it encodes.

Changing any of the other basic video settings may result in a DVD movie that won't play on a DVD player. If you want to change the other settings, you should change the preset, which will update these settings.

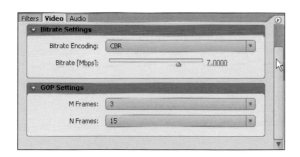

9 In the **Export Settings** dialog box, scroll down until you can see the **Bitrate Settings** area.

Currently, this preset has a Constant Bitrate setting of 7.0000 Mbps. This means every second of your DVD movie will play with the same bitrate. Notice the Estimated File Size setting, in the lower-right corner of the Export Settings dialog box, shows 1.02 MB/Sec. (That's 1,020 KB/Sec.)

Premiere Pro 2 allows you to change the bitrate to any value from 1.5 to 9. The bitrate has a direct impact on the size and quality of the finished movie.

A 1.5 Mbps bitrate is extremely low, and you can fit a two- to three-hour movie on a single DVD, but the quality will suffer. On the other hand, a 9 Mbps bitrate will have much higher quality. However, many DVD players have problems playing anything greater than 7 or 8 Mbps. And, truth be told, the quality difference between 7 and 9 Mbps will hardly be noticed. For this reason, 8 Mbps is recommended as the highest bitrate.

Note: It's recommended you do not change the GOP settings, shown below the Bitrate Settings area (unless you are extremely well versed in GOP interframe compression).

10 Click the **Bitrate Encoding** pop-up menu, and choose **VBR, 1 Pass**.

When you choose variable bitrate encoding, Premiere Pro 2 allows you to define the minimum, target, and maximum bitrates. Notice the Estimated File Size setting has dropped, when compared with CBR encoding, to 919.92 KB/Sec (or .91992 MB/Sec).

The drop in estimated file size demonstrates the power of variable encoding. Instead of encoding each frame of video at the same constant bitrate, variable encoding allows Premiere Pro 2 to scrutinize each frame of video and economize the bitrate used. Variable bitrates can result in higher-quality video within the same file size—at the expense of processing time, however.

The Minimum Bitrate setting is the lowest bitrate you are willing to let Premiere Pro 2 use. For example, on simple titles and frames without motion, Premiere Pro 2 may be able to achieve the same high quality even with a bitrate of 1.5 Mbps.

On the other hand, in complex frames with a lot of detail, Premiere Pro 2 will increase the bitrate to the Maximum Bitrate setting.

The Target Bitrate setting is the overall *average* for which you'd like Premiere Pro 2 to strive.

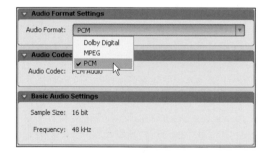

11 In the **Export Settings** dialog box, select the **Audio** tab. Make sure **Audio Format** is set to **PCM**.

DVDs can have one of three audio formats: Dolby Digital, MPEG, and PCM. Each has its advantages and disadvantages. Many users prefer Dolby Digital for its good compromise of quality and file size. Regrettably, Premiere Pro 2 comes with only three trial uses of the Dolby Digital format. (You can purchase more.) If trial uses were not a factor, we would recommend Dolby Digital audio.

Of the remaining two audio formats, MPEG takes up considerably less file space but is not as compatible as PCM audio in NTSC countries. (If you're in a PAL country, feel free to choose MPEG.) For a complete list of the audio options and their features, see the sidebar following this exercise.

---

12 Click **OK** to return to the **DVD Burn** dialog box.

At this point, you have specified your encoding settings, so you are ready to burn! Depending on your computer and burner, this process may take from 10 to 30 minutes.

Note: If you want to burn and have available DVD media and a DVD burner, click Burn in the next step. If you have chosen to export to a folder and have free hard drive space, you can also click Burn.

---

13 In the **DVD Burn** dialog box, click **Burn**.

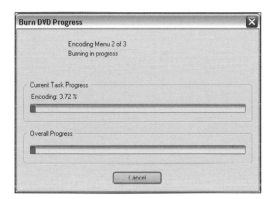 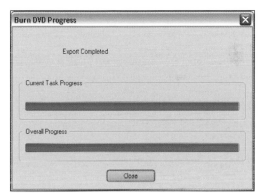

As soon as you click Burn, Premiere Pro 2 opens the Burn DVD Progress dialog box. This displays the current progress of your DVD exporting. When exporting is done, the dialog box will simply say Export Completed. (After days and months of toiling over your project, some kind of fanfare would have been nice!)

---

14 Choose **File > Save**, or press **Ctrl+S**. Choose **File > Close** to close this project.

Congratulations! You have just exported your DVD movie, complete with menus and animated backgrounds. In addition, you learned the options available when exporting a DVD, how to select encoding presets, and how to customize the settings to your liking.

If you decide to venture off the beaten path and customize the encoding settings, it is recommended you tweak only the quality and bitrate settings. The remainder of the settings are specific to the DVD format, and changing them can create expensive drink coasters but useless DVD movies. (In other words, changing any of the other settings may result in a disc that won't play in a DVD player.)

AC3 Versus PCM Versus MP2 Audio Formats

Call it the Battle of the Acronyms. The DVD format supports three types of audio: Dolby Digital (AC3), uncompressed PCM, and MPEG Layer II. Each format has advantages and disadvantages:

Dolby Digital (AC3) audio: Dolby Digital Audio is a highly compressed audio format stored in an AC3 file. Dolby can be stereo or surround, and it allows you to change the bitrates from 128 to 384 KB/Sec. Many editors settle on 256 KB/Sec as a good compromise of quality and file size. If you plan to burn surround sound, then you must choose Dolby Digital (AC3). Also, make sure your sequence has 5.1 channels of audio. Because of its blend of high quality and efficient file sizes, the AC3 format is the most popular for DVDs and is recommended.

PCM audio: Uncompressed PCM audio is often stored as a WAV or AIFF sound file. PCM audio is enormous in size, often ten times the file size of AC3 and MP2 files. Compressed AC3 or MP2 audio can sound just as good as PCM while taking up less disk space. You should use PCM audio if AC3 is not available or if you plan to further edit the DVD movie. (Whether you should further edit your DVD movie is an entirely different can of worms!)

MPEG Layer II (MP2) audio: The MP2 format is not the same as MPEG-3 (the format to which you "archive" your "purchased" music). For NTSC DVDs, the MPEG audio is not officially supported, although most DVD players will play it. Just to be safe, for maximum compatibility with NTSC DVDs, MP2 is not recommended. PAL DVD players do support MP2 audio, and this audio format is perfectly acceptable for PAL DVDs.

Understanding DVD Formats

You're at the store looking for DVDs to burn your movies. While staring at the rows and rows of disc options converging into infinity, you become confused and disoriented. The walls start to spin, and you become dizzy. As you stagger to the floor, you manage to gasp, "How do I know which disc to purchase? Heeeelp!"

When purchasing DVDs, you have two primary considerations: What format does your DVD burner support, and what format does your DVD player support?

Of course, sometimes the DVD player playing the disc is not your own—and more often than not, you have no way of knowing the DVD player model. So you need to pick a format for maximum compatibility on any number of players. The compatibility issues break down into two categories: formats and capacities.

Understanding the DVD+R and DVD-R Formats

Currently, two competing DVD-burning formats exist: DVD+R and DVD-R. Your DVD burner may support only +R or may support only –R. Some DVD burners can burn to both formats and are indicated as **DVD±R**. Any disc that says **+R** or **–R** can be written to only *once*. That means, once you burn a movie onto these discs, it is "locked," and you can never modify or update the DVD.

However, with **rewritable DVDs**, you can write to and erase the DVDs many times. Rewritable discs are indicated with a *W* suffix, such as **DVD+RW** or **DVD-RW**. If your burner supports both, it is written as **DVD±RW**.

Some DVD players support only one or the other, and some support both. Most players on store shelves at this point in time support both formats. But, will your client have an up-to-date player? Not likely. Anecdotal evidence suggests that DVD-R is winning the compatibility war. Then again, you will run into some older models that play only DVD+R.

For maximum compatibility, you can always burn one of each format—as long as your burner supports ±R. Or, you can keep a stack of "test discs" handy, pass them out to your clients when you first meet them, and ask them to test the disc on their player. (Bonus: You can use this disc as a sales tool and add your logo and a quick commercial about your company. Who knows, they may hand the disc off to a friend who is in the market for a videographer.)

Even though the ability to rewrite discs is alluring, RW discs have the lowest odds of compatibility. Here is a list of the formats and their compatibility percentage: DVD-R (93%), DVD+R (89%), DVD-RW (80%), DVD+RW (79%).*

Understanding DVD Capacity

Currently, most of the discs on the store shelf can hold about 4.7 GB of data. These are called **DVD 5** discs (they hold *almost* 5 GB of data). All DVD burners and players support DVD 5, which is a one-layer, one-sided disc.

Dual-layered discs provide nearly twice the data capacity of a single layer. These discs are called **DVD 9** and hold about 8.5 GB of data. All DVD players can play dual-layered discs, but only some burners are capable of burning to these types of discs.

A rare format, which you may find only at specialized retailers, is **DVD 10**, which holds about 8.75 GB of data. These discs are single-layered but double-sided; data is written to both sides of the disc. However, it's not as neat as it sounds—you are prompted to flip the disc over when burning or playing. (However, some newer megaplayers will do this internally.)

Most rare of all are **DVD 18** discs, which are dual-layered and dual-sided. These discs hold about 15.9 GB. As with DVD 9 dual-layered discs, make sure your DVD burner supports dual layers before purchasing these discs.

You can purchase all of these disc capacities in each of the four main formats: DVD+R, DVD-R, DVD+RW, and DVD-RW. When in doubt, go with the DVD 5 (4.7 GB) DVD-R discs, which provide maximum compatibility across a wide range of players and burners.

This entire chapter was dedicated to just one of many exporting methods. Premiere Pro 2 also allows you to export your finished movie to your video camera, to a VCR, and to a variety of Web formats, still images, and audio files. In addition, in this chapter you got a taste of the Export Settings dialog box; in the next chapter you will learn how to really maximize its features for exporting to the Web.

* Numbers "borrowed" from **www.videohelp.com/dvd.htm**

13

Exporting to Files and Tape

Beyond exporting to DVDs, as you did in Chapter 12, *"Authoring DVDs,"* Adobe Premiere Pro 2 can export to a variety of formats, including video cameras, still images, and Web movies. When you export to DV (**D**igital **V**ideo) videotape, for example, exporting is a relatively straightforward task. However, when you plan to export to a movie file, whether it's for the Web, CD playback, or an archive file on your hard drive, you have to consider some additional settings. For example, in Chapter 12, *"Authoring DVDs,"* when you exported to DVD, you didn't get to choose the format of the movie—it was a DVD movie, and that was that. But when you export to any other type of file, you can choose between formats such as Apple QuickTime, Windows Media, Real RealMedia, and Macromedia Flash. You can also specify different frame sizes, frame rates, audio qualities, and many more settings. This chapter will walk you through exporting to the most common formats and explain how to choose the settings to optimize your movie quality.

Understanding the Basics of Exporting

Exporting is the act of copying your finished sequence from Premiere Pro 2 to another format. Similar to exporting DVDs in Chapter 12, *"Authoring DVDs,"* Premiere Pro 2 will export only *one sequence* at a time. As you did in the previous chapter, if you want to export multiple sequences, you should nest them into a single sequence.

The marketing hyperbole tells you Premiere Pro 2 can export to dozens of formats. Although this is true, most of the formats fall into one of five mediums:

Videotape: This exports the video via the IEEE-1394 port (also called FireWire or i.Link).

High-quality DV movie on your hard drive: This is useful when you want to reuse the DV file in a future Premiere Pro 2 project.

Still images: This is useful when you want to edit a frame of video in Adobe Photoshop or a similar image-editing application. You can use this format for Web pages, but Premiere Pro 2 lacks the sophistication and compression options available in Photoshop.

Audio files (no video): This is useful when you want to burn audio to a music CD or reuse the audio file in a future Premiere Pro 2 project.

Movies for Web or CD playback: This is a broad category including a handful of formats and uses.

Each of these mediums may encompass dozens of formats. Except for videotape, the mediums result in the creation of a file on your hard drive. Likewise, except for videotape, the mediums each require you to specify additional settings. Throughout this chapter, you will learn the most useful settings for each medium.

Exporting to Videotape

Exporting a sequence to DV tape is a useful way to archive your projects. Rather than keeping them as huge files on your hard drive, sometimes it's more cost effective to export the finished product to DV tape, label it, and stick the tape in a shoe-box somewhere. (Forgive us, we mean store it in a highly professional, fireproof, humidity-controlled tape storage unit.)

You can also export to tape if you want to hand off the finished product to another editor to use in a future project. Tapes are **platform independent**—meaning, you can export to a tape on a Windows computer and then import the tape onto a Mac. Exporting to tape keeps your video in the highest-possible quality, which makes it ideal for importing into future projects on any platform capable of editing DV.

The downside to exporting to tape is that you lose the ability to reedit the video. To borrow a Photoshop term, the video on tape is flattened. If there is a title or transition you want to remove—so sorry. Any work you did on your sequence can no longer be undone or removed.

Recording a sequence to DV tape is straightforward. (At least, when the hardware and the software are communicating properly, it *should* be straightforward.) To export directly to a DV device, such as a camcorder or VCR (**V**ideo **C**assette **R**ecorder), you need to have the device connected to the computer via the IEEE-1394 port, also called FireWire or i.Link.

If a DV device is properly connected, you can export a sequence by choosing **File > Export > Export to Tape**. And that's all it takes. You have no format options or presets to choose. In fact, in most cases Premiere Pro 2 will activate your DV VCR or DV camera automatically—just make sure the camera is in playback mode—and handle the start and stop recording functions. You don't have to lift a finger.

Of course, if you feel like lifting a finger, the **Export to Tape** dialog box lets you specify a few export options before the process of recording begins. Here are some of the options:

Activate Recording Device: Unless you have a DV device Premiere Pro 2 does not support, you should normally turn on this check box. This will automatically start and stop your DV device for you.

Assemble at timecode: When selected, Premiere Pro 2 will start recording at the exact spot on the tape you specify. Premiere Pro 2 handles rewinding or fast-forwarding to the timecode you specify. Usually you will not select this option, and Premiere Pro 2 will start recording at the current spot on the tape.

Delay movie start by: Some DV devices need a brief period of time between receiving the video signal and recording it. (Only a few DV devices will need this check box turned on. Refer to your device's manual to see what the manufacturer recommends.)

Preroll: Some DV devices need additional time to get up to the proper tape-recording speed. (You've probably seen this on your "dinosaur" VHS VCR.) To be honest, this option doesn't always work as advertised. In Exercise 1, you'll discover a handy workaround.

Abort after/Report dropped frames: A **dropped frame** occurs when the computer system is having a hard time delivering all 30 fps (frames per second) to your DV device and a frame is accidentally skipped (or "dropped"). Some editors can handle a dropped frame or two (after all, $1/30$ of 1 second may be hard to notice); others will want to halt the export as soon as a single frame is dropped.

Render audio before export: Instead of trying to render the audio on the fly, as the sequence is exporting, you can tell Premiere Pro 2 to do its "render homework" before exporting begins. The more Premiere Pro 2 renders in advance, the less work it has to do during export. The downside is you'll have to wait while it renders. (But audio renders *extremely* quick, so you don't have to wait long.)

Because each DV device is different, learning which options result in a successful export may be a matter of trial and error. Luckily, as DV technology matures, the communication between computer and device is becoming more standardized, resulting in fewer hardware incompatibilities.

If you experience performance issues or communication problems between your attached DV device and Premiere Pro 2, you can tweak a few additional settings to help maximize your computer's resources when previewing your programs. You can find these settings in the **Playback Settings** dialog box.

Configuring DV Playback

If you're working on a DV project, you can preview the sequence on a DV camcorder or DV VCR. Within Premiere Pro 2, you can specify how both the video and audio should play back when a DV device is connected. You can configure these options in the **Playback Settings** dialog box. For example, if your video stutters during playback, it could be a sign your computer is having trouble trying to output real-time previews to both your computer monitor and your DV device. The **Playback Settings** dialog box allows you to choose to which devices previews should be output.

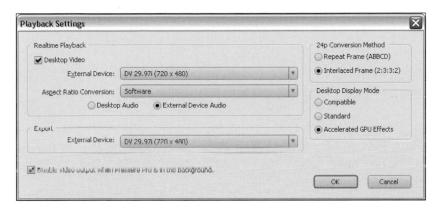

You can access the **Playback Settings** dialog box by clicking the **Output** button in the **Program Monitor**. Here is a basic rundown of the options:

Desktop Video: When this check box is turned on, Premiere Pro 2 does its best to play back the sequence in the **Program Monitor**.

External Device: If Premiere Pro 2 detects an attached DV device, you can choose to preview the video on the external device while editing. Or you can choose **None** from the **External Device** pop-up menu. When you choose **None**, the video will not preview on an attached device, even if connected.

Aspect Ratio Conversion: This option specifies how Premiere Pro 2 tries to correct the preview if you are watching a widescreen project on a 4:3 device, or vice versa. These options apply only to attached DV devices. If you are not experiencing abnormally fat or thin video on your attached DV device, leave the conversion set to **None**. Unless you are positive your DV device has hardware support, choose **Software**. This is more taxing on Premiere Pro 2 but provides maximum compatibility with DV devices.

Desktop Audio/External Device Audio: This specifies whether your audio should play through your computer speakers or your attached DV device while editing. Many editors who choose to watch the attached DV device while editing will play their audio via their DV device. However, the audio coming from your computer speakers is not in sync with the video previewing on the attached DV device. For this reason, it is recommended you send both audio and video previews to the same location.

External Device: This export option allows you to specify which attached device should be used for exporting the finished program. Most editors have only one device to choose from, so this option is moot.

24p Conversion Method: This specifies which 24p (pull-down) method Premiere Pro 2 uses. This setting applies to you only if you have a 24p camera. If you don't have a 24p camera, this option won't affect your projects. If you do have a 24p camera, choose **Interlaced Frame 2:3:3:2** unless you are experiencing performance issues during playback, in which case you can choose **Repeat**

Frame. (For information on 24p and pull-down, refer to Chapter 16, *"Working with 16:9, HDV, and 24p Video."*)

Desktop Display Mode: This option applies when you are previewing on your computer monitor *only* and specifies how, if at all, Premiere Pro 2 should rely on your computer's graphics card to help display video. You should choose one of these options based on the type of graphics card you have: First, **Compatible** is for older graphics cards. Second, **Standard** uses the hardware capabilities of your graphics card. Finally, GPU (**G**raphics **P**rocessing **U**nit) is a feature of graphics cards that helps the computer do the math to display complex effects. If your card has GPU acceleration, **Accelerated GPU** means Premiere Pro 2 relies on the GPU to accelerate rendering and improve playback.

There's no right or wrong way to set up your system for previewing DV playback. None of these options will affect your quality. They help give you maximum flexibility when editing and optimize your computer's real-time performance during the editing process.

The best way to use these settings is to learn through testing. And lastly, keep in mind unless you have specialized hardware, odds are the default settings are going to suit your system just fine, so don't lose any sleep over these confusing hardware choices.

In the next exercise, you will learn how to export a sequence to DV tape.

NOTE:

Using Third-Party Products

Some users purchase Premiere Pro 2 as part of a bundle with a third-party capture card. The third-party card acts as a middleman between Premiere Pro 2 and the DV/HDV (**H**igh-**D**efinition **V**ideo) camera or VCR, providing added functionality beyond the built-in capabilities of Premiere Pro 2.

These third-party products are designed to "plug into" Premiere Pro 2, which means the product works transparently in conjunction with Premiere Pro 2. That is, if it's working properly, you shouldn't know it's there.

As part of its transparency, the third-party product often has its own windows and menus. As a result, the illustrations and options throughout this chapter may differ from those on your system. If you own a third-party capture card, please refer to the documentation provided by the manufacturer whenever possible. The concepts taught throughout this chapter should apply equally, but you may need to select different options recommended by the manufacturer.

EXERCISE

1 | Recording to a DV Device

When your DV hardware (camcorder or VCR) is properly communicating with Premiere Pro 2, you can export to tape with the click of a single button (maybe two). You should use this export method when you want to send your finished sequence to DV tape, either for archiving or for accessing quickly in a future project. Sending to a DV device keeps your sequence in the highest-possible quality.

Note: If you have a DV device, turn it on, put it in playback mode, and connect it to the computer via FireWire/i.Link before launching Premiere Pro 2, just to be safe. Please note if you do not have a DV device properly connected to your computer, you may not be able to complete some of the steps in this exercise.

---

1 On the **Welcome Screen**, click **Open Project**. In the **Open Project** dialog box, navigate to the **c:\exercise_files\chap_13** folder, click **exercise01.prproj** to select it, and click **Open**.

---

2 Choose **File > Save As**. Navigate to the **c:\exercise files\dutch_harbor** folder. Name the file **dutch harbor promo.prproj**, and click **Save**.

Note: If a previous version of dutch harbor promo.prproj already exists, you may be asked to replace it. Click Yes.

Before recording to tape, you should first make sure Premiere Pro 2 and your attached DV device are properly communicating. You can do this via the Playback Settings dialog box, as described previously.

---

3 In the **Program Monitor**, click the **Output** button. In the pop-up menu, choose **Playback Settings**.

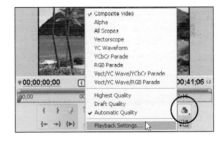

---

4 In the **Playback Settings** dialog box, make sure **Realtime Playback > External Device** and **Export > External Device** are set to your attached DV device. Also, make sure the **External Device Audio** radio button is selected. Click **OK**.

These settings make sure you can preview your project and export it to your attached DV device.

Note: If you do not have a properly attached DV device, these settings may be unavailable to you. Depending on your DV device properties, your options may differ slightly from those shown here.

Chapter 13 : **Exporting to Files and Tape** | 397

5 In the **Program Monitor**, click the **Play In to Out** button. After previewing and hearing your audio on the attached DV device, click the **Stop** button.

If Premiere Pro 2 is communicating with your DV device, you should be able to see and hear the video/audio via the attached device.

You are now ready to export your project to DV tape. Before you do, it is useful to insert black video at the start of your sequence, which is called a **header**. A header of black prevents the sequence from starting at the beginning of the tape, which can result in frame drop or other unwanted glitches.

Also, a header of black video allows your device some time to get up to speed before the real video starts playing, called **preroll**. (Not all devices require this, but it never hurts to be safe when recording the finished product to tape.)

---

6 Choose **File > New > Black Video**.

This adds a still image of pure black to the Project panel. Remember, this isn't really *video*. Rather, it's a still image of black, but like any still image in Premiere Pro 2, you can stretch it to play as video for as long as you require.

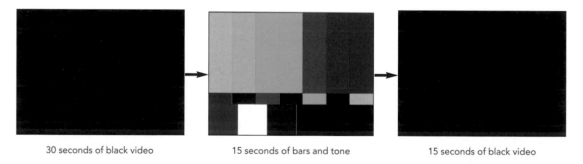

| 30 seconds of black video | 15 seconds of bars and tone | 15 seconds of black video |

If you plan to submit your tape to a post-production house or to another broadcast outlet, a standard practice is to record a 1-minute header consisting of black video, then colored bars with audio tone, and then black again.

---

7 Choose **File > New > Bars and Tone**.

You now have two clips, Black Video and Bars and Tone, in your Project panel. Before adding them to the sequence in the Timeline panel because they basically are still images, you can specify their duration directly in the Project panel.

8 In the **Project** panel, right-click the **Bars and Tone** clip, and choose **Speed/Duration**. In the **Clip Speed / Duration** dialog box, click the **Duration** value, and type **1500**. Click **OK**.

This changes the duration of the Bars and Tone clip to 15;00 (15 seconds).

9 In the **Project** panel, right-click the **Black Video** clip, and choose **Speed/Duration**. In the **Clip Speed / Duration** dialog box, click the **Duration** value, and type **10000**. Click **OK**.

This changes the duration of the Black Video clip to 1;00;00 (1 minute).

Note: In the Clip Speed / Duration dialog box, the duration will change to 00;01;00;02 automatically. This is because your project is really playing at 29.97 fps. Try as you might, you won't be able to get to exactly 00;01;00;00, and that's perfectly normal.

Now your clips are the proper duration, so it is time to insert them at the beginning of the sequence.

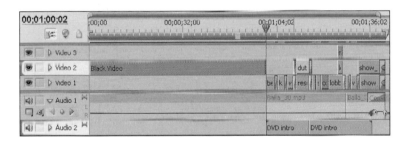

10 At the top of the **Timeline** panel, click the **DVD intro** tab to bring that sequence to the foreground.

11 Drag the **Timeline CTI** (Current Time Indicator) to the beginning of the sequence. In the **Project** panel, right-click the **Black Video** clip, and choose **Insert**. Press the **backslash** (\) key to zoom the sequence to fit inside the **Timeline** panel.

The Insert command inserts the clip into the target track, beginning at the CTI.

Now it is time to insert the Bars and Tone clip; however, you want to insert it starting at 30 seconds.

00;00;30;00		;00;00	00;00;32;00	00;01;04;02

●	▷ Video 3	
●	▷ Video 2	Black Video
●	▷ Video 1	be k v
◄)	▽ Audio 1	Baila_30.n

12 Click the **Timeline** panel **timecode** display, and type **3000** to move the Timeline CTI to **00;00;30;00**.

●	▷ Video 3			
●	▷ Video 2	Black Video	Bars and Tone	Black Video	dut
●	▷ Video 1			be k v res
◄)	▽ Audio 1			Baila_30.mp3
◄)	▷ Audio 2		Bars and Tone	DVD intro

13 In the **Project** panel, right-click the **Bars and Tone** clip, and choose **Overlay**.

This **overlays** (overwrites) anything on the target track, starting at the CTI.

OK, you now have 30 seconds of black video, 15 seconds of bars and tone, and 15 seconds of black video before your sequence actually begins. You are *finally* ready to export to tape.

14 At the top of the **Timeline** panel, select the **DVD intro** tab to bring that sequence to the foreground.

Tip: Before exporting to tape—or to any format, for that matter—it is a good idea to select the sequence you want to export. This ensures you are not accidentally exporting the wrong sequence or another clip.

15 Choose **File > Export > Export to Tape**. In the **Export to Tape** dialog box, make sure **Activate Recording Device** is turned on. Also, make sure **Report dropped frames** and **Render audio before export** are turned on.

All systems are go. However, this is the real deal—this is not a drill. If you don't want to overwrite what you currently have on your DV tape, then *don't* click Record. If you don't want to record at this stage, skip to Step 17.

16 If you want to record to tape, click the **Record** button.

Before the recording begins, Premiere Pro 2 has to render all your audio and video files. This may take a couple of minutes, depending on your processor and depending on how much you've already rendered. (All of those red render lines at the top of the Timeline panel have to turn green before Premiere Pro 2 can record the sequence to tape.)

After rendering is complete, if everything is working properly, Premiere Pro 2 should automatically start recording and stop recording when playback is done.

---

17 Click the **Close** box to close the **Export to Tape** dialog box. (If you did not record, click **Cancel** to close the dialog box.)

---

18 Choose **File > Save**, or press **Ctrl+S**. Leave **dutch harbor promo.prproj** open for the next exercise.

If we stripped from this exercise the advanced options of checking your playback settings and adding black video and bars and tone, the actual exercise would have been about two steps long. As you can see, exporting to tape is a no brainer in Premiere Pro 2. And, as an added bonus, you learned a few tips and tricks for delivering your video to broadcast facilities and production houses.

Exporting to tape is the only export medium not resulting in a file on your hard drive (besides burning to DVD disc). The other methods require additional options and settings in order to create an optimized movie on your hard drive.

Exporting a DV Movie File

When exporting a DV movie, an alternative method to employ is to export the DV movie to a file on your hard drive, rather than DV tape. This gives you all the benefits of preserving the video in its native high-quality format, without needing an attached DV device.

You have an even better reason to export to a DV file. For example, let's say you produce a weekly television program. You have created an effects-intensive show opening you plan to use at the start of every show. If you export the show opening to a DV movie file, all the rendering takes place at the time of export. This means you can import the file into future projects, and no rendering is required. In fact, Premiere Pro 2 cannot distinguish between this file and a file captured from your DV camera. As far as Premiere Pro 2 is concerned, as long as the file is in the DV format, it is a DV movie, and no rendering is required.

The downside is the movie is flattened. Similar to exporting to DV tape, you can no longer undo edits made in the movie. You can definitely *edit* the movie as you would edit any clip, but you can't remove a title, transition, and so on. As far as Premiere Pro 2 is concerned, it's just a single video clip.

Exporting a DV file is nearly as simple as exporting to DV tape. Because the DV format is so rigid, you really have no choices to make. In fact, as opposed to other formats, you want to try your best to *not deviate* from the DV standard—even the slightest change can cause the file to not comply with the DV format and thus require extra rendering time.

In the next exercise, you will walk through each setting to ensure your DV movies are exported in the pure DV format. Afterward, you will save your export settings so you can reuse the preset whenever you export to a DV file in the future.

2 | Saving DV Movie Export Settings

Exporting to a DV movie file allows you to import the file into other projects. Premiere Pro 2 will recognize the file as a DV file and will not require rendering in your DV projects. This allows you to reuse a complex section of video repeatedly, without rendering each time. However, the trick in exporting to a DV movie file is to make sure your options are perfectly matched to the DV specification. Even the slightest deviation can cause the file to seem foreign to Premiere Pro 2 and cause unnecessary rendering. In this exercise, you will walk through the steps of specifying the correct DV settings and then save those settings for quick reference in future projects.

1 If you followed the previous exercise, **dutch_harbor_promo.prproj** should still be open in Premiere Pro 2. If it's not, click **Open Project** on the **Welcome Screen**. Navigate to **c:\exercise_files\chap_13** folder, click **exercise02.prproj** to select it, and click **Open**.

2 Choose **File > Save As**. Navigate to the **c:\exercise_files\dutch_harbor** folder. Name the file **dutch_harbor_promo.prproj**, and click **Save**.

Note: If a previous version of dutch_harbor_promo.prproj already exists, you may be asked to replace it. Click Yes.

One of the decisions to make when exporting a file to your hard disk is to answer this question: "Do you want to export the entire sequence or just a portion of the sequence?" If you want to export just a small section of the sequence, you can do this by resizing the work area bar.

In this case, the sequence you currently have open has a 1-minute header of black video and bars and tone. You do not need to export this portion of the sequence, so you can use the work area bar to exclude the header.

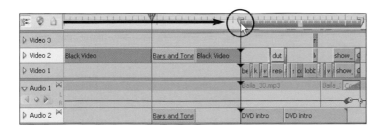

3 In the **Timeline** panel, click and drag the left handle of the work area bar, and snap it to the beginning of the first clip on Track **Video 1**, which is where the "real" video starts playing.

Currently, your Timeline panel is active because you just moved the work area bar. However, in your other projects, before you export to a movie file, it's extremely important the Timeline panel is active. Otherwise, you may end up exporting the last element you clicked, such as a clip in the Project panel.

4 With the **Timeline** panel active, choose **File > Export > Movie**. In the **Export Movie** dialog box, click **Settings**.

This opens the Export Movie Settings dialog box. In the next series of steps, you will walk through each screen of the dialog box to ensure compliance with the DV format.

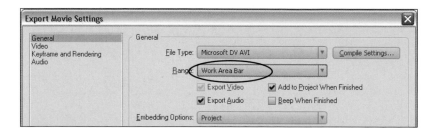

5 In the **Export Movie Settings** dialog box **File Type** pop-up menu, choose **Microsoft DV AVI**. In the **Range** pop-up menu, choose **Work Area Bar**. Make sure the following check boxes are turned on: **Export Video**, **Export Audio**, and **Add to Project When Finished**.

Note: As shown in the illustration here, the Export Video check box is dimmed; however, if you squint, you can see it is turned on. When exporting to a movie, Premiere Pro 2 "locks" the Export Video option so you can't uncheck it. (After all, what good is a movie without video?)

The Embedding Options pop-up menu is optional. It's not part of the DV format, so it's a matter of taste. This option tells Premiere Pro 2 to remember the name of the project, which allows you to use the Edit Original command after importing the finished file into future projects.

The Compile Settings button has some handy features if you plan to export to Adobe Encore DVD. If you have created sequence markers, you can request that the finished file maintain those markers. Encore DVD can read the markers and convert them into chapter points. Again, this is an optional feature and has no bearing on the DV format.

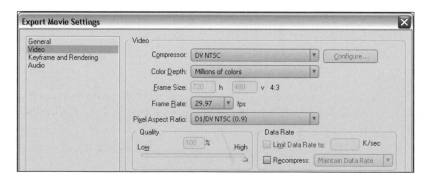

6 In the left side of the **Export Movie Settings** dialog box, click **Video** to view the video settings. From the pop-up menus, set **Compressor** to **DV NTSC**, set **Color Depth** to **Millions of Colors**, set **Frame Rate** to **29.97 fps**, and set **Pixel Aspect Ratio** to **D1/DV NTSC (0.9)**.

The Quality and Data Rate settings have no effect when exporting to the DV format, so you can ignore them.

Tip: If you are creating a PAL DV, your compressor will be DV PAL, the Frame Rate setting will be 25.00 fps, and the Pixel Aspect Ratio setting will be D1/DV PAL (1.067). Besides these settings, all other settings outlined in this exercise apply to PAL DV.

---

7 In the **Export Movie Settings** dialog box, turn off the **Recompress** check box.

Tip: When exporting DV movies from DV projects, it is important to turn off the Recompress check box. When the Recompress check box is turned on, Premiere Pro 2 will render every frame of video as it makes your movie. If this check box is turned off, Premiere Pro 2 will not rerender any video that is already in the DV format, which results in decreased render times.

8 In the left side of the **Export Movie Settings** dialog box, click **Keyframe and Rendering**. Set **Bit Depth** to **8-bit**, and set **Fields** to **Lower Field First**. Turn off the **Optimize Stills** check box.

The options in the Keyframe Options area at the bottom of this dialog box do not have any effect on DV files.

9 In the left side of the **Export Movie Settings** dialog box, click **Audio**. From the pop-up menus, set **Compressor** to **Uncompressed**, set **Sample Rate** to **48000 Hz**, set **Sample Type** to **16-bit**, set **Channels** to **Stereo**, and set **Interleave** to **1/2 Second**.

The DV format allows you to use 32,000 Hz (**Hertz**) audio, but 48,000 is the most common. (And why not? It's slightly better quality.) On the other hand, if you're absolutely, positively, 100 percent sure your source clips are 32,000 Hz and you will be using the DV file in 32,000 Hz projects only, then you can switch the Sample Rate setting to 32000 Hz.

Now you are done specifying your settings to ensure DV compatibility. Premiere Pro 2 allows you to save all these settings as a template for quick reference in future projects.

10 In the **Export Movie Settings** dialog box, click **Save**. In the **Save Export Settings** dialog box **Name** field, type **DV NTSC 48 Work Area**. If you'd like, type a description to remind you when to use these settings, as shown in the illustration here. Click **OK**. In the **Export Movie Settings** dialog box, click **OK**.

11 In the **Export Movie** dialog box, navigate to the **c:\exercise_files\chap_13** folder. In the **File name** field, type **dvd_intro**. (Premiere Pro 2 will automatically append the **.avi** extension.) Click **Save**.

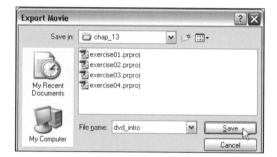

While the movie renders, the Rendering dialog box appears. When rendering is complete, the clip automatically imports into the Project panel. This is now a DV file like any other on your hard drive and can be imported into future projects.

12 Choose **File > Save**, or press **Ctrl+S**. Leave **dutch harbor promo.prproj** open for the next exercise.

The export settings you saved in this exercise will stay on your system until you remove them, which means you can use the setting preset in all your future projects. To access the preset, simply click Load in the Export Movie Settings dialog box.

While following this exercise, you may have noticed a handful of other file types and compressor settings. It is rare to deviate from the settings covered in this exercise, and usually only advanced users do that. For most users, the only time to use the Export Movie dialog box is when exporting a DV file. For 99 percent of the other types of movies you can export, such as movies for the Web or CD, you should export from the Adobe Media Encoder, which you will learn about after Exercise 3.

3 | Exporting Still Images and Audio Files

Oh sure, Premiere Pro 2 can export still images and audio files. And yes, it's extremely simple to do. But truth be told, Premiere Pro 2 is not a stellar performer in either category. For example, if you want to export images for use on a Web page, you can specify only GIF. In addition, Premiere Pro 2 lacks the options to optimize the image for easy Web viewing. The best workflow for exporting still images in Premiere Pro 2 is to export in the highest-quality image (TIF) and then import it into an application such as Photoshop. Similarly, with audio, you can export it to an uncompressed audio format and edit it further in an audio-editing application, such as Adobe Audition. This exercise walks you through some of the most important options when exporting images and audio files.

1 If you followed the previous exercise, **dutch_harbor_promo.prproj** should still be open in Premiere Pro 2. If it's not, click **Open Project** on the **Welcome Screen**. Navigate to **c:\exercise_files\chap_13** folder, click **exercise03.prproj** to select it, and click **Open**.

2 Choose **File > Save As**. Navigate to the **c:\exercise files\dutch_harbor** folder. Name the file **dutch harbor promo.prproj**, and click **Save**.

Note: If a previous version of dutch harbor promo.prproj already exists, you may be asked to replace it. Click Yes.

In the next series of steps, you will export a frame of video from the sequence in the highest possible quality. Maintaining the high quality allows you to edit the image in applications such as Photoshop.

3 At the top of the **Timeline** panel, select the **DVD Intro** tab to bring the sequence to the foreground. Drag the **Timeline CTI** to **00;01;06;11**.

This is a good frame to use as an example for exporting a still image because it has motion (the arm of the kayaker is moving). Images with motion require an additional step to prevent artifacts due to interlaced video.

4 With the **Timeline** panel still selected as the active panel, choose **File > Export > Frame**. In the **Export Frame** dialog box, click **Settings**.

This opens the Export Frame Settings dialog box, which looks suspiciously

like the Export Movie Settings dialog box. Don't be fooled—they're basically the same. However, you can choose only still images from the File Type pop-up menu.

5 In the **Export Frame Settings** dialog box, choose **TIFF** from the **File Type** pop-up menu.

6 In the **Export Frame Settings** dialog box, click **Video**. In the **Pixel Aspect Ratio** pop-up menu, choose **Square Pixels (1.0)**.

The next two sentences are *very* important, so grab your highlighter (unless this is a library rental). If you plan to use the still image in future Premiere Pro 2 projects, leave the aspect ratio as D1/DV NTSC (0.9). If you plan to edit the image for use on the Web, change the aspect ratio to Square Pixels (1.0).

Also, if you want to export your frame of video with an alpha channel, change Color Depth to Millions+ of colors. This will save the image with an alpha channel that can be interpreted in Photoshop.

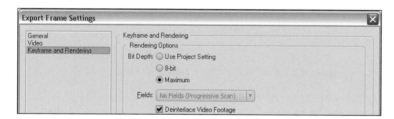

7 In the **Export Frame Settings** dialog box, click **Keyframe and Rendering**. For **Bit Depth**, click the **Maximum** radio button to select it. Turn on the **Deinterlace Video Footage** check box. Click **OK**.

This image is not deinterlaced. Notice the combing on the paddle.

This image is deinterlaced.

The top image is not deinterlaced. The bottom image is deinterlaced.

Deinterlacing is the process of discarding one field of video. Previously, you learned video is comprised of two fields. If a frame of video has a lot of motion, the fields can result in interlacing artifacts such as **combing**, as shown in the illustration here on the left. This effect is especially noticeable on the paddle.

When an image has a lot of motion, deinterlacing can help resolve the combing effect. However, the disadvantage of deinterlacing is that, along with one field of video, you lose half of the picture detail. As shown in the illustration here in the middle, observe how deinterlacing lowered the quality of the Digital Juice logo.

What is the moral of the story? If your frame doesn't have motion, deinterlacing is not required. If your frame has motion or fine lines such as those found in text and logos, as shown in the two illustrations here on the right, you have to decide whether deinterlacing is worth the loss of image detail. Look again at the kayaker—can you notice a loss in image detail?

---

8 In the **Export Frame** dialog box, navigate to **c:\exercise_files\chap_13**. In the **File name** text box, type **kayaker**, and click **Save**.

The kayaker TIF image is exported to the hard drive and automatically imported into the Project panel.

Newly created TIF image

Original frame of video

9 In the **Project** panel, double-click the **kayaker** clip to open it in the **Source Monitor**.

As shown in the illustration here, compare the newly created frame with the original frame in the sequence. Notice how the new frame appears a bit too thin? (The Digital Juice "sphere" looks more egg-shaped in the left image.)

Premiere Pro 2 thinks the new image has a pixel aspect ratio of 0.9, even though you specified 1.0. This is causing it to display thinner than it really is. You can easily rectify this by changing the clip's interpretation in Premiere Pro 2.

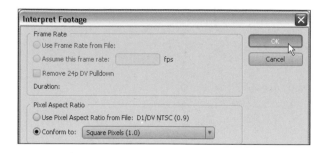

10 In the **Project** panel, make sure the **kayaker** clip is still selected. Choose **File > Interpret Footage**. In the **Interpret Footage** dialog box, change the **Pixel Aspect Ratio > Conform to** pop-up menu to **Square Pixels (1.0)**.

Immediately in the Source Monitor, you should see the image shift in aspect ratio, and the image now looks normal again. (Notice the sphere of the Digital Juice logo is back to a perfect circle.)

What did you just do? In Step 10, you chose a pixel aspect ratio of 1.0. So, in this step, you made sure Premiere Pro 2 knew this image had a 1.0 ratio.

Why did Premiere Pro 2 interpret it incorrectly? Premiere Pro 2 tries to be helpful. Anytime you import a still image containing the same frame size of DV video (720 x 480 pixels), Premiere Pro 2 thinks, "Aha! This must be an image from DV video because it is the same size as DV video." So, Premiere Pro 2 *assumes* it has a pixel aspect ratio of 0.9, just like DV video.

Tip: If your still images are displaying either too fat or too thin, try changing the interpretation method of Premiere Pro 2; this often fixes the issue.

---

11 In the **Timeline** panel, select the **DVD intro** tab to make it the active panel. Choose **File > Export > Audio**.

Few options are available when exporting audio. The best workflow is to export it in the highest-quality format possible and then edit the file further in a program such as Audition.

---

12 In the **Export Audio** dialog box, click **Settings**.

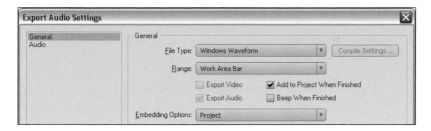

13 In the **Export Audio Settings** dialog box, make sure the **File Type** pop-up menu is set to **Windows Waveform**. Change the **Range** pop-up menu to **Work Area Bar**. Make sure the **Add to Project When Finished** check box is turned on and the **Embedding Options** pop-up menu is set to **Project**.

14 In the **Export Audio Settings** dialog box, click **Audio**. Apply the settings shown in the illustration here to your project. Click **OK**.

15 In the **Export Audio** dialog box, navigate to **c:\exercise_files\chap_13**. In the **File name** text box, type **dutch_harbor_audio**. Click **Save**.

A rendering box appears briefly (audio renders quickly). After the audio file is successfully exported to your hard drive, it is imported into the Project panel.

You can use this audio clip in any of your future projects, or you can burn the file to a music CD if you have burning software. (Alas, Premiere Pro 2 will not do this for you.)

16 Choose **File > Save**, or press **Ctrl+S**. Leave **dutch harbor promo.prproj** open for the next exercise.

Premiere Pro 2 is capable of delivering your still images and audio files in the highest-quality format possible. This is good news when you want to continue to edit these files in their respective applications, such as Photoshop or Audition. However, Premiere Pro 2 is not very sophisticated at creating still images for use in Web pages or music files for use in MP3 players, for example.

Even though Premiere Pro 2 may not be the most robust application for exporting still images to the Web, it does one task very well—and that's exporting *movies* to the Web, supporting all of the major formats. To do this, Premiere Pro 2 relies on a completely different exporting method, the Adobe Media Encoder.

Understanding the Adobe Media Encoder

So far, all of the files you have exported in this chapter have been using the same Premiere Pro 2 dialog box. However, movies for the Web, CDs, and the like, get their own special exporting dialog box, called the **Adobe Media Encoder**.

You can also use the **Adobe Media Encoder** for exporting files to your hard drive, but you should not use the files for editing in future projects. Instead, the Adobe Media Encoder excels at providing **delivery formats**, which are formats in which the final video should be watched. Whereas the other export methods create files you can use to reedit, the Adobe Media Encoder formats are heavily compressed and not ideally suited for editing.

Use the Adobe Media Encoder when you want to export movies for playback on the Web, small movies for e-mailing, MPEG-1 VCD and MPEG-2 SVCD (for creating video CDs, which are different from DVDs), high-quality movies for PowerPoint presentations, movies for burning to a data CD, or any other use where file size is a top priority.

The most common formats the Adobe Media Encoder can export to include Windows Media Video/Audio, QuickTime, RealMedia, and Flash. All of these formats are capable of delivering high-quality video. Although some editors will (freely) give you opinions on which ones *they* think are the best formats, truth be told, they are all good formats. Instead of worrying which format has the highest quality, you should base your decision on compatibility with your audience. Are you delivering to Windows or Mac computers? Or, if you are exporting movies to a company Web site, is there a defined protocol for movie formats?

Using the Export Settings Dialog Box

When you choose **File > Adobe Media Encoder**, Premiere Pro 2 opens the **Export Settings** dialog box. (Why it's not just called **Adobe Media Encoder** is beyond us!) You will recognize the **Export Settings** dialog box from Chapter 12, *"Authoring DVDs."* You used this to customize your DVD encode settings. In the previous chapter, you dealt with only a few options pertaining to exporting a DVD. Now it's time to learn the other features of the **Export Settings** dialog box.

The **Adobe Media Encoder**...I mean, the **Export Settings** dialog box, has three primary sections: the **Export Settings** area, the output options area, and **Source/Output** preview area. The following sections describe each one and how you can use them in the **Adobe Media Encoder** workflow.

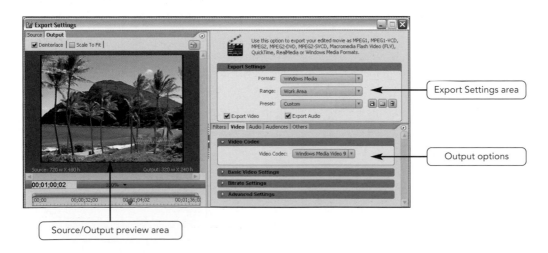

Exploring the Export Settings Area

Typically, you start in the **Export Settings** area and begin by choosing the desired format. All other options available will stem from the format setting you choose here. Within each format, you can specify an encoding preset based on the audience requirements.

WM9 NTSC 1024K download	WM9 PAL 1024K download
WM9 NTSC 128K download	WM9 PAL 128K download
WM9 NTSC 256K download	WM9 PAL 256K download
WM9 NTSC 32K download	WM9 PAL 32K download
WM9 NTSC 512K download	WM9 PAL 512K download
WM9 NTSC 64K download	WM9 PAL 64K download
WM9 NTSC streaming modem	WM9 PAL streaming modem
WM9 NTSC streaming	WM9 PAL streaming

More than 50 preset choices are available just for the Windows Media format.

As with the DVD presets you experienced in Chapter 12, *"Authoring DVDs,"* each format may have from 20 to 50 preset options. The presets are often labeled for a target "audience." What separates one audience from another? It usually depends on how the user will watch the movie, such as via a CD drive, Internet connection, or fast network.

For example, if you are making a movie to play across your corporate network, then size isn't a primary concern because your users will have speedy connections to the file. You can safely choose a preset resulting in a much larger movie, such as **WM9 NTSC 1024K download**.

If your target audience will be users at home with a slow Internet connection, then download size is *the* limiting factor, and you should choose a preset resulting in a small file size, such as **WM9 NTSC 64K download**.

For a detailed explanation of what all those numbers mean, see the following sidebar.

NOTE:

Watching the Incredible Shrinking Movie

So how exactly does the **Adobe Media Encoder** achieve such small file sizes? And what's the deal with all those numbers in the presets—1024K, 28K, 256K, 64K, and so on?

Those numbers refer to the bitrate of the resulting file. You got an introduction to bitrates in Chapter 12, *"Authoring DVDs."* As you may recall, the **bitrate** is the amount of data playing back per second. The bitrate directly impacts the ultimate file size because a large amount of data per second x lots of seconds = large file size.

For example, 1024K is 1,024,000 bps (**bits per** second). DVDs usually fall around 7,000,000 bps. CDs and network servers can play back a 1,024-kbps (**kilobits per** second) bitrate without breaking a sweat. This is not so for dial-up modems. Recognize the term 56K? That's 56,000 bps, the maximum bitrate the modem can handle.

The bitrate, however, is nothing more than the product of it parts. These ingredients together define the bitrate:

Video codec: Every codec (**c**ompressor/**dec**ompressor) compresses differently, using different algorithms and logic. Some codecs keep video pristine but result in high bitrate. Others are great at compressing heavily for low bitrates, but the video quality is subpar. The ideal codec finds a harmony between video quality and bitrate.

continues on next page

Watching the Incredible Shrinking Movie *continued*

Frame rate: DV NTSC video plays at 29.97 fps (or 25.0 for PAL DV). If you lower the frame rate, fewer frames need to be played, which requires a lower bitrate. At frame rates less than 12 to 15, your eye can detect individual frames, and the illusion of animation is lost.

Frame width x height: The size of the output "frame" relates directly to the number of pixels. Smaller frames have fewer pixels and therefore require a lower bitrate.

Bitrate mode: A CBR (**C**onstant **B**it **R**ate) compresses the data to a fixed rate. A VBR (**V**ariable **B**it **R**ate) scans each frame and determines the maximum bitrate required.

Quality: Some formats don't let you specify the quality amount. Instead, the quality is a byproduct of the bitrate divided by the frame size and frame rate. In other words, if you lower the frame size or frame rate, the quality increases in order to maintain the same bitrate amount.

Think of a file's bitrate like a water balloon. (Stay with us on this analogy; it's going somewhere!) As you squeeze one part of the balloon, the water increases in the other part. The amount of water remains the same; you're simply distributing the water differently in the balloon.

Similarly, as you reduce (squeeze) the frame size or frame rate of a file, the quality increases. Like the amount of water in the balloon, the file size (amount of data) remains the same; you're just distributing the bits differently in the file. More bits are dedicated to the quality, and fewer bits are dedicated to the frame size or frame rate.

Using the **Adobe Media Encoder** presets takes the guesswork out of specifying these different options. Many of the presets are tuned to find the "sweet spot," balancing quality and file size.

Exploring the Output Options

After you define the export settings, you can move on to the output options. It's crucial you first define your format and preset because each format has its *own* output options. So each time you change the format, the output options change as well.

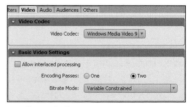
Windows Media options

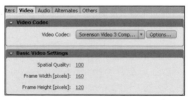
QuickTime options

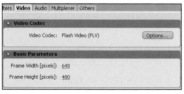
Flash options

As shown in the illustration here, different options are available for each format. Keep in mind these are just a tiny morsel of options available to each format. Within each format, you may see an additional 50 options you can customize to your liking.

At the top of the output options, you will see tabbed dividers. Each format has its own tabs—for example, the Flash format has a **Multiplexer** tab. The Windows Media format has an **Audiences** tab, whereas QuickTime calls it **Alternates**.

If you begin by choosing a proper preset in the **Export Settings** area, you shouldn't have to specify *any* of these settings. Instead, each preset defines every option for that format. Remember, the presets are nothing more than a group of saved options, available for quick reference later, like a bookmark.

Many editors begin with a preset and then further refine the options to suit their needs. Once you define the settings and options you like to use most often, you can then save your own preset for easy access in future projects.

Exploring the Source/Output Preview Area

New to Premiere Pro 2 is a **Source/Output** preview area, which displays what your final output will look like. This is an incredibly massive, immense, huge timesaving device. In the "old" days, you had to tweak your settings and hope for the best. If you didn't like it, you had to go back and tweak it some more and, again, hope for the best. In between each tweaking, there was rendering. Lots and lots of rendering. Now, you can preview immediately what your finished file will look like before rendering!

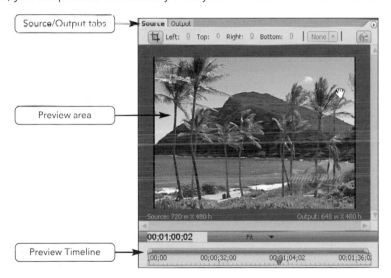

As the name implies, the **Source/Output** preview area shows you both the source view and the output view. You can alternate between the two views by selecting the **Source** or **Output** tabs in the upper-left corner. As you make changes to the export format and options, the changes will appear immediately in the preview area.

Another helpful option Premiere Pro 2 added is the ability to crop your video in the **Source** preview area. For example, notice how the DV video clip in the illustration shown here has a stripe of black on its far left and far right sides? You can use the crop feature to exclude this video. Or, if you want to create a fake "widescreen" look, you can crop off 50 pixels from the top and bottom of the source clip.

At the bottom of the **Source/Output** preview area is the **Preview Timeline**. This allows you to advance the CTI to any frame of video so you can see what the final output will look like.

Now you have a good grasp of how the **Adobe Media Encoder** works, so it's time to try it for yourself.

Exporting to Web Movie

Whenever you want to export to a destination format (the final format the viewer will watch the movie in), then the **Adobe Media Encoder** is the way to go for exporting. The **Adobe Media Encoder** lets you choose between the most popular Web formats. Finding the format you like best may take time. Once you decide on the format, then you pick a preset based on the audience or delivery method. If you plan to burn to CD, so someone can play the movie on their computer, then you can choose a preset with a high bitrate. On the other hand, if users need to download the movie over the Internet, then you have to compromise quality for a smaller bitrate and file size. In this exercise, you will learn how to export a Web movie.

1 If you followed the previous exercise, **dutch_harbor_promo.prproj** should still be open in Premiere Pro 2. If it's not, click **Open Project** on the **Welcome Screen**. Navigate to the **c:\exercise_files\chap_13** folder, click **exercise04.prproj** to select it, and click **Open**.

2 Choose **File > Save As**. Navigate to the **c:\exercise files\dutch_harbor** folder. Name the file **dutch harbor promo.prproj**, and click **Save**.

Note: If a previous version of dutch harbor promo.prproj already exists, you may be asked to replace it. Click Yes.

3 In the **Timeline** panel, select the **DVD intro** tab to bring the panel to the foreground. Choose **File > Export > Adobe Media Encoder**.

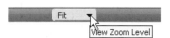

4 In the **Export Settings** dialog box, click the **Source** tab to view the source video. Click the **View Zoom Level** button, and choose **Fit**.

No matter how big your source video is, the Fit zoom level reduces the preview so it can display entirely within the preview area. If you enlarge the preview area, the Fit zoom level increases to match.

When the Export Settings dialog box opens, you will notice the preview area is black. This is because your sequence has 1 minute of black at the beginning. The timecode display indicates you are currently viewing frame 00;00;00;00. So, everything will look black until you move the CTI to the 1-minute mark.

5 In the **Export Settings** dialog box, click the blue timecode display, and type **10000**.

This advances the CTI to 00;01;00;02, and the preview area displays a frame of video. (Just like in Exercise 1, this is the closest you can get to 00;01;00;00 because of the 29.97 frame rate of NTSC video.)

The first step in exporting your movie with the Adobe Media Encoder is to decide on the export format.

---

6 In the **Export Settings** dialog box, click the **Format** pop-up menu, and choose **Windows Media**. Click the **Range** pop-up menu, and choose **Work Area**. Click the **Preset** pop-up menu, and choose **WM9 NTSC 256K download**.

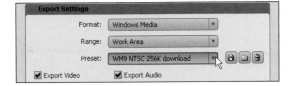

To translate the preset, WM9 means Windows Media v.9; NTSC means NTSC video format; 256K means 256 kilobits/second, which is the bitrate; and download means it's ideally suited for downloading.

Tip: Just because this preset says "download" doesn't mean it can be downloaded only. Rather, this is just giving you an idea of what this preset is used for usually. However, you can burn the resulting file to CD, e-mail it, or put it on a network server. The same is true for all the presets. Premiere Pro 2 is trying to suggest the best use, but what you do with the file is your own business!

The next step, when exporting a DV sequence with the Adobe Media Encoder, is to specify the part of the image you want to export, such as trimming off an unwanted area of the screen from the top, left, right, or bottom. This is called **cropping**.

When you're exporting video originating from a DV camera, frequently you'll see black bars along the sides of the video. That's just a by-product of video cameras. You can remove these within the Adobe Media Encoder by using the cropping feature so the black bars don't show up on your finished output.

---

7 In the **Export Settings** dialog box **Source** tab, click the **Crop** button.

This puts the Source preview area in crop mode and displays a cropping boundary around the Source preview area, with handles in the corners. To crop, change any of the cropping values (Left, Top, Right, or Bottom) at the top of the Source tab, or click and drag any side or corner handle of the cropping boundary.

8 In the **Export Settings** dialog box **Source**
preview area, click and drag the left cropping
boundary to the right until the **Left** cropping setting is **8**. Then, click and drag the right cropping
boundary to the left until the **Right** cropping
value is **8**.

Now that you've specified the format, preset, and
crop area, you are ready to preview the output
and tweak the options to your liking.

9 In the **Export Settings** dialog box, click the **Switch to Output** button to bring the **Output** tab to the
foreground.

Clicking this button is the same as clicking the Output tab. Clicking the button again will return you to
the Source tab.

When previewing the output, it is helpful to view it at its true, final size. This allows you to see the finished file as an audience member will see it.

10 In the **Export Settings** dialog box, click the **View Zoom Level** pop-up menu, and choose **100%**.

Notice on the edges of your Output preview area, you can still see bars of black. Note these are not the
same strips of black from the DV video. Rather, these are the "empty" areas left behind as a result of
your cropping.

It may help to think of it like this: Cropping video is like taking an eraser to the video. Even though
you've "erased" the video you don't want, the empty canvas behind still shows. (And that canvas happens to be black.)

To rectify this, you can use the Scale to Fit option, which enlarges the video until the height or width fits
within the frame.

11 In the **Export Settings** dialog box **Output** tab, turn on the **Scale to Fit** check box.

You may have to squint and press your nose up against your computer monitor to see the difference, but the video enlarged ever so slightly, and it now fills most of the empty canvas. If you have trouble comparing, try turning the Scale to Fit check box off and on.

Even after turning on Scale to Fit, you'll see a sliver of black on the sides of the Output preview. You can further trim the Output preview area by reducing the Frame Width setting.

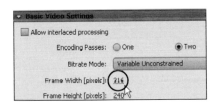

12 In the **Export Settings** dialog box output options, click the **Frame Width [pixels]** value, and type **316**.

The empty areas of the canvas have effectively been "trimmed" by reducing the size of the Output preview area frame.

Tip: Some formats may return a (very helpful!) "unknown" error message if you attempt to export an odd number of pixels for the width or the height. (The engine compressing the video likes to work in "groups" of pixels, and it doesn't like having remainders when dividing. The solution is to simply choose an even integer for the width and height values.)

Before moving on to the other output options, take a second to make sure the output video options are tailored to your liking.

13 In the **Export Settings** dialog box output options, change **Frame Rate [fps]** to **15**, and make sure the **Pixel Aspect Ratio** pop-up menu is **Square Pixels (1.0)**. Also, make sure the **Allow interlaced processing** check box is turned off.

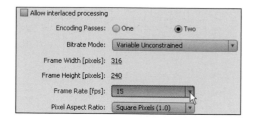

Reducing the frame rate is a great way to keep the picture quality while reducing file size. (After all, if you reduce the number of frames displaying per second by half, you will dramatically reduce the file size.) Especially for Web downloads, you have little need to keep the video playing at 29.97 fps—although anything less than 15 or 12 may look choppy and the "illusion of motion" will be lost.

If the final destination is going to be a computer screen, make sure Pixel Aspect Ratio is 1.0 and the Allow interlaced processing check box is turned off.

---

14 In the **Export Settings** dialog box **Advanced Settings**, change **Average Video Bitrate [kbps]** to **100.00**.

The bitrate tells Premiere Pro 2 how much data it should try to squeeze in each second of video. In this case, we used 100 so the movie would be easier to download for people with slower Internet connections. To learn more about tweaking the bitrate, see the sidebar following this exercise.

The Keyframe Interval setting doesn't have any relation to the animation keyframes you created in Chapter 8, *"Animating Effects."* Rather, this value specifies how frequently the finished movie stores a complete frame of video. Decreasing the interval can improve video quality but significantly impacts the overall file size. To lower file size, increase the interval.

---

15 In the **Export Settings** dialog box, select the **Audio** tab to view the audio options.

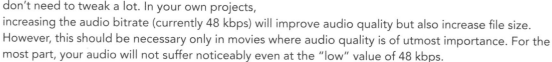

Actually, the settings listed are preferred, and you don't need to tweak a lot. In your own projects, increasing the audio bitrate (currently 48 kbps) will improve audio quality but also increase file size. However, this should be necessary only in movies where audio quality is of utmost importance. For the most part, your audio will not suffer noticeably even at the "low" value of 48 kbps.

---

16 In the **Export Settings** dialog box, select the **Audiences** tab to view the audience options.

The Output option should be set to Compressed, unless you want to output a massively huge uncompressed file. (Now why go and do a thing like that?)

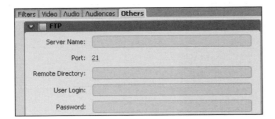

17 In the **Export Settings** dialog box, select the **Others** tab to view the other options.

In this tab, you can set up your file to automatically upload itself to an FTP (**F**ile **T**ransfer **P**rotocol) server. In addition, you can save these settings as part of a preset, so you have to specify them only once.

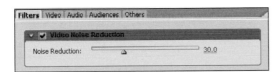

18 In the **Export Settings** dialog box, select the **Filters** tab to view the filter options. Click the **Video Noise Reduction** check box to turn on noise reduction, and if necessary, drag the slider value to **30.0**.

The noise reduction adds a heavy blur (of sorts) to the Output preview area. The idea behind noise reduction is that sharp and contrasting pixels are harder to encode, which results in larger file sizes. Groups of smooth color encode to smaller sizes.

When you add noise reduction, Premiere Pro 2 attempts to eliminate video noise by smoothing out the image. Also, know that noise reduction adds a hefty amount of rendering time, so use it only if you think it's necessary.

19 In the **Export Settings** dialog box **Filters** tab, click the **Video Noise Reduction** check box to turn off noise reduction.

The last option to consider, before outputting, is whether to deinterlace. As you noticed in Exercise 3, when exporting still images, deinterlacing can prevent combing artifacts. However, deinterlacing achieves this by discarding one of the two fields—so the outputted movie doesn't have as much detail as the original. So the question remains, should you deinterlace?

As a matter of personal preference, we vote Deinterlace: Yes. After all, because video for the Web is so heavily compressed, a lot of detail is already lost in the compression stage alone. Additional detail loss because of deinterlacing is practically negligible. Plus, the upside is your frames will have smoother edges and not show combing artifacts.

Note: This is a matter of opinion—not the de facto standard.

20 In the **Export Settings** dialog box, click the timecode display, and type **12507**. (This takes you to a timecode of 00;01;25;07.) If necessary, in the **Output** tab, click the **Deinterlace** check box to turn on deinterlacing.

As shown in the illustration here, this frame of video, which has swift motion, is a good example of how deinterlacing can help. Notice the before and after previews. When deinterlacing is off (left) the woman's face and shoulder appear to be seen in double. This is because you are viewing both fields at once.

When interlacing is on (right), you don't see any such motion artifacts. If you look closely, you can see some of the fine detail in the Digital Juice logo is lost, but you may find this modest loss in detail worth the cost of deinterlacing.

Now that you have specified all of your settings, you may want to save this preset for future use.

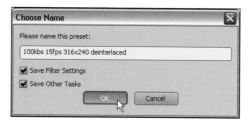

21 In the **Export Settings** dialog box, click the **Save Preset** button. In the **Choose Name** dialog box, in the **Please name this preset** field, type **100kbps 15fps 316x240 deinterlaced**. Turn on the **Save Filter Settings** and **Save Other Tasks** check boxes. Click **OK**.

It's always helpful to include the "major" values when naming a preset so you can quickly understand it later. In this case, the preset name says, "Bitrate of 100 kbps, frame rate of 15 frames per second, frame size of 316 x 240, and deinterlaced video."

Also, saving the filter settings and other tasks means Premiere Pro 2 will remember your noise reduction and FTP options.

It's finally time to export your movie!

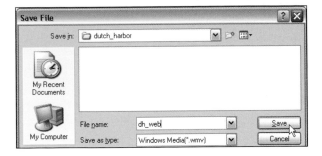
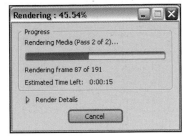

22 In the **Export Settings** dialog box, click **OK**. Navigate to **c:\exercise_files\dutch_harbor**, and in the **File name** text box, type **dh_web**. Click **Save**.

As soon as you click Save, Premiere Pro 2 begins the process of rendering. Remember, you specified a two-pass encoding process so Premiere Pro 2 will analyze the video in the first pass and then start all over again to encode on the second pass. Depending on your system, this may take upward of 5 to 10 minutes.

23 When rendering is complete, click the Windows **Start** button, and choose **Run**. In the **Open** text box, type **c:\exercise_files\ dutch_harbor**. Click **OK**. In the **Folder** dialog box, double-click **dh_web.wmv** to preview your finished movie.

While previewing, watch the picture quality and frame rate with a critical eye. Do you notice the frame rate was dropped in half? Is the picture quality acceptable at 100 kbps? Does the audio quality seem to suffer, or is it acceptable?

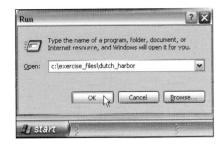

24 In Premiere Pro 2, choose **File > Save**, or press **Ctrl+S**. Choose **File > Close** to close this project.

Encoding movies for playback on the Web, CD, and other media is a highly specialized process. Entire bookshelves are dedicated to just this topic. What you have learned in this exercise are basic encoding properties and general rules of thumb. But for every rule, a reason exists for breaking the rule. Don't be afraid to venture out to try your own encoding settings.

Also, keep in mind you have just seen a single format—you can choose from another half dozen. Although some of the settings may have different names or present themselves slightly differently from format to format, the principles you learned in this exercise apply to any format.

As a disclaimer to this exercise, you should know many of the settings are based on personal opinion. One person's "acceptable audio quality of 48 kbps" is another person's "ugh—you chose *that*?" In the end, finding the right encoding value is up to you—and it can be different with each project. For a practical look at achieving the best mix of file size and quality, see the following sidebar.

NOTE:

Finding the Bitrate Sweet Spot

No magic formula will tell you the proper bitrate to use in your encoding sessions. Rather, it's all a matter of taste. Like snowflakes, no two movies export alike. Some movies have more action, and some have more static images. In addition, each audience is different. The following are some helpful tips to help you find the right blend of file size and picture quality.

Multiple Exports

In reality, the process of creating a Web movie doesn't end after the first export. Like many things in life, it's hard to get it right on the first try. Many editors will continue to export additional versions until they find the bitrate amount that is *just right*.

A popular workflow is to set a 5- to 10-second work area and continually export and reexport, fine-tuning the bitrate each time. (It's just like firing cannonballs in naval warfare. Did we lose you in that analogy? Sorry.)

To help reduce the amount of time it takes to make multiple exports, you can set the workflow to a small segment of 5 to 10 seconds. Once you find the bitrate that works best for you, then set **Range** back to **Entire Sequence**, and render the puppy.

Frame Rate Versus Picture Quality

If you're looking to save space, start with the frame rate. As mentioned previously, you can drop the frame rate by as much as half, and it may not be noticeable. Because you don't require as much data in the frame rate, this allows for the picture quality to increase while maintaining the same bitrate.

You can also free even more bitrate by reducing the frame size. This too would allow more bitrate to be dedicated toward quality picture compression. However, most editors use this as a last resort because nobody wants video the size of a postage stamp.

Working Backward from File Size

Perhaps you have an idea of the maximum file size you're willing to create. You can work backward and figure out the bitrate you should use, in kilobits per second (kbps).

For example, let's say you want a file no more than 6 MB (6,000 KB). Your movie is four minutes long (240 seconds). Quick math says that's 6000 ÷ 240 = 25 KB per second. To convert kilo*bytes* to kilo*bits*, multiply that number by 8. (There are 8 kilobits in 1 kilobyte.)

In other words, 25 x 8 = 200 kbps. If you want the audio to encode at 48 kbps, then that takes away from the total kilobits available, so you have 200 – 48 = 152 kbps remaining for the video.

Now you know to set the bitrate level at 152 and then tweak the frame rate, frame size, and other options until you find a happy compromise at this bitrate.

Lastly, you should know the **Estimated File Size** display in the bottom of the **Export Settings** dialog box is notoriously a bad judge of file size. You will actually achieve better results by doing your own math, as explained in this sidebar.

This marks an important step in your Premiere Pro 2 education. You have now taken a project from scratch all the way through exporting it to DVD, back to tape, and to the Web. Along the way you modified the project in just about every way conceivable. Thus ends your journey with Dutch Harbor Resort and Casino.

But your Premiere Pro 2 education is not yet finished. Despite knowing every nook and cranny of editing video, adding effects and transitions, and exporting in Premiere Pro 2, you haven't crossed one major frontier—capturing digital video.

In the next chapter, you will learn the proper workflow and options for capturing video from a DV camera. And because you understand the concepts of storing files on a hard drive, specifying project preferences, and setting In and Out points, the actual process of capturing will be a breeze, as you will find out in the next chapter.

14

Capturing Digital Video

When you capture video from your video camera, Adobe Premiere Pro 2 saves the video as a file on your hard drive, in a location you specify. Premiere Pro 2 gives you the ability to divide a videotape into multiple small files, which makes it easier to quickly find a specific scene. When capturing, you can provide additional information about each file you capture, such as a name, shot number, and scene number. Once the file has been saved, it is treated like any other clip you have imported in previous chapters: You tell Premiere Pro 2 where to find the file, and the project links to it. And because the captured video is saved to your hard drive like any other file, you can use the video in multiple projects—just as long as you don't delete the file from your computer. In this chapter, you will learn the workflow and options for capturing digital video and how the **Capture** panel assists you in the overall workflow of capturing video.

Understanding the Capture Workflow

Capturing is the process of transferring audio and video footage from a video camera to your computer. The audio and video captured from a video camera become a file on a hard drive, and you can import it into Premiere Pro 2 as a clip. The primary steps in the capture workflow are connecting a video camera to your computer, specifying your capture settings in the **Capture** panel, and capturing the video or audio as a file. The following sections describe each step of this process.

Connecting a Video Camera to Your Computer

The type of video camera you own defines how (and *if*) it can be connected to your computer. You have many, many formats and varieties of cameras to choose from at the consumer level, but they tend to fall into three groups. These include video cameras that can record to digital tape (miniDV, Digital8, HDV, DVCam, and DVCPro), analog tape (VHS, SVHS, and VHS-c, 8 mm, and Hi-8), and disc (DVD and memory stick).

Premiere Pro 2 is capable of communicating and transferring video directly from most video cameras that record to digital tape. This is thanks to a special type of cable that connects your camera to your computer, called IEEE-1394 (also called FireWire or i.Link). FireWire is a digital cable. The information that is sent across the cable does not degrade like analog cables. When using a FireWire cable, the image that is sent from the camera is identical to what the computer receives on the other end. Because of this, your video remains at full quality. (Analog formats can suffer degradation, known as **generation loss**, each time they are transferred over an analog cable.)

Beyond keeping your video in pristine format, FireWire has the added benefit of transferring additional device information, such as the time-code, device make and model, and so on. This means when you plug a DV (**D**igital **V**ideo) camera into your computer, Premiere Pro 2 recognizes the camera and knows how to talk with it. In addition, Premiere Pro 2 can send commands to the camera, such as rewind, fast-forward, record, play, and so on. This is called **device control** and is at the heart of the compatibility between Premiere Pro 2 and DV cameras.

To successfully capture from most digital cameras, the camera must have a FireWire port for sending video out, and the computer must have a FireWire port for receiving video in. If you have this type of setup, you need no additional hardware or software to capture video in Premiere Pro 2.

If you have a camera that records to analog tape, then you need some way to convert the analog video into digital video. This can be in the form of an **analog-to-digital converter**, which is a separate device receiving analog video from your camera and sending it out as digital video to Premiere Pro 2. Another option is to purchase an **analog capture card**, which is hardware that installs in the back of your computer and digitizes the analog video to a digital file. However, you may have to use the software that comes with the analog capture card, instead of using Premiere Pro 2 to capture the video.

If you have a camera that records to disc, such as a DVD disc or memory stick, then odds are Premiere Pro 2 cannot communicate with your camera (unless your camera has FireWire output, which is not typically found on these types of video cameras). In this case, you need to use your own method to get the video onto your computer, such as connecting via USB (**U**niversal **S**erial **B**us) or copying the files from DVD to your hard drive. Keep in mind this type of video is nonstandard and taxes Premiere Pro 2 and your computer more than standard digital video.

At the "prosumer" level, if you are using HD (**H**igh-**D**efinition) or other professional formats, then you should purchase a professional capture card, usually called an SDI (**S**erial **D**igital **I**nterface). This has special inputs to keep up with the high quality and demanding file size requirements of professional formats. Premiere Pro 2 comes with the ability to communicate with many third-party SDI cards.

Of all the formats listed previously, Premiere Pro 2 is designed to work, out of the box, with video cameras and VCRs (**V**ideo **C**assette **R**ecorders) with FireWire output. All other formats will require additional hardware or software. For a complete list of certified third-party hardware, visit the Adobe Web site.

Specifying Capture Settings in the Capture Panel

After you've verified your DV camera is properly connected and communicating with Premiere Pro 2, the next step is to use the **Capture** panel to specify capture settings, such as the playback settings during capture, capture format, capture location, and device control. You can access all these settings via the **Capture** panel. The following are descriptions of these settings:

Capture format: You can specify the format of the captured video. In the **Capture** panel **Settings** tab, click the **Edit** button to access the **Project Settings** dialog box shown in the illustration here. If you are capturing HDV (**H**igh-**D**efinition **V**ideo) footage, you can change the capture format from **DV Capture** to **HDV Capture**.

Note: The **Settings** button shown here will be displayed only if you have a DV camera or VCR turned on and connected.

Playback settings: Premiere Pro 2 lets you specify, in the **DV Capture Options** dialog box, whether you would like to watch and listen to the audio/video on your desktop (computer monitor and speakers) while previewing and during cap-

ture. The **DV Capture Options** dialog box is available only if you have a DV camera or VCR turned on and connected to your computer. You can open it via the **Capture** panel **Settings** tab by clicking the **Edit** button and clicking the **Settings** button.

It takes a little extra effort on the part of your computer to play the video on the monitor at the same time the video is captured on your hard drive. Although most computers can handle the burden without breaking a sweat, if you are experiencing performance problems during capture, these playback settings are the first place to start in order to lighten the load.

Capture locations: You can specify the location on your hard drive for the captured video. In the **Control** panel **Settings** tab, you can use the **Audio** and **Video** pop-up menus to specify the same directory as the project, the **My Documents** folder, or a custom location. If you've given your project its own directory on your hard drive, then you may find it useful to capture to the same folder as the project. This way, all your files are conveniently located in one location.

On the other hand, some editors like to keep all their projects in a "project directory" and capture all their footage to a separate "footage directory." The advantage to organizing your files in this manner is the ability to quickly find any video clip, without trying to remember which project directory it is in. In this instance, you would specify a custom capture location by clicking the **Browse** button.

By default, Premiere Pro 2 will capture to your **My Documents** folder. To be honest, this isn't ideal. For most people, the **My Documents** folder resides on their system's C drive. You'll get improved performance by capturing to a separate hard drive, other than your primary C drive. (In this book, the only reason we chose C is because it is a common location found on most computers.) For maximum performance, you should leave the application files on one hard drive and the assets (audio, video, and graphics) on a second hard drive. This can prevent bottlenecks and slow-downs because your processor can access two different hard drives simultaneously, instead of waiting for a single hard drive to do two tasks.

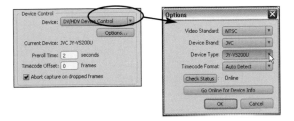

Device control: Although all digital devices use a shared language to communicate with Premiere Pro 2, each device has its own "accent." Premiere Pro 2 sometimes has to communicate slightly differently with devices from different manufacturers, for example. Luckily, Premiere Pro 2 has a wealth of knowledge about many devices and their particular quirks. The **Device Control** settings allow you to define the exact make and model of your device, so Premiere Pro 2 knows whether it needs to do anything special to compensate for known behaviors of your device. In the **Capture** panel **Settings** tab, click the **Options** button to specify the exact make and model of your digital video camera or VCR.

If your device isn't listed—don't worry. Your device is probably too new or just hasn't been certified to work with Premiere Pro 2 yet, which isn't the end of the world. Odds are it will still work; it just hasn't been put on the list yet. You may have to choose a similar device from the same manufacturer or choose a more "generic" device setting.

Once you've specified your capture settings, it's time to capture from your video camera.

Capturing Audio and Video as a File

Premiere Pro 2 allows you to capture an entire videotape as one massive file or divide the video-tape into multiple, smaller files. The advantage of capturing one big file is that you can find all the video you might use in one file. In addition, the capture process is quicker because Premiere Pro 2 doesn't need to take time to divide the videotape into smaller segments. Instead, all of the capturing can take place in one pass.

The disadvantage of capturing one big file is that a massively large file sometimes can bog down the computer. Think of it like juggling—it's easier to juggle three tennis balls than one bowling ball. In addition, if you plan to use only 3 minutes of a 60-minute tape, then you are wasting a lot of hard drive space. And finally, if you import the long clip into the **Source Monitor**, trying to find the particular 30-second segment of a 60-minute clip is the proverbial needle in a haystack.

For this reason, many editors opt to capture their videotape as multiple, smaller files. The main advantages are file size and response times. Smaller files take up much less room. (A 1-minute DV clip might be 216 MB, whereas a 1-hour DV clip could be 13,000 MB!) In addition, when you import a smaller file into a project, Premiere Pro 2 can analyze, scan, and "digest" smaller files much more quickly than large files. And lastly, if you divide the smaller file into 20 clips, then you should be able to quickly find what you are looking for because you can see each clip in your **Project** panel.

The disadvantage of capturing to smaller files is the capture process takes a bit longer. With each file, Premiere Pro 2 has to rewind, pause, play, and stop your video camera. Most would agree this is a minor nuisance when compared to the many advantages.

No matter which method you use, you must capture your file(s) in the **Capture** panel.

Working in the Capture Panel

The **Capture** panel is responsible for communicating with your DV camera or VCR. It sends commands to play, stop, rewind, and so on. The **Capture** panel provides controls, similar to those found in the **Source Monitor**, for setting **In** and **Out** points around the portions of videotape you want to capture. The **Capture** panel also lets you specify vital information about each clip, such as the tape name and clip name.

Controlling and Previewing a DV Device

The most important function of the **Capture** panel is to communicate with your DV device (camera or VCR). This allows Premiere Pro 2 to control the device so it can capture any scene by rewinding to the desired section of videotape, initiating playback, and stopping playback after saving the file to hard drive.

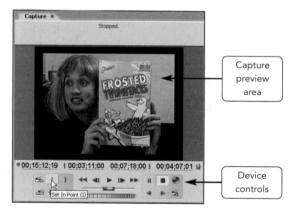

Capture preview area

Device controls

At the bottom of the **Capture** panel, you will find device controls similar to those in the **Source Monitor** and **Program Monitor**. The device controls allow you to play, pause, stop, fast-forward, and rewind your DV device. The preview area displays what is currently playing on your device. When capturing, you can either capture video on the fly, as it plays, or use **In** and **Out** points.

Capturing on the fly is the most basic method for capturing. First, you begin playback by clicking the **Play** button. During playback, if you see a section of video you want to capture, click the **Record** button. When you want to stop capturing, click the **Stop** button.

The downside of capturing on the fly is you may be a little "slow on the draw" when clicking the **Record** button. By the time you get around to recording, the vital part of the clip may have already passed.

Capturing with **In** and **Out** points is a more methodical approach to capturing. Just as you set **In** and **Out** points in the **Source Monitor**, you can set **Media In** and **Media Out** points on the videotape. These points aren't really put *on the videotape*, but Premiere Pro 2 mentally records the position of each **Media In** and **Media Out** point. When you tell Premiere Pro 2 to capture the video, it rewinds the camera to the **Media In** point and stops capturing after it reaches the **Media Out** point.

The advantage is you can continuously revise your **In** and **Out** points until you are ready to capture. The disadvantage is the process of capturing can take longer because you have to watch the video while you set your points, and then you have to watch it again as Premiere Pro 2 rewinds and captures.

Specifying Clip Data

Each time you capture a clip, Premiere Pro 2 asks you to provide information about the clip. At a minimum, you must name your clip so Premiere Pro 2 knows what to call the file when it stores it on your hard drive. The name you provide is the name of the file. For example, a name of **Josie First Birthday** will result in the file name **Josie First Birthday.avi**.

In addition to the clip name, Premiere Pro 2 allows you to provide more information, as shown in the illustration here. Although these other categories of data are not required, it is *highly* recommended you always include a tape name so you can recapture the video if the file is accidentally (or purposefully) deleted from your computer.

For example, when you try to recapture the clip, Premiere Pro 2 will prompt you, "Please insert tape: Holland Vacation Apr 28th." If you don't include a tape name, Premiere Pro 2 will say, "Please insert tape." Uh-oh, which tape? You may find yourself a year from now sifting through a shoebox of miniDV tapes trying to remember what day Jacob fell in the canal. (Don't worry; he made it out OK.)

As a bonus, when you include any of this additional information, Premiere Pro 2 stores it with the file. You can view the clip's data in Adobe Bridge. In addition, you can use Adobe Bridge to search for any word in the clip data. The more verbose you are when adding clip data, the easier it will be to search and find a clip a year from now.

In the next exercise, you will learn how to use all the functions of the **Control** panel and see how they fit into the overall workflow of successfully capturing digital video.

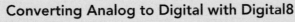

NOTE:

Converting Analog to Digital with Digital8

Unlike digital video, which can communicate with the existing hardware on your computer, analog video requires additional hardware in order to be captured by Premiere Pro 2. As described previously, this can be in the form of an external analog-to-digital converter or an analog capture card installed in your computer. However, one more device warrants consideration when converting analog to digital: the Sony Digital8 (D8) video camera. This marvelous little invention records in digital format, but it records to your standard, run-of-the-mill 8 mm or Hi8 tape. Even better, D8 video cameras output to FireWire.

Not impressed, you say? Consider this: Perhaps you have some old Hi8 or 8 mm tapes lying around the house. You can purchase an inexpensive Sony D8 camcorder to use exclusively as a VCR. Truth be told, the camera recording quality is only so-so, but this has no effect on the playback quality of existing tapes, so your tapes are transferred at their original quality.

With D8 video cameras, you can transfer your old analog tapes digitally with all the advantages of FireWire: complete device control and lossless quality. And best of all, it doesn't require any additional hardware; as far as Premiere Pro 2 is concerned, it's 100 percent real digital video. If you are migrating from Hi8/8 mm to DV, these D8 camcorders make excellent additions to your video-editing gear.

One caveat: When D8 cameras first came out, all were capable of playing analog tapes and sending them out digitally via FireWire. However, in recent years, Sony has segmented their D8 cameras. Now, only *some* can play analog tapes. If you're shopping for a D8 camera as an inexpensive analog-to-digital converter, make sure you get a model with analog playback.

1 | Preparing for Capture

Before you begin capturing from your DV device, you must first verify Premiere Pro 2 and your device are communicating properly. You must also decide where to save the files on your hard drive. After you address these two issues, you can begin capturing. In this exercise, you will specify your capture locations and device capture properties so Premiere Pro 2 knows what type of video camera or VCR you are using and can communicate properly.

Note: To have access to some of the settings and dialog boxes shown in this exercise, you will need to have a DV device (camera or VCR) available.

---

1 Connect a DV device to your computer via the FireWire port. Make sure your camcorder is in **Playback/VCR/VTR** mode. (Different brands use different naming conventions.) Insert a tape—one with existing footage you can capture—into your device.

Tip: Use an AC power adapter for a DV camera when capturing. This should prevent the camera from going into a "standby" or "sleep" mode, as well as prevent the battery from running out in the middle of a capture.

---

2 If the Windows XP **Digital Video Device** dialog box appears, select **Edit and Record Video using Adobe Premiere Pro**, and click **OK** to launch Premiere Pro 2 automatically. If the dialog box does not appear, launch Premiere Pro 2 manually.

Note: If this dialog box does not appear, do not worry. Your system may be configured so this dialog box is deactivated.

3 On the **Welcome Screen**, click **New Project**.

4 In the **New Project** dialog box, choose the preset matching the format of the source video you will capture.

Here's a tip you haven't heard in a while: When creating a new project in Premiere Pro 2, you should choose the preset matching the format of the video you are going to capture. For many of you, this will be the same as the format of the DV device. For others with more advanced video cameras, you will have to choose between standard and widescreen formats. The preset tells Premiere Pro 2 what type of video to expect and how to properly set up the project settings.

5 In the **New Project** dialog box, click the **Browse** button, and navigate to the **c:\exercise_files\chap_14** folder. In the **Name** text box, type **exercise01**, and click **OK**.

Note: If you are feeling adventurous, you can choose your own location. For example, if you have a second hard drive just for capturing, feel free to specify that location.

6 Choose **File > Capture**.

Tip: If you see the word Stopped at the top of the Capture panel, this is a good indication Premiere Pro 2 has already detected and communicated with your DV device. In this case, the device is reporting to Premiere Pro 2 that playback is stopped. If you don't see this indicator, it can be a sign your computer is having some hardware issues and Premiere Pro 2 cannot "find" the attached FireWire device.

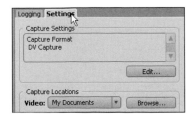

7 In the **Capture** panel, select the **Settings** tab to bring the settings to the foreground.

You can tackle the Settings tab of the Capture panel by working from the top down. The first setting is to make sure the capture settings are correct. These tell Premiere Pro 2 what type of video to expect, such as DV or HDV.

8 In the **Capture** panel, click the **Edit** button. In the **Project Settings** dialog box, make sure the **Capture Format** pop-up menu correctly lists your type of device.

You can find these settings at the project level; the project preset you chose specifies these settings. Ideally, they should already be correct.

Note: The Settings button shown in the illustration here will be visible only if you have a DV camera or VCR attached.

9 In the **Project Settings** dialog box, click the **Settings** button. In the **DV Capture Options** dialog box, make sure all **During Preview** and **During Capture** check boxes are turned on. Click **OK**.

This ensures you will be able to see and hear the video and audio on your desktop (computer monitor and speakers) while playing and capturing from the video camera. If you experience problems while capturing, such as stuttering video, you should consider turning off these previews.

---

10 In the **Project Settings** dialog box, click **OK** to return to the **Capture** panel.

The next item in the Settings tab you should specify is the capture location. This determines where on your hard drive the captured files are saved.

11 In the **Capture** panel, make sure the **Video** and **Audio** pop-up menus are set to **Same as Project**.

If you would like to specify your own capture location, click the Browse button, and choose the location. As described previously in this chapter, capturing to your My Documents folder is not recommended.

Note: For video captured from a DV device, the audio and video are stored in the same file. For DV files, specifying a different audio location has no effect. The video location will be used when saving the file.

Last, you should make sure Premiere Pro 2 is speaking the right language with your DV device; you can do this by specifying the device control. This determines what commands Premiere Pro 2 sends to your device to control playback, rewind, and so on.

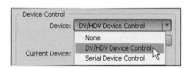

12 In the **Capture** panel, make sure the **Device** pop-up menu correctly lists your type of DV device.

13 In the **Capture** panel, click the **Options** button. In the **Options** dialog box, use each of the pop-up menus to select your device video standard, brand, and type. If your device type isn't listed, choose the closest model available. Click **OK**.

Your options may differ from those shown in the illustration here.

Tip: For up-to-date information on approved devices, click the Go Online for Device Info button. This opens a browser that takes you to the Adobe Premiere Pro 2 Third-Party Hardware Compatibility Web page.

14 In the **Capture** panel, turn on the **Abort capture on dropped frames** check box.

When the hard drive is having a hard time keeping up with the video streaming in from the DV device, sometimes an occasional frame will be "forgotten" or skipped—this is called a **dropped frame**.

When the Abort capture on dropped frames check box is turned on, Premiere Pro 2 will abort the capture process if it detects a frame was dropped. No file will be saved to disk, and you will be notified.

Depending on the demands of the project, some editors are willing to leave this check box turned off. After all, 1 frame in 30 may not be noticeable to the human eye. When this check box is turned off, Premiere Pro 2 will continue to capture but will notify you at the end of any problems. The file will be saved to your hard drive.

With all the available settings now specified, your DV device should be communicating with Premiere Pro 2. To verify, you can try using the device controls in the Capture panel and see whether your DV device responds accordingly.

15 At the bottom of the **Capture** panel, click **Play** to begin playback of your DV device.

Ideally, your device should start playing, and you should see a smooth preview in the Capture panel.

16 While the DV device is playing, click the **Fast-Forward** button, and then click the **Rewind** button to verify you are able to properly control these functions from within Premiere Pro 2.

17 At the bottom of the **Capture** panel, click **Stop** to stop playback of your DV device.

Tip: Some DV cameras and VCRs will have their life spans significantly reduced when paused for long periods of time because the recording heads will be engaged too long. However, some of the "pro-sumer" DV devices come with mechanisms that disengage the recording heads during extended pause modes—which doesn't reduce the life span of the device. When in doubt, don't pause for a long time.

18 In the **Capture** panel, click the **Close** box.

---

19 Choose **File > Save**, or press **Ctrl+S**. Leave **exercise01.prproj** open for the next exercise.

This exercise was all about making sure Premiere Pro 2 is properly communicating with your DV device and making sure you are saving captured files to the chosen location. These settings are stored with the project. You will have to do this only once per project. If you create a new project, you will have to specify the settings again. However, Premiere Pro 2 tends to remember a few of the important settings, such as your DV device make and model.

You have properly specified all your capture settings. The next step is to preview and capture video and audio from your DV device.

NOTE:

Why Have a Dedicated Drive?

What's the big deal about having an extra hard drive? Why not just capture to the **My Documents** folder on your main hard drive?

For starters, capturing and playing digital video taxes your hard drive quite heavily. (You try displaying 30 still images per second for hours at a time and see how well you do!) However, while capturing, your operating system may need to access Premiere Pro 2 program files or other system files. This can cause a data bottleneck because Premiere Pro 2 is trying to save large digital video files to the same drive the operating system is trying to access. Picture the Three Stooges getting stuck in a doorway.

A second hard drive, dedicated exclusively for audio and video storage, allows Premiere Pro 2 to capture without being interrupted by the operating system processes. This can result in fewer (or zero) frames dropped during capture and much smoother performance.

Another advantage of having a second hard drive is data security. If your primary hard drive (knock on wood) ever crashes, your data on the second drive should not be affected. Sure, reinstalling the Windows operating system is tantamount to oral surgery without anesthesia, but at least you won't lose hours and hours of Premiere Pro 2 projects.

Yet another advantage is that storage drives tend to be much larger than system drives. And keep in mind hard drives will perform slower as they get full. So filling up your primary drive with video affects not only video playback performance but also all files and applications on that hard drive. (And you don't want to be put in the unenviable position of deciding which application you need to remove from your system because you don't have room to capture Josie's pony-riding lessons.)

Don't despair if you have only one drive. With today's technology, a single, reasonably fast hard drive may have no noticeable problems during video capture. When you're ready to take your editing system to the next level, a second hard drive is a must.

2 | Capturing Video and Audio

Capturing is the process of transferring audio and video from a DV camera or VCR and saving the footage as a file on your hard drive. Premiere Pro 2 provides a few different methods for capturing. You can record video on the fly, as your DV device plays. This is similar to hitting the **Record** button on your home VCR while watching television. The capture starts when you hit **Record** and stops when you hit **Stop**. The DV device doesn't pause or wait. It just keeps playing. A second method for capturing is to specify **Media In** and **Media Out** points. Premiere Pro 2 then communicates with your DV device to rewind the tape and capture only the section of video you have specified. In this exercise, you will get to experience both capture methods.

---

1 If you followed the previous exercise, **exercise01.prproj** should still be open in Premiere Pro 2. If it's not, click **Open Project** on the **Welcome Screen**. Navigate to **c:\exercise_files\chap_14** folder, click **exercise01.prproj** to select it, and click **Open**.

Note: The project file exercise01.prproj will exist only if you followed the previous exercise because the project settings need to be tailored to your format of video camera. If you skipped Exercise 1, go back and perform at least Steps 1 through 5 in order to create a new project.

---

2 If necessary, choose **File > Capture** to open the **Capture** panel.

The easiest way to capture video and audio is to record on the fly. As your DV device plays, click the Record button when you see something you want to capture. When you're done, click the Stop button.

3 In the **Capture** panel, click **Play** to play the DV device.

4 As the DV device plays, click the **Record** button to begin the recording process.

As the media is captured to your hard drive, the Capture panel displays information about the capture, such as the duration, number of dropped frames, and remaining disk space.

---

5 To stop capturing, click the **Stop** button, or press the **Esc** key.

As soon as you stop capturing, Premiere Pro 2 displays the Save Captured Clip dialog box. This is where you can name the clip and include additional information.

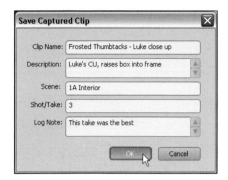

6 In the **Save Captured Clip** dialog box, type an appropriate name in the **Clip Name** text box. Click **OK**.

If you would like to supply additional information, feel free to do so. This information is also stored with the clip and can be used for searching in Adobe Bridge.

7 In the **Capture** panel, click the **Close** box.

Not only is the file saved to your hard drive, but Premiere Pro 2 also imports the clip into your project. This clip in the Project panel is now a movie clip like any other you've used. Even though the clip was imported into this project, you can still use it in any other project, as long as you remember where the file is saved.

Well, that was almost *too* easy. Capturing video and audio on the fly is extremely simple. In the next series of steps, you will learn how to specify Media In and Media Out points.

8 Choose **File > Capture**.

Specifying Media In and Out points is like specifying In and Out points in the Source Monitor. Set the Media In point, set the Media Out point, and then tell Premiere Pro 2 to rewind and capture it.

9 In the **Capture** panel, click **Play** to play the DV device.

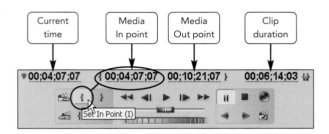

Current time | Media In point | Media Out point | Clip duration

▼00;04;07;07 { 00;04;07;07 } 00;10;21;07 } 00;06;14;03

Set In Point (I)

10 When you see the frame of video you want to start capturing, click the **Set In Point (I)** button.

We have a few issues to point out here: First, nothing is being recorded yet, and the video does not stop playing. You can continue to update your Media In point by clicking the button again and again as the DV device plays. Also notice the Media In timecode displays the timecode of the videotape at the time you click the Set In Point button.

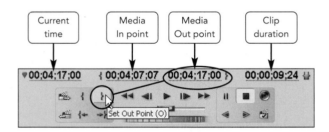

Current time | Media In point | Media Out point | Clip duration

▼00;04;17;00 { 00;04;07;07 00;04;17;00 } 00;00;09;24

Set Out Point (O)

11 When you see the frame of video where you want to stop capturing, click the **Set Out Point (O)** button.

This time, the Media Out timecode displays the timecode at the time you click the Set Out Point button. Also, notice the In to Out duration, as shown in the illustration here, is 00;00;09;24.

One of the advantages of using the Set In Point (I) and Set Out Point (O) buttons is nothing has been captured to tape yet. You've specified only the points you'd like to capture. This gives you the added bonus of being able to update the Media In or Out points before you capture.

For example, let's say you clicked the Set In Point (I) button 1 second too late. Instead of rewinding and clicking the Set In Point (I) button again, you can click and drag the Media In timecode wherever you want.

12 Position your cursor over the **Media In** timecode, and click and drag it 30 frames to the left.

Just like the other timecodes throughout Premiere Pro 2, you can click and drag, or you can click the text and type a new value such as −30 to set the Media In point 30 frames to the left. As shown in the illustration here, notice the In to Out duration is now 00;00;10;24.

13 In the **Logging** tab of the **Capture** panel, click the **In/Out** button to capture the Media In to Media Out duration.

If Premiere Pro 2 and your DV device are communicating properly, Premiere Pro 2 should automatically rewind your videotape to the Media In point and handle all the functions of starting and stopping playback. When the clip is captured successfully, Premiere Pro 2 will ask you to name the clip.

14 In the **Save Captured Clip** dialog box, type an appropriate name in the **Clip Name** text box. Click **OK**.

If you can see the Project panel (behind the floating Capture panel), you will notice the second clip has been imported into the project.

Premiere Pro 2 has **frame-accurate** DV device control, which means the clip you just captured starts on the exact frame you specified and ends on the exact frame you specified. This means you can recapture this clip 10 years from now, and the result will be an exact duplicate, down to 1/30 of a second (unless we have hologram cameras by then).

15 In the **Capture** panel, click the **Close** box.

---

16 Choose **File > Save**, or press **Ctrl+S**. Leave **exercise01.prproj** open for the next exercise.

You just learned the two quickest methods for capturing video and audio in Premiere Pro 2. No matter which method you choose, the result is the same: a file on your hard drive and a clip in your Project panel.

So far, all of the capturing you have done has been one clip at a time. In other words, you tell Premiere Pro 2 to capture one clip, and it does. You then specify the next clip, and it does. And so on. However, you can use another method of capturing called **batch capturing**, which will capture as many clips as you'd like in one session. You set the ball rolling and walk away. When you return, all the clips you requested will be imported into your Project panel. You will learn how to do this in the next exercise.

NOTE:

Learning to Live with the DV Video File Size

Here's an often-asked question: "I don't have 13 GB of hard drive space, so can I capture my DV video at a lower setting, or a smaller size, to fit more on my hard drive?" Here's the short answer: No, you can't.

Here's the long answer: No, you *really* can't.

In Chapter 12, *"Authoring DVDs,"* you learned you can resize MPEG-2 files for DVD based on bitrate and quality; lowering the bitrate results in a smaller file size, which saves hard drive space.

Unfortunately, digital video is not nearly as flexible. Video captured via FireWire can be captured at one size and one size only. There's no compromising with digital video. You must capture it at its best quality and its maximum size. The advantage of capturing digital video is its ease because you never have to specify any quality settings. The disadvantage is its inflexibility; if you're low on hard drive space, you're out of luck.

Understanding Batch Capture

Instead of capturing one clip at a time, **batch capturing** allows you to capture many clips—as many as you'd like—in one session. For example, perhaps you want to capture 20 scenes. You specify each of the 20 scenes you want, and then you tell Premiere Pro 2 to start capturing. You can walk away and go have lunch. When you return, you will have 20 new clips sitting in your **Project** panel, ready to edit. To batch capture media from your DV device, you must log your clips.

Understanding How to Log Clips

Logging is the process of reviewing your videotape and specifying which portions of the tape you'd like to capture. Logging creates a list of clips you plan to capture. These clips, known as **offline clips**, are added to the **Project** panel, but they contain no video or audio. They are just placeholders, specifying which clips you plan to capture. Once you have finished logging all your clips, you can select them all—or just select the ones you want to capture—and batch capture them all at once.

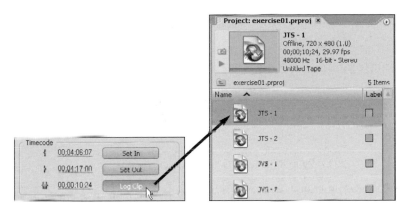

When logging in Premiere Pro 2, you set **Media In** and **Media Out** points, but instead of capturing them right away, you click the **Log Clip** button in the **Capture** panel. This logs them to the **Project** panel and creates an offline clip, representing the clip to be captured, as shown in the illustration here. The offline clip stores every bit of information you provided about the clip, such as clip name, tape name, shot/take, description, and so on. The offline clip is stored in the **Project** panel until you are ready to batch capture the clips and magically turn them into real, living clips (just like Pinocchio!).

If you change your mind about any clips you've logged, you can simply delete them in the **Project** panel, and they will not be captured. In addition, you can choose to batch capture all the clips or select only the clips you want to capture at this time.

In the next exercise, you will log several clips and then batch capture them all at once.

3 | Logging Clips for Batch Capture

Logging lets you specify clips you plan to capture at a later point. This allows you to sift through an entire tape and decide which takes you want to use. For example, instead of capturing all three takes of a scene, you can log each one but then capture only the best one. In addition, instead of waiting for the capture, you can log an entire clip and then begin the process of batch capturing. All the clips will be batch captured in one session, without you having to micromanage the process, so to speak. When you return, all your offline log clips should be online clips, ready to edit. In this exercise, you will learn how to log clips from tape and batch capture them all at once.

---

1 If you followed the previous exercise, **exercise01.prproj** should still be open in Premiere Pro 2. If it's not, click **Open Project** on the **Welcome Screen**. Navigate to the **c:\exercise_files\chap_14** folder, click **exercise01.prproj** to select it, and click **Open**.

Note: The project file exercise01.prproj will exist only if you followed Exercise 1 because the project settings need to be tailored to your video camera's format. If you skipped Exercise 1, go back and perform at least Steps 1 through 5 to create a new project.

---

2 Choose **File > New > Bin**. When the **Bin** appears in the **Project** panel, type **Captured Clips** to name the clip.

---

3 If necessary, choose **File > Capture** to open the **Capture** panel.

In the Capture panel, before capturing or logging, you can specify whether you would like your captured clips placed in a bin. You do this by using the Logging tab.

---

4 In the **Capture** panel, select the **Logging** tab to bring it to the foreground. In the **Log Clips To** box, choose the **Captured Clips** bin.

All the clips you log/capture will be placed in the Captured Clips bin.

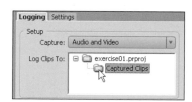

Before you begin logging, you should first specify a tape name. This is especially helpful if you plan to log multiple times at once. When capturing, Premiere Pro 2 will prompt you to put in a specific tape. All logged clips from that tape will be captured. Then, you will be prompted to enter the next tape, and so on.

Even if you plan to batch capture only one tape, typing a tape name is still vital, so you can quickly find the tape a year from now if you need to recapture the clip.

5 In the **Capture** panel **Tape Name** text box, type an appropriate name for the tape you will be logging.

Ideally, the tape name you choose should match what is written on the outside of the tape or its cassette case. This way, in a year from now, when Premiere Pro 2 says, "Please insert tape: Chili Pepsi," there will be no guessing as to which tape you need to use.

---

6 In the **Capture** panel, click the **Play** button to play your DV device.

To log your clips, you must first specify a Media In and Media Out point for each clip.

7 In the **Capture** panel, during playback, click the **Set In** button.

The Set In and Set Out buttons in the Logging tab are the same as the Set In Point and Set Out Point buttons you used in the previous exercise. The main advantage is they are closer to the Log Clip button.

8 In the **Capture** panel, during playback, click the **Set Out** button.

9 In the **Capture** panel, during playback, click the **Log Clip** button.

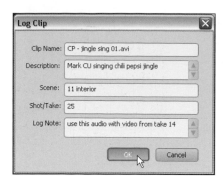

10 In the **Log Clip** dialog box, in the **Clip Name** text box, type a name, and then include any additional information you would like stored with the file. Click **OK**.

As soon as you click OK, an offline clip appears in the selected bin. You can now continue to log your next clips.

---

11 While the videotape plays, click the **Set In** button. At the end of the desired scene, click the **Set Out** button. Click the **Log Clip** button. In the **Log Clip** dialog box, type an appropriate name in the **Clip Name** text box. Repeat this step for as many clips as you would like to log from the current tape.

We have two important points to make here: First, as you name and provide additional information about the clip, Premiere Pro 2 *pauses* playback. This allows you to take as long as you need (for you slow typers) so you don't miss any crucial video while entering clip data.

Second, as soon as you finish typing clip data, Premiere Pro 2 automatically starts playback again (on most DV devices). This prevents you from having to start and stop yourself. The only mouse clicks you need to worry about are the In, Out, and Log buttons.

When you are done logging, you must return to the Project panel to issue the Batch Capture command. Even though this takes you right back to the Capture panel, you must first select the clips, in the Project panel, that you want to batch.

---

12 In the **Capture** panel, click the **Close** box.

13 In the **Project** panel **Captured Clips** bin, hold down the **Ctrl** key and click each clip you would like to batch capture to select the files.

Tip: You can also hold down the Shift key to select the range of clips you would like to capture.

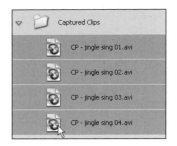

14 With the clips still selected, choose **File > Batch Capture**.

This opens the Batch Capture dialog box. Before capture begins, Premiere Pro 2 asks you whether you want to capture your video with handles of extra frames. For example, if you specified 30, Premiere Pro 2 would capture an extra 30 frames before each clip and an extra 30 frames after each clip. This is helpful if you are afraid you missed vital video at the beginning or end of each clip. In this case, you will leave the Capture with handles check box turned off.

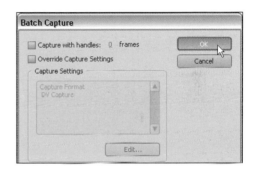

Premiere Pro 2 also asks you whether you want to override the capture settings and choose your own. Because you spent so much time in the Settings tab, this isn't required for this project. However, this feature is useful when you are working in a nonstandard project (like 320 x 240 pixels) and you want to capture DV video in 720 x 480 pixels. You can override the project's capture format and choose the DV capture format.

15 In the **Batch Capture** dialog box, click **OK**.

Premiere Pro 2 will next prompt you to insert the tape. In this case, there's only one tape, and it's probably already inserted in your DV device.

16 If the capture tape is not inserted in the DV device, insert it now. Click **OK**.

As soon as you click OK, Premiere Pro 2 rewinds the camera (or fast-forwards, depending on the position of the logged clips) and captures each clip one at a time. You don't have to do anything between each capture. When the batch capture is finished, Premiere Pro 2 displays a prompt.

17 In the **Batch Capture** dialog box, click **OK**.

18 In the **Capture** panel, click the **Close** box.

In the Project panel, each offline clip is turned into an online video and audio clip. These clips are now ready for editing.

19 Choose **File > Save**, or press **Ctrl+S**. Leave **exercise01.prproj** open for the next exercise.

Batch capturing allows you to plan ahead and decide exactly which clips you want to capture—and which ones you don't—by logging an entire tape (or, as much of a tape as you feel like logging). Even though batch capturing requires more work up front, in the long run, you will see a net gain in the time saved. After all, you don't have to wait around while clips capture.

Here's a useful tip: Some users report problems with batch capture when they have their screensavers turned on. It's a good idea to disable your screensaver when either capturing from or exporting to DV devices in Premiere Pro 2.

As if batch capture wasn't helpful enough, Premiere Pro 2 provides one last method for capturing video, called scene detection. This is like batch capture, but instead of *you* logging clips, Premiere Pro 2 analyzes your tape and does it for you.

Using Automatic Scene Detection

The last method of capturing in Premiere Pro 2 you have yet to learn is scene detection. When the **Scene Detect** check box is turned on, Premiere Pro 2 plays back your entire videotape and records each scene as a different clip. If you have 30 scenes on a videotape, that's 30 different clips saved to your hard drive and imported into your project.

Instead of manually logging **In** and **Out** points, you can use the scene detection feature to do this for you. Premiere Pro 2 analyzes the video for scene breaks as indicated by the tape's time/date stamp. The **time/date stamp** is the date and time the video was recorded on tape. Virtually all video cameras have a time/date stamp feature. Normally, this information is hidden to the editors, but Premiere Pro 2 can read in the data via FireWire.

Here's how it works: Every time you begin recording footage on DV tape, the video camera remembers the date and time you started recording—down to the second. Premiere Pro 2 scans the videotape and detects each instance of discontinuity in the time stamp.

For example, say you stopped recording a scene at 3:11 p.m. You fixed the actor's microphone and then started recording again at 3:14 p.m. Premiere Pro 2 realizes the time/date stamp has a gap and interprets this as a new scene. Basically, each time you pause or stop the video camera, Premiere Pro 2 creates a new scene. However, if you keep the video camera rolling and shoot a new scene without stopping or pausing the video camera, Premiere Pro 2 cannot discern this as a unique scene because there is no gap in the time/date stamp.

In the next exercise, you will discover the luxury of batch capturing with scene detection.

Oh, sure, you thought batch capturing was pretty easy. But that required you to log your own clips. If you aren't picky about the scenes you capture and if you have plenty of hard drive space, consider capturing with scene detection. Premiere Pro 2 automatically analyzes your tape as it plays. Each time it finds a break in the time/date stamp, it knows you must have paused or stopped the camera. It then logs and captures this to a new file on your hard drive and imports it as a clip in your project. Scene detection works whether you are capturing an entire tape or just a section between specific **In** and **Out** points. In this exercise, you will use scene detection to automate the batch-capture process.

Note: Scene detection may work only if you've specified the date and time of your camera. (Otherwise, the camera won't "stamp" the video since it doesn't know the date or time.)

---

1 If you followed the previous exercise, **exercise01.prproj** should still be open in Premiere Pro 2. If it's not, click **Open Project** on the **Welcome Screen**. Navigate to **c:\exercise_files\chap_14** folder, click **exercise01.prproj** to select it, and click **Open**.

Note: The project file exercise01.prproj will exist only if you followed Exercise 1 because the project settings need to be tailored to your format of video camera. If you skipped Exercise 1, go back and perform at least steps 1 through 5 to create a new project.

---

2 If necessary, choose **File > Capture** to open the **Capture** panel.

3 In the **Logging** tab of the **Capture** panel, turn on the **Scene Detect** check box.

Before using scene detection, just like every other capture method, you should first specify your tape name and, in this case, a generic clip name.

---

4 In the **Capture** panel **Tape Name** text box, type an appropriate name for the tape you are about to capture. In the **Clip Name** text box, type a generic tape name.

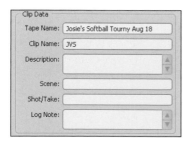

When using scene detection, you will not be given the opportunity to name each clip, so it's best to use a generic name. In addition, Premiere Pro 2 will append consecutive numbers to the end of each clip name—such as My Clip 01, My Clip 02, My Clip 03, and so on.

Now it is time to use scene detection to capture video from your camera. If you want to use scene detection to automatically log and capture a specific section of the videotape, you should first Set In and Set Out points around the desired section of tape.

On the other hand, if you want to use scene detection to capture the entire tape, you can do this with the click of a single button: Tape. When you click the Tape button, Premiere Pro 2 starts capturing at the current tape position. If you want to start at the beginning of the tape, it's up to you to rewind to the start of the tape.

5 In the **Capture** panel, click the **Tape** button.

Premiere Pro 2 will rewind to the beginning of the tape. As it plays, it automatically turns each detected scene into a separate clip in the Project panel.

6 To stop scene detection, click the **Stop** button, or press the **Esc** key.

7 In the **Project** panel, click the **Close** box.

Each detected scene is now shown as a clip in your Project panel. Just like the other clips you've captured, they are ready to be edited.

8 Choose **File > Save**, or press **Ctrl+S**. Choose **File > Close** to close this project.

Using scene detection can be a huge timesaving device. Rather than logging each clip yourself, Premiere Pro 2 does all this work for you. The downside is you do not get an opportunity to specify clip data customized to each clip. Also, scene detection will continue until it reaches the end of the tape, which requires ample hard drive space, or until you tell it to stop.

Congratulations! You have now learned the basics of every function of Premiere Pro 2—from capture to export, there's not a task you haven't learned to accomplish. However, just because you have the finished DVD in your hands, or you've given the tape to the client, doesn't mean you are done. As you learned in kindergarten, you have to be sure to put away your toys when you're done playing with them. In the grown-up realm of video editing, this includes properly storing and archiving your projects so you can edit them in the future while freeing up valuable hard drive space. In the next chapter, you'll learn all about the thrill-a-minute world of project archiving.

15

Archiving Projects

Even though you've taken your project from conception all the way through export, your journey is not quite complete. You still have to decide how—if at all—you would like to save the project for future use; this is called **archiving**, and it is the last phase of the production process. The goal of archiving is to back up projects and source clips for editing at a later time while maintaining the highest-quality possible. If you don't plan to edit your project again, you can delete the media files and free up the hard drive space for your next project. However, many editors, especially corporate, broadcast, and wedding videographers, need to keep their projects indefinitely, just in case the client requests another copy or wants to make changes later. Proper archiving will ensure maximum quality, efficient media storage, and the ability to re-create a project with ease. In this chapter, you will learn the different archiving options and how your archive method affects the hard drive space or disc space required.

Understanding Archiving

Archiving refers to the process of storing your files for long durations, with the express purpose of being able to reuse them later. The goal of archiving is to store your project and media files in a format that allows you to quickly create them again without having to compromise quality and that takes up as little hard drive space as possible.

Why bother archiving? When you complete a project, you have two options for the original files on your hard drive: You can delete them, or you can store them for future use.

"Nah, I'll never need this project again." If you delete all the files on your hard drive, you free up lots of hard drive space. However, when the president of Local Business Incorporated calls you a year from now and asks you to replace their old logo with their new logo, you cannot re-create the project. You have deleted all the files, so you'll have to start from scratch.

"I'll keep the project on my hard drive, along with all the files, and never get rid of it." If you save every file on your hard drive, you'll be able to quickly open and make changes to the original project at any point later. But this ties up valuable hard drive space.

For many editors, this is quite a conundrum, and it highlights the importance of archiving. Sure, both solutions described are legitimate; nothing is wrong with deleting your projects, and nothing is wrong with storing them on your hard drive in perpetuity. But both methods are dangerous—after all, what if you *do* need to edit that deleted project again? Or what if your hard drive crashes, and that project you've been storing for 5 years is gone forever?

Properly managing projects and the files needed to re-create those projects provides the best of both worlds: efficient and minimum use of hard drive space with the ability to reedit a project 10 years from now.

When archiving a project, the two most important questions are, "Will it use little hard drive space?" and "Can you reedit the original project?" Three basic options are available to you for archiving projects for future use. Some methods will use zero hard drive space, and others will allow you to reedit the original project with ease. The following sections break down the advantages and disadvantages of each option.

Storing the Finished Program on DV Tape

Some editors choose to save a finished copy of their movie on DV (**D**igital **V**ideo) tape. After all, the biggest benefit of using FireWire is the ability to transfer files digitally. This means (theoretically) no loss in quality each time you transfer video to and from tape. Once the project is finished, you can export the movie to DV tape, and it will retain its original quality. If you need to reuse this movie, you can just capture it and insert it into a future project.

As shown in the illustration here, the advantage of this method is you can delete every file associated with the project after transferring it to tape. This takes up 0 MB (**M**ega**B**ytes) on your hard drive. You can't get any more efficient use of storage space than that.

The downside is you can never reedit the original project again. Do you want to remove a transition? Too bad. Do you want to change a logo or graphic?

Can't do it. The movie is like any other video on tape. The only way you can reuse the movie is to capture it like regular video, and even then you are extremely limited in what you can do to it.

You should use this option only when you are *absolutely* positive you'll never need to edit the original project again.

Storing All Files on Your Hard Drive or on DVD

If you want maximum flexibility to reedit a project quickly, then you can store the project file, and all the files with it, on your hard drive or on removable media such as DVD, an external USB (**U**niversal **S**erial **B**us) drive, and so on.

This option takes up massive amounts of hard drive space; a 1-hour project and its source video will take up at least 13 GB (about three or four standard DVDs). On the other hand, when it comes time to reedit the project, you have the original project file and every clip needed to re-create the project.

This method is best used when you have gobs of storage space or when the project is small enough to back up onto DVDs. (See the note after this section for a discussion of DVD movie discs versus DVD-ROMs.)

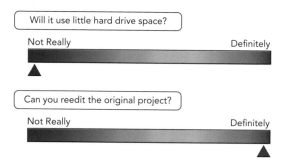

Will it use little hard drive space?

Not Really   Definitely

Can you reedit the original project?

Not Really   Definitely

NOTE:

DVD Movie Discs Versus DVD-ROMs

In this chapter, we stated that storing 1 hour of digital video requires at least three DVDs. But in Chapter 12, *"Authoring DVDs,"* you read that an hour of video could easily be exported to a single DVD. So which is it—three DVDs or one DVD?

First, it's important to understand DVDs have two different personalities. Some DVDs are turned into DVD-ROMs, and they act like mini–hard drives. Other DVDs become mini–movie players, such as the DVD movies you rent at the video store.

When you export a sequence to a DVD movie disc, the video is converted and saved as a highly compressed MPEG-2 movie, which is playable in a home DVD player. Because you've thrown away so much data in order to squeeze the sequence onto the DVD, it's not ideal for reediting in future projects.

Video files saved to a DVD-ROM are kept as computer files—stored like any other file on your hard drive. When you put a DVD-ROM into a computer DVD drive, you can see the original files and their extensions, just like you were viewing any other folder of your hard drive.

DVD-ROM files are not compressed like DVD movie discs, so they keep their original format and size. The original DV movie takes up 13 GB for 1 hour of video, so a standard 4.7 GB DVD-ROM (single-sided, single-layer) would need three discs to store all the video files.

To make a long story short, you should use DVD movie discs for delivering final playback to an audience. You should use DVD-ROMs for storing files you may want to reedit.

Storing Only the Project File, Graphics, and Audio Files

This option advocates backing up *only* the project file, graphics, and any external audio files (such as MP3 music files). So, what does this option suggest you delete? You should delete *all* your video clips captured from a DV/HDV (**H**igh-**D**efinition **V**ideo) tape. Just make sure you never erase or overwrite your tapes so you can recapture the video clips if needed later.

Because you delete all the video files and keep only a handful of tiny files, this option gets high marks for using little hard drive space. In addition, because you keep the original project and associated files, you can reedit the project at any point down the road. So this option also gets high marks for being "reeditable."

This option is a bit more sophisticated, so take a minute to consider what is included in a project file, and what is kept on the hard drive, whenever you import clips.

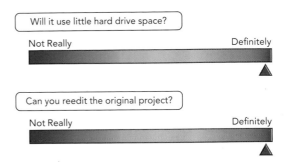

As shown in the illustration here, say you have a typical 1-hour program containing an average amount of graphics, music, and video files. As you've (we hope) learned, the items on the left are stored *inside* the project file. They exist only in the project. The total size of the project file—and all the bins, sequences, and titles—is about 5 MB, give or take a few megabytes. The items on the right reside entirely on the hard drive. The Adobe Premiere Pro 2 project file only *links* to video, audio, and graphic files.

As you can see, the video clips take up the lion's share of the storage space. In fact, all the other files and clips combined can fit on a USB drive or CD. When you delete the video files, you are freeing up 98 percent of the space required for this project.

Now you may be thinking, "Wait a minute. How can I delete *all my video files* and still be able to reedit the project?" When you capture digital video via FireWire, Premiere Pro 2 remembers the timecode of every clip. In other words, it remembers the exact starting and ending point on the tape, so it knows how to find that clip, with an accuracy of 1/30 of a second. This is true for every video transferred via FireWire. Even when you delete the video from your hard drive, Premiere Pro 2 keeps offline files as "placeholders." The original video is gone, but Premiere Pro 2 still remembers every clip you used and where on the tape each clip lived.

Preventing Timecode Breaks

A year from now, when Premiere Pro 2 tries to recapture your original clip, it does its best to find the exact spot on the tape from where the original clip came. However, if you have a break in the timecode, Premiere Pro 2 has trouble locating the clip. Here is a primer on timecode, including how to prevent breaks:

What is the timecode? A tape's timecode is similar to the timecode of the Premiere Pro 2 sequences you have been editing; the beginning is 00;00;00;00, and the end is…well, the end of the tape. (Many durations of tapes are available for purchase.) The timecode is like a map, helping Premiere Pro 2 know whether it needs to rewind or fast-forward to find the clip on the tape.

Where does the timecode come from? Nearly all tapes come *without* timecodes. The camera creates the timecode as it records video. When you push the camera's **Record** button, the camera asks itself, "Is there an existing timecode? If so, I'll continue the timecode." This is a **continuous timecode**, and it is good.

However, if the camera can't find any existing timecode, then it says, "Hmm. This must be a new tape. I'll start the timecode at 0 seconds." This is a **timecode break**, and it is bad.

Why are timecode breaks bad? Most cameras restart the timecode at 00;00;00;00 if a timecode break is detected. Let's say you have a captured video clip that resides on the tape at 00;00;03;11. If you have a timecode break, then you might have *more than one* instance of 00;00;03;11. This causes Premiere Pro 2 to get confused—which instance of 00;00;03;11 is the correct one? Odds are, it will guess wrong, and you'll end up with the wrong clip being captured.

What causes timecode breaks? Have you ever videotaped something, and then said, "Let's watch that in the camera's handy-dandy LCD monitor"? You then stop recording and play back the clip. After the clip finishes, you accidentally let the tape play too long, and it plays beyond the existing timecode.

"OK, let's try that take again. Places, everyone." When you put the camera back in record mode and hit the **Record** button, no timecode exists—because you played the tape beyond the end of the last take—and a new timecode is created. This is the most common cause of timecode breaks.

How can you prevent timecode breaks? Everyone wants to watch what they just recorded; it's human nature. If you're going to do this, here are two tips for preventing timecode breaks: First, every time you record a scene, let the camera roll for an extra 5 seconds before turning it off. This way, if you must watch what you just filmed, you have lots of padding. If you stop the camera on the existing timecode, then the camera will pick up where it left off and keep the timecode *continuous*.

Second, when you first buy a tape, you can put the camera in record mode and walk away. This is called **striping** and will ensure continuous timecode on the tape before you use it. This isn't necessary if you follow the previous tip, but it can protect you from accidentally breaking the timecode by miscuing a tape in your camera.

Armed with the project file and the original videotape(s), you can recapture every video clip in the project. Premiere Pro 2 will automatically rebuild the sequence(s) by replacing the placeholders with the real video clips. The finished product will be 100 percent identical to the original project.

This method does have some caveats: Along with the project file, you need to retain the irretrievable files. Irretrievable files are those that cannot be recaptured via FireWire or magically brought back to life once they are deleted from your hard drive.

For example, a still image you scanned from a photo album may not be easily re-creatable. You could rescan the image, but you don't have any guarantee you could re-create the same image. Odds are, the next time you scan the photograph it would be different in some respects (size, position, color, and so on). In this sense, the original photograph is irretrievable.

Other examples of irretrievable files include music and graphics. Fortunately, these types of files usually take up little space, and they can fit on a single CD or live in a small corner of your hard drive indefinitely. (That is, 20 MB on a 200,000 MB hard drive probably won't break the storage bank.)

The other caveat is you must have a continuous timecode on your DV/HDV tapes. In other words, you cannot have any breaks or gaps in the timecode—this confuses Premiere Pro 2 when trying to rewind and fast-forward the tape. What causes a break in the timecode? See the following sidebar.

To assist you in each of these methods, Premiere Pro introduces the **Project Manager**, which you'll learn how to use in the next section.

Using the Project Manager

You can use the **Project Manager** to create a new project from an existing project for the purposes of archiving the project and necessary files. When creating a new project, you are given two options in the **Project Manager**: You can copy all the necessary files to a single location, making it easy to round up all the media and create a backup on DVD, or you can create a new trimmed project, copying only the portions of the audio and video clips used in the project. You can find both of these tools in the same **Project Manager** dialog box. Depending on which option of the **Project Manager** you are using, different choices are available.

Understanding How to Create a New Trimmed Project

The first option you'll see in the **Project Manager** dialog box is **Create New Trimmed Project**. This option results in a new project file (in a destination of your choosing). However, instead of including all the video and audio clips, the new project file includes only the *used* portions of your clips. For example, if you captured a 5-minute video clip but used only 1 minute, the newly created clip will be only 1-minute long. The unused material of each clip is "trimmed off" and not copied to the new location.

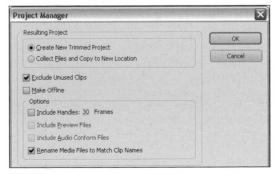

When you have **Create New Trimmed Project** selected, a few other options are available to you:

Exclude Unused Clips: This option will not make trimmed copies of any clips you are not using. In other words, if a clip is in the **Project** panel but not in a sequence, it doesn't get copied. (As a certain author's grandpappy says, "Why copy a file you ain't usin'?")

Make Offline: This option does not copy any clips captured within Premiere Pro 2, such as DV/HDV clips. Instead, Premiere Pro 2 creates an empty placeholder for each DV/HDV clip, called an **offline clip**. You can then use batch capture, as you learned in Chapter 14, *"Capturing Digital Video,"* to recapture the offline clips.

Also note, all other clips—those that can't be re-created from digital videotape—are still copied to the new location when the Make Offline check box is turned on.

Include Handles: When you create a trimmed project, Premiere Pro 2 includes only the portions of the clips you are using. However, to be safe, sometimes it's useful to add an extra second of padding before and after the clip (just in case you want to add a transition later). Including handles will add as many frames as you'd like to the beginning and end of your trimmed clips.

Rename Media Files to Match Clip Names: If you've renamed some clips in the **Project** or **Timeline** panel to help keep your sequences organized, then the newly created trimmed clips will be saved with the name you've given them, instead of their original file names.

Collecting Files and Copying Them to New Location

When you choose the **Collect Files and Copy to New Location** option in the **Project Manager** dialog box, all external clips—audio, video, and graphics—are copied to a new folder along with the project. (The title clips, as you may recall, reside inside the project file, so they too are copied with the project.) This option is useful if you plan to save all your files to removable storage, such as a DVD, external hard drive, and so on.

When you select **Collect Files and Copy to New Location**, you get a couple of other options. You get the same **Exclude Unused Clips** check box, as described previously, and you get two new options:

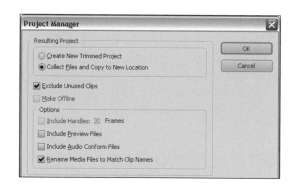

Include Preview Files: When copying the source files, you can also choose to copy the rendered files. This prevents you from having to rerender when you open the project in its new location.

Include Audio Conform Files: Similar to the previous option, this copies all the converted audio files, so you won't lose any time **conforming** (converting) them again in the new project.

The **Project Manager** is extremely simple. In the next exercise, you will learn how to create trimmed copies of all your clips.

EXERCISE

1 | Creating a Trimmed Project

A **trimmed project** reduces the storage size of the project and its linked files. When you create a trimmed project, Premiere Pro 2 copies each clip to a new location—but it copies only the portion of the clip being used. This helps reduce file size dramatically. After all, if you have no plans to use the entire source clip again, you may safely discard the portion of the clip you are not using. In this exercise, you will create a trimmed project with the **Project Manager**.

1 On the **Welcome Screen**, click **Open Project**. In the **Open Project** dialog box, navigate to the **c:\exercise_files\chap_15** folder, click **exercise01.prproj** to select it, and click **Open**.

2 Choose **File > Save As**. Navigate to the **c:\exercise_files\dutch_harbor** folder. Name the file **dutch harbor promo.prproj**, and click **Save**.

Note: If a previous version of dutch harbor promo.prproj already exists, you may be asked to replace it. Click Yes.

3 Choose **Project > Project Manager**.

4 In the **Project Manager** dialog box, select **Create New Trimmed Project**.

This option results in a new project and copies of your original clips. However, it copies only the "used" portions of any clip.

For example, if your project contains a 10-minute source clip but you are using only 1 minute of the clip in a sequence, then only the 1 minute portion of the clip will be copied. The unused remainder of the clip will be discarded. This can dramatically reduce file sizes.

5 In the **Project Manager** dialog box, turn on the **Exclude Unused Clips** check box to ignore unused clips.

This option ignores any clips not being used in a sequence. This is another feature that helps reduce the resulting file size.

6 In the **Project Manager** dialog box, turn on the **Include Handles** check box to add handles. Change the value to **30 Frames**.

This adds 30 frames to the beginning and end of any trimmed clip. For example, if your trimmed clip is only 30 seconds long, the copied version will be 32 seconds long: 1 second at the start of the clip plus the 30-second clip plus 1 second at the end of the clip.

Adding handles gives you flexibility if you need to reedit a clip or if you decide you want to add a transition at the start or end of a clip. It basically just gives you a bit more flexibility, and an extra 2 seconds won't dramatically increase the file size.

---

7 In the **Project Manager** dialog box, click the **Browse** button to change the destination of the new project and trimmed clips.

---

8 In the **Browse For Folder** dialog box, navigate to the **C** directory, and click **exercise_files** to select the folder. Click **OK**.

This copies the newly created files into a subfolder of the selected folder. When you create trimmed versions, the new subfolder name will start with the word Trimmed_ and be followed by the current project name: Trimmed_dutch harbor promo.

---

9 In the **Project Manager** dialog box, click the **Calculate** button to determine how large the resulting files will be.

Premiere Pro 2 indicates the current project takes up 1.8 GB. The new file, after trimming clips and excluding the unused clips, is 729.1 MB. This is less than half of 1.8 GB (which is the same as 1,800 MB).

---

10 In the **Project Manager** dialog box, click **OK** to copy the new clips and project file.

After you click OK, the Project Manager Progress dialog box displays a progress bar. When rendering is done, you can view the exercise_files folder to see the newly created subfolder.

---

11 Click the **Windows XP Start** button, and choose **Run**. In the **Run** dialog box, type **c:\exercise_files** in the **Open** text box to open this folder for viewing.

Tip: You can also navigate to this folder by double-clicking the My Computer icon on your Desktop.

---

12 In the **c:\exercise_files** folder, double-click the **Trimmed_dutch harbor promo** folder to view its contents.

Tip: You can also navigate to this folder by double-clicking the My Computer icon on your Desktop.

In this folder, you are able to see copies of all your clips. If you compare many of them to their original counterparts (in c:\exercise_files\media_files), you will discover the copy is much smaller because the clips have been trimmed.

Name ▲	Size	Type
coral_reef.jpg	41 KB	JPEG Image
DaReggaeMon_30.mp3	470 KB	MP3 audio file (mp3)
dutch harbor promo.prproj	1,942 KB	Adobe Premiere Pro...
Dutch Harbordutch_harbor_logo.psd	940 KB	Adobe Photoshop I...
DVD intro.wav	6,329 KB	Wave Sound
DVD map.wav	8,157 KB	Wave Sound
DVD map_001.wav	1,403 KB	Wave Sound
eruptologist.avi	53,958 KB	Video Clip
historian.avi	58,650 KB	Video Clip
historian_001.avi	48,155 KB	Video Clip

Also notice some clips, such as historian.avi and historian_001.avi, have been split into two versions. Because you were using two different sections of the original clip, Premiere Pro 2 trimmed the original into two smaller versions. The size of the two trimmed versions is still smaller than the original; in addition, if you need to recapture these clips, say, a year from now, you no longer have to capture the entire original clip. Instead, you can capture the two trimmed versions as separate clips.

---

13 In the c:\exercise_files\Trimmed_dutch harbor promo folder, double-click **dutch harbor promo.prproj** to open the newly created project.

Note: You haven't made any changes to the project you already have open in Premiere Pro 2, but if you are prompted to save changes to the old project, click No.

---

14 After the new project opens, select the **DVD history** tab at the top of the **Timeline** panel.

---

15 Drag the **Timeline CTI** (**C**urrent **T**ime **I**ndicator) to the beginning of the sequence. Press the **spacebar** to begin playback. After a few seconds of watching the video, press the **spacebar** again to stop playback.

Your newly trimmed project should be nearly identical to the original project. All the sequences, when played, should look the same. However, the primary difference, which should be transparent to you, is the project links to all the newly copied clips, instead of the old clips.

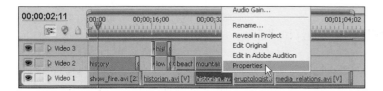

16 In the **Timeline** panel, right-click the second **historian.avi** clip on Track **Video 1**.

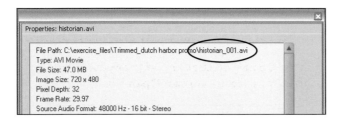

Even though the clip is still *labeled* historian.avi, behind the scenes it really points to the newly created clip called historian_001.avi in the Trimmed_dutch harbor promo folder.

This underscores that all the clips in this project are the trimmed copies. You could now delete all the original files, and this new project would not be affected. (This is just an example; don't really delete the exercise files!)

---

17 Choose **File > Save**, or press **Ctrl+S**. Choose **File > Close** to close this project.

With a trimmed version of all your clips in place, you can archive the files as described previously in this chapter. For example, you can choose to copy the trimmed project and clips to removable media, such as a CD, DVD, or USB drive.

As described previously in this chapter, the Project Manager also has the option Collect Files and Copy to New Location. This is essentially the same action you just took—but without the trimming. Collecting, rather than trimming, is useful if you think you may still use some of the unused source video. On the other hand, if your project is completely finalized and you are positive you will not need to reuse the footage, then trimming the project, as shown in this exercise, is the most efficient option.

In this exercise, the resulting files could have fit on a CD. Of course, in the real world you will be working with much larger projects. Even after trimming, the resulting trimmed project and clips will require multiple DVDs. To prevent this, you can delete the video files and keep only the project file, which is the third archiving method described previously in this chapter. The Project Manager will do this for you, if you ask it nicely. You'll learn how to do this in the next exercise.

---

2 | Making Offline Projects

What do you do if trimming the project doesn't reduce the file size enough? Perhaps you crave even more storage savings. Fortunately, the **Project Manager** has an additional feature to turn all your DV/HDV clips into offline clips. When the new project and its files are copied, Premiere Pro 2 will *not* copy any DV/HDV clips. Instead, it will create offline placeholders for these types of clips. You can then fit the resulting files on a single CD and batch capture the offline clips whenever you'd like.

---

1 On the **Welcome Screen**, click **Open Project**. In the **Open Project** dialog box, navigate to the **c:\exercise_files\chap_15** folder, click **exercise02.prproj** to select it, and click **Open**.

---

2 Choose **File > Save As**. Navigate to the **c:\exercise_files\dutch_harbor** folder. Name the file **dutch harbor promo.prproj**, and click **Save**.

Note: If a previous version of dutch harbor promo.prproj already exists, you may be asked to replace it. Click Yes.

Note: You can see this project contains only the DVD history sequence. This was the only sequence containing clips captured via a DV device.

---

3 Choose **Project > Project Manager**.

4 In the **Project Manager** dialog box, select **Create New Trimmed Project**.

This is the only option allowing you to make offline video clips.

5 In the **Project Manager** dialog box, make sure both the **Exclude Unused Clips** and **Make Offline** check boxes are turned on.

As before, this does not copy any unused clips. This creates offline placeholders out of all clips captured with device control, such as DV/HDV.

6 In the **Project Manager** dialog box, turn on the **Include Handles** check box. Change the value to **30 Frames**.

Even though the resulting video clips will be offline, when you recapture them, say, a year from now, they will be recaptured with an extra second before and after each clip.

7 In the **Project Manager** dialog box, click the **Browse** button. In the **Browse For Folder** dialog box, navigate to the **C** directory, and click the **exercise_files** folder to select it. Click **OK**.

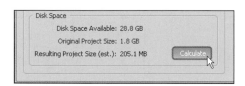

8 In the **Project Manager** dialog box, click the **Calculate** button to determine how large the resulting files will be.

Similar to the previous exercise, Premiere Pro 2 indicates the current project takes up 1.8 GB on the hard drive. However, in this exercise, the resulting project will take up only 205.1 MB. In the previous exercise, when copying the video clips, the resulting file took up 729.1 MB.

9 In the **Project Manager** dialog box, click **OK** to copy the new clips and project file.

10 Click the **Windows XP Start** button, and choose **Run**. In the **Run** dialog box, type **c:\exercise_files** in the **Open** text box. Click **OK**.

Just like the previous exercise, Premiere Pro 2 copies all the trimmed files to a folder in the c:\exercise_files folder. However, because of the folder you created in the previous exercise, Premiere Pro 2 may have renamed the new folder with a _001 suffix, such as Trimmed_dutch harbor promo_001.

---

11 In the **c:\exercise_files** folder, double-click the **Trimmed_dutch harbor promo_001** folder to view its contents.

Note: If you performed the previous exercise, then the resulting folder may be named Trimmed_dutch harbor promo.

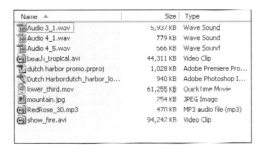

This folder contains significantly fewer files compared to the previous exercise. Instead, Premiere Pro 2 copied only the irretrievable files: audio, graphics, and non-DV clips.

---

12 In the current folder, double-click **dutch harbor promo.prproj** to open the newly created project.

Note: You haven't made any changes to the project you already have open in Premiere Pro 2, but if you are prompted to save changes to the old project, click No.

---

13 After the new project opens, in the **Timeline** panel, drag the **CTI** to the beginning of the **historian.avi** sequence. Press the **spacebar** to begin playback. After a few seconds of watching the video, press the **spacebar** again to stop playback.

During playback, you will notice the DV-captured clip of the actor speaking shows as offline in the Program Monitor. In the Project panel Video bin, you will also notice the video clips show as offline.

As shown in the illustration here, this is a prime example of which types of clips become offline and which types stay online. Notice the title text Clay Potter is still online. Also notice the pink lower third is still online. This is because these two clips didn't come from a DV device, so Premiere Pro 2 knows to keep them around.

---

14 Choose **File > Save**, or press **Ctrl+S**. Choose **File > Close** to close this project.

You can now take this project and all the newly trimmed clips and store them on a CD or leave them on your hard drive in a special archive folder.

What do you do with the original files? Delete 'em! Delete them all. When it comes time to reedit this project 10 years from now, simply pop the original videotapes back in your DV camera or VCR (**V**ideo **C**assette **R**ecorder) and batch capture the offline video clips. Simple. Of course, in this archival method, the absolutely worst thing you can do is to erase, lose, or ruin your original videotapes. But, being the smart editor you are, you've got them stored in a temperature- and humidity-controlled tape vault, right? Right.

Congratulations, you've reached another milestone. Oh sure, archiving projects isn't as sexy or glamorous as, say, adding effects or authoring DVDs. But proper project management can save you money in storage costs and time when trying to re-create a project a year from now. In fact, this book may have just paid for itself!

So far, all of the chapters have taken you through the features and options found within the most common formats of video editing—standard DV video. But what if you are using other formats such as widescreen DV or HDV? The next chapter will walk you through the useful project settings when using these other formats.

16

Working with 16:9, HDV, and 24p Video

So far in this book, you have been working with run-of-the-mill, regular DV (**D**igital **V**ideo). This is the vanilla flavor of DV and is used by 90 percent of people with DV cameras. However, other flavors of DV are becoming more popular. For example, some widescreen cameras change the width-to-height ratio of the video screen from 4:3 to 16:9. Some HDV (**H**igh-**D**efinition **V**ideo) cameras shoot in HDV. And some DV cameras shoot 24 fps (**f**rames **p**er **s**econd), instead of the typical 29.97 of NTSC (**N**ational **T**elevision **S**ystems **C**ommittee) DV.

Adobe Premiere Pro 2 supports each of these DV variances. Ideally, as long as you choose the proper project presets, you shouldn't have to make any other changes. Premiere Pro 2 will know how to process the video "behind the scenes" so you can focus on editing your projects. In this chapter, you will learn the subtle nuances of each flavor of DV ice cream.

Understanding Standard DV

Beyond the regular DV format, three other varieties of DV exist: widescreen, HDV, and 24p (**p**ull-down). Regular DV cameras are by far the most common format. If you have a camera format in one of the other three DV varieties, then sometimes you will have special considerations and unique project presets to specify in Premiere Pro 2. To help you understand how each of the other formats compares to the regular format, it's a good idea to start by defining the regular format.

It's important to note the regular format is different depending on where you live. NTSC is the video format of the United States, Japan, and most of the Americas. PAL (**P**hase **A**lternation **L**ine) is the video format just about everywhere else.

The following table outlines the primary differences between the two formats (for a definition of each property, refer to Chapter 1, *"Getting Started"*):

Standard NTSC DV Versus Standard PAL DV		
Property	**NTSC DV**	**PAL DV**
Frame size	720 x 480 pixels	720 x 576 pixels
Frame rate	29.97 fps	25 fps
Timebase	30 fps	25 fps
Pixel aspect ratio	0.9	1.067

Now you know the settings of the standard DV format in your country, so it's time to begin venturing off the beaten path and comparing the standard format to the other varieties of DV.

Working with 16:9 Video

Widescreen video is commonly referred to as **letterbox** or **16:9** because its ratio is 16 to 9; in other words, you get 16 pixels horizontally for every 9 pixels vertically. This results in a "shoebox" frame shape.

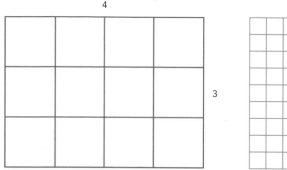

Regular DV   Widescreen DV

The only difference between widescreen and regular DV video is the shape of the frame. The shape of the standard definition frame is like that of your average television set—mostly square. You will see this written as 4:3 because there are 4 horizontal pixels for every 3 vertical pixels.

This is simple so far, right? Well, here's the kicker: Both formats have the *same number of pixels*. That's right. Even though the 16:9 format is wider than the regular 4:3 format, they have the same number of pixels across.

Huh? How can that be? How can a frame of significantly wider video have the same number of pixels? Well, the answer lies in the pixel aspect ratio, which defines the shape of *each pixel*.

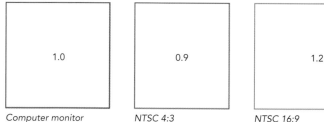

Computer monitor   NTSC 4:3   NTSC 16:9

A computer monitor has a perfectly square pixel with a 1.0 pixel aspect ratio—its width ÷ height is exactly 1.0. A pixel of 4:3 NTSC DV video has a 0.9 aspect ratio because it is slightly skinnier than a perfect square. And a pixel of 16:9 NTSC DV video has a 1.2 aspect ratio because it is slightly fatter than a perfect square. (By the way, PAL 4:3 has a 1.067 pixel aspect ratio, and PAL 16:9 has a 1.422 pixel aspect ratio.)

So when you butt together the same number of pixels in a row, you end up with a widescreen frame, simply because each pixel is wider. Whether you are using 4:3 or 16:9, *you always have the same number of pixels*.

In Premiere Pro 2, you don't need to do anything special to capture 16:9 widescreen DV. Premiere Pro 2 will automatically detect the format, and it will know to display the pixels slightly wider than regular pixels.

When creating a 16:9 project, the only special step you must take is to choose a widescreen project preset when loading your project. As you learned eons ago in this book, it's best to pick a project format to match the video you'll be editing. If you shot your video in 16:9, then create a 16:9 project. Once you've done this, Premiere Pro will take care of the rest.

When you are previewing a 16:9 project on an external DV device, you may need to take an extra step to get your video to display with the correct pixel aspect ratio. Premiere Pro 2 allows you to adjust the DV playback settings to prevent 16:9 video from becoming squeezed when displayed on a 4:3 television monitor.

16:9 project in Premiere Pro

Standard 4:3 television screen

No aspect ratio conversion

Aspect ratio conversion

As shown in the illustration here, if a 16:9 frame is displayed without aspect ratio conversion, the video appears squeezed as it is displayed on a standard 4:3 television screen. When the proper aspect ratio is applied, Premiere Pro 2 reduces the output a little bit so you can see the entire 16:9 frame within the 4:3 screen. This is similar to how a widescreen Hollywood movie looks when you watch it on a 4:3 screen.

In the next exercise, you will learn how to change the aspect ratio conversion in the playback settings and also how to change a project preset after you've begun working on a project.

1 | Creating a 16:9 Project

If you're shooting 16:9 video, it's important to choose a 16:9 project preset in Premiere Pro 2. This ensures the project "canvas" is wide like your video so you can view the entire image. But if you've mistakenly created a 4:3 project when working with 16:9 video, your 16:9 clips will be cropped (cut off) on the sides. This poses a problem because Premiere Pro 2 doesn't let you change project settings once you've started a new project.

Instead of having to rebuild your entire project from scratch, you can implement a simple solution: You can create a new 16:9 project and import the old 4:3 project into the new project. *Voila!* In this exercise, you will convert a 4:3 project into 16:9 and also make sure the playback settings are tuned properly for displaying on an attached 4:3 DV device.

Note: It is helpful to attach a DV device before starting this exercise, but it is not required.

---

1 On the **Welcome Screen**, click **Open Project**. In the **Open Project** dialog box, navigate to the **c:\exercise_files\chap_16** folder, click **exercise01.prproj** to select it, and click **Open**.

---

2 In the **Project** panel, double-click **wide.avi**.

In the Source Monitor, you can see the wide.avi clip is a 16:9 widescreen clip. However, this project is a 4:3 project. In the Program Monitor, you can see the far-left and far-right edges of the clip are being cropped.

Because you cannot change the project size, the solution is to create a new 16:9 project and import this existing project. This changes the canvas of the Program Monitor to the correct ratio of 16:9.

---

3 Choose **File > New > Project**. If prompted to save changes, click **No**.

---

4 In the **New Project** dialog box, choose the **DV – NTSC > Widescreen 48kHz** project preset.

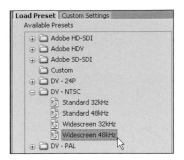

5 Click the **Browse** button to specify the location in which the project should be saved. In the **Browse For Folder** dialog box, navigate to the **c:\exercise_files\chap_16** directory. Click **OK**.

6 In the **New Project** dialog box **Name** textbox, type **widescreen**, and click **OK**.

This opens a new widescreen project. You can see in the Program Monitor the familiar shoebox shape of the 16:9 frame. The next step is to import the errant 4:3 project.

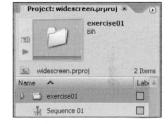

7 Choose **File > Import**. Navigate to **c:\exercise files\chap_16** directory, and click **exercise01.prproj** to select it. Click **Open**.

This imports the exercise01 project as its own bin in the Project panel.

8 Click the **arrow** icon to the left of the **exercise01** bin icon to view its contents. In the **exercise01** bin, double-click **Sequence 01** to open it in the **Timeline** panel.

You can now see the entire widescreen frame of video in the Program Monitor.

The last step is to ensure the widescreen video is being displayed properly on an attached 4:3 television monitor.

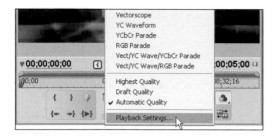

9 In the **Program Monitor**, click the **Output** button. Choose **Playback Settings**.

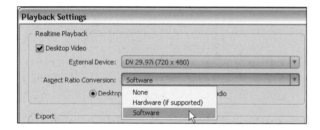

10 In the **Playback Settings** dialog box, click the **Aspect Ratio Conversion** pop-up menu, and choose **Software**. Click **OK**.

You should now see a correct 16:9 widescreen preview in your attached DV device.

Tip: If your DV device is intelligent enough to do its own aspect ratio conversion, then choose Hardware (if supported). If your device doesn't do its own conversion or if you're not sure, choose Software. The Software option is a smidge more taxing on your system because Premiere Pro 2 must do the math instead of your DV device—but it's better than no conversion.

Note: You may need to have an attached DV device to access this pop-up menu.

11 Choose **File > Save**, or press **Ctrl+S**. Choose **File > Close** to close this project.

Dealing with 16:9 video isn't a mystery. Premiere Pro 2 handles nearly every task for you—all you have to do is make sure the aspect ratio is correct on your attached DV device.

Even though this exercise didn't discuss it, you can also import 4:3 video into a 16:9 project. However, this is not necessarily recommended because the 4:3 video is not wide enough to fill the 16:9 frame.

This exercise dealt with widescreen video of the standard definition variety. Premiere Pro 2 also supports high-definition widescreen video. However, *all* HDV is widescreen, so it is redundant to say "hi-def widescreen." In the next section, you will look at issues relating to HDV.

Working with HDV

Walk into any electronics store, and you will likely see a mammoth 60-inch HD (**H**igh **D**efinition) television set prominently displayed. Unless you have more than a $1,000 to spend, odds are you have a regular, SD (**S**tandard **D**efinition) television set in your home.

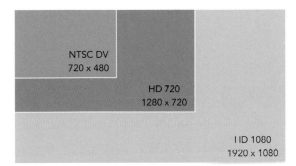

The primary difference between SD video and HD video is the frame size. Standard NTSC DV is 720 x 480 pixels (PAL DV is 720 x 576 pixels). SD is the size of most televisions. HD frame sizes are almost always 1280 x 720 pixels (called **HD 720**) or 1920 x 1080 pixels (called **HD 1080**). Notice the substantial difference between HD 720 and HD 1080—this increases the requirements for processing, displaying, and storing HD 1080.

Geeky note: The true pixel size of HD 1080 is 1440 x 1080. However, this format uses a pixel aspect ratio of 1.333, so its pixels are wider. Effectively, 1440 x 1.333 creates a frame size of 1920 x 1080.

Shooting HD can be costly—from the high-end camera equipment to the massive computing horsepower required. If you are using true HD, you will need a special capture device called an SDI (**S**erial **D**igital **I**nterface), which allows you to transfer high-quality HD video to your computer. Premiere Pro 2 is happy to work with this type of video but cannot do so without costly SDI equipment and lots and lots of computing power. (Lots.)

To bring HD to the masses, a new format has emerged, HDV. HDV is a blend of HD frame sizes at the storage sizes of DV. HDV is shot on cameras that cost as much as high-end DV cameras, can

record to DV tapes, and can even be captured by Premiere Pro 2 using FireWire, just like a DV camera. HDV's main benefit is low-cost video acquisition.

You may be thinking, "How can so many pixels be recorded to tape yet result in files the same size as standard DV files?" The answer lies in MPEG-2 compression. Just like the DVDs you author, HDV is highly compressed. Nonvital information about each frame is thrown out in order to reduce the overall file sizes. It's the innovation of compression that has made HDV an affordable, viable format for independent videographers.

Premiere Pro 2 is the first version of Premiere to extend native support for HDV. This means you can capture and edit without the need for additional hardware or software. However, this is part truth, part marketing hype.

Despite the compression, which results in smaller file sizes and the ability to record a large number of pixels on a standard DV tape, the requirement to play back HDV is still much greater than standard DV video. What you gain in quality, you lose in performance.

Without getting too technical, it's important to know your computer has to work a lot harder to "unravel" HDV video during editing and playback. For smooth playback, an extremely fast processor and separate hard drive are required.

When it comes to exporting HDV, Premiere Pro 2 allows you to edit in HDV mode so you can export your project back to HDV tape. Or, you can export HDV to the Web at any frame size or frame rate you desire. (But, honestly, who has an Internet connection fast enough to download HDV video on the fly?)

If you plan to export to DV, brace yourself for some bad news. HD DVDs are not yet supported by Premiere Pro 2 or Encore DVD. Instead, the Adobe Media Encoder will reduce your video to the standard DV size when authoring a DVD. So, you have to export your HDV movie to a high-quality movie file on your computer and then use third-party DVD-authoring/burning software with support for the HD DVD format.

Another geeky note: Odds are, HD DVD players are hitting store shelves as you read this book. There are competing HD DVD formats, and it's hard for Adobe to predict which format will be more popular. Once the formats duke it out and a clear winner is established, Adobe can extend support for HD DVDs, probably in the next release of Premiere Pro.

How well can your system play HDV? The next exercise will put your system to the test as you walk through the steps of removing a blue background in order to create transparency around an actor. (This is called a **bluescreen effect**.)

2 | Creating an HD 1080 Bluescreen

Because of the large size of HD 1080 video—1920 x 1080 pixels—you can get some decent results when trying to remove a bluescreen background. This is a process called **bluescreening** and is done daily at Hollywood studios. (Granted, they use super-advanced software programs costing two arms and three legs.) However, don't get discouraged because you can achieve decent results with Premiere Pro 2. In this exercise, you will get a chance to test your system and see how well it performs with HD 1080 video, as well as see how well you can remove a bluescreen background.

Note: If you are using the trial version of Premiere Pro 2, you may not be able to follow this exercise because the trial version does not permit you to edit HDV MPEG-2 video.

---

1 On the **Welcome Screen**, click **Open Project**. In the **Open Project** dialog box, navigate to the **c:\exercise_files\chap_16** folder, click **exercise02.prproj** to select it, and click **Open**.

---

2 Choose **File > Save As**. Navigate to the **c:\exercise files\chap_16** folder. Name the file **HDV 1080i**, and click **Save**.

Handsome devil

In the Program Monitor, you can see a frame of the HDV video you are going to "bluescreen."

If you are fortunate enough to have a second computer monitor, Premiere Pro 2 allows you to use the second monitor as playback for your HDV project.

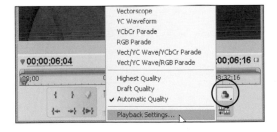

Playback Settings

Realtime Playback
☑ Desktop Video
External Device: Monitor:2 (1024 x 768) 8-Bit BGRA
Aspect Ratio Conversion: Hardware (if supported)

3 In the **Program Monitor**, click the **Output** button, and choose **Playback Settings**. In the **Playback Settings** dialog box, choose an appropriate **External Device** setting if an extra device is listed. If you have no additional external device, then choose **None**. Click **OK**.

If Premiere Pro 2 detects a compatible external device, it will appear in this menu. This example uses a second computer monitor as a playback monitor, like a television. The option to export playback on a second computer monitor appears with HDV projects only. When working in standard DV projects, you will not see this menu choice.

It's time to start testing the performance of your system. First you'll test how well your system can play this clip, without any effects applied to it.

4 In the **Program Monitor**, click the **Play** button to play the entire clip.

If you are lucky, your system played this clip with relatively little stutter. The hard drive and processor speed, as well as the amount of available memory, will affect playback.

In the Timeline panel, this video clip is on Track Video 2. On Track Video 1, underneath this clip, is a background that will be revealed once you "hide" the blue background.

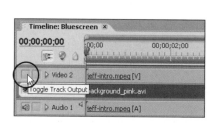

5 In the **Timeline** panel, click the **Toggle Track Output** toggle to turn off the display of Track **Video 2**.

When you turn off Track Video 2, you can see the pink background clip behind it on Track Video 1. This is a standard-definition, regular NTSC DV clip. This tiny, pink square swimming in an empty sea of black should give you an appreciation for how much larger HD video is than regular DV video.

Placing SD video in an HD project does not always yield acceptable results. If you want this SD video clip to play full screen, you have to blow it up more than 200 percent. That will create pixilation and blurriness. But what the heck...let's try it!

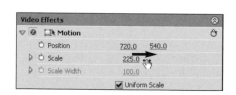

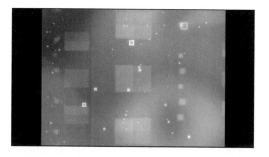

6 On Track **Video 1**, click the **background_pink.avi** clip to select it. Choose **Window > Effect Controls**. Click and drag the **Scale** value up to **225.0**, until it (vertically) fills the frame.

Tip: Some background clips, like this one from Digital Juice, yield acceptable results when scaled to greater than 100 percent because they are blurry and ambiguous in content to start. However, you definitely will not be so lucky if you are importing video from a DV camera.

Even though you've increased the size of the background clip, its 4:3 shape doesn't match the project's 16:9 widescreen shape—so you'll see black areas along each side. You can cheat by making Premiere Pro 2 *think* this clip is a widescreen clip.

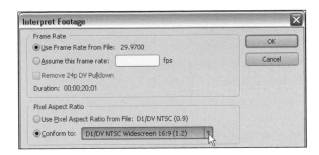

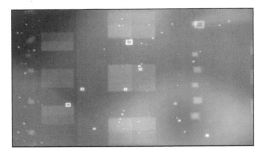

7 In the **Project** panel, right-click the **background_pink.avi** clip, and choose **Interpret Footage**. In the **Interpret Footage** dialog box, change the **Pixel Aspect Ratio > Conform to** pop-up menu to **D1/DV NTSC Widescreen 16:9 (1.2)**. Click **OK**.

You have just created a poor man's widescreen. Premiere Pro 2 now thinks this clip is a 16:9 clip, and it adjusts the clip to fill the entire widescreen HDV 1080 frame.

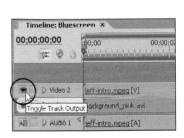

8 In the **Timeline** panel, click the **Toggle Track Output** toggle to turn on the display of Track **Video 2** so you can see the bluescreen HDV clip again. Drag the **Timeline CTI** (Current Time Indicator) to the beginning of the sequence.

With the background properly set up, it's time to push your system a bit further by adding a bluescreen effect to this clip.

When adding a bluescreen, it's important to get your blue background as "true blue" as possible. This clip, as you can see, is a bit dark and hazy, which isn't ideal for bluescreening. Applying color correction to your clip will improve the results of your bluescreen effect.

9 In the **Effects** panel, expand the **Video Effects > Adjust** folder to view its contents. Drag the **Auto Contrast** effect to the **jeff-intro.mpeg** clip on Track **Video 2**.

10 In the **Effects** panel, expand the **Video Effects > Keying** folder to view its contents. Drag the **Blue Screen Key** effect to the **jeff-intro.mpeg** clip on Track **Video 2**.

This effect has default parameters you can tweak to improve the bluescreen result. If you look closely, you can see some of the white squares showing through my sweater, especially around my right shoulder.

Tip: Keying is an informal term for compositing two images by removing color (or luminance) from one image to reveal another image behind it.

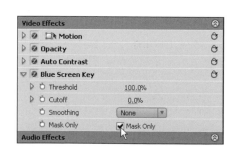

11 Choose **Window > Effect Controls** if the **Effect Controls** panel is not already in the foreground. In the **Effect Controls** panel, expand **Blue Screen Key** to view its properties. Click the **Mask Only** check box to turn on masking.

The mask shows a cutout of your key. Pure-white areas are completely opaque, and gray or translucent areas are semiopaque. The goal when fine-tuning a key with a mask is to create a completely solid white cutout.

12 In the **Effect Controls** panel, click and drag the **Blue Screen Key Threshold** value to **50.0%**.

The threshold controls the range of blue color that determines the transparent area of the clip. In other words, it helps make "sort-of blue" colors become transparent.

At a 50 percent threshold, you can see you've eliminated the dark "halo" around me. While dragging the value, you may have noticed the background pink appears brighter because some of the "sort-of blue" areas of the back wall are now transparent.

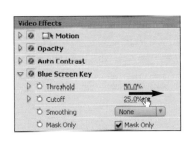

13 In the **Effect Controls** panel, click and drag the **Blue Screen Key Cutoff** value to **25.0%**.

The cutoff value specifies the opacity of the nontransparent (opaque) areas. Dragging the value to the right increases the opacity of the nontransparent region.

14 In the **Effect Controls** panel, change the **Blue Screen Key Smoothing** pop-up menu to **High**.

Smoothing specifies the amount of "softening" applied to the boundary between transparent and non-transparent areas of the clip.

Tip: Leave the smoothing set to None if you want sharp edges.

Original

Final

15 In the **Effect Controls** panel **Blue Screen Key** effect, turn on the **Mask Only** check box to view the composite image.

Comparing the final result to the original parameters, you can see the key is much cleaner. No halo appears around me, and my sweater is no longer semitransparent.

Now it's time for the moment of truth. It's time to play the clip and see how well your system handles a 1080 HDV clip with two effects.

---

16 In the **Program Monitor**, click the **Play** button to preview the entire sequence.

If your system did not perform decently, you may have experienced stuttering video and lagging audio during playback. These types of performance issues are indicative of how hard it is for Premiere Pro 2 to play even a brief 6 seconds of HDV.

---

17 Choose **File > Save**, or press **Ctrl+S**. Choose **File > Close** to close this project.

In this exercise, if your computer seemed to gasp for air while playing the HDV movie and effects, you're not alone. HDV is demanding of your system—from the processor to the hard drive to the memory. Although Premiere Pro 2 will gladly play HDV movies on your computer system, to really become an efficient editor you may need to look beyond the built-in capabilities of Premiere Pro 2.

NOTE:

Cineform's Aspect HD

The good folks in the Adobe marketing department like to hype the "native support" built into Premiere Pro 2 for HDV. However, as this past exercise may have proven to you, native support doesn't always equate to sufficient playback performance.

To smoothly play HDV material, the best solution available is Cineform Aspect HD. This product "plugs into" Premiere Pro 2 so you can continue to edit in Premiere Pro 2, with Aspect HD's presence being transparent. In fact, you may not even realize it's there because Premiere Pro 2 should continue to behave as normal. But when you play back and edit HDV material, you will be using the "brains" of Aspect HD instead of the regular Premiere Pro 2 brains.

continues on next page

Cineform's Aspect HD *continued*

Aspect HD's literature boasts, "On a 3GHz P4, Aspect HD will edit three streams of 1080i video on a Premiere Pro 2 Timeline—including effects, transitions, and titles—without dropping a frame." Compare that to the previous exercise, where you were playing a single, stuttering video clip. In addition, Aspect HD extends support for more varieties of HD/HDV not supported by Premiere Pro 2.

Do you need Aspect HD to edit HDV? No. If you are rarely using HDV in your normal workflow, then you can probably suffer through the HDV performance provided by Premiere Pro 2. But if you own an HDV camera and are editing HDV all the time, then Aspect HD should be a no-brainer. The time you save in rendering and playback will be worth the cost alone.

You can find out more about Aspect HD at **www.cineform.com**.

Working with 24p

Some newer cameras shoot 24 fps of video instead of the typical 30 fps of regular NTSC video. This is called **24p**. Motion picture movies are shot on film at 24 fps, so the goal is to create a more "film-like" look to the video. (Whether it works is a whole separate can of worms, with entire books dedicated to the subject.) The **p** stands for **progressive** because each frame of video comprises one big field. This is unique from regular DV video, where each frame of video comprises two fields.

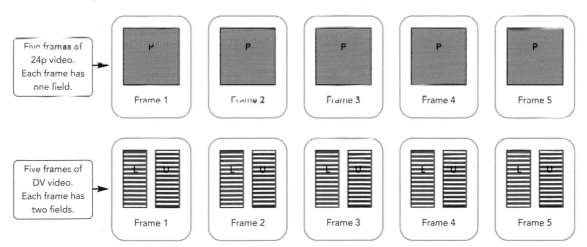

To understand what makes 24p unique, begin by comparing it to the "regular" variety of DV NTSC video, the video standard in the United States. Each frame of NTSC video comprises two fields. Half of the information is stored on the **lower** field, and the other half is stored on the **upper** field. The fields are interlaced—like teeth of a comb or a zipper. The two fields combine to make one complete frame. (This was described in Chapter 1, "*Getting Started.*")

The difference between fields describes only one difference. Another important difference is the frame rate. DV NTSC video has a frame rate of 30 fps. It's actually 29.97 fps, but humans like to round up to make things easier, so it is labeled 30 fps. (To make things easy, 30 fps will be substituted throughout this section.) All NTSC tapes record at 30 fps.

When using a 24p camera, the camera's internal "brain" processes what it sees through the lens at 24 fps. But when the video is recorded to tape, it must be recorded at the NTSC rate of 30 fps. This poses a problem—the camera is giving 24 frames, but the tape expects 30. Where do you get the extra six frames?

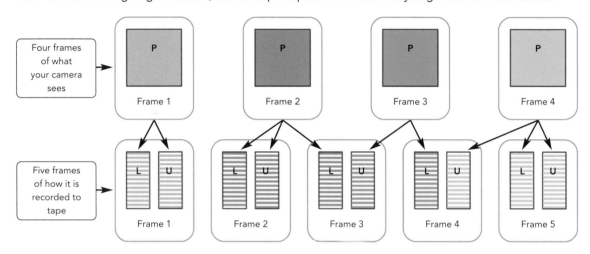

The extra six frames come from "doubling" some of the 24p frames, as shown in the illustration here. This takes place through a process called **2:3 pull-down**. To help illustrate 2:3 pull-down, the frames of 24p have been color-coded. You can see the first (lavender) 24p frame is divided into *two* fields. The second frame (blue) is divided into *three* fields. And so on. Hence you have the name **2:3**.

If you count each color, you will see two lavenders, three blues, two greens, and three oranges...a cadence of 2-3-2-3 over and over. If you do this 24 times per second, you will end up with 30 interlaced frames.

NTSC footage shot in 24p mode is recorded on DV tape at 30 fps, thanks to your friend, 2:3p. When capturing 24p footage, Premiere Pro 2 captures it like regular DV 30 fps video.

Even though the file is captured at 30 fps, Premiere Pro 2 recognizes it is supposed to be 24p, so it does special processing during playback. When playing back the clips in the **Source Monitor** or **Program Monitor**, Premiere Pro 2 removes the 2:3p so you can work in the true frame rate of 24 fps.

If you are working with 24p footage, then you should select a 24p project preset in Premiere Pro 2. This will ensure the frames of video display and play correctly. In addition, it will ensure the **Time Ruler** (also called the **timebase**) has 24 fps.

When you send a 24p project to NTSC DV tape, the 2:3p is reintroduced so the movie conforms to the 30 fps NTSC DV standard. (Remember, NTSC DV is *always* 30 fps.)

On the other hand, if you are exporting to the Web, you can specify your video be 24p, and the resulting files will play at 24 fps. (Web movies are more flexible than DV tapes, and you can choose any frame rate you want when exporting a movie to the Web.)

You can also use the 24p format to author progressive-scan DVDs. In this workflow, you have to export the file from Premiere Pro 2 and then use Encore DVD to create a 24p progressive-scan DVD.

Congratulations, you have reached the end of one of the more technically challenging chapters. We hope you made it out unscathed, with your brain still intact. Understanding the many different varieties of video is difficult even for video professionals.

Deep down, this chapter was a primer, helping you make sense of the different kinds of digital video. Luckily, with Premiere Pro 2, you don't need to do much differently. Instead of worrying about turning on special options or customizing your own settings, you should be able to pick a project preset and hit the ground running. Ideally, everything will work no matter the format, and you will not have to modify your workflow.

Extending built-in support to HDV cameras is but one of many new features in Premiere Pro 2 and is generating a lot of interest among independent movie makers. Beyond HDV support, the good folks at Adobe also focused their attention on improving the integration with other Adobe products, such as Adobe After Effects and Adobe Audition, which you will read about in the next chapter.

17

Integrating with Other Adobe Applications

Adobe Premiere Pro 2 now makes it easier than ever to share video and audio clips with other applications in the Adobe Production Studio, especially Adobe After Effects, Adobe Photoshop, and Adobe Audition. Until now, sharing clips between applications required you to export your work from one application before you could import it into another. Premiere Pro 2 now offers **Adobe Dynamic Link**, a feature of the Adobe Production Studio, which provides the ability to create a "live link" between an After Effects composition and a clip in Premiere Pro 2. This means changes you make to the After Effects composition update in Premiere Pro 2 immediately, without rendering. Furthermore, you can preview the composition in real time. If you've ever suffered through the pseudo-integration between After Effects and Premiere Pro in the past, this new feature is absolutely earth shattering. In addition, Premiere Pro 2 builds upon the integration already present with Photoshop for editing still images and with Audition for editing sound files. In this chapter, you will walk through the most common ways to share clips with all applications in the Adobe Production Studio.

Understanding the Integration Workflow

When the folks at Adobe speak of "integration," they are basically talking about sharing files with ease between other Adobe applications. Premiere Pro 2 has features to integrate specifically with After Effects, Photoshop, and Audition. Unique menu commands allow you to launch any of these applications and seamlessly share a single file between the applications. When you save a file in one application, it updates in the other.

Premiere Pro 2 can also import clips from Adobe Illustrator, but that's not true integration; rather, it's akin to importing any other type of clip. No menu commands are specific to Illustrator files.

In addition, Premiere Pro 2 can export a file type that can be used by Adobe Encore DVD, but the integration isn't as explicit. Rather, you export a file from one application, and the other application can read it. This is akin to importing any other type of clip, and it is not true integration either.

Integration means you have the ability to edit a clip from a Premiere Pro 2 project in one of the other applications without having to export first. You can make changes to the clip in the other application, and your changes will be reflected in Premiere Pro 2 immediately.

Typically, you will complete your project as thoroughly as you can in Premiere Pro 2 and then fine-tune a video clip or edit an audio clip, for example, in one of the other Adobe Production Studio applications. It doesn't always have to be the final step, but it's usually the safest workflow because you don't want to spend hours tweaking a clip in After Effects only to decide it needs to change after further editing in Premiere Pro 2.

Each application in the Adobe Production Studio offers a different level of integration with Premiere Pro 2. Take a moment to read how each application integrates with Premiere Pro 2.

Integrating with After Effects

Of all the applications Premiere Pro 2 integrates with, none has been given more attention than After Effects 7. In Premiere Pro 2, Adobe went to great lengths to ensure you can easily share clips between the two applications.

What's it for? After Effects, if you're new to the Adobe Production Studio, is for animating graphics and creating advanced effects. It's like the **Effect Controls** panel on steroids. It's not as good at raw editing as Premiere Pro 2, but it's *light years* better in the type of effects you can create, and its keyframe animation capabilities are much more sophisticated.

How does it integrate? Premiere Pro 2 integrates with After Effects 7 in two ways. First, you can cut and paste clips between a Premiere Pro 2 sequence and an After Effects sequence. (In After Effects they're called **compositions**.) This method is best for copying a clip into After Effects and doing advanced effects work on the clip. When done working on the clip in After Effects, you can copy the clip and paste it back into Premiere Pro 2.

The downside to this method is that all effects used on the clip must be available to both applications. If you do some fancy graphics work in After Effects, the effects you used may not be available in Premiere Pro 2 (because After Effects is much more advanced than Premiere Pro 2). When you paste the clip back into Premiere Pro 2, you will lose many of your effects because Premiere Pro 2 doesn't support them. For example, if you use the **Particle Playground** effect, an effect found only in After Effects, the effect will not be applied to the clip when you paste the clip into Premiere Pro 2.

To prevent this, you should export your After Effects composition to a movie and import the movie into Premiere Pro 2 like any other clip. This requires rendering, but it's better than nothing!

However, a much better way of integrating with After Effects 7 exists, which is available to you only if you own the complete Adobe Production Studio. You can use the new **Adobe Dynamic Link** feature, which allows you to share the clip between the two applications without having to copy and paste or export and render. You don't even have to worry about the effects being available to each application. Any changes you make in After Effects are automatically updated in Premiere Pro 2—and you don't even need to save your After Effects project! The clip in Premiere Pro 2 updates instantaneously.

You can preview the linked clip in the **Source Monitor**, set **In** and **Out** points, add it to a sequence, and use any of the other tools you've learned to edit it. As far as Premiere Pro 2 is concerned, it's a regular clip.

The copy-and-paste method does not require the Adobe Production Studio to be installed. However, the **Adobe Dynamic Link** option is available only if you've installed the Adobe Production Studio. We'll walk you through how to use both methods later in this chapter.

TIP:

Learning After Effects 7

The purpose of this chapter is to show you how to integrate video content between Premiere Pro 2 and other Adobe applications, including After Effects 7. For more information about how to use After Effects 7, use the **free 24-hour pass to the lynda.com Online Training Library** provided in the introduction of this book, and check out the following video-based training resources:

After Effects 7 Essential Training
with Lee Brimelow

After Effects 7 New Features
with Lee Brimelow

Or, check out the following book from the Hands-On Training series:

After Effects 7 Hands-On Training
by Chad Fahs and Lynda Weinman
Published by lynda.com/books and Peachpit Press, available May 2006
ISBN: 0321397754

Integrating with Photoshop

What's it for? Photoshop is for editing still images. It is one of the, if not *the*, most advanced image-editing tool available on the market. For example, although the Premiere Pro 2 **Titler** panel is fully featured, it has only a smidgeon of the feature set you get for making text in Photoshop. Many of the color correction tools you've learned to use in Premiere Pro 2 are also available in Photoshop, so the leap may not be that difficult.

How does it integrate? Premiere Pro 2 provides the ability to open a new Photoshop document directly from within Premiere Pro 2. This feature launches Photoshop for you and creates a new Photoshop document with the same size and aspect ratio of your current Premiere Pro 2 project. It also imports the Photoshop document as a clip in the Premiere Pro 2 **Project** panel. You can toggle between the applications. As you save changes to the Photoshop document, they are automatically updated in Premiere Pro 2, without you having to reimport the clip each time.

As a reminder, since you learned this many chapters ago, when you import a Photoshop file, you can choose to import all the layers as a Premiere Pro 2 sequence, import a single layer, or merge the layers as a flat image before importing.

Photoshop integration with Premiere Pro 2 does not require the Adobe Production Studio.

TIP:

Learning Photoshop CS2

The purpose of this chapter is to show you how to integrate video content between Premiere Pro 2 and other Adobe applications, including Photoshop CS2. For more information about how to use Photoshop CS2, use the **free 24-hour pass to the lynda.com Online Training Library** provided in the introduction of this book, and check out the following video-based training resources:

Photoshop CS2 Essential Training
with Michael Ninness

Photoshop CS2 for the Web Essential Training
with Tanya Staples

Enhancing Digital Photography with Photoshop CS2
with Chris Orwig

Or, check out the following book from the Hands-On Training series:

Adobe Photoshop CS2 for the Web Hands-On Training
by Tanya Staples
Published by lynda.com/books and Peachpit Press
ISBN: 0321331710

Integrating with Audition

What's it for? Audition is for advanced audio editing. Although Premiere Pro 2 has many tools and effects for working with audio, sometimes you'll need to use advanced techniques to edit your audio. For example, your audio file might be suffering from hard-to-isolate clicks and pops or extreme background noise you are unable to remove using the basic effects found in Premiere Pro 2.

How does it integrate? You can select an audio clip in Premiere Pro 2 and choose **Edit In Audition**. This launches Audition and allows you to perform advanced audio editing on the audio clip. Furthermore, the "new" clip you are working on in Audition replaces the "old" clip in Premiere Pro 2. Each time you save the clip in Audition, the audio automatically updates in Premiere Pro 2. In this workflow, you can continue to edit the audio multiple times, over and over.

Audition integration with Premiere Pro 2 does not require the Adobe Production Studio.

Integrating with Illustrator

What's it for? Illustrator is great for creating vector artwork and hand-drawn illustrations. (Vector artwork is comprised of lines, rather than the pixels found in still images.) The major advantage of Illustrator is that empty areas of the Illustrator canvas are converted to transparent areas in Premiere Pro 2. Because many companies supply their logos in vector artwork, this is handy when you want to "overlay" the logo on top of existing video in Premiere Pro 2.

How does it integrate? You can save files in Illustrator and import them into Premiere Pro 2 like any other graphic clip. If you want to edit the clip, you can choose **Edit Original**, which launches Illustrator. You can then work on the Illustrator file and save your changes, which will show up immediately in Premiere Pro 2.

However, calling this true integration is sort of cheating because its capabilities are nothing beyond what you can do with any other type of clip in Premiere Pro 2. Unlike Photoshop graphics, you cannot initiate a new Illustrator graphic from Premiere Pro 2, and you cannot automatically create Illustrator files with the correct pixel size and aspect ratio.

Illustrator "integration" with Premiere Pro 2 does not require the Adobe Production Studio.

TIP:

Learning Illustrator CS2

The purpose of this chapter is to show you how to integrate video content between Premiere Pro 2 and other Adobe applications, including Illustrator CS2. For more information about how to use Illustrator CS2, use the **free 24-hour pass to the lynda.com Online Training Library** provided in the introduction of this book, and check out the following video-based training resources:

Illustrator CS2 Essential Training
with Jeff Van West

Integrating with Encore DVD

What's it for? Encore DVD is Adobe's powerful DVD-authoring and DVD-burning software. Remember the two-menu DVDs you created in Chapter 12, "Authoring DVDs"? Encore DVD gives you unlimited menu capabilities. Beyond additional menus, you can create advanced navigation controls to move the user from one chapter to the next. You can also assign any button on the DVD remote control to take the user to a new chapter. And you can create your own templates and backgrounds and gain complete control over the menu objects.

How does it integrate? It doesn't actually integrate very well. The best workflow for combining Premiere Pro 2 and Encore DVD is to finish your sequence in Premiere Pro 2 and export it to an MPEG-2 or AVI file that Encore DVD can use.

In this sense, it's really not integration because it's a one-way road; you export from Premiere Pro 2 to a file that can be imported into Encore DVD. But you can't go from Encore DVD to Premiere Pro 2. If you want to make changes to the file you exported, you have to export the whole file again.

With that said, it's not all doom and gloom. In fact, many editors prefer the advanced authoring controls found in Encore DVD over the simple templates found in Premiere Pro 2. Keep in mind both applications will result in equal-quality DVDs. However, the amount of flexibility and control you have over the DVDs is what separates Encore DVD from Premiere Pro 2.

Being able to export to an Encore DVD format does not require the Adobe Production Studio.

In the following exercises, you will walk through integration procedures for the three applications truly integrated with Premiere Pro 2: After Effects, Photoshop, and Audition.

Copying and Pasting Between Premiere Pro 2 and After Effects 7

After you have completed the main editing phase of your movie in Premiere Pro 2, you may want to create some effects requiring the advanced graphics capabilities of After Effects. Premiere Pro 2 provides two ways for you to integrate your project with After Effects. The first method, which you will learn in this exercise, is to copy and paste clips between the two applications. (Exercise 2 will walk you through the second method.)

Note: This exercise requires After Effects to be installed.

---

1 On the **Welcome Screen**, click **Open Project**. In the **Open Project** dialog box, navigate to the c:\exercise_files\chap_17 folder, click **exercise01.prproj** to select it, and click **Open**.

---

2 Choose **File > Save As**. Navigate to the c:\exercise_files\dutch_harbor folder. Name the file **dutch harbor promo.prproj**, and click **Save**.

Note: If a previous version of dutch harbor promo.prproj already exists, you may be asked to replace it. Click Yes.

The first step is to cut a clip from the Premiere Pro 2 Timeline panel so you can paste it into After Effects.

---

3 In the **Timeline** panel, select the **DVD intro** tab to bring it to the foreground. Click the **coral_reef.jpg** clip on Track **Video 1** to select it. Choose **Edit > Cut**.

Using Cut will copy the clip to memory, as well as remove it from the Timeline. This leaves a gap on the Timeline, which you will later fill with a new clip (after you add visual effects to the clip in After Effects).

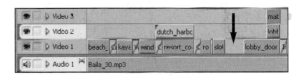

To make sure your After Effects workspace closely resembles the one shown in this book, you will use the Standard workspace in After Effects.

---

4 If necessary, start After Effects. In After Effects, choose **Window > Workspace > Standard**.

To paste the clip into After Effects, you must have an After Effects sequence already started (called a **composition** in After Effects).

---

5 In After Effects, choose **Composition > New Composition**.

When creating a new composition in After Effects, you have to define the settings—much like you do when creating a new project in Premiere Pro 2. Just like Premiere Pro 2, you can choose a preset specifying all the essential options, such as frame size, pixel aspect ratio, and frame rate.

---

6 In the **Composition Settings** dialog box, from the **Preset** pop-up menu choose **NTSC DV**. Click **OK**.

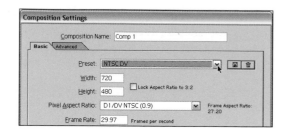

7 In After Effects, select the tab at the top of the **Timeline** panel to make it the active panel.

After Effects allows you to paste a clip from Premiere Pro 2 only inside an existing composition. So this step ensures the composition inside the Timeline panel is currently active before you paste.

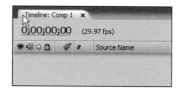

8 In After Effects, choose **Edit > Paste**.

This pastes the coral_reef.jpg clip from Premiere Pro 2 into the Composition panel.

Tip: You will notice the Timeline panel in After Effects is not divided into tracks like the Timeline in Premiere Pro 2. Instead, it's divided into layers, like Photoshop. If you are new to After Effects, this may be a confusing concept. Feel free to pick up a copy of *After Effects 7 Hands-On Training* available at **www.lynda.com**. (Another shameless plug!)

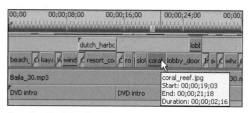

Premiere Pro Timeline

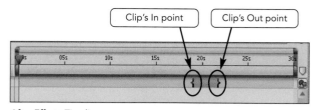

After Effects Timeline

When you paste a clip from Premiere Pro 2 into After Effects, the clip is pasted to the exact point in time it exists in the Premiere Pro 2 sequence.

For example, as shown in the illustration here, in Premiere Pro 2 (left), coral_reef.jpg starts at 19;03 and ends at 21;18. In After Effects (right), the Time Ruler above the composition shows the clip's In and Out points are at the same points in time.

9 In the After Effects **Timeline** panel, drag the **CTI** (**C**urrent **T**ime **I**ndicator) to the beginning of the composition. Press the [key to snap the clip to the **CTI**.

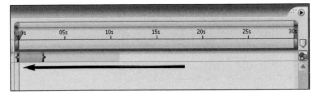

Tip: In After Effects, the [keyboard shortcut moves the entire clip and snaps its In point to the CTI. You should now be able to see the coral_reef.jpg clip in the After Effects Composition panel. This is similar to the Program Monitor in Premiere Pro 2.

10 In the After Effects **Time Controls** panel, click the **Play** button to preview the clip in the **Composition** panel. After the clip plays, click the **Stop** button to stop playback.

Tip: During playback, you may notice how slow After Effects seems to play. This is because it is displaying your video in extremely high quality. This highlights a major difference between Premiere Pro 2 and After Effects. Premiere Pro 2 is tuned to quickly display your video in real time. After Effects is built to display the highest-quality image, especially when adding effects.

At this point in the workflow, you can begin working on this clip in After Effects. You can add masks, complex animation motions, motion blurs, effects, transparency modes…the list goes on and on.

Note: Once you are done working on the clip in After Effects, you can paste it into Premiere Pro 2. However, only the effects found in both applications will be pasted. This means many of the effects you've created in After Effects will not paste into Premiere Pro 2, so you may lose much of your work. This underscores the danger of the copy-and-paste method of sharing clips between Premiere Pro 2 and After Effects.

Instead of copying and pasting into Premiere Pro 2, the safer method is to export it to a movie file from After Effects and then import it like a regular clip into Premiere Pro 2. To demonstrate this, a "smoke" effect has been applied to the coral_reef.jpg clip using the Particle Playground effect in the professional edition of After Effects. This has been rendered to a file you can now import into Premiere Pro 2.

11 In After Effects, choose **File > Exit**. If prompted to save your changes, click **No**.

You will return to Premiere Pro 2 and import the movie exported from After Effects.

---

12 In Premiere Pro 2, choose **File > Import**. In the **Import** dialog box, navigate to the **c:\exercise_files\chap_17** directory, click **smoke.avi** to select it, and click **Open**.

You will replace the old coral_reef.jpg clip—actually the gap created where you cut coral_reef.jpg—with the newly imported clip.

---

13 In the **Project** panel, drag the **smoke.avi** clip to the gap on Track **Video 1**. As you drag, be sure to snap it to the start of the gap.

Because the movie was exported from After Effects with the same duration, the clip should snugly fit inside the entire gap.

---

14 Drag and snap the **Timeline CTI** to the beginning of the **smoke.avi** clip on Track **Video 1**. Press the **spacebar** to play and preview the new clip. When the clip is finished playing, press the **spacebar** to stop playback.

As the clip plays, look for the subtle smoke effect rising from the lower hill. This is but one example of the advanced types of effects you can create with After Effects.

---

15 Choose **File > Save**, or press **Ctrl+S**. Choose **File > Close** to close this project.

The copy-and-paste integration between After Effects and Premiere Pro 2 is helpful but has its limitations. Remember, if a clip has an effect applied to it, the effect must be found in both applications, or it will not be pasted. For this reason, the best workflow is to copy from Premiere Pro 2 and paste into After Effects. Then, export a separate movie file from After Effects and import it like a regular clip into Premiere Pro 2. When exporting from After Effects, you can create a DV movie file, which will make Premiere Pro 2 happy.

This is one method of integrating Premiere Pro 2 and After Effects. Next, you will learn the Adobe Dynamic Link method, which is ten times faster but requires the Adobe Production Studio.

2 | Creating a Dynamic After Effects Link

This exercise demonstrates another method available to you for sharing clips between Premiere Pro 2 and After Effects. The **Adobe Dynamic Link** is a new feature requiring absolutely zero rendering and exporting. Unlike the copy-and-paste method, shown in the previous exercise, you don't have to worry about which effects are shared between the two applications. All your effects in the After Effects composition appear immediately—no matter what—in Premiere Pro 2.

Note: This exercise requires the Adobe Production Studio to be installed.

1 On the **Welcome Screen**, click **Open Project**. In the **Open Project** dialog box, navigate to **c:\exercise_files\chap_17** folder, click **exercise02.prproj** to select it, and click **Open**.

2 Choose **File > Save As**. Navigate to the **c:\exercise_files\dutch_harbor** folder. Name the file **dutch harbor promo.prproj**, and click **Save**.

Note: If a previous version of dutch harbor promo.prproj already exists, you may be asked to replace it. Click Yes.

In this exercise, you will create an Adobe Dynamic Link to an existing After Effects composition. Remember, unless you have the Adobe Production Studio, you will not be able to follow these steps.

3 Choose **File > Adobe Dynamic Link > Import After Effects Composition**.

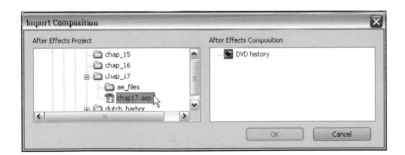

4 In the **Import Composition** dialog box, navigate to **c:\exercise_files\chap_17**, and click **chap17.aep** to select it. In the right side of the dialog box, click the **DVD history** After Effects composition to select it, and click **OK**.

You have just selected an After Effects project titled chap17.aep. The right side of the Import Composition dialog box shows you all the available compositions within the project. In this case, the chap17.aep After Effects project has only one composition, DVD history.

This imports the After Effects composition into the Premiere Pro 2 Project panel. It appears with a special icon to indicate it is an Adobe Dynamic Link clip.

5 In the **Project** panel, double-click the **DVD history Adobe Dynamic Link** clip to open it in the **Source Monitor**.

You can edit an Adobe Dynamic Link clip like any other clip you've used throughout this book. You can set In and Out points, add effects and transitions, and so on.

6 In the **Source Monitor**, click the **Toggle Take Audio and Video** toggle until the **filmstrip** icon displays.

By default, the Adobe Dynamic Link clips have both audio and video. However, in this case, you have no audio to use, so the Toggle Take Audio and Video feature tells Premiere Pro 2 to use only the video portion of this clip.

7 In the **Timeline** panel, select the **DVD intro** tab to bring it to the foreground. Drag the **Source Monitor** preview down to the gap on Track **Video 1**, and snap it to the **Timeline CTI**.

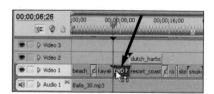

8 Press the **spacebar** to play the sequence. After the **Adobe Dynamic Link** clip plays, press the **spacebar** again to stop playback.

You probably noticed the playback was not completely in real time. In fact, your system may have slowed down considerably while playing this clip. But look at this as the glass being half full: Performance was compromised, but you didn't have to render anything from After Effects! Being able to see unrendered After Effects compositions instantaneously is a huge benefit.

Another benefit to the Adobe Dynamic Link feature is the ability to make changes to this clip in After Effects and see your changes update immediately in Premiere Pro 2.

---

9 In the **Timeline** panel, right-click the **DVD History Dynamic Link** clip on Track **Video 1**, and choose **Edit Original**.

If After Effects is not already running, this command launches After Effects. The project containing this composition automatically opens. You can now make changes to this composition in After Effects.

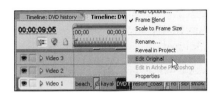

---

10 In the After Effects **Timeline** panel, click the **arrow** icon next to **Layer 1** to expand its properties.

You should recognize the Transform properties for this clip because they are identical to the Premiere Pro 2 fixed effects. In After Effects, the fixed properties of each clip appear in the Timeline panel, instead of in the Effect Controls panel. However, changing the values of the properties is the same in both applications.

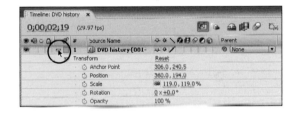

---

11 In the After Effects **Timeline** panel, click and drag the **Scale** value to **200%**.

Tip: In Chapter 4, *"Adding Graphics,"* we cautioned you to avoid scaling an image to greater than 100 percent, whenever possible. This image, however, is an Illustrator file, which is comprised of lines and shapes (called **vector artwork**) rather than a grid of pixels like a Photoshop file (called **raster artwork**). In After Effects, unlike Premiere Pro 2, you can scale vector artwork to any size, and you will never see pixilation, blurriness, or jagged edges.

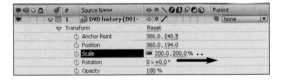

Unlike After Effects, Premiere Pro 2 treats all image files as raster artwork. Therefore, the rule of thumb is a bit more complex: In Premiere Pro 2, avoid scaling any image to greater than 100 percent. In After Effects, scale only vector artwork to greater than 100 percent.

---

12 Switch back to Premiere Pro 2. Snap the **Timeline CTI** to the beginning of the **DVD History Dynamic Link** clip.

Without doing anything, you should see the clip automatically update in the Premiere Pro 2 Program Monitor. Behold the incredible power of Adobe Dynamic Link!

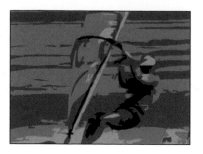

---

13 Choose **File > Save**, or press **Ctrl+S**. Choose **File > Close** to close this project.

---

14 Switch to After Effects, and choose **File > Exit**. When prompted to save changes, click **No**.

In the good old days of video editing, you had to export a movie from After Effects and import it into Premiere Pro 2. If you didn't like what you saw, you had to repeat the process of "review and change" over and over, like Sisyphus doomed to roll his giant boulder up that hill for all eternity. (See, you're also learning Greek mythology!)

Time is money—and there's no bigger time-saver in Premiere Pro 2 than Adobe Dynamic Link. Alas, it only comes with the Adobe Production Studio. But, in the world of time and money—if you're in the business of frequently sharing clips between Premiere Pro 2 and After Effects—the timesavings alone can justify the added expense of the Adobe Production Studio.

Whether or not you own the Adobe Production Studio, Premiere Pro 2 makes it easy to integrate with Photoshop as well. In the next exercise, you will create a Photoshop document directly from within Premiere Pro 2.

VIDEO: | **illustrator.mov**

In the previous exercise, you may have recognized the wind surfer clip from your Dutch Harbor Resort and Casino projects. The stylized look was created using the new **Live Trace** option in Illustrator CS2. Although Illustrator doesn't directly integrate with Premiere Pro 2 or After Effects, you can still use Illustrator's capabilities to create unique looks, such as the one in the previous exercise.

To learn more about how this effect was created using Premiere Pro 2, Illustrator, the Adobe Bridge, and After Effects (whew!), check out **illustrator.mov** in the **videos** folder on the **Premiere Pro 2 HOT DVD-ROM**.

3 | Integrating with Photoshop

You can apply many of the effects to Photoshop that you can apply to a still image in Premiere Pro 2. In fact, it is often better to apply the effect in Photoshop because then Premiere Pro 2 doesn't have to create the effect. This reduces the workload on Premiere Pro 2 and can improve playback performance. You can create titles, for example, easily in Premiere Pro 2, but you get a wider array of tools for making advanced graphics in Photoshop.

Photoshop, now more than ever, integrates tightly with the video creation process. You can create new Photoshop documents directly in Premiere Pro 2. You can also use new video preview features in Photoshop to view your images via an attached DV (**D**igital **V**ideo) device. In this exercise, you will learn how Photoshop integrates into your video production workflow.

---

1   On the **Welcome Screen**, click **Open Project**. In the **Open Project** dialog box, navigate to the **c:\exercise_files\chap_17** folder, click **exercise03.prproj** to select it, and click **Open**.

---

2   Choose **File > Save As**. Navigate to the **c:\exercise_files\dutch_harbor** folder. Name the file **dutch harbor promo.prproj**, and click **Save**.

Note: If a previous version of dutch harbor promo.prproj already exists, you may be asked to replace it. Click Yes.

You can create a new Photoshop document directly from within Premiere Pro 2. The document takes on the frame size and pixel aspect ratio of your current project.

---

3   Choose **File > New > Photoshop File**.

Before working on the Photoshop document, you must name and save it.

---

4   In the **Save Photoshop File As** dialog box, type **clouds** in the **File name** box. Click **Save**.

This automatically launches Photoshop and creates a new Photoshop file.

Note: When Photoshop starts, depending on your preferences, you may see a warning about pixel aspect ratio correction. This alerts you that the Photoshop preview has been modified to match your Premiere Pro 2 project settings. (This is a great feature, so don't be scared!) Click OK.

A blank Photoshop document opens. The Photoshop document automatically matches the size of your project and even displays the title and action safe margins to help you if you are creating text.

Short of giving a full-blown Photoshop lesson, in this exercise you will create some simple clouds you can use as a background behind a logo in Premiere Pro 2.

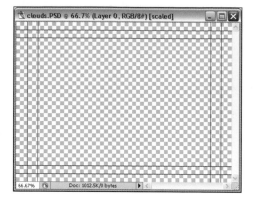

5 In Photoshop, choose **Window > Swatches** to open the color swatch library.

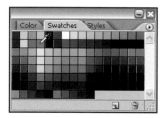

6 In the Photoshop **Swatches** palette, click the **Cyan** swatch.

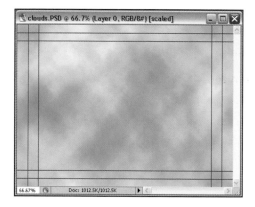

7 Choose **Filter > Render > Clouds**.

8 Choose **File > Save**, or press **Ctrl+S**.

9 Switch to Premiere Pro 2.

In the Premiere Pro 2 Project panel, you should see the clouds.PSD clip, as well as the effect you created.

10 In the **Timeline** panel, select the **dutch_harbor_logo** tab to bring that sequence to the foreground.

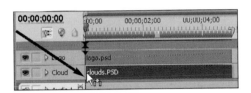

11 In the **Project** panel, drag the **clouds.PSD** clip to the beginning of Track **Cloud** in the **Timeline** panel.

You know, for a two-step cloud effect, that's not half bad!

Not only can you create new Photoshop documents from within Premiere Pro 2, but you can also modify existing documents, without having to export or reimport the clips.

12 In the **Logo** track, right-click **logo.psd**, and choose **Edit in Adobe Photoshop**.

This opens the document in Photoshop for editing. For example, let's say you would like to add an outer glow. Sure, you could do this in Premiere Pro 2—but it can be less taxing on your system if you add effects in Photoshop. (This way, the effect is built into the picture, and Premiere Pro 2 doesn't have to do any extra math.) In addition, Photoshop often provides more control and flexibility than some of the Premiere Pro 2 effects.

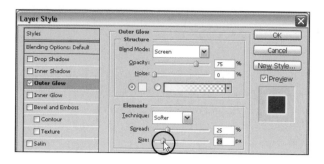

13 In Photoshop, choose **Layer > Layer Style > Outer Glow**. In the **Layer Style** dialog box, click the **Spread** slider, and drag it to **25%**. Click the **Size** slider, and drag it to **29px**. Click **OK**.

This style creates a glow around the image. Spread increases the boundaries of the glow (it "spreads" it out), and Size specifies the amount of blur.

---

14 Choose **File > Save**, or press **Ctrl+S**.

---

15 Switch to Premiere Pro 2. Drag the **Timeline CTI** to the beginning of the sequence.

In the Premiere Pro 2 Program Monitor, you should see the logo.psd clip updated automatically.

---

16 Choose **File > Save**, or press **Ctrl+S**. Choose **File > Close** to close this project.

---

17 Switch to Photoshop, and choose **File > Exit**. If prompted to save changes, click **No**.

As you've experienced, the integration between Premiere Pro 2 and Photoshop allows you to share a single image between the applications without having to export and reimport between each change. In fact, Photoshop CS 2 now contains a video export feature allowing you to preview your document on an attached DV device. (However, you have to close Premiere Pro 2 to see this because only one device can have "control" of the FireWire port at a time.) This allows you to see what your document will look like on an attached video monitor without ever leaving Photoshop.

Beyond After Effects compositions and Photoshop documents, Premiere Pro 2 also has equally tight integration with Adobe's audio-editing application, Audition. It's similar to the Photoshop integration, which you'll discover for yourself in the next exercise.

---

4 | Integrating with Audition

Audition performs advanced audio editing. Its features are incredibly rich and powerful. The audio editing you have learned in Premiere Pro 2 is the tip of the tip of the iceberg when it comes to Audition. Sometimes you run into an audio glitch Premiere Pro 2 alone can't solve, such as background noise you are incapable of removing. This is where Audition comes into play. In the overall workflow, you typically will work with Audition after the editing phase is complete.

Note: This exercise requires Adobe Audition 2.

---

1 On the **Welcome Screen**, click **Open Project**. In the **Open Project** dialog box, navigate to the c:\exercise_files\chap_17 folder, click **exercise04.prproj** to select it, and click **Open**.

---

2 Choose **File > Save As**. Navigate to the **c:\exercise_files\dutch_harbor** folder. Name the file **dutch harbor promo.prproj**, and click **Save**.

Note: If a previous version of dutch harbor promo.prproj already exists, you may be asked to replace it. Click Yes.

Audition has many tools available for eliminating unwanted background noise. In Chapter 10, *"Working with Audio,"* you learned how to use effects in Premiere Pro 2 to eliminate unwanted noise. This exercise demonstrates an alternative method of removing background noise using integration with Audition.

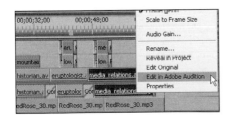

3 In the **Timeline** panel, select the **DVD history** tab to bring it to the foreground. On Track **Audio 1**, right-click the **media_relations.avi** clip, and choose **Edit in Adobe Audition**.

This opens the audio clip in Audition. However, before Audition opens, Premiere Pro 2 renders the audio to a new clip. This takes place "behind the scenes" automatically, so you don't have to manually export the audio clip to use it in Audition.

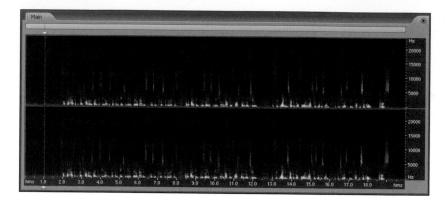

4 In Audition, choose **Window > Workspace > Frequency Space Editing**.

This view displays a color spectrum of the audio by its frequency. To make a long story short, the yellow and red colors represent the actor's voice, whereas the purple noise all around represents the background noise. (This is a generalized description of the spectral frequency display, which you can read all about in the Audition Help file.)

5 In Audition, choose **Effects > Restoration > Hiss Reduction (Process)**.

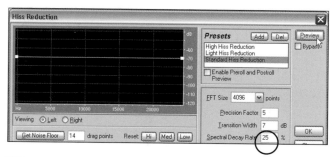

6 In the **Hiss Reduction** dialog box, select the **Standard Hiss Reduction** preset. In the **Spectral Decay Rate** box, type **25**. Click **Preview** to listen to the results before finalizing the effect.

During playback of the preview, you can turn the Bypass check box on and off to compare the before and after versions of the effect.

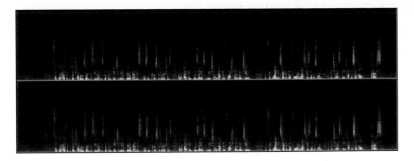

7 In the **Hiss Reduction** dialog box, click **OK** to accept the effect.

Although the result is still not perfect, it is dramatically better—all with the click of a simple preset. This is just a taste of what Audition is capable of doing.

---

8 In Audition, choose **File > Save**, or press **Ctrl+S**. Switch to Premiere Pro 2.

Without having to render or export, your changes automatically update in Premiere Pro 2. In the Project panel, you can see the new audio clip. In addition, the original audio clip has been automatically replaced in the Timeline with the new version.

---

9 Drag the **Timeline CTI** to the beginning of **media_relations.avi** on Track **Video 1**. In the **Program Monitor**, click the **Play** button to preview the new audio.

During playback, you should hear the new audio clip—and little (or none) of the original background noise.

---

10 Choose **File > Save**, or press **Ctrl+S**. Choose **File > Close** to close this project.

---

11 In Audition, choose **File > Exit**. If prompted to save changes, click **Yes**.

If you've ever processed your Premiere Pro audio in a separate audio-editing application, this workflow is nothing short of amazing. In the past, the simple task of sharing audio used to require multiple steps of rendering and exporting. In addition, after you manually imported the audio into the Project panel, you had to remove the audio clip in the Timeline and manually replace it. This was a long, arduous process.

With the integration between Premiere Pro 2 and Audition 2, what used to be about ten steps now can be performed in one. Not only is this a huge timesaving feature, but the advanced audio tools found in Audition make this an invaluable product for any video editor.

Now that you've learned the primary applications Premiere Pro 2 integrates with, you will next get to work with Encore DVD, one of the applications that doesn't integrate as well with Premiere Pro 2. However, this doesn't mean you can't use them together—it only means you won't find the same level of back-and-forth sharing as with After Effects, Photoshop, and Audition.

---

5 | Exporting to Encore DVD

Premiere Pro 2 doesn't truly integrate with Encore DVD—not in the sense Premiere Pro 2 integrates with After Effects, Photoshop, and Audition. Rather, when you want to author DVDs with intricate menu and navigation controls in Encore, you have to export a movie from Premiere Pro 2. You can choose to export as a DV AVI file or as an MPEG-2 file. Alas, that's where the integration ends. There's no modifying in Encore DVD and opening in Premiere Pro 2. It's a one-way road, from Premiere Pro 2 to Encore DVD, and that's where the road ends.

If you give Encore DVD a DV AVI file, it will have to convert it to an MPEG-2 file before burning to DVD. But if you give Encore DVD an MPEG-2 file, it won't have to render it again. Many editors choose to export an MPEG-2 file from Premiere Pro 2, because it requires one less rendering step. In this exercise, you will walk through the steps of exporting an MPEG-2 file to Encore DVD.

---

1 On the **Welcome Screen**, click **Open Project**. In the **Open Project** dialog box, navigate to the **c:\exercise_files\chap_17** folder, click **exercise05.prproj** to select it, and click **Open**.

---

2 Choose **File > Save As**. Navigate to the **c:\exercise_files\dutch harbor** folder. Name the file **dutch harbor promo.prproj**, and click **Save**.

Note: If a previous version of dutch harbor promo.prproj already exists, you may be asked to replace it. Click Yes.

When authoring DVDs in Premiere Pro 2, you can create markers equating to chapter points. (Like tracks on a CD, you can skip from chapter to chapter.) You can embed these markers in the file you export, and they will show up as chapter points in Encore DVD.

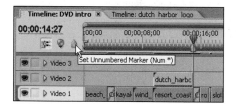

3 In the **Timeline** panel, select the **DVD intro** tab to bring it to the foreground. Drag the **Timeline CTI** to **00;00;14;27**. In the **Timeline** panel, click the **Set Unnumbered Marker** button.

This places a marker at the CTI. You will notice this is different from the DVD markers you set in Chapter 12, *"Authoring DVDs."* The DVD markers in Premiere Pro 2 are not used by any applications outside Premiere Pro 2. The names are confusing, but just remember: DVD markers exist only in Premiere Pro 2, and you can use other markers in Encore DVD.

4 Double-click the marker you just created in the **Time Ruler**. In the **Marker** dialog box, type **1** in the **Chapter** text box. Click **OK**.

Encore DVD will not recognize the markers unless you name the marker in the Chapter text box.

5 Drag the **Timeline CTI** to **00;00;26;18**. In the **Timeline** panel, click the **Set Unnumbered Marker** button.

6 Double-click the marker you just created in the **Time Ruler**. In the **Marker** dialog box, type **1** in the **Chapter** text box. Click **OK**.

Now that you have created markers to be used as chapter points, it is time to export the MPEG-2 file. This will be a familiar process because you use the same Adobe Media Encoder you learned about in Chapter 13, "*Exporting to Files and Tapes.*"

7 In the **Timeline** panel, select the **DVD intro** tab to bring the sequence to the foreground. Choose **File > Export > Adobe Media Encoder**.

8 In the **Export Settings** dialog box, from the **Format** pop-up menu choose **MPEG2 DVD**. From the **Range** pop-up menu, choose **Entire Sequence**. From the **Preset** pop-up menu, choose **NTSC DV 4:3 High Quality 7Mb CBR 1 Pass**.

As you did the last time you used the Adobe Media Encoder, you will start with a preset and then tweak the video properties to your liking.

9 In the **Export Settings** dialog box **Video** tab, change the **Bitrate Encoding** pop-up menu to **VBR, 2 Pass**. Change **Minimum Bitrate [Mbps]** to **1.5000**. Change **Target Bitrate [Mbps]** to **6.0000**. Change **Maximum Bitrate [Mbps]** to **8.0000**.

As you learned earlier in this book, a VBR (**V**ariable **B**it **R**ate) can improve compression efficiency by allowing the encoder to lower the bitrate with easy frames of video and increase it with complex frames.

10 In the **Export Settings** dialog box, select the **Audio** tab. Change the **Audio Format** pop-up menu to **PCM**. Click **OK**.

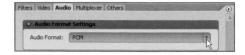

Ideally Dolby Digital (AC3) is the preferred format, but Premiere Pro 2 comes with only three trial uses of this format. Luckily, Encore DVD allows unlimited use of the Dolby Digital audio format when authoring a DVD.

For this reason, it's best to export your Premiere Pro 2 movie with PCM format because this audio format is uncompressed. This keeps your audio in its highest-quality setting so you can cleanly convert it in Encore DVD.

---

11 In the **Save File** dialog box, navigate to the **c:\exercise_files\dutch_harbor** directory. Leave the **File name** as **DVD intro**, and click **Save**.

Note: Depending on your system speed, this may take up to 5 minutes for both passes to complete.

On your hard drive, you now have a file ready to be imported into Encore DVD.

12 Launch Encore DVD. On the **Welcome Screen**, click **New Project**.

Upon starting a new project in Encore DVD, you may be asked to choose the television standard for this project. If so, choose NTSC, and click OK.

13 In the **Save As** dialog box, navigate to the **c:\exercise_files\dutch_harbor** folder. In the **File name** textbox, type **dutch harbor**, and click **Save**.

 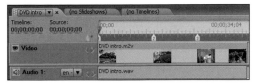

14 Choose **File > Import As > Timeline**. In the **Import as Timeline** dialog box, hold down the **Ctrl** key, click **DVD intro.m2v**, and then click **DVD intro.wav**. Click **Open**.

This places both items in the Encore DVD Project panel. In addition, this creates a new Timeline with the audio and video clips already placed inside the Timeline panel. You can see the DVD chapter points that were converted from the Premiere Pro 2 markers.

Even though you've already exported the video in MPEG-2 format, sometimes Encore DVD wants to use a slightly different MPEG-2 format. You can explicitly tell Encore DVD to *not* transcode the file because you've already supplied it in a high-quality, DVD-ready format.

---

15 In the Encore DVD **Project** panel, click the **DVD intro.m2v** video to select it. Choose **File > Transcode > Transcode Settings > Don't Transcode**.

Your Encore DVD project is now set up for you to begin work. You've exported the highest-possible quality video from Premiere Pro 2, and you've specified no further transcoding is required.

---

16 In Encore, choose **File > Exit**. If prompted to save changes, click **Yes**.

---

17 In Premiere Pro 2, choose **File > Save**, or press **Ctrl+S**. Choose **File > Close** to close this project.

As you can see, the integration between Premiere Pro 2 and Encore DVD is a tad lacking. But at least you now know how to export your movies from Premiere Pro 2 in the best format possible. This will save you gobs of time, as well as prevent your video quality from degrading because of mismatched settings.

You've now seen how Premiere Pro 2 integrates with the other applications in the Adobe Production Studio. For additional learning resources, including books and video training for Adobe applications (and much more!), use the free 24-hour pass to the lynda.com Online Training Library provided in the introduction of this book, and check out our video-based training tutorials.

Insert a fanfare of horns because you have just finished not only another chapter but the entire book! You have learned every facet of the video-editing process, as well as learned about the new features found only in Premiere Pro 2. Along the way you received step-by-step instructions and practical tips you can use in the real world, long after this book is collecting dust on your shelf (or being sold on eBay—let's be honest).

Just because you're done with the book doesn't mean the learning has to end. Be sure to check out the bonus chapters on multi-camera editing and Adobe Clip Notes, two incredible new features, available as PDFs on the accompanying DVD-ROM.

Technical Support and Troubleshooting FAQ

If you run into problems while following the exercises in this book, you might find the answer in the "Troubleshooting FAQ" section. If you don't find the information you're looking for, use the contact information provided in the "Technical Support Information" section.

Troubleshooting FAQ

Q When I open one of the exercise project files (such as **exercise01.prproj**), Adobe Premiere Pro 2 says it can't find certain files. If I click **Cancel** or **Skip** or **Offline**, all the video and audio in the project shows as offline. Why?

A When Premiere Pro 2 opens an exercise project file, it expects to find all the video, audio, and graphic files in the **c:\exercise_files\media_files** directory. You may have copied the exercise files to a drive other than the C drive, and Premiere Pro 2 is asking you to help find the file.

Close the project, and *do not save* if prompted. Reopen the project, and you may be asked to find the files again. Navigate to the directory where you chose to copy the files, and select the file it is asking you to find. When you find the first file, Premiere Pro 2 will usually find most (if not all) of the other missing files.

If you are not prompted to find the files again, you may have made them permanently offline. The easiest solution is to recopy the exercise file from the **Premiere Pro 2 HOT DVD-ROM**. (Be sure to turn off its read-only flag.)

Q When I attempt to save one of the exercise project files, why do I get a **Project Save Error** dialog box that says "Could not open the project file with write access"?

A The project file may still be set to **read-only** mode (this is sometimes the default for files copied from DVDs). You can choose **File > Save As** and save the project with a new name. You may also choose to exit Premiere Pro 2 and use **My Computer** to find the exercise file on your hard drive; when you find the file, right click it, and choose **Properties**. Turn off the **read-only** check box.

Q When I attempt to open one of the exercise project files, why do I get an error that says, "The project could not be loaded; it may be damaged or contain outdated elements"?

A This is usually caused by trying to open a Premiere Pro 2 project with an earlier version, such as 1.x. You can download a trial version of Premiere Pro 2 from **www.Adobe.com**.

Q I am not able to import HDV video or files with **.mpg** or **.m2v** extensions, and I receive an error. Why?

A The trial version of Premiere Pro 2 is not able to import or capture HDV (**H**igh-**D**efinition **V**ideo) or MPEG files—which frequently have an **.mpg** or **.m2v** extension. You must either purchase the full version of Premiere Pro 2 or use another product to convert your video to an AVI format that Premiere Pro 2 will open.

Q Why am I not able to open **c:\exercise_files\chap_16\exercise02.prproj**?

A This exercise uses HDV video. You may be using the trial version that doesn't allow you to use HDV video. See the previous answer.

Q Why am I not able to open any of the .prproj exercise files from **c:\exercise_files\chap_18**?

A These exercises use MPEG video. You may be using the trial version that doesn't allow you to use MPEG video.

Q Why don't I hear any audio? I hear audio in the **Source Monitor** but not once I put the file in the **Timeline** panel.

A Premiere Pro 2 may be trying to play the audio out via an attached DV (Digital Video) camera or VCR (Video Cassette Recorder). Choose **Project > Settings > General**, and click the **Playback Settings** button. Make sure all audio options are set to play audio through your desktop speakers instead of the attached DV device.

Q Why does my video stutter or appear to jerk during playback?

A A few different sources can cause this problem: incompatible display drivers, slow hard drive speeds, or a system without enough resources. You can try upgrading to the latest graphic display drivers provided by your graphics card manufacturer. Also, make sure your graphics card is certified as being compatible with Premiere Pro 2; check out the third-party certification list at **www.adobe.com/products/premiere/dvhdwrdb.html**.

If you suspect a slow hard drive, try freeing up space on your hard drive by deleting unnecessary files. Hard drives work best with more than 80 percent free space. Also try defragmenting your hard drive (**Start > All Programs > Accessories > System Tools > Disk Defragmenter**).

If you suspect a slow system, try closing all unnecessary applications, as well as nonessential processes running in the system tray (in the lower-right corner of your monitor). Temporarily disable any antivirus software that may be slowing the system. Turn off any screensavers, and remove any wallpaper backgrounds on your **Desktop**. (Right-click the **Desktop**, and choose **Properties**.) If you are an advanced Windows XP user, also increase your paging file sizes to their maximum amounts.

This can also be caused by systems not capable of displaying video to both the **Program Monitor** and an attached DV device. Disable the preview on one or the other; choose **Project > Settings > General**, and click the **Playback Settings** button.

Q Rendering seems slow. Why?

A Rendering, like going to the gym, yields results only after a long, long wait. Rendering is based on the speed of your computer and the complexity and duration of the video being rendered. Apart from optimizing your system (see the previous answer), you can't do much except use the work area to reduce the portion of the **Timeline** panel you are rendering.

Q During exporting to tape, the export suddenly stops for no reason. What gives?

A This often happens when your computer goes into screensaver mode. Disable the screensaver. (Right-click the Desktop, and choose **Properties > Screen Saver**.)

Q Why does my Program Monitor look blocky or pixilated during playback?

A This is completely normal; Premiere Pro 2 has to lower the quality of playback to accommodate the speed of your system. This is only a preview artifact, and it shouldn't be apparent on the final output to tape, DVD, or Web movie.

Q Why do my still images appear to flicker or flutter when displayed on a television?

A Unlike your still images—which have a much higher resolution—televisions do a poor job of displaying thin, horizontal lines. This results in strobing images. Add a slight blur to your still image, such as using the **Anti-Flicker Filter** in the **Effect Controls** panel. Or, if that is not strong enough, try adding a **Fast Blur** from the **Effects** panel.

Q Why am I dropping frames during capture from my DV camera?

A This is usually caused by a hard drive that cannot keep up with the demands of digital video. (It gets overwhelmed by all 30 frames per second—sometimes it loses a couple; imagine Lucy at the assembly line in the chocolate factory.) Try capturing to the fastest drive in your system. Sometimes external drives are not fast enough to capture, even though they can play back without any problem. In addition, some system drives are not fast enough to capture and run applications at the same time. It is best to have a dedicated hard drive separate from your primary system drive.

Q Premiere Pro 2 does not recognize my attached video camera. What should I do?

A Two things are required for Premiere Pro 2 to connect to your video camera: First, your computer must have an OHCI-compliant FireWire port. Second, your camera must have a FireWire port. If your camera has a USB (**U**niversal **S**erial **B**us) port, then Premiere Pro 2 will not recognize it. If you have a USB camera, you'll have to manually copy the files from your camera to your hard drive by yourself. (The USB video camera should show up as an external drive in **My Computer**.)

Q Video from my digital camera seems dark. What should I do?

A Video monitors display colors differently than your computer monitor does. What looks normal on a video monitor may appear dark on a computer display. The best solution is to view the video on a television or attached DV camera. If you plan to export the video to the Web, then you can use many of the color correction tools to improve the brightness of your video clips. (See Chapter 9, "*Correcting Color.*")

Technical Support Information

The following sections list some technical support resources you can use if you need additional help.

lynda.com

If you run into any problems as you work through this book, check the companion Web site for updates: **www.lynda.com/books/HOT/pp2**

If you don't find what you're looking for on the companion Web site, send Jeff Schell an e-mail: **pp2hot@lynda.com**

We encourage and welcome your feedback, comments, and error reports.

Peachpit Press

If your book has a defective DVD, please contact the customer service department at Peachpit Press: **customer_service@peachpit.com**

Adobe Technical Support

If you're having problems with Premiere Pro 2, please visit the Adobe Technical Support Center: **www.adobe.com/support/**

B

Premiere Pro 2 Resources

Adobe Premiere Pro 2 users have many great resources to mine for information about the product. You have ample choices among a variety of newsgroups, conferences, and third-party Web sites that can really help you get the most out of the new skills you've developed by following the exercises in this book. In this appendix, you'll find the best resources for further developing your skills with digital video and Premiere Pro 2.

lynda.com Training Resources

lynda.com

lynda.com is a leader in software books and video training for Web and graphics professionals. To help further develop your skills in digital video and Premiere Pro 2, check out the following training resources from **lynda.com**.

Video Training CDs and the Online Training Library

lynda.com offers video training as stand-alone CD and DVD products and through a subscription to the **lynda.com Online Training Library**™.

For a free, 24-hour pass to the **lynda.com Online Training Library**™, register your copy of the *Adobe Premiere Pro 2 Hands-On Training* book at the following link: **www.lynda.com/register/HOT/pp2**

Note: This offer is available for new subscribers only and does not apply to current or past subscribers of the **lynda.com Online Training Library**™.

To help you build your skills with Premiere Pro 2, check out the following video-based training tutorials at **lynda.com**:

Digital Video Principles
with Larry Jordan

Premiere Pro 2 Essential Training
with Jeff Schell

Premiere Pro 2 New Features
with Jeff Schell

After Effects 7 Essential Training
with Lee Brimelow

After Effects 7 New Features
with Lee Brimelow

Photoshop CS2 Essential Training
with Michael Ninness

Photoshop CS2 for the Web Essential Training
with Tanya Staples

Enhancing Digital Photography with Photoshop CS2
with Chris Orwig

Illustrator CS2 Essential Training
with Jeff Van West

Flash Professional 8 Essential Training
with Shane Rebenschied

Flash Professional 8 Beyond the Basics
with Shane Rebenschied

Flash Professional 8 Video Integration
with Lee Brimelow

Flash User Experience Best Practices
with Robert Hoekman Jr.

Photoshop CS2 and Flash 8 Integration
with Michael Ninness

Books

The **Hands-On Training** series was originally developed by Lynda Weinman, author of the revolutionary book *Designing Web Graphics*, first released in 1996. Lynda believes people learn best from doing and developed the **Hands-On Training** series to teach users software programs and technologies through a progressive learning process.

Check out the following books from **lynda.com**:

Adobe After Effects 7 Hands-On Training
by Chad Fahs and Lynda Weinman
lynda.com/books and Peachpit Press
ISBN: 0321397754

Adobe Dreamweaver 8 Hands-On Training
by Daniel Short and Garo Green
lynda.com/books and Peachpit Press
ISBN: 0321293894

Macromedia Flash Professional 8 Hands-On Training
by James Gonzalez
lynda.com/books and Peachpit Press
ISBN: 0321293886

Macromedia Flash Professional 8 Beyond the Basics Hands-On Training
by Shane Rebenschied
lynda.com/books and Peachpit Press
ISBN: 0321293878

Adobe Photoshop CS2 for the Web Hands-On Training
by Tanya Staples
lynda.com/books and Peachpit Press
ISBN: 0321331710

Adobe InDesign CS2 Hands-On Training
by Brian Wood
lynda.com/books and Peachpit Press
ISBN: 0321348729

Designing Web Graphics.4
by Lynda Weinman
New Riders
ISBN: 0735710791

Flashforward Conference

Flashforward is an international educational conference dedicated to Macromedia Flash. Flashforward is hosted twice annually by Lynda Weinman, founder of **lynda.com**. Flashforward provides the best conferences for Flash designers and developers to present their technical and artistic work in an educational setting.

For more information about the Flashforward conference, visit **www.flashforwardconference.com**.

Online Forums

These are some online forums you may find useful:

DMN Forums: I am proud to be one of the cohosts of the Adobe Premiere Pro user group on this Web site. You'll find me there answering all sorts of questions. (**www.dmnforums.com**)

Creative Cow: This is another top-notch forum for users to ask questions of knowledgeable professionals. (**www.creativecow.net**)

Adobe User-to-User Forum: Nobody from Adobe responds on this board, but you'll find a handful of amazingly smart folks fielding questions here. (**www.adobeforums.com**)

Adobe Resources

The following are some Adobe resources you may find useful:

Adobe Production Studio Resource Center: This is a jumping-off point for many of the following resources. (**www.adobe.com/studio/psguide/resources.html**)

Adobe Production Studio Curriculum Guide: This site offers free guides and source materials for the Adobe Production Studio. This site is aimed at high-school and college courses but is free to the public. (**www.adobe.com/education/instruction/curriculum/dv_curriculum.html**)

Adobe video and audio primers. You can find PDF primers on a wide variety of topics dealing with audio and video production here. (**www.adobe.com/motion/primers.html**)

Tips & tutorials: This site contains hundreds of how-tos, quick tips, and expert tutorials provided by Adobe. (**http://studio.adobe.com/us/tips**)

Third-party hardware compatibility: This page lists hardware devices, such as cameras, capture cards, sound cards, graphic cards, and DVD burners that have been certified as compatible with

Premiere Pro 2. (**www.adobe.com/products/premiere/dvhdwrdb.html**)

Downloads: This page has updated patches, fixes, and other freely available downloads for Premiere Pro 2 and other Adobe products. (**www.adobe.com/support/downloads/main.html**)

Support: This site has official Adobe technical documents addressing known bugs, issues, and support bulletins. (**www.adobe.com/support**)

Adobe Studio Exchange: This is an exchange site allowing you exchange files, effects, actions, extensions, and plug-ins for a wide range of Adobe products. Note: Premiere Pro 2 users may not get much use out of this; however, users of Adobe Photoshop, Adobe Illustrator, and Adobe After Effects will find a wealth of helpful files. (**http://share.studio.adobe.com**)

Motion Design Center: This is Adobe's new site of galleries, articles, interviews with industry professionals, and tutorials covering the world of motion design. It's mostly dedicated to Flash, After Effects, Photoshop, and other Web development products. (**www.adobe.com/motiondesign**)

Third-Party Web Sites

The following are some third-party Web sites you may find useful:

JeffSchell.com: I may be biased in the matter, but I think this is an excellent Web site! Sign up for monthly tutorials, ask questions of the author, and find out about additional Premiere Pro 2 training. (**www.jeffschell.com**)

Digital Juice: This contains hundreds of royalty-free animated backgrounds, lower thirds, and overlays for use in your video projects. (**www.digitaljuice.com**)

Wikicities: This is a wiki community for Premiere Pro users to share their knowledge. If you are looking for troubleshooting help, this is the place to start. (**http://ppro.wikicities.com**)

StevenGotz.com: This site contains a collection of links and original content for video editors. (**www.stevengotz.com**)

Powers of Story: Editing your video and audio is only part of creating a compelling product. Being able to tell a good story is equally important. This site talks about the power of a compelling story. (**www.powersofstory.com**)

Wrigley Video Productions: Here you'll find free video tutorials and a user forum. (**www.wrigleyvideo.com**)

2Writers.com: This site offers free downloadable utilities for use with Premiere Pro. (**www.2writers.com/download.htm**)

VideoHelp.com: This is one of the best sites for learning all about DVD authoring. This is the home of the excellent Bitrate Calculator (**www.videohelp.com/calc.htm**), which determines the optimal bitrate settings for your DVD movie based on duration and DVD size. (**www.videohelp.com**)

About How to Shoot Good Video: This is About.com's guide for shooting good video. It's a wonderful resource that explains some of the basic rules of shooting. (**http://desktopvideo. about.com/od/editing/ht/goodvideo_ro.htm**)

Sonnyboo: This site contains free goodies for indie filmmakers, such as full-screen images of FBI-type warnings: "The following preview has been approved for all audiences," which is the type of full-screen image you see while watching a rental movie. (**www.sonnyboo.com**)

GreatDV.com: Here you'll find wonderful tips for pre-production, production, and post-production, ranging from setting up the proper lighting to getting excellent bluescreen results. (**www.greatdv.com**)

Index

Numbers

A

Page numbers beginning with "DVD:" refer to bonus Chapters 18 and 19, found on the HOT DVD.

B

Page numbers beginning with "DVD:" refer to bonus Chapters 18 and 19, found on the HOT DVD.

Page numbers beginning with "DVD:" refer to bonus Chapters 18 and 19, found on the HOT DVD.

Page numbers beginning with "DVD:" refer to bonus Chapters 18 and 19, found on the HOT DVD.

Page numbers beginning with "DVD:" refer to bonus Chapters 18 and 19, found on the HOT DVD.

Page numbers beginning with "DVD:" refer to bonus Chapters 18 and 19, found on the HOT DVD.

G

H

I

Page numbers beginning with "DVD:" refer to bonus Chapters 18 and 19, found on the HOT DVD.

J–K

L

M

Page numbers beginning with "DVD:" refer to bonus Chapters 18 and 19, found on the HOT DVD.

Page numbers beginning with "DVD:" refer to bonus Chapters 18 and 19, found on the HOT DVD.

Q–R

Page numbers beginning with "DVD:" refer to bonus Chapters 18 and 19, found on the HOT DVD.

Page numbers beginning with "DVD:" refer to bonus Chapters 18 and 19, found on the HOT DVD.

U–V

Page numbers beginning with "DVD:" refer to bonus Chapters 18 and 19, found on the HOT DVD.

W

X–Y–Z

Page numbers beginning with "DVD:" refer to bonus Chapters 18 and 19, found on the HOT DVD.

THIS SOFTWARE LICENSE AGREEMENT CONSTITUTES AN AGREEMENT BETWEEN YOU AND, LYNDA.COM, INC. YOU SHOULD CAREFULLY READ THE FOLLOWING TERMS AND CONDITIONS. COPYING THIS SOFTWARE TO YOUR MACHINE OR OTHERWISE REMOVING OR USING THE SOFTWARE INDICATES YOUR ACCEPTANCE OF THESE TERMS AND CONDITIONS. IF YOU DO NOT AGREE TO BE BOUND BY THE PROVISIONS OF THIS LICENSE AGREEMENT, YOU SHOULD PROMPTLY DELETE THE SOFTWARE FROM YOUR MACHINE.

TERMS AND CONDITIONS:

1. GRANT OF LICENSE. In consideration of payment of the License Fee, which was a part of the price you paid for this product, LICENSOR grants to you (the "Licensee") a non-exclusive right to use the Software (all parts and elements of the data contained on the accompanying DVD-ROM is hereinafter referred to as the "Software"), along with any updates or upgrade releases of the Software for which you have paid on a single computer only (i.e., with a single CPU) at a single location, all as more particularly set forth and limited below. LICENSOR reserves all rights not expressly granted to you as Licensee in this License Agreement.

2. OWNERSHIP OF SOFTWARE. The license granted herein is not a sale of the original Software or of any copy of the Software. As Licensee, you own only the rights to use the Software as described herein and the magnetic or other physical media on which the Software is originally or subsequently recorded or fixed. LICENSOR retains title and ownership of the Software recorded on the original disk(s), as well as title and ownership of any subsequent copies of the Software irrespective of the form of media on or in which the Software is recorded or fixed. This license does not grant you any intellectual or other proprietary or other rights of any nature whatsoever in the Software.

3. USE RESTRICTIONS. As Licensee, you may use the Software only as expressly authorized in this License Agreement under the terms of paragraph 4. You may physically transfer the Software from one computer to another provided that the Software is used on only a single computer at any one time. You may not: (i) electronically transfer the Software from one computer to another over a network; (ii) make the Software available through a time-sharing service, network of computers, or other multiple user arrangement; (iii) distribute copies of the Software or related written materials to any third party, whether for sale or otherwise; (iv) modify, adapt, translate, reverse engineer, decompile, disassemble, or prepare any derivative work based on the Software or any element thereof; (v) make or distribute, whether for sale or otherwise, any hard copy or printed version of any of the Software nor any portion thereof nor any work of yours containing the Software or any component thereof; (vi) use any of the Software nor any of its components in any other work.

4. THIS IS WHAT YOU CAN AND CANNOT DO WITH THE SOFTWARE. Even though in the preceding paragraph and elsewhere LICENSOR has restricted your use of the Software, the following is the only thing you can do with the Software and the various elements of the Software: THE ARTWORK CONTAINED ON THIS DVD-ROM MAY NOT BE USED IN ANY MANNER WHATSOEVER OTHER THAN TO VIEW THE SAME ON YOUR COMPUTER, OR POST TO YOUR PERSONAL, NON-COMMERCIAL WEB SITE FOR EDUCATIONAL PURPOSES ONLY. THIS MATERIAL IS SUBJECT TO ALL OF THE RESTRICTION PROVISIONS OF THIS SOFTWARE LICENSE. SPECIFICALLY BUT NOT IN LIMITATION OF THESE RESTRICTIONS, YOU MAY NOT DISTRIBUTE, RESELL OR TRANSFER THIS PART OF THE SOFTWARE NOR ANY OF YOUR DESIGN OR OTHER WORK CONTAINING ANY OF THE SOFTWARE on this DVD-ROM, ALL AS MORE PARTICULARLY RESTRICTED IN THE WITHIN SOFTWARE LICENSE.

5. COPY RESTRICTIONS. The Software and accompanying written materials are protected under United States copyright laws. Unauthorized copying and/or distribution of the Software and/or the related written materials is expressly forbidden. You may be held legally responsible for any copyright infringement that is caused, directly or indirectly, by your failure to abide by the terms of this License Agreement. Subject to the terms of this License Agreement and if the software is not otherwise copy protected, you may make one copy of the Software for backup purposes only. The copyright notice and any other proprietary notices which were included in the original Software must be reproduced and included on any such backup copy.

6. TRANSFER RESTRICTIONS. The license herein granted is personal to you, the Licensee. You may not transfer the Software nor any of its components or elements to anyone else, nor may you sell, lease, loan, sublicense, assign, or otherwise dispose of the Software nor any of its components or elements without the express written consent of LICENSOR, which consent may be granted or withheld at LICENSOR's sole discretion.

7. TERMINATION. The license herein granted hereby will remain in effect until terminated. This license will terminate automatically without further notice from LICENSOR in the event of the violation of any of the provisions hereof. As Licensee, you agree that upon such termination you will promptly destroy any and all copies of the Software which remain in your possession and, upon request, will certify to such destruction in writing to LICENSOR.

8. LIMITATION AND DISCLAIMER OF WARRANTIES. a) THE SOFTWARE AND RELATED WRITTEN MATERIALS, INCLUDING ANY INSTRUCTIONS FOR USE, ARE PROVIDED ON AN "AS IS" BASIS, WITHOUT WARRANTY OF ANY KIND, EXPRESS OR IMPLIED. THIS DISCLAIMER OF WARRANTY EXPRESSLY INCLUDES, BUT IS NOT LIMITED TO, ANY IMPLIED WARRANTIES OF MERCHANTABILITY AND/OR OF FITNESS FOR A PARTICULAR PURPOSE. NO WARRANTY OF ANY KIND IS MADE AS TO WHETHER OR NOT THIS SOFTWARE INFRINGES UPON ANY RIGHTS OF ANY OTHER THIRD PARTIES. NO ORAL OR WRITTEN INFORMATION GIVEN BY LICENSOR, ITS SUPPLIERS, DISTRIBUTORS, DEALERS, EMPLOYEES, OR AGENTS, SHALL CREATE OR OTHERWISE ENLARGE THE SCOPE OF ANY WARRANTY HEREUNDER. LICENSEE ASSUMES THE ENTIRE RISK AS TO THE QUALITY AND THE PERFORMANCE OF SUCH SOFTWARE.

SHOULD THE SOFTWARE PROVE DEFECTIVE, YOU, AS LICENSEE (AND NOT LICENSOR, ITS SUPPLIERS, DISTRIBUTORS, DEALERS OR AGENTS), ASSUME THE ENTIRE COST OF ALL NECESSARY CORRECTION, SERVICING, OR REPAIR. b) LICENSOR warrants the disk(s) on which this copy of the Software is recorded or fixed to be free from defects in materials and workmanship, under normal use and service, for a period of ninety (90) days from the date of delivery as evidenced by a copy of the applicable receipt. LICENSOR hereby limits the duration of any implied warranties with respect to the disk(s) to the duration of the express warranty. This limited warranty shall not apply if the disk(s) have been damaged by unreasonable use, accident, negligence, or by any other causes unrelated to defective materials or workmanship. c) LICENSOR does not warrant that the functions contained in the Software will be uninterrupted or error free and Licensee is encouraged to test the Software for Licensee's intended use prior to placing any reliance thereon. All risk of the use of the Software will be on you, as Licensee. d) THE LIMITED WARRANTY SET FORTH ABOVE GIVES YOU SPECIFIC LEGAL RIGHTS AND YOU MAY ALSO HAVE OTHER RIGHTS, WHICH VARY FROM STATE TO STATE. SOME STATES DO NOT ALLOW THE LIMITATION OR EXCLUSION OF IMPLIED WARRANTIES OR OF INCIDENTAL OR CONSEQUEN-TIAL DAMAGES, SO THE LIMITATIONS AND EXCLUSIONS CONCERNING THE SOFTWARE AND RELATED WRITTEN MATERIALS SET FORTH ABOVE MAY NOT APPLY TO YOU.

9. LIMITATION OF REMEDIES. LICENSOR's entire liability and Licensee's exclusive remedy shall be the replacement of any disk(s) not meeting the limited warranty set forth in Section 8 above which is returned to LICENSOR with a copy of the applicable receipt within the warranty period. Any replacement disk(s)will be warranted for the remainder of the original warranty period or thirty (30) days, whichever is longer.

10. LIMITATION OF LIABILITY. IN NO EVENT WILL LICENSOR, OR ANYONE ELSE INVOLVED IN THE CREATION, PRODUCTION, AND/OR DELIVERY OF THIS SOFTWARE PRODUCT BE LIABLE TO LICENSEE OR ANY OTHER PERSON OR ENTITY FOR ANY DIRECT, INDIRECT, OR OTHER DAMAGES, INCLUDING, WITHOUT LIMITATION, ANY INTERRUPTION OF SERVICES, LOST PROFITS, LOST SAVINGS, LOSS OF DATA, OR ANY OTHER CONSEQUENTIAL, INCIDENTAL, SPECIAL, OR PUNITIVE DAMAGES, ARISING OUT OF THE PURCHASE, USE, INABILITY TO USE, OR OPERATION OF THE SOFTWARE, EVEN IF LICENSOR OR ANY AUTHORIZED LICENSOR DEALER HAS BEEN ADVISED OF THE POSSIBILITY OF SUCH DAMAGES. BY YOUR USE OF THE SOFTWARE, YOU ACKNOWLEDGE THAT THE LIMITATION OF LIABILITY SET FORTH IN THIS LICENSE WAS THE BASIS UPON WHICH THE SOFTWARE WAS OFFERED BY LICENSOR AND YOU ACKNOWLEDGE THAT THE PRICE OF THE SOFTWARE LICENSE WOULD BE HIGHER IN THE ABSENCE OF SUCH LIMITATION. SOME STATES DO NOT ALLOW THE LIMITATION OR EXCLUSION OF LIABILITY FOR INCIDENTAL OR CONSEQUENTIAL DAMAGES SO THE ABOVE LIMITATIONS AND EXCLUSIONS MAY NOT APPLY TO YOU.

11. UPDATES. LICENSOR, at its sole discretion, may periodically issue updates of the Software which you may receive upon request and payment of the applicable update fee in effect from time to time and in such event, all of the provisions of the within License Agreement shall apply to such updates.

12. EXPORT RESTRICTIONS. Licensee agrees not to export or re-export the Software and accompanying documentation (or any copies thereof) in violation of any applicable U.S. laws or regulations.

13. ENTIRE AGREEMENT. YOU, AS LICENSEE, ACKNOWLEDGE THAT: (i) YOU HAVE READ THIS ENTIRE AGREEMENT AND AGREE TO BE BOUND BY ITS TERMS AND CONDITIONS; (ii) THIS AGREEMENT IS THE COMPLETE AND EXCLUSIVE STATEMENT OF THE UNDERSTANDING BETWEEN THE PARTIES AND SUPERSEDES ANY AND ALL PRIOR ORAL OR WRITTEN COMMUNICA-TIONS RELATING TO THE SUBJECT MATTER HEREOF; AND (iii) THIS AGREE-MENT MAY NOT BE MODIFIED, AMENDED, OR IN ANY WAY ALTERED EXCEPT BY A WRITING SIGNED BY BOTH YOURSELF AND AN OFFICER OR AUTHO-RIZED REPRESENTATIVE OF LICENSOR.

14. SEVERABILITY. In the event that any provision of this License Agreement is held to be illegal or otherwise unenforceable, such provision shall be deemed to have been deleted from this License Agreement while the remaining provisions of this License Agreement shall be unaffected and shall continue in full force and effect.

15. GOVERNING LAW. This License Agreement shall be governed by the laws of the State of California applicable to agreements wholly to be performed therein and of the United States of America, excluding that body of the law related to conflicts of law. This License Agreement shall not be governed by the United Nations Convention on Contracts for the International Sale of Goods, the applica-tion of which is expressly excluded. No waiver of any breach of the provisions of this License Agreement shall be deemed a waiver of any other breach of this License Agreement.

16. RESTRICTED RIGHTS LEGEND. Use, duplication, or disclosure by the Government is subject to restrictions as set forth in subparagraph (c)(1)(ii) of the Rights in Technical Data and Computer Software clause at 48 CFR § 252.227-7013 and DFARS § 252.227-7013 or subparagraphs (c) (1) and (c)(2) of the Commercial Computer Software-Restricted Rights.at 48 CFR § 52.227.19, as applicable. Contractor/manufacturer: LICENSOR: LYNDA.COM, INC., c/o PEACHPIT PRESS, 1249 Eighth Street, Berkeley, CA 94710.